PRAISE FOR GRANTLEE

'Engagingly written ... one of the most
nuanced portraits to date'
The Australian

'Vivid, detailed and well written'
Daily Telegraph

'A staggering accomplishment that can't be missed by
history buffs and story lovers alike'
Betterreading.com.au

'A free-flowing biography of a great Australian figure'
John Howard

'Clear and accessible ... well-crafted and
extensively documented'
Weekend Australian

'Kieza has added hugely to the depth of knowledge about
our greatest military general in a book that is timely'
Tim Fischer, *Courier-Mail*

'The author writes with the immediacy of a fine
documentary ... an easy, informative read, bringing
historic personalities to life'
Ballarat Courier

ALSO BY GRANTLEE KIEZA

Hudson Fysh

The Kelly Hunters

Lawson

Banks

Macquarie

Banjo

The Hornet (with Jeff Horn)

Boxing in Australia

Mrs Kelly: The Astonishing Life of Ned Kelly's Mother

Monash: The Soldier Who Shaped Australia

Sons of the Southern Cross

Bert Hinkler: The Most Daring Man in the World

The Retriever (with Keith Schafferius)

A Year to Remember (with Mark Waugh)

Stopping the Clock: Health and Fitness the George Daldry Way

(with George Daldry)

Fast and Furious: A Celebration of Cricket's Pace Bowlers

Mark My Words: The Mark Graham Story

(with Alan Clarkson and Brian Mossop)

Australian Boxing: The Illustrated History

Fenech: The Official Biography (with Peter Muszkat)

GRANTLEE KIEZA

The Remarkable
Mrs Reibey

ABC
BOOKS

CONTENT WARNING:
Aboriginal and Torres Strait Islander people should be aware that *The Remarkable Mrs Reibey* contains descriptions, images and names of people now deceased. This book also contains descriptions of frontier violence that may be confronting or disturbing for some readers.

 The ABC 'Wave' device is a trademark of the Australian Broadcasting Corporation and is used under licence by HarperCollins*Publishers* Australia.

HarperCollins*Publishers*
Australia • Brazil • Canada • France • Germany • Holland • India
Italy • Japan • Mexico • New Zealand • Poland • Spain • Sweden
Switzerland • United Kingdom • United States of America

HarperCollins acknowledges the Traditional Custodians
of the land upon which we live and work, and pays respect
to Elders past and present.

First published in Australia in 2023
by HarperCollins*Publishers* Australia Pty Limited
Gadigal Country
Level 13, 201 Elizabeth Street, Sydney NSW 2000
ABN 36 009 913 517
harpercollins.com.au

A catalogue record for this book is available from the National Library of Australia

ISBN 978 0 7333 4150 2 (paperback)
ISBN 978 1 4607 1340 2 (ebook)

Cover design by Lisa Reidy
Cover images: Mary Reibey, watercolour on ivory miniature, ca. 1835 (FL1048687) courtesy
Mitchell Library, State Library of New South Wales; Sydney from the western side of the Cove,
ca 1803. Evans, George William, 1780–1852 (FL3234336) courtesy State Library of New South Wales
Author photograph by Milen Boubbov
Typeset in Bembo Std by Kelli Lonergan
Printed and bound in Australia by McPherson's Printing Group

MIX
Paper | Supporting responsible forestry
FSC® C001695

For Jude McGee, with my eternal thanks

Prologue

THE SUMMER SUN bathed the English market town of Stafford in a soft evening glow as a teenage girl cantered a stolen horse along a country lane towards a public execution: hers.

A public notice in a newspaper had warned everyone who lived around Stafford to keep an eye out for a valuable brood mare taken from a paddock near Chester, about eighty kilometres away. Fourteen-year-old Molly Haydock[1] prayed that the local sheriff wouldn't drag her off the bay horse, beat her senseless and then try to ensure she met an even worse fate. In the north of England in 1791, horse thieves were hanged by the neck until dead.

With her life on the line, this high-spirited orphan was wearing the clothes of a teenage boy and going by the name of a dead male friend. In this guise, Molly thought she might evade the law, at least in the short term. Appearing as a boy would make it easier for her to blend into her surrounds. And there was less chance of a boy being robbed or raped by the pistol-toting highwaymen who were preying on travellers throughout England.

It wasn't hard for the desperate girl to swap genders in the public eye, because she had yet to reach puberty; folklore suggested that girls matured later in the cold north of England than in the south.[2] As Molly cantered below the beech and elm trees on a mare worth a princely £10, her small, slight, flat-chested frame was garbed in a baggy labourer's smock. On her feet were worn leather boots, and a cloth cap was pulled low over her cherubic round face and reddish brown hair. Local girls parted their hair down the middle, so Molly had parted hers on the side like the boys did, in case the cap came off.[3]

Molly was an endless source of aggravation for her respectable middle-class family, and the press would soon brand her a 'lively lass'.[4] At various times throughout the next couple of years, Molly Haydock would be known as Mary, with the surname Etticks, Haddock or Haydock, and James, with the surname Barrow, Borrow, Burrough or Burrows. Then, most famously, she became Mary Reibey*, the richest woman in Australia.

---

* Pronounced Rabey

Chapter 1

FROM THE TIME Mary Reibey was born as Molly Haydock in the old Norman town of Bury, Lancashire, she had to fight a grim battle for survival.

When she came into the world on 12 May 1777,[1] Britain was in the midst of embracing a mesmerising Age of Enlightenment, but the infinite wonders being unveiled by science were struggling against the ceaseless human despair of poverty and crime. The rebellion by the united colonies of America was strangling British trade, and inflation was rampant. Meanwhile, the Industrial Revolution was making the rich richer while destroying the lives of the poor, tearing apart communities and befouling the environment.

With a population of four thousand, Bury was on the outskirts of the bustling city of Manchester, the second largest in Britain after London. A starving agricultural workforce was being pressed into grim, damp, overcrowded streets blighted by poor sanitation, as a shortage of doctors battled outbreaks of typhoid, cholera and smallpox. The nearby city of Liverpool was Britain's main slaving port; by the time of Molly's birth, Liverpool's ships had carried more than a million slaves[2] from West Africa across the Atlantic to the plantation owners of the Caribbean.

A shroud of coal smoke was descending over the county of Lancashire, which was central to the Industrial Revolution. Fields and farms were surrendering to steam engines in what the English poet William Blake would later call 'dark Satanic mills':

the cramped sweatshops that turned Bury into a major centre for textile manufacturing. Working conditions were abhorrent. Children as young as four were forced to work in the mills; many others were pushed downwards into stifling coalmines, or upwards into a claustrophobic nightmare as chimney sweeps.

In Lancashire, the infant mortality rate was among the highest in the counties of a rapidly imploding Britain, and life expectancy for those who survived infancy was among the lowest. As Molly's mother Jane Haydock[3] cradled her baby on that May day in 1777, she knew the odds were stacked against her. Two of the newborn's infant sisters had perished. To survive, Molly would need to be a fighter.

LIFE WAS CHEAP IN BRITAIN in 1777. Disease lurked in every breath, and the legal statutes known as 'The Bloody Code' listed more than two hundred offences that carried the death penalty. Most of them were rooted in poverty and hunger, and included such crimes as cutting down a tree, stealing a rabbit, or collecting the spoils from a shipwreck.

The spectacle of public executions drew large crowds of people who created a carnival atmosphere. Boiling, burning and beheading had been common punishments in the Middle Ages, and burning carried over into Molly's lifetime – six women were reduced to ashes in Britain while tied to stakes in the years surrounding her birth – though public hanging had become the principal punishment for capital crimes.[4] Most of the hangings in Molly's county occurred on the wilds of Lancaster Moor. A cart would carry the condemned and their coffins from the prison at Lancaster Castle to the gallows on the moor outside the town's southern gate, sometimes stopping at the Golden Lion public house so that those awaiting execution could have a farewell drink.[5] As the prisoners were forced up ladders and then fell to their deaths at the end of ropes, cheers and jeers would erupt from the crowds.

Youth was no protection from the gallows. The year before Molly was born, a Gloucester girl, Susannah Underwood, was hanged for setting fire to a barn and a haystack. The local newspaper criticised the appalling manners of the terrified, weeping fifteen year old, who had refused to shake hands with her master and accuser before the hangman bound her arms for the execution.[6]

In the halls of Westminster, though, there was a growing movement among British politicians to make hangmen redundant. Banishing British criminals by transporting them to distant shores was seen as a humane alternative to breaking their necks, and a way to make money for the Crown from their forced labour. In fact, Britain had sent convicts and prisoners of war across the Atlantic for two hundred years, forcing them to toil in the American colonies for the Empire – until 4 July 1776, when the Declaration of Independence curtailed all that. Britain's prisons had been overcrowded for years, and by the time of Molly's birth they had become so crowded that ships left over from the Seven Years War with France choked the Thames as floating prison hulks.

King George III and his ministers wanted to establish a new overseas penal colony and another source of raw materials. The government sought a meeting with Joseph Banks, the young president of the Royal Society, Britain's foremost academy of the sciences. They wished to discuss his travels in the South Pacific and the places he had visited there – especially New South Wales in the vast, far-off land known as New Holland.

Seven years before Molly Haydock's birth, Banks had helped to finance one of the great scientific voyages of history aboard a small converted coal transport vessel, the *Endeavour*, under the command of Lieutenant James Cook, a towering Yorkshireman with a withering gaze. Together the pair had changed the course of history, recording details of lands, peoples, plants and animals that were previously unknown to Europeans, as Cook mapped much of what to them was a new world, including the east coast of New Holland. In April 1770, at a place that Cook named Botany Bay in honour of Banks's scientific work, the *Endeavour*'s skipper introduced himself to a wary Indigenous population by shooting a Gweagal man in the leg after the local people had brandished spears at the Europeans. While Cook had seen large

Joseph Banks pictured not long before Mary's birth – William Dickinson (engraver) after a painting by Sir Joshua Reynolds. *National Portrait Gallery, Canberra*

tracts around Botany Bay that looked like 'barren heath', he'd also found deep black soil that he thought was 'Capable of producing any kind of grain'.[7]

The three-year travels of the *Endeavour* had resulted in Great Britain claiming vast territories for her Empire. Ever since Banks had returned to London, he'd been the toast of the scientific world; he'd brought back more than thirty thousand plant specimens, along with stories of cannibals in New Zealand and sensual delights in Tahiti (then called Otaheite), and vivid descriptions of the 'kangooroo',[8] swifter than a greyhound as it bounded about on its hind legs.

On the very day Molly Haydock was born, thousands of miles away on the far side of the globe, Cook – now a Royal Navy captain – was in command of another converted coal ship. The HMS *Resolution* was breezing through the turquoise waves of the spectacular Tongan archipelago, which was adorned with white-sand beaches and palm trees. Serene and sublime, the chain of tropical islands seemed to be waving a welcome. On a previous visit, Cook had named the archipelago 'The Friendly Isles' for the warm greetings he'd received there, but the Pacific could be a dangerous place – and murder was in the air. The captain dropped anchor off the tiny Tongan island of Nomuka. In this remote paradise, he and his crew were blissfully unaware of a plot to butcher them.

With Britain's war in America going badly, Cook was leading his third voyage of discovery to find territories for his monarch. The voyage had started almost a year earlier, when two ships had left Plymouth on England's south-west coast. Like the smaller *Endeavour*, the 462-tonne *Resolution* had started its life as a North Sea collier sailing out of Whitby in Cook's home county of Yorkshire. The ship's first lieutenant was John Gore, who had shot and killed a Maori warrior and a kangaroo on the *Endeavour* voyage, and the ship's master was the salty-tongued William Bligh,[9] the stocky, red-faced son of a Plymouth customs officer. Lieutenant Charles Clerke, who had also sailed on the *Endeavour*, was commanding the voyage's second ship: the 299-tonne *Discovery*, another Whitby-built collier. One of Clerke's midshipmen was George Vancouver, who would later chart and name much of Canada's Pacific west coast.

At Nomuka, the Great Chief Finau – a tall, thin man Cook estimated to be about thirty years old – invited the captain to sail to another island, Lifuka, where the British visitors were treated to a display of dancing that Cook said 'whould [sic] have met with universal applause on a European Theatre'.[10] The Tongan chief planned to lure the British visitors to a convenient location, kill them and loot the ships. However, due to infighting among the local chiefs, the plot was never carried out. Cook sailed on towards Hawaii.

MOLLY HAYDOCK'S FAMILY were respectable middle-class people or 'yeomen' with small landholdings and money. Her father James,[11] a weaver,[12] could trace his roots back to the fourteenth century. In 1740, Molly's grandfather Thomas

Haydock had married Mary Bracewell of Goosnargh, a town where the old farmhouse Chingle Hall was said to be haunted by the ghosts of priests killed for refusing to denounce Catholicism during the Protestant Reformation. At the age of twenty-two, Molly's father married twenty-year-old Jane 'Jinny' Law at the Church of St Mary the Virgin in nearby Blackburn, Lancashire.[13] Jane's family had lived around Blackburn for at least two hundred and fifty years. Their first child, Betty,[14] was born in 1772. She and Molly were the only Haydock children to survive infancy.

On 29 May 1777, Molly was baptised. Two years later her father died in a fall from a horse,[15] and her mother moved away, leaving her two daughters with relatives. As far as Molly and her family were concerned, the little girls had been orphaned.[16] Molly felt a sense of abandonment that stayed with her all her life. She grew up on Darwen Street, Blackburn, in the terrace house of her widowed grandmother Alice Law.[17] She formed a close and loving bond with Alice and the family's nurse.[18]

Molly had been just a year old when Captain Cook's heavy-handed dealing with indigenous people caught up with him at Kealakekua Bay on Hawaii Island. Plagued by a maddening stomach complaint, he had started making rash decisions while tensions with the local people escalated. When a group of locals took one of Cook's small boats, he tried kidnapping the King of Hawaii, Kalaniʻōpuʻu, in order to retrieve it.

On the morning of 14 February 1779, Cook arrived on shore with a company of armed marines and encouraged Kalaniʻōpuʻu to walk with him to the wooden boats the British had left on the shore. A melee ensued. Just as Cook had done at Botany Bay nine years before, he fired his musket. This time he killed a man. Cook and the redcoats were immediately swamped by a tsunami of furious Polynesians.[19] As William Bligh watched the skirmish through a spyglass from the deck of the *Resolution*, Cook was clubbed to the sand and then stabbed in the neck. He fell face first into the water, where he bled to death.

A month after Cook's death, Sir Charles Bunbury[20] opened a parliamentary committee to look into the question of convict transportation. On 10 April 1779, Bunbury presented to the House of Commons an official summation of recent testimony from Joseph Banks.[21] Botany Bay was Banks's preferred site for a convict settlement. He explained that as it was about seven months' voyage from England there was no chance of any convict escaping and returning home. There would be 'little probability of any opposition from the natives', Banks said. During his stay there in 1770, he'd seen 'very few, and did not think there were above fifty in all the neighbourhood, and had reason to believe the country was very thinly peopled'.

Banks had no doubt that sheep and oxen would thrive at Botany Bay, because there was plenty of fresh water from what would be called 'Cooks River', and the grass was long and luxuriant. The weather was mild and moderate, the climate similar to that of Toulouse 'in the south of France'.[22] There was an edible wild spinach, and the area abounded in fish and stingrays. There was also an 'abundance of timber and fuel, sufficient for any number of buildings which might be found necessary', and there appeared to be no beasts of prey.[23]

AT HER GRANDMOTHER'S home in Blackburn, Molly Haydock grew into a well-loved but sometimes too-active child with a heart inclined towards kindness. She befriended a deaf and speech-impaired girl, and would delight her playmate with dancing and games. From infancy she accompanied Granny Law to services in the chapel where her parents had married and where Reverend Thomas Harkie delivered the weekly sermon.

It was in that church, when Molly was four years old, that her mother's younger sister, Penelope Law,[24] married Adam Hope,[25] a woollen draper. Penelope and Adam volunteered to raise Molly's ill-tempered older sister Betty as one of their own children, while Molly stayed with the grandmother she adored. Molly found Betty obnoxious from an early age.

Though displaced by the trauma of her father's death and her mother's departure, Molly was surrounded by sensible, literate people. The yeoman class had money to invest in land and factories, and in the education of their families. As bright as a button, and with a fondness for figures and hard work, Molly read books on English, Greek and Roman history. She was taught to write in a neat cursive. Most likely she was educated at home: the local grammar school didn't take girls, though its headmaster, the Reverend Samuel Dean, regarded her as a well-behaved and popular lass. Spelling wasn't her strength, but she could think logically and make herself understood. She most likely did some work in a clerical position at a shopfront in Bury, and she developed a lifelong passion for numbers.[26] The world around her provided a lasting education too.

When Molly was nine, rumours began to circulate around England about the government's plans to empty its prisons by sending a 'First Fleet' of convicts and free settlers to the great southern land. Captain Arthur Phillip – a 49-year-old naval

Captain Arthur Phillip, 1786, painted by Francis Wheatley,
State Library of NSW FL3153744

veteran and former spy whose smile was missing a front tooth[27] – was chosen to lead a voyage that would establish the first European settlement in New Holland. After consultation with Phillip's mentor Joseph Banks, Home Secretary Lord Sydney[28] appointed Phillip as the Governor-Designate of New South Wales, and he was given command of the mission to settle Botany Bay on a handsome salary of £1000 a year.[29] Not only would he be building a prison settlement, but he would also be establishing, by an act of Parliament, the colony of New South Wales,[30] with hopes that the frontier community would strengthen Britain's strategic position in the Pacific against the Dutch and the Spanish, promote trade with Asia, and become a lucrative colonial outpost for London. Phillip organised for his portrait to be painted, and the artist Francis Wheatley captured the image of a small, olive-skinned man with a pear-shaped head, holding a document inscribed with 'New South Wales, 1787'.[31]

On Monday, 7 May, as Molly was about to celebrate her tenth birthday in Blackburn, Phillip arrived at Portsmouth to take command of the eleven ships in the First Fleet. There would be two Royal Navy escort ships, the HMS *Sirius* and HMS *Supply*, six convict transports, the *Alexander, Charlotte, Friendship, Lady Penrhyn, Prince of Wales* and the *Scarborough*, and three store ships, the *Borrowdale, Fishburn* and *Golden Grove*. They had been lying at the Motherbank, a shallow sandbar off the north-east coast of the Isle of Wight. The contingent of ships would be the largest ever to sail into the Pacific Ocean, with between 750 and 780 convicts, and around 550 crew, marines and family members.[32] On 13 May 1787, the fleet weighed anchors with a fresh breeze behind it and left Spithead on the Solent River in Hampshire for what would be an eight-month journey south.[33]

Two weeks later, Molly's mother Jane died in Cheshire. The undertaker John Forster sent the bill for the funeral to Molly's uncle Adam Hope. Forster charged £1 7 shillings for Jane's 'coffon' and 5 shillings threepence for 'lining the same' with flannel.[34]

On 5 August, the First Fleet reached Rio de Janeiro. The clothes of the convict women had become infested with lice, so those garments were burnt and replaced by some made from rice sacks. Water, food and more clothing was taken on board, and the ships reached Cape Town on 13 October. There the officers bought plants, seeds and farm animals, including one bull, one male calf, five cows, one stallion, three mares, three colts, forty-four sheep, thirty-two pigs, four goats, and poultry. The horses were for the governor's use when the fleet reached Botany Bay – everyone else would have to walk or march. The prison settlement was intended to be a place of strict confinement; if anyone wanted to use a boat, they would need Phillip's permission.

As the overcrowded ships lurched into the westerly winds of the Southern Ocean on their final leg of the voyage, they were battered by violent storms. The vessels were lashed by mountainous waves, and the convicts were cold, wet and deathly afraid in the cramped holds. Terrified cattle were knocked over in their pens and badly injured.

Finally, the *Supply*, the fastest of the eleven ships, reached Botany Bay on 18 January 1788, with the others following over the next three days. The fleet had covered twenty-four thousand kilometres with the loss of forty-eight lives – considered minimal collateral damage for the time.

After eight months at sea, Phillip found Botany Bay underwhelming. He quickly decided it was unsuitable for the settlement, as the wide waterway was too open and unprotected against storms, and the water too shallow for the ships to anchor close to shore. Much of the surrounding countryside was of barren, sandy soil. Phillip sailed a few kilometres north to an inlet James Cook had named after Sir George Jackson, one of the Lords Commissioners of the British Admiralty. Cook had not explored the inlet but when Phillip sailed into Port Jackson he 'had the satisfaction of finding the finest harbour in the world, in which a thousand sail of the line may ride in the most perfect security'.[35] There was a good stream of fresh water, too, and he named the cove where he anchored after Lord Sydney.[36] On the evening of 26 January 1788, Phillip oversaw the raising of the Union Jack there. His marines fired volleys, and he and his officers made

Entrance of Port Jackson, 27 January 1788, William Bradley drawings from his journal *A Voyage to New South Wales*, ca. 1802. *State Library of NSW FL1113868*

toasts to the King's health and the future of this new colony.[37] After Phillip sent word of the mission's success with the ships returning to England, a Second Fleet was soon organised with more convicts and settlers.

In Sydney, convicts were on the bottom rung of the social ladder – and many in authority saw convict women as the dirt on that rung. This was despite the fact that few of them were dangerous criminals. More than eighty per cent had been convicted of petty theft as the result of hunger and necessity, for which they'd received woefully disproportionate sentences: months in British prisons followed by years of hard labour thousands of miles from home and loved ones. Yet their reputations were tarnished as they were labelled 'whores', 'loafers' and 'degenerates'. It was a stereotype promoted by military officers, judges, parsons, governors, doctors and the wives of the establishment.[38]

Soon after the erection of basic huts for the prisoners, one of the convict women on the First Fleet was moved to write of the 'disconsolate situation' in what she called 'this solitary waste of the creation'.

As for the distresses of the women, they are past description, as they are deprived of tea and other things. They were indulged in the voyage by the seamen, and as they are all totally unprovided with clothes, those who have young children are quite wretched. Besides this, though a number of marriages have taken place, several women, who became pregnant on the voyage, and are since left by their partners, who have returned to England, are not likely even here to form any fresh connections ... the inconveniences since suffered for want of shelter, bedding, &c., are not to be imagined by any stranger. However, we have now two streets, if four rows of the most miserable huts you can possibly conceive of deserve that name. Windows they have none, as from the Governor's house, &c., now nearly finished, no glass could be spared so that lattices of twigs are made by our people to supply their places. At the extremity of the lines, where since our arrival the dead are buried, there is a place called the church-yard; but we hear, as soon as a sufficient quantity of bricks can be made, a church is to be built, and named St. Philip, after the Governor ...[39]

The marine captain Watkin Tench,[40] who had been a prisoner of war in the fight with the Americans and then volunteered for service in the new colony at Botany Bay, wrote that even though men and women had been kept apart on the First Fleet ships, 'when landed, their separation became impracticable, and would have been, perhaps, wrong. Licentiousness was the unavoidable consequence, and their old habits of depravity were beginning to recur. What was to be attempted? To prevent their intercourse was impossible; and to palliate its evils only remained. Marriage was recommended ...'[41] Some of the settlers and soldiers gladly became bigamists, forgetting about wives left behind in England. Governor Phillip's judge advocate, the marine captain David Collins[42] – whose wife was in London – would have two children with Ann Yeates, a milliner who had escaped a death sentence for a burglary in York when that sentence was commuted to seven years' transportation.

Life was hazardous for all the new arrivals in Sydney, but even more dangerous for the First Peoples, whose lives would never be the same. Europeans brought calamities for which the Eora people, those who inhabited the coastal areas around Sydney Cove, had no resistance: smallpox, influenza, measles, tuberculosis and sexually transmitted diseases. Collins was appalled at the damage done:

> The number that it swept off, by their own accounts, was incredible. At that time a native was living with us; and on our taking him down to the harbour to look for his former companions, those who witnessed his expression and agony can never forget either. He looked anxiously around him in the different coves we visited; not a vestige on the sand was to be found of human foot; the excavations in the rocks were filled with the putrid bodies of those who had fallen victims to the disorder; not a living person was anywhere to be met with. He lifted up his hands and eyes in silent agony for some time; at last he exclaimed, 'All dead! All dead!' and then hung his head in mournful silence.[43]

On a visit to Broken Bay, north of Sydney, Collins found many places where his path was covered with the skeletons of Aboriginal people. The same spectacle met him in the hollows of most of the rocks of that bay.[44]

AT THE HOME OF Molly Haydock's grandmother in Lancashire, a great deal of community interest was centred around the construction of the nearby St John the Evangelist Church of England. A local cotton baron, Henry Sudell, stumped up £4000: half of the construction cost.[45] On 31 July 1789,[46] Molly held the tiny hand[47] of her three-year-old cousin David Hope[48] as the church was consecrated and a stone marker was unveiled.

By then, Arthur Phillip was eighteen months into the toughest job of his life. The land around the primitive settlement was proving unsuitable for farming, and John Hunter[49] – who had commanded one of the First Fleet ships, the *Sirius* – had gone upriver in search of more fertile country, mapping places now known as Five Dock Bay and Iron Cove. Very little of the wheat brought from England had vegetated, while most of the rest had been destroyed by weevils. There were few skilled farmers among the convicts, and though some crops took root, they were assailed by autumn thunderstorms, mice, and ants. Prized cattle, brought from Cape Town, ran away. Phillip feared his little settlement would starve.[50] To discourage stealing from the dwindling food stores at Sydney Cove, he had hanged eleven men since the fleet's arrival.

In Blackburn in 1790, finding enough to eat wasn't a problem for Molly – but soon the hangman's noose would loom large over her, too. After Granny Law became desperately ill and could no longer care for her, there was what Molly later called a stunning change in her own 'situation'. She had felt abandoned by the loss of her parents and now the guiding light of her young life was about to dim for good. Relatives sent Molly to work in service as a maid at a local boarding school,[51] a common practice of middle-class families to teach girls how to sew, cook and clean.[52] Molly's sister Betty had a foul temper but she did as she was told. Molly made her own rules. In June 1791, she ran away from the school.

The respectable girl from the established family had always been headstrong, but now she went haywire. Soon she was running for her life.

Chapter 2

T HE ENORMITY OF MOLLY'S crime hit her as soon as
she reached the town of Stafford. She realised that the good
people there had instantly become suspicious of this small, skinny
boy trying to sell a fine bay horse for half a year's wages. In the
late 1700s, suspicion was a useful trait in England's north. Seamen
from the Liverpool slave ships had little regard for the welfare
of the local communities, and smugglers abounded on the local
canals. Until recently, military gangs had roamed the narrow
cobblestone streets, pressing – or kidnapping – the unwary into
service on warships for the fight against America and soon they
would start again for wars with France. Highwaymen preyed on
the unwary. Reports of crime travelled fast along the dirt roads of
Britain – especially reports on the theft of horses, which were so
valuable to everyday life.

Molly would later claim that she'd simply become so bored
with sewing and other chores at the boarding school that she'd
taken the horse for a frolic.[1] Yet the facts contradict this story:
she had spent weeks fending for herself in a vagabond existence,
and in Stafford she was hoping to make fast money in a strike for
youthful independence. Rather than a childish lark, her scheme
had taken considerable planning and subterfuge. She'd assumed
the identity of James Borrow, a lad she had once known; he'd
been a few weeks older than her and had recently died.[2]

Molly would go on to claim that she'd left Blackburn in June
1791 in company with a girl who had convinced her to run away.

They'd lived rough and by their wits, walking together through the summer warmth to the town of Chester – eighty kilometres south-west – before parting ways. Molly's story was that she'd then walked alone towards Stafford – another eighty kilometres south-east, on the way to London – when a man with two horses had overtaken her. He'd pleaded with her to ride one for him, then on reaching Stafford he'd panicked and ridden off, leaving Molly to answer an avalanche of questions.[3]

That's not the way other witnesses remembered it. A ten-year-old brood mare belonging to John Sorton Hughes, a glove merchant, had been taken from a field on the outskirts of Chester on Friday, 11 August 1791, four days after the funeral of Molly's grandmother Alice Law. Despite having spavin – or swelling – on one leg and evidence of recent swelling on another, the valuable breeding horse turned up the next night: it was eighty kilometres away in Stafford, underneath a scrawny lad.

Stafford was a staging post on the busy road linking the industrial centres of Birmingham and Wolverhampton with Manchester and Liverpool, and Molly wasn't keen to linger under the suspicious gaze of the locals. She didn't yet know that Hughes had placed advertisements in his local newspaper, the *Chester Chronicle*, asking for information about his stolen mare.[4] The horse was a fair age but still had a few years of breeding in her.

Towards evening on the twelfth, Molly rode the horse to Stafford's Swan Inn. Before she'd even given her alias to the innkeeper, Robert Silvester, she asked him if he'd like to buy the mare.[5]

Silvester noticed that this boy spoke in a very low tone and kept his head down.

'What's your name, lad?' the innkeeper asked.

'James Borrow, sir.'[6]

Because of Molly's Lancashire accent, he thought she'd said 'Burrow'.

'And why in God's name are you trying to flog me this old nag?'

'It belongs to my Uncle Darbin,' Molly explained rather unconvincingly. 'He lives five miles from Chester. He asked me to sell her because I'm good at selling them. Beautiful horse, sir.'[7]

Silvester eyed the mare warily, noting that it was 'a Bay horse with a longish tail'. He wasn't in the market for a horse – and certainly not one from an itinerant seller. 'Don't want the horse, lad,' he told Molly with a bite in his tone. 'Best you get about your business quick smart. And take that bag of bones too. Be off with you.'

Selling a stolen horse was tougher than Molly had anticipated. She just wanted to get rid of it and get away with some gold coins before she had to answer too many more questions. Resilient and tenacious, she hung around Silvester's stable all night, out of his view, until the golden glow of daybreak offered a new day with new opportunities.

At 5 a.m., in the half-light, Molly approached Francis Emborton, the stable groom at the inn. She told him that he could have the horse cheap for a quick sale.[8]

'No thanks, lad,' he said curtly, 'I'd rather take my chances at the horse market than with her.'

Molly told the groom he must be mad – she lied and said the horse was only a little past four years of age and a bargain for thirteen quid.

Nothing about this added up for the experienced horseman. He opened the mare's mouth to look at her aged teeth. 'This bloomin' thing's as old as me,' he said.[9] He started to smell a rat, thinking that he was in the presence of someone 'so young' yet somehow 'an old, old offender'. He examined the juvenile horse trader 'more strictly'. 'Tell me, boy,' he snapped, 'how does it happen that someone as young as you should be entrusted with selling a horse?'

'I've s-s-sold horses before,' Molly stammered, and Emborton knew it was a lie. 'I sold another horse for my uncle for more money than he could have got for her. He asked me to sell this one too.' Then she quickly changed the subject. 'It's four pounds for the saddle and bridle.'

Emborton told the boy to get away from the inn.

Molly walked the horse further into Stafford. She approached the local baker, John Commander – who, living up to his name, was taking nonsense from no one, especially this weedy stripling trying to sell him a horse. Before Molly could talk up the mare's worth, Commander grabbed the youngster by the scruff of the neck and called out to a passing yeoman, William Moore, that he'd caught a horse thief red-handed.[10] Molly struggled and protested, but Commander's thick hands had been kneading dough for years, and his fingers gripped like iron locks.

Moore interrogated Molly fiercely, and she told him that she'd bought the mare from her uncle 'John Borrow', a grocer who lived somewhere called 'Darbin'. Leaving Molly in Commander's clutches, Moore went to find a carrier from Chester, who said he'd never heard of anyone fitting that description. A blind man could see through the urchin's lies.

Moore turned up the heat. 'Horse stealing is a hanging offence, so tell the truth!'

Molly stammered, 'I'm James Borrow,' and added that her uncle John ran the Black Crow Inn and had a side business hiring out a post-chaise coach.

'Black Crow?' the carrier asked. 'Never heard of it. There's no such place, you little beggar.'

Molly could feel the noose tighten. 'No, no no-oo. Not the Black Crow, that's not it,' she spluttered. 'I bought the horse from Thomas Lyster. He has the White Lyon Inn at the back of the exchange in Chester.'[11]

The volunteer lawmen had heard enough. They dragged Molly kicking and screaming to the dilapidated and stinking Staffordshire County Gaol, located at the town's North Gate, where they handed her over. The constables tossed her into a crowded cell that reeked of human waste and the collective misery of the worst offenders in that part of Britain. The cells could hold up to fifty inmates at a time. Some had been confined for months awaiting trial; others knew they would eventually 'climb the ladder to bed', a euphemism for being hanged, and had nothing to lose. Joe Rogers, a burglar from London, had been waiting five months for his appointment with the Grim Reaper. Molly was surrounded by despair. Britain's foremost prison reformer John Howard, who had been inspecting the Crown's gaols for a House of Commons select committee, had recently visited Stafford's county gaol and found its conditions to be deplorable.[12] A new county prison in nearby Foregate field was underway but not yet complete.

Not only was the old prison falling apart but so was the composure of many of Molly's fellow inmates as they were trapped in this nightmare. Yet Molly's facade still did not crack. She couldn't convince the authorities that the horse was rightfully hers, but she managed to convince them and her fellow prisoners that she was a boy named James. It was a very good thing her cellmates didn't discover that she was a girl or that her name was Molly: 'a molly' was eighteenth-century prison slang for a male kept by men and other boys for sexual practices, and a 'molly house' was a brothel where men met for sex with one another.[13]

On 18 August, six days after Molly had ridden into town on the bay mare, John Hughes, nephew of the Chester glove merchant, identified his uncle's property by her markings and spavins.[14] The three accusers – John Commander, William Moore and the younger Hughes – appeared before Stafford's mayor, John Wright Esquire, to swear oaths that 'James Burrow' had stolen the horse. Molly had never been so frightened in all her short life.

LIFE WAS ALSO GRIM at Sydney Cove for Governor Arthur Phillip and his struggling colony.

As governor, Phillip had brought with him six handwritten pages, composed by Lord Sydney, that were his 'Instructions' from King George III 'with the advice of his Privy Council'.[15] Phillip was officially 'Captain-General and Governor-in-Chief of the territory called New South Wales', which extended from the northern 'extremity Territorial of the coast, called Cape York' to the southern extremity – the bottom of the island now called Tasmania and of all the country inland to the west, 'as far as the one hundred and thirty-fifth degree of east longitude [about midway through the Australian continent] ... and including all the islands adjacent in the Pacific Ocean'.[16]

The Instructions made no mention of protecting or even recognising Aboriginal land, although modern scholars estimate there were as many as one and a quarter million occupants of the continent at that time.[17] Largely because of Joseph Banks's testimony about New Holland being sparsely populated and the government's designs upon the territory, Britain had decided that New South Wales was *terra nullius* – that is, it belonged only to the first people who claimed it formally under a European understanding of the law. Phillip, however, was instructed to 'endeavour by every possible means to open an Intercourse with the Natives and to conciliate their affections, enjoining all Our Subjects to live in amity and kindness with them. And if any of Our Subjects shall wantonly destroy them, or give them any unnecessary Interruption in the exercise of their several occupations, it is our Will and Pleasure that you do cause such offenders to be brought to punishment according to the degree of the Offence.'[18] The original Instructions contained several revisions; for instance, the word 'Savages' was crossed out and replaced with 'Natives'.[19]

In September 1789, Henry Hacking[20] – the violent, heavy-drinking quartermaster from the *Sirius* – may have been the first colonist to kill a local. While hunting on the north shore of the harbour, Hacking fired into a group of Eora people. He either killed or wounded two men,[21] who were carried away by their companions.

Throughout June 1790, five ships of the Second Fleet arrived at Sydney Cove after a voyage of eleven months. But rather than improving Phillip's situation, they made it even more trying.

The *Lady Juliana* carried only convict women and girls including London sex workers and many hardened criminals, as well as thirteen-year-old Mary Wade,[22] who had been convicted of highway robbery. The ship gained a reputation as a 'floating brothel'. The Scottish steward John Nicol[23] recalled that 'when we were fairly out to sea, every man on board took a wife from among the convicts, they nothing loath'. Nicol had fallen for Sarah Whitlam of Lincoln, a convicted shoplifter, as soon as he knocked the rivet out of her chains, and she bore his son on the voyage.[24] Richard Alley, the ship's surgeon, formed a relationship with the convict Ann Mash,[25] also known as Ann Marsh, who had been transported for stealing a bushel (25 kilograms) of wheat.

While official reports said that the women on board the *Lady Juliana* were often noisy, unruly and drunk, and sometimes fought among themselves, the ship was kept clean, and the women were given free access to the deck as well as fresh food obtained at all their ports of call.

When the ship sailed into Port Jackson on 3 June 1790, it was the first vessel to arrive there since the First Fleet two and a half years earlier. At least one of the women was happy with the way they'd been treated on the voyage: 'We arrived here safe after a long voyage, in very good health, thanks to our good agent, [Lieutenant Thomas Edgar] on board, and the gentleman in England who sent us out, as we had everything that we could expect from them, and all our provisions were good ... Five or six [children] were born on board the ship; they had great care taken of them, and baby linen and every necessary for them were ready made to be put on.'[26] There had been five deaths on board. Two hundred and twenty-two women – many of them pregnant – and seven babies were off-loaded. Phillip saw them only as a further drain on his meagre resources, while Marine Lieutenant Ralph Clark – a man partial to flogging noncompliant women prisoners[27] – bemoaned the arrival of more 'damned whores'.

Two weeks later the storeship *Justinian* arrived, followed a week later by the pitiful living dead aboard the *Surprize*, *Neptune* and *Scarborough*. The British Government had hired the three ships from a slave transport company,[28] which had agreed to a fee to get the prisoners to Sydney Cove dead or alive. Captain William Hill, of the New South Wales Corps, sailed on the *Surprize* and was appalled that the slave traders contracted for the transports used the same 'barbarous' restraints from that evil business. Convicts were constrained by short iron bolts that made it impossible to extend either leg from the other more than an inch or two. 'Thus fettered,' Hill lamented, 'it was impossible for them to move but at the risk of both their legs being broken.'[29] The three overcrowded ships had left England with a combined total of just over a thousand convicts; more than a quarter died on the journey.

The *Neptune* also carried passengers such as the pugnacious young lieutenant John Macarthur,[30] his wife Elizabeth,[31] and their infant son Edward.[32] Macarthur could find a fight anywhere; even before they had set off, he'd become involved in a heated dispute with the *Neptune*'s commander, Captain Thomas Gilbert, over the size and state of his family's cabin. Gilbert had been the master of the *Charlotte* in the First Fleet. Macarthur publicly ridiculed him as a scoundrel, and the two fought a duel at the Fountain Tavern on the Plymouth docks[33] – though both missed.[34] Macarthur used an ally, Evan Nepean, the Under Secretary of State for the Home Department, to have Gilbert replaced on the ship. While their cabin was still cramped, the Macarthur family travelled in much greater comfort than the convicts on board, who were starved, beaten, and almost constantly chained and confined below deck. The crew withheld food from the prisoners with plans to sell it in Sydney. It was all too much for Macarthur, so he transferred to the *Scarborough* with his family.

Captain Hill bemoaned what he called the 'villainy, oppression, and shameful peculation of the masters of two of the transports'.

> The bark I was on board of was, indeed, unfit, from her make and size, to be sent so great a distance; if it blew but the most trifling gale she was lost in the waters, of which she shipped so much; that, from the Cape, the unhappy wretches, the convicts, were considerably above their waists in water ... In this situation they were obliged, for the safety of the ship, to be pen'd down; but when the gales abated no means were used to purify the air by fumigations, no vinegar was applied to rectify the nauseous steams issuing from their miserable dungeon ... even when attacked by disease their situations were not altered, neither had they any comforts administered. The slave trade is merciful compared with what I have seen in this fleet.[35]

Reverend
Richard Johnson,
Chaplain to the
Settlement in
New South Wales,
1787, painted
and engraved by
Garnet Terry,
State Library of NSW
FL8805784

When the ships arrived in Sydney, the convicts – half-naked, famished and filthy – were riddled with lice, and more than half of them were reported to be desperately ill. Many could not walk; some could not move.

The Reverend Richard Johnson, chaplain of the First Fleet, went aboard the vessels to minister to the dying. He broke down later as he explained that the wretched sight on the *Surprize* was 'truly shocking to the feelings of humanity'.[36] Many of the feeble prisoners were riddled with scurvy. One man was beset with what must have been '10,000 lice upon his body and bed'.[37] Others were lying in pools of their own filth, suffering from violent fevers, projectile vomiting, and diarrhoea. The stench was so offensive that the reverend had to race back above deck to retch. He was told that the conditions on board the *Scarborough* and *Neptune* were even worse, and not to venture there. Some of the corpses were cast naked upon the shore and left there for a time. Other prisoners who couldn't walk were thrown overboard into the water by the crew like empty crates. A few of the convicts, barely alive, crawled on hands and knees down the gangplank to dry land, while others were carried by hardier friends.[38] Five hundred of the prisoners arrived desperately ill; shortly afterwards, another 124 of them died. It would have been kinder if they had been hanged in Britain.

Arthur Phillip was appalled. Soon he was writing to his mentor Joseph Banks back in London that his health was 'gone' and that he was 'worn out'.[39] The penal settlement around Sydney Cove had become hell on earth.

To make things even more difficult for Phillip, he had incurred the wrath of the Eora.

While they initially had great respect for him, partly because Phillip was missing the same front tooth that the Eora knocked out of their young warriors in initiation ceremonies, that respect waned. After several skirmishes and deaths on both sides, Phillip decided to kidnap some of the Eora men to force a truce, and to ascertain more about the local peoples, their numbers, and their intentions towards the settlers.

The brutal kidnappings took place in the surf on the northern side of Port Jackson at Manly, a place Phillip had named in honour of the 'manly' bearing of the Eora. The first victim, a peaceful man named Arabanoo, died of smallpox that had taken hold among the Indigenous people who had no resistance to imported diseases. Phillip then sent orders to kidnap more of the men and two more, Colebee – a Gadigal man, and Bennelong,[40] of the Wangal clan – were wrestled down, tied up and held prisoner at Government House. Both eventually escaped, though before his flight to freedom Bennelong formed a friendship of sorts with Phillip, or as much as a prisoner could with his captor.

Other Eora men demanded justice or 'payback' for the cruel treatment of their people. On 7 September 1790, four months after Bennelong's escape, Phillip was invited to a celebration thrown by the local people at Manly: a feast of whale meat.

Bennelong was on the beach to greet them, a huge, friendly smile across his face, but soon Phillip was surrounded by other warriors. Then an Eora man, Willemering,[41] speared Phillip in the shoulder, making sure that he did not kill the leader of the invaders but only punished him for the crimes of the new settlers. Phillip required emergency treatment from the colony's assistant surgeon, William Balmain,[42] but did not order any retaliation, perhaps sensing himself that justice had been done. He and Bennelong restored their friendship and Phillip built Bennelong a hut on an eastern point of Sydney Cove.[43]

Three months later, the Europeans blamed another Eora man, the fearsome warrior Pemulwuy, for the spearing death of Phillip's gamekeeper, John McIntyre, a convict with a reputation for cruelty to the First Peoples.[44]

THE STAFFORDSHIRE COUNTY GAOL was as putrid as a convict ship and just as deadly. Prisoners jostled with each other in overcrowded chaos, their body odour and bad breath becoming one great stink as they tramped about to ease their nerves or sat in the straw over the cool, hard flagstones. Molly was thankful for one thing: there hadn't been any medical checks. When she lifted her smock to use the grimy, crusted 'seats of ease' – the stomach-churning toilet bins – she was careful to keep the secrets of her body hidden.

Mayor John Wright had compiled the sworn, signed testimony against Molly, written by a clerk in elegant script on legal parchment. The evidence was rolled together and tied with ribbon, and a note was written on the reverse: 'Informations ags Jas Burrow for Horse stealing, 18th Augt 1791'.[45] James Burrow was committed to stand trial at the Summer Assizes, to be held six days later. Molly would have to spend those days with her life hanging in the balance. She kept up her disguise, refused to seek help from what was left of her family, and prepared to face court.

The Stafford Assizes, part of the Oxford Circuit, were held at the local courthouse in March and August each year. Visiting judges from the halls of Westminster would arrive amid pomp and circumstance, and decide the fate of the unfortunates who appeared before them, based on the testimony of accusers with their 'Informations, Depositions and Confessions'. Eleven days after William Moore and John Commander had collared her, Molly would appear with thirty-five other prisoners before either Sir James Eyre[46] or Mr Justice John Heath.[47] Six women were named on the list, while Molly was still listed as James Burrow, a labourer from the parish of St Mary's in Stafford. No one believed her story about coming from Chester, so she was listed as a local.

Molly was then grouped with the ten prisoners set to face the fearsome Justice Heath, a fifty-five year old who had spent all his adult life in the law and was renowned for his 'quickness of apprehension, accuracy of discrimination, and strength of judgment'.[48] His powers of observation must have temporarily deserted him on 24 August 1791, as he apparently had no idea that the accused horse thief James Burrow, nervously trembling before him, was a fourteen-year-old girl. Heath was known as a 'hanging judge', and his contemporaries regarded his sentences as 'Draconian'. 'If you imprison at home,' Heath once told a colleague, 'the criminal is soon thrown upon you, hardened in guilt. If you transport, you corrupt infant societies, and sow the seeds of atrocious crimes over the habitable globe. There is no regenerating of felons in this life, and for their own sake as well as the sake of society, I think it better to hang.'[49] This, then, was the man who would decide whether little Molly Haydock lived or died.

The arrival of the judges into the Staffordshire County Gaol was designed to create a sense of awe and reverence for the unwavering justice and absolute power of God and King. It was heralded by the tolling of bells and the blowing of trumpets as twenty sheriff's men in ceremonial dress, armed with gilded javelins, led each judge's majestic, slow-rolling carriage up the high street and into Gaol Square, with its crumbling grey walls, that seemed to reek of fear and despair. On 24 August, the noise of Justice Heath's arrival echoed off the stone walls and floors of the grim cells. For many of the prisoners, the sound was as ominous as that of approaching boot heels would be on their day of execution. For those not facing the judge, though, the Summer

Assizes heralded a holiday and the entertainment of public executions at nearby Sandyford.

As Justice Heath took his place in the courthouse that day, Staffordshire's sheriff, Moreton Walhouse, brought out the ten defendants under guard. They walked through the decaying stone corridors and across the open square into the courthouse. The summer sun shone brightly on Molly's face, and she wondered

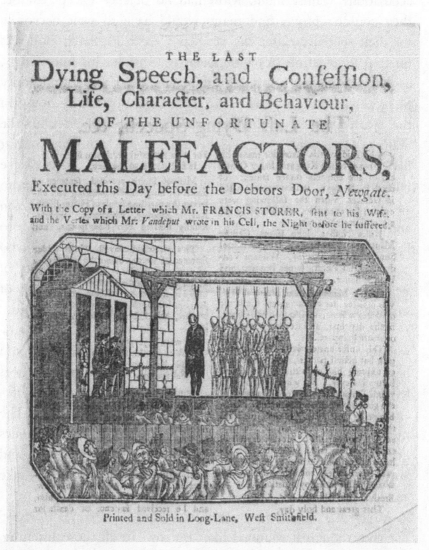

Public Hanging in England: The Last Dying Speech and Confession, Life, Character, and Behaviour of the Unfortunate Malefactors, 1785. *The Lewis Walpole Library, Yale University*

how much longer she would feel its comforting warmth. Inside the foreboding courtroom, with its dark wood panelling and oak dock, attendants had spread herbs and flowers to mask the stench of the unwashed accused. To ward off lice and fleas, some court officials and witnesses wore rags soaked in vinegar around their ankles.

One after the other, the prisoners were called to answer the accusations against them. Most had no defence except excuses they couldn't prove, and many would have to wait nervously for their sentences after the verdicts were read. Sarah Bull was on trial for stealing from John Harris, 'without his knowledge', a silver watch worth forty shillings. Jane Watt was found guilty of breaking into and stealing from an empty dwelling house in the nearby village of Enville – after having escaped from the Stafford Gaol, where she had been a long-term inmate.[50] Watt had made off with velvet waistcoats, linen shirts, silver sleeve buttons, a silk handkerchief, cotton stockings and two muslin aprons. Ann Thompson was convicted of pinching yards of cotton and nankeen. Priscilla Cockin was said to have twice set fire to haystacks. Tom Jones was convicted of being a highwayman who had taken a silver pistol from a traveller. Job Bratt was guilty of stealing twenty-four iron locks, while John Brough was guilty of stealing lead weight from the Marquis of the County of Stafford.

The horse theft allegedly committed by young James Burrow was the robbery of greatest value that Mr Justice Heath would hear that day. As Molly was called to stand in the dock, her legs felt like rubber. In solemn tones befitting the gravity of a life-and-death situation, the bailiff announced to the court that: 'The Jurors for our Lord the King upon their oath present that James Burrow, labourer of the Parish of Saint Mary … with force and arms … a Bay Mare of His Price of ten Pounds … did steal take and lead away against the peace of our said Lord the King.'[51]

Molly was asked to state her name and age. 'James Borrow,' she said, though it sounded like 'Burrow' to all those listening. 'Fourteen years.' In a voice as firm as she could muster, she said she was not guilty. But four citizens of good repute – baker John

Commander, groom Francis Emborton, yeoman William Moore and innkeeper Robert Silvester – provided evidence that this boy had stolen the horse. The younger John Hughes testified that the mare in question was his uncle's and that it had been taken from a common on the outskirts of Chester. The men's names were signed on a piece of parchment and witnessed by two justices of the peace.[52]

The jury briefly considered the evidence. Molly knew the word was coming, but when the foreman delivered it, she felt it as a blow to her heart: 'Guilty!'

Her knees knocked as Justice Heath eyed her dispassionately. A bailiff placed a piece of black cloth on the judge's bewigged head, then Heath uttered lines that he knew by heart. 'James Burrow, the law is that thou shalt return to the place whence thou camest and from thence be carried to the place of execution where thou shalt be hanged by the neck 'til thy body be dead. And the Lord have mercy upon thy soul.' The judge's words hit like the crack of Molly's neck breaking.

The chill of the grave ran through her body. A gaoler's hand clutched at her shoulder, and as her knees gave way he half threw her out of the dock and into the courtyard.

On a parchment charge sheet, a bailiff wrote, 'Guilty.' Later, a court clerk added, 'To be hanged: No goods.' Poor little Molly, terrified and apparently friendless, had not a single possession to leave behind except the boys' clothing on her scrawny back.

Chapter 3

A S MOLLY FRETTED OVER how she would spend the last days of her all-too-brief life, she continued to maintain her disguise. She found a corner of the cell in which to huddle and cry. There was little charity in those crowded cells – in fact, prisoners spared the death penalty would mock those about to dance with a rope.

Hangings were taking place all over Britain. On the day that Molly was convicted and sentenced, a hundred kilometres away at the Warwickshire Assizes, six men were also sentenced to hang; one of them was so overcome that he had to be dragged from the dock, writhing and screaming.[1] The day after Molly was condemned, a murderer was hanged on a moor outside Shrewsbury. A week later, a large crowd gathered there to see the execution of a man convicted of sacrilege after he stole linen and silver items from a chapel.[2] The rope squeezed his throat until his face went purple and then black, and he lost control of his bowels and bladder before dying.

As each day surrendered to night, and darkness drowned out whatever light there was in Molly's cell, fear clawed at her heart. When she closed her eyes and tried to rest, she wondered what eternal sleep was like. Her parents were dead; her grandparents were dead. Now the little girl with no goods and no one in the world to watch over her was waiting for her own cruel death, surrounded by strangers. She longed to go home, but instead she would be going to the gallows at Sandyford Bridge, just south of Stafford, where bodies were dumped in shallow graves.

There was, however, a glimmer of hope: British judges were beginning to agree that transporting convicts to New South Wales was an acceptable way to curtail the number of executions. Six prisoners had been sentenced to death in Stafford on the day Justice Heath passed judgement on Mary, but even he was softening. Soon after Molly was sentenced, Heath gave the murderess Jane North an unconditional pardon after a surgeon – who hadn't been able to give evidence at her trial – finally examined her and declared she'd been insane at the time of the killing.[3] As was the judicial practice of the time, following death sentences, a magistrate began the appeal process to commute some of the other death sentences in Stafford; he prepared a document for 'The King's most excellent Majesty' recommending 'diverse favourable circumstances' for some of the prisoners on death row as 'fit subjects' to receive pardons on 'several conditions … if your majesty shall so think fit'. Not long after the sentences were handed down, Heath, going against his stated principle to hang as best practice, recommended mercy for that odd, frail little horse thief James Burrow, taking into account 'the tender age of the prisoner'.[4] Heath recommended that the burglar Jane Watt be transported across the seas 'for the term of her natural life', and that the highwayman Tom Jones, the sheep stealer William Greenough, and the horse thief James Burrow all be sent to New South Wales too, but each for the term of seven years.[5]

News that some of the death sentences were being commuted spread quickly through the Stafford cells. The prospect that her life was likely to be spared lifted Molly from her torpor, despite her grim living conditions. Even before the King or his minions had responded to Heath's recommendations, their approval was thought to be a certainty. On 2 September 1791, the *Chester Chronicle* reported on the mercy of the court and claimed that among those saved from a meeting with the hangman was 'James Burrough, a youth of 15 [sic]' who had been condemned for 'stealing a valuable mare, lately advertised in our *Chronicle*, the property of Mr. Sorton [Hughes], of this city'.[6]

Around this time, Molly's ruse was finally exposed by a prison doctor – and Arthur Phillip was partly to blame. Back in 1787, when Phillip had been preparing to transport the first batch of convicts to Botany Bay, he'd told Evan Nepean, at the Home Office, that unless the prisoners were washed and clothed properly before being loaded onto the ships, there was a great danger that the crews would run away to 'avoid fatal distemper'.[7] In Stafford four years later, a prison doctor was called to examine all those not to be hanged, and the prisoners queued to be washed and scrubbed clean of filth and lice. It was inevitable that Molly's secret would be laid bare.

News of her cross-dressing made her something of a minor celebrity. Within days, the tiny felon was making headlines right across Britain – in Derby, Northampton, Ipswich, Newcastle, Reading, Chester, and all the way to London.[8] On 5 September 1791, amid news reports about the doings of Monsieur Robespierre during the revolution in France, and of the Indian general Tipu Sultan's war with the British, this item appeared in Thomas Aris's *Birmingham Gazette*: 'A discovery of a singular nature was made, it is said, in Stafford gaol a few days ago. A prisoner who was convicted and condemned for horse-stealing, but since reprieved (under the name of James Burrough) proves to be a woman; she has lain in the dungeon with near 50 male prisoners since the 18th of August, without any kind of suspicion arising among them of her sex. She now says her name is Mary Etticks.'[9] 'Etticks' may have been the way a gaoler heard Mary say the surname 'Haydock' in a strong northern accent; soon her surname would be written as 'Haddock' in the convict muster,[10] and perhaps 'Molly' morphed into 'Mary' to avoid the use of the slang term in prison. From now on she used the name 'Mary Haydock' even if prison officials were careless in the way they recorded it. The revelation of her true gender also required her speedy removal from among the male prisoners to a cell used to house the female convicts.

While Mary's life was spared, she and her fellow inmates could only watch on helplessly as the county sheriff and his guards collared one of her former cellmates, the burglar Joe Rogers, pinioned his arms and led him away for execution on 10 September. As Mary fretted over the condemned man's pleas, her sister Betty was looking forward to a prosperous future. The day after the execution, at the St Mary the Virgin Church in Prestwich, just up the road from Bury, Mary's nineteen-year-old sister married[11] Charles Foster,[12] a thirty-year-old wheelwright from Bolton.

Eight days later, a Stafford court official signed a document stating that the convict still officially known to the legal system as James Burrow was to be transported to 'the eastern coast of New South Wales or some one of the other islands adjacent' for the term of seven years.[13] Two justices of the peace from Stafford, John Williamson and Joseph Dickenson, were directed to organise the transportation.

Mary was breathing easier, but she knew she still had an arduous journey ahead to New South Wales – a place that the prisoners had heard was a godforsaken hellhole. Mary finally got word out to her aunt Penelope Hope that she was in a terrible bind.

IN THE DAYS AFTER MARY'S reprieve, ships of an eleven-strong Third Fleet carrying about two thousand more convicts were arriving in Sydney. There were 182 deaths among the prisoners, though the conditions were not as barbaric as on the Second Fleet. On board the *Queen*, which had sailed from Cork, was the first contingent of Irish convicts to come direct from that land: 126 men and boys, and 22 women and girls.

On the same day as the *Queen*'s arrival, 26 September 1791, an expedition organised by Joseph Banks and led by George Vancouver came across what is now known as Western Australia. Three days later, Vancouver formally claimed King George Sound – now the site of the city of Albany – for the British. The adventurer Archibald Menzies,[14] one of the men on the expedition, wrote to his patron Banks:

Here we remained a fortnight which gave me an opportunity of examining the Country in various excursions round the Sound – making a copious collection of its Vegetable productions, particularly the Genius BANKSIA which are here very numerous. The Climate appears to be exceeding favourable – the soil tho' light is good and productive of a vast variety of Vegetables particularly inland where the Country appears chiefly covered with wood diversified with pleasing pasturage & gentle raising hills ... we saw no Natives or Quadrupeds of any kind during our stay, tho' some recent traces of the former were very evident in two deserted Villages at the head of the Sound.[15]

In Sydney, Governor Phillip had started apportioning parcels of land to settlers and pardoned convicts for farming. He had selected an area upriver from Sydney as the best site for a large farm; the local Dharug people called the area 'Burramatta', which the Europeans heard as 'Parramatta'. Phillip initially named it Rose Hill. He gave the convicted burglar James Ruse[16] twelve hectares[17] to cultivate there, and it produced a bumper crop of corn, the first grown in the new colony. Phillip had another reason to feel optimistic: he wrote to Sir Philip Stephens, the First Secretary of the Admiralty, to say that the great number of sperm whales seen off the coast of New South Wales gave reason to hope that whaling could become a major industry for the infant colony.[18]

A Fourth Fleet had begun transporting convicts. As Mary awaited her fate, the *Pitt* was nearing Rio de Janeiro on its way to Sydney Cove. It carried a company of the New South Wales Corps to replace the marines in the prison settlement. Leading the Corps was the new Lieutenant-Governor of New South Wales: portly, round-faced Francis Grose,[19] a 33-year-old army major who had inherited his looks from his father, a rotund dealer in antiques and rare books whose own father had sold jewellery to the King. As a youngster Grose had twice been wounded in the war against the American rebels, and he'd been invalided home on half pay.

Lieutenant Governor Francis Grose. *National Library of Australia*
nla.obj-136080725

An affable man who tried to avoid conflict, he'd jumped at the opportunity to command the Corps on full pay, even though he was still troubled by his wounds and the posting was in a frontier settlement on the other side of the world. With Arthur Phillip's health in decline and requiring a return to England, Grose was to take charge of the colony until a more experienced, permanent governor could be appointed.

The *Pitt* had left Yarmouth Roads, on the Isle of Wight, on 17 July 1791. On board were 410 convicts (352 men and boys, and 58 women and girls), as well as the Corps soldiers, and the wives and children of free passengers and convicts. One of the convicts was a Scottish artist, Thomas Watling, who had been charged with forging guinea notes. He denied the charge, but rather than risk conviction and possible execution he'd asked to be transported; his sentence was fourteen years in New South Wales.

Early in the voyage there was apocalyptic thunder and lightning. Smallpox broke out after the ship left Cape Verde in the central Atlantic, and seven crewmen, thirteen soldiers, five of the soldiers' wives, five of their children, fifteen convicts, and two of the convicts' children died.[20] Many of those onboard became plagued by ulcerated legs.

When the *Pitt* reached Cape Town, Watling simply ran away and hid until Grose and the others had sailed for New South Wales. 'YOUR loved Watling is at liberty!' the escapee gushed in a letter from his hiding place to Marion Kirkpatrick, the maiden aunt in Dumfries who had raised him. 'True,' he wrote, 'I am in a remote clime, where Slavery wields her iron sceptre, and where slaves are at this moment attending me – yet blessed be Divine Mercy, I enjoy freedom! – I that but yesterday had the ignominious epithet convict adhibited to my name, am again myself! to-day all nature seems renovated. The sun that has [been] clouded for three years has regained his splendour, and the meads their verdure.'[21] Watling told Aunt Marion that his senses were all absorbed in the 'most pleasing delirium … that ever was poured upon mortal man.'[22]

ALTHOUGH MARY HAD disgraced her yeoman family, Aunt Penelope and Uncle Adam Hope began to attempt a rescue mission. Despite her high spirits, they knew the family's little runaway was still a young, frightened girl better suited to the bosom of a loving, extended family than chained below deck on a hell ship. They gathered together as many upstanding community members of Bury and Blackburn as they could, to vouch for Mary's character and to claim that her escapade had just been a good-natured lark that had resulted in a terrible misunderstanding.

On 5 November 1791, Adam Hope, woollen draper, and 'others hereunto subscribed residents in the Town of Blackburn',[23] signed what they called a 'humble' petition appealing 'to the King's most excellent Majesty'. The signatories were all men and comprised a surgeon, a 'gentleman', a tea dealer, cotton manufacturers, linen drapers, merchants, attorneys, a tallow chandler and soap boiler, and two church ministers including Samuel Dean, Headmaster of the Free Grammar School. The petition 'most respectfully Sheweth That Mary Haydock (a girl only fourteen years of age) was convicted at the last Stafford assizes of Horse-stealing for which she is now under sentence of transportation for 7 years to parts beyond the seas.'[24] It continued:

> That the said Mary Haydock being a poor helpless Orphan was prevailed on by another young girl to leave her situation in the month of June last, and in order that they might not be discovered they purchased Boys Clothes and changed their names: the said Mary Haydock then assuming the name of James Burrow – that they immediately came for Chester and the next day they parted – that the said Mary Haydock (then Burrow in boy's clothes) on her way to Stafford was accidentally overtaken by a man with 2 horses who desired her to ride one and he would please her and that the man fearing a discovery left her in Stafford with the horse and she showing inexperience in offering it for sale was apprehended upon suspicion of having stolen it, and committed to the prison there under the name James Burrow.[25]

The petitioners claimed that it did not appear as though Mary had 'any hand in the original Act of stealing the horse but that she has been drawn in by the wicked contrivance of some evil minded person or persons to share solely the whole blame of the business; and when the circumstances of her very tender years is considered it appears still more unlikely to your Petitioners that she alone could have formed a scheme so daring as that of stealing a Horse, but that the business must at least have been suggested to her by some evil disposed person or persons.'

The petitioners implored the King that they had 'known the said Mary Haydock from her Infancy she being a Native of Blackburn but could never suppose her capable of committing any such offence, that of stealing a horse especially as she had

had a good education and every endeavour has been used by her lately deceased Grandmother in whose custody she was for some time to enjoin her to the practice of every moral religious duty'.[26] They added, 'Your Petitioners therefore most humbly pray that your Majesty considering the pitiable situation of her, the said Mary Haydock, will be graciously pleased to extend to her your royal pardon and forgiveness, so that she may not be doomed to a miserable exile, but be freed from her present miserable confinement, and again be restored to her relations and friends.'[27]

The petition was passed on with a covering letter to Henry Dundas, Britain's Secretary of State, by Thomas Harkie, the Anglican minister at Blackburn. The Reverend Harkie couldn't speak for Mary's character – she had become an infrequent visitor to church, after all – so he pleaded her case on behalf of parishioners he knew.

> Nov. 5th, 1791
> Sir, I transmit to you the enclosed petition accompanied
> with the request of the friends of the unhappy young Girl
> who is the object of it ... Not knowing the young girl
> personally I could not with propriety put my name to the
> Petition. Her relations in this town are very respectable
> people, and I hope her extreme youth will entitle her to the
> royal Mercy.
>
> THOS HARKIE

The appeals were earnest, heartfelt and forceful. Justice Heath was having none of that nonsense, though – he was certain that the theft had required a degree of cunning. Two weeks after the petition was signed, Heath compiled a long report on the 'Case of Mary Haydock' and sent it to Lord Grenville, the new Secretary of State for Foreign Affairs and a future prime minister. Heath told Grenville that there had already been a 'Capital Respite' in the case and that he was not recommending any further extension of mercy.[28] It was of great surprise to him that the prisoner he had tried under the name 'James Burrow' was 'according to the Petition presented to his Majesty … a Girl of the name of Mary Haydock'.[29]

Justice Heath took Grenville through all the detailed witness statements in the Mary Haydock case. The judge laid them out in logical detail and summarised them with a compelling argument.

> The Jury found the prisoner guilty on the Evidence and
> I was then and still continue to be perfectly satisfied
> with the Verdict. On compassion to the tender age of the
> prisoner, I humbly recommended her as a proper object
> of the royal Mercy so that her Punishment might be
> mitigated to Transportation. I have perused the Petition
> presented to his Majesty praying a free pardon on the
> suggestion of her perfect innocence. I am humbly of the
> opinion that there is no grounds for this suggestion, and
> I am afraid that on the contrary from the artful manner
> with which she conducted herself that there is so much
> reason to suspect with [groom] Frances [Emborton] that
> she is an old offender or at least that it is not her first
> offence. If there were any respectable persons who would
> take charge of her and enter into the cognizance that she
> shall not commit any Felonies for 4 or 5 years to come, I
> think that she might be justly entitled to the Royal Mercy.
> Otherwise come, I am humbly of the opinion that under
> the present circumstances it is more advantageous for the
> prisoner herself and expedient for the Public example
> that she should be transported. All which is most humbly
> submitted to the royal Wisdom and Consideration.
>
> I am My Lord
Your most Obedient
Humble Servant
JOHN HEATH[30]

The petitioners, all men, since they were the only ones with any influence at that time in England, had begged for Mary's release, but it seems that none were willing to wager their reputations on a promise that she wouldn't reoffend. The girl had been fending for herself for five months and had now spent three of those alongside criminals, some of them condemned. Some of her relatives were well established in the Church and in business; she had cousins who would become doctors, and another branch of her family, the Walmsleys, were well-known lawyers. Mary's family ultimately decided that they couldn't take her back into their care and that a few years of hardship might chase the wildness from her soul.

Meanwhile Grenville had much weightier issues to deal with than the fate of a cross-dressing teenage horse thief. Arthur Phillip was sending him some of the strange animals 'known in England by the name of "kangaroo"'[31] and soon Grenville would receive letters from Phillip requesting guidance on how to apportion more land to members of the colony's military and civil administration.[32] Phillip was in poor health, suffering from kidney stones and other ailments, and thoroughly sick of New South Wales – he told Grenville that he wanted to go home.[33]

MARY HAD BEEN IN PRISON for eight long months when another ship of the Fourth Fleet, the merchant vessel *Kitty*, left Portsmouth for Sydney on 6 April 1792. Most recently the ship had delivered 113 slaves to Morant Bay, Jamaica, after having collected them from the infamous Cape Coast Castle on the Gold Coast of West Africa in what is now Ghana.

While Mary awaited transportation, she was allowed visitors. Her bond with Aunt Penelope grew stronger as the prospect of a long absence made the heart grow fonder. Prisoners were permitted to have money and possessions, and Penelope gave Mary gifts of clothing and cash before her departure. Betty was not so kind, though, and a rift between the sisters turned into a chasm.

Desperate for any chance to win her freedom, Mary was deceived by a conman who charged her two guineas to help swing her release. She never saw him or the gold coins again. Instead, she and other prisoners were moved from Stafford's gaol to London's Newgate Prison, 250 kilometres south-east, and assigned to travel on the next ship of the Fourth Fleet heading to New South Wales: an East Indiaman cargo vessel, the *Royal Admiral*, forty metres long and twelve wide. East Indiamen were the largest merchant vessels of the time, built to carry passengers and cargo under charter to the East India trading companies. The Royal Admiral was 919 tons and had three decks.

Convicts assigned to the *Royal Admiral* came from counties throughout England, Scotland and Wales. A newspaper in Bath reported that on 14 May 1792: '54 transports [convicts], of whom five were women, were removed from Newgate on board a Lighter, to be conveyed to the *Royal Admiral*, lying at Gravesend, and bound for Botany Bay. It is hoped the above transports may be useful hands in the whale fishery of New South Wales. Mary Haddock [sic], an active lass of only sixteen years [sic], who was capitally convicted at the last Stafford assizes for horse-stealing, under the name of James Barrow [sic], has had her sentence mitigated to a seven years visit to Botany Bay.'[34] Before dawn a general muster took place at Newgate and Mary bade farewell to her fellow prisoners. She and the others were marched from the prison to Blackfriars Bridge by the city guard, where the lighter was waiting to receive them. Two weeks later 102 more convicts were sent from Newgate down the river in preparation for the voyage.[35] Other prisoners were moved from the Exmouth gaol to Portsmouth via the Anger County Gaol in Wiltshire to also sail on the *Royal Admiral*.[36] The women and girls on board were keenly aware that they were vastly outnumbered by men and boys.

On 14 May 1792, the same day that Mary was loaded onto the ship, twenty-one soldiers of the New South Wales Corps marched on board as guards.[37] Three years earlier, Captain William Bligh – who had sailed on Cook's final voyage – had been taken prisoner by some of his crew on HMS *Bounty* near Tonga and set adrift in a small launch with eighteen of his supporters. In one of the greatest feats of navigation ever recorded, he'd guided the small boat to safety in Timor, 6500 kilometres away, after an astonishing voyage of two months. The New South Wales Corps would make sure there was no way that convicts could take control of the *Royal Admiral* on the way to New South Wales.

Despite the lessons about overcrowding and disease that should have been learnt from previous voyages, the prisoners – 49 women and girls, and 297 men and boys – were packed in tight with the soldiers and almost a hundred crewmen, the free passengers and children. Six of the convicts were young: three boys and three girls. Five of the convict women and girls were pregnant, including the teenage Loveridge sisters, Mary[38] and Priscilla, described as being of 'the Gypsey Tribe';[39] both had been sentenced to transportation for stealing three gowns and a large quantity of linen from a Berkshire house.[40] There were also more than a dozen passengers deemed crucial for the development and survival of the infant colony, including William Peat, a master carpenter travelling with his wife Phoebe and their infant daughter Mary; Thomas Allen, a master miller; and an experienced Scottish farmer, John Jamieson,[41] travelling with his wife Mary and their two young sons. Henry Hacking – who, after shooting two Eora people, had returned to England on the Dutch vessel *Waaksamheid* – had joined the *Royal Admiral*'s crew as the second master.

The *Royal Admiral* was owned by London shipping baron Thomas Larkins, from one of the most prominent families doing business with the East India Company. Before its departure, he came on board to pay the crew three months' wages,[42] normal procedure to quell any unrest among them. Under the transport contract, Governor Phillip had agreed to pay Larkins's agent, George Brown, £2754 12 shillings and 4 pence after the safe arrival of the convicts in Port Jackson.[43] The contractors were to supply food, basic clothing and bedding, and to do their best to keep the prisoners alive. The already cramped ship brought nine months of provisions for the convicts, flour and livestock for the settlement, spare masts, and limestone ballast that could be used in building at Sydney Cove.[44]

Two days after Mary came on board, the *Royal Admiral*'s skipper, Essex Henry Bond,[45] weighed anchor at Gravesend and set sail along the south coast of England.[46] A week later, Mary saw what she was told was the Isle of Wight, and Captain Bond anchored the vessel in a sheltered bay, St Helens Roads. Fresh water, salted beef, vegetables, bread and ale were taken on board. On 30 May, Captain Bond set sail, passing Torbay as he headed for the prison settlement of Sydney Cove, twenty thousand kilometres away. In a thick fog, the *Royal Admiral* passed the Eddystone Lighthouse off the coast of Cornwall.[47]

Two years earlier, Captain Bond had sailed the vessel to China for the East India Company. On this voyage he was planning to off-load the convicts at Port Jackson, sell many of the goods he was carrying for his own trade, then sail on to China to load more tea for Britain. Some of the convicts were convinced that China was close to New South Wales and that they could quickly walk there if they escaped their bonds – that was if they survived the voyage.

Chapter 4

STORIES OF THE HORROR voyages to New South Wales had spread like the plague through the British prison system,[1] terrifying many of the convicts before they boarded the transport ships bound for the prison camp they still called Botany Bay. The news had not spread widely back in Britain that the site had been changed to Sydney Cove. It was a relief to Mary when she found conditions on the *Royal Admiral* much more comfortable than she had imagined. Women and girls weren't shackled like the men and boys, who had chains around their feet and hands, and they were given more freedom to move around the deck, to inhale the salty spray and celebrate a small degree of independence on the high seas. All the convicts were allowed out of the prison rooms and into the fresh air for an hour's daily exercise, and divine service was held each Sunday. Still, there was always a looming threat of floggings or worse for the misbehaviour of both convicts and crewmen, and the soldiers would brandish their muskets as a warning against any hint of mutiny.

Although conditions were strict and spartan, there was at least food, clothing and shelter. For many of the poorer convicts, transportation was their ticket out of starvation, and conviction a lifesaver. Rations were meagre and usually unappetising, but no one starved, nor did they have to steal to survive, though they were occasionally punished for the pilfering of stores. Livestock was regularly killed for meat. There was boiled beef and pork, pea soup, and oatmeal with a little sugar and butter. There was fresh water and, if that ran out, Spanish red wine.

The prisoners were corralled into smaller, more manageable groups under guard in prison holds below deck. They were then supplied with uniforms. Many of the poorer convicts had emerged from prison wearing nothing but rags, while wealthier convicts could bring clothing with them to sell at high prices in Sydney. On board the *Royal Admiral*, all of the prisoners were issued with coarse, loose-fitting garments known as 'slops', so named because they looked sloppy and seemed to have been designed for further humiliation. Many prisoners, both women and men, had their hair cropped short to guard against lice on the ship. Each prisoner was given a straw mattress wrapped in tightly woven material called ticking, a pillow of similar construction, a thin woollen blanket, and a bar of soap to wash themselves. Bedding was regularly aired. During the voyage they would face everything from tropical heat to mountainous waves and blasts of Antarctic wind when they reached the Southern Ocean.

The prison quarters below deck were hot and stuffy, with people pressed in beneath low ceilings. After almost no time the holds stunk to high heaven. The latrines involved a plank with holes in it atop a series of buckets; these would be emptied over the side of the ship at regular intervals, but the nauseating smell lingered and enveloped everyone like a fog. Prisoners who had never developed sea legs found their stomachs at the mercy of the wind and waves, and vomit often stained the floor. The bases of the masts ran through the prison holds, loudly creaking and groaning all day and night under the power of the wind. Convicts slept in rows of double bunks, and Mary – being young, agile and not pregnant – slept on top with the floorboards of the upper deck inches from her face. At night the prisoners sang ditties and told stories of the terrors and curiosities that awaited them in the great southern land, such as the bounding kangaroo.

Captain Bond took great pains to see that there was much less fraternisation between crew and convicts than there had been on previous voyages – such as that of the 'floating brothel', the *Lady*

Juliana, in 1790. A row of spikes between the segregated quarters was designed to prevent any secret liaisons, and while a heavily barred hatch on the deck let in a little sunlight and air for the prisoners during the day, it was battened down at night, giving the convict quarters the ambience of a tomb.

Bond had a genuine affinity with the *Royal Admiral*. He had first sailed on it way back in 1777 when the ship was newly built and he was a fourteen-year-old servant. He'd worked his way up the ranks by serving on several ships of the East India Company, and when he was at last given his first command, it was on the *Royal Admiral* in 1789.[2]

He ran a tight ship, but disease, death and disobedience were part of maritime life. Just two days into the voyage to Sydney, when the *Royal Admiral* was near the Isles of Scilly, a cat-o'-nine-tails lashed six times across the back of seaman Joe Hall after he was found to be drunk and disorderly.[3] The following day, a sailor named Kirk fell overboard in rough seas and drowned.[4]

Among the crew was Dr Richard Alley, appointed by the Commissioners of the Navy at 12 shillings and sixpence a day until his arrival back in England, on top of his pay as a naval surgeon.[5] He was to oversee the ship's convicts and to assist its doctor, John Syme. Alley had papers for Governor Phillip that outlined the provisions the ship was carrying for the use of the Sydney settlement. The papers also explained that the *Royal Admiral* had been chartered by the East India Company to bring home tea, requiring it to be in China by January 1793.[6] It would have to make good time to Sydney and leave promptly.

Alley had last sailed to Sydney on the *Lady Juliana*. After that voyage, he had lived with the convict Ann Mash in Sydney until he'd decided to leave for England – and leave her holding their baby. Ann was six months pregnant when Alley took off on a Dutch transport ship.[7] Three months later, on 5 June 1791, she gave birth to their daughter Charlotte Maria Alley, who only lived for five days.[8] Now a bereaved single mother, and an angry one at that, Ann accused Ann Flavelle – with whom she shared a convict hut – of stealing baby linen and other goods. The accused received twenty-five lashes across her bare back.[9] Ann would rise above her circumstances and like many of the women in this frontier town, prosper as a businesswoman in Sydney.

THE GREAT ROLLING GREY ocean intrigued Mary and all the others unused to sea travel. As brisk winds pushed the *Royal Admiral* south towards the Cape of Good Hope, Mary heard that among the men there were cases of venereal disease and that some had ulcerated legs from untreated old sores.[10] Some of the prisoners began coughing ferociously with consumption. Dr Syme worked overtime tending to the sick, and Captain Bond had the ship's carpenter John Blundel and the other tradesmen performing frequent maintenance as the vessel made good time down the Atlantic.

George Thompson, who filled the roles of gunner and inspector of convicts,[11] won the respect of Mary and all the other souls on board as he regularly had the decks washed with oil of tar while ensuring that the prison holds were fumigated and kept as clean as possible.[12] Still the vastness and turbulence of the water and the uncertainty of what would happen in their prison destination was unsettling for all the prisoners, especially the youngest. Some cried often. Of a small, lost-looking girl with a broad accent who fitted Mary's description, Thompson wrote in Latin: '*Quis talio fando temperate lachrymis* – Who can shed tears in such a way?'[13] According to the convict James Lacey, 'The greatest praise falls short of what this gentl'n [Thompson] deserves for his unremitted attention to the health and comfort of the unhappy men under his care, his sea stock, purchased at his own expense, being at all times dedicated to the use of any of them whose situation seemed to require it.'[14] Lacey was overjoyed at finding the treatment of the prisoners in 'every respect far superior to what from the outset we were led to expect', although he was dismayed that convict women and girls – such as young Mary Haydock – seemed to be given more freedom to move around the ship than Lacey's wife, Sarah, who travelled with him as a free woman.[15]

Some of the crew tried to hoard provisions, but Lacey recorded that the 'excellent' purser Richard Halliday, was 'a gentl'n who, by his strict attention, prevented many frauds being practised on the provisions of the convicts by those employ'd to deliver it'.[16] Anyone caught stealing from the stores was whipped, and Bond did not discriminate, having soldier James Parr receive a dozen lashes for falling asleep on guard duty.[17] Despite such punishments, Lacey believed that Bond, Thompson and some of the other soldiers and crew were 'very human, good men'. Bond sometimes ordered extra rations for the convicts in order to maintain their health and spirits. However, Lacey believed that 'not having tasted the bitter cup of affliction themselves' some officers on the ship were 'apt to view us wretched beings with more contempt than is necessary, or than their services deserved, being at all times employed in the most slavish part of the ship's duty'.[18]

By 12 June 1792, the *Royal Admiral* was off the Portuguese island of Madeira. Five days later, Mary saw the Canary Islands off the north-western coast of Africa.[19] As Bond turned the ship south-west towards the Cape Verde Islands, he heard that some of the convicts were hatching a plan to overpower the soldiers and take command of the vessel. Lacey complained that the accusations were fraudulent – formulated by a convict who was being bullied and wanted revenge.[20] But Bond lined up eight of the accused conspirators and had the alleged ringleader lashed thirty-six times with the cat, blood running down his back in rivulets. The other seven convicts received twenty-four lashes each.[21] Their howls echoed around the ship, and Mary and the others could only whisper about the brutality lest their complaints be overheard by the officers.

Below deck under the summer sun near the equator, Mary sometimes found the conditions stifling. Yet she was more comfortable than many of the other passengers, especially the pregnant women and girls.[22] A month after leaving England, the sixteen-year-old burglar Mary Loveridge gave birth to a daughter, Charlotte, off the coast of Gambia in western Africa.[23] Captain Bond, authorised to perform religious services, baptised the child, praying that she would not fall into sin like her mother. Later in the voyage he would baptise Priscilla Loveridge's baby.[24]

Although the ship had taken on large quantities of fresh vegetables before leaving England, the diet on board was inadequate. Bond ordered the surgeon, Alley, to give special provisions to those unfortunates who showed signs of scurvy – whose gums swelled and burst, and whose teeth became loose. Left untreated, the scurvy would destroy joints and make it impossible for sufferers to stand up. Bond instructed Dr Syme to dole out malt and wort, the sugary liquid extracted from the mashing process in making beer and whisky. Syme also gave cider, and spruce beer to those showing symptoms of the dreaded mariners' curse. Even some of the convicts, passengers and crew who didn't have scurvy were putting their hands up for the cider and beer.[25] Some of the sick were beyond help. Not long after Mary observed the *Royal Admiral* sail past another ship, the *Brothers of Liverpool*, off the coast of Guinea, the body of Thomas Smalley – a convict who had died shaking and rattling with fever – was committed to the deep.[26] The corpse was sewn into a hammock, weighted with ballast, and dropped over the side after a short service performed by the captain.

A week later, on 10 July 1792, the ship crossed the equator. Celebrations were held among the crew, with one of them dressed as King Neptune to mark the occasion. By the time Mary saw the archipelago of Trinidade and Martim Vaz on 19 July, thirty-two convicts and eight sailors were being treated for scurvy, fever or dysentery, and the body of another convict, William Barlow, had been weighed down and slid overboard into a watery grave.[27]

IN SYDNEY, the arrival of the storeship *Britannia* on 26 July was a cause for great rejoicing. Sydney only had twenty-four days' worth of salt meat left in the stores, and a month's delay for the ship could have been calamitous for the colony. Under the command of part-owner William Raven[28] and with an ambitious first mate, a young man named Thomas Reibey,[29] the *Britannia* berthed in Sydney after a passage of twenty-three weeks from

Falmouth.[30] The convicts and settlers in Sydney now numbered 4639, and the *Britannia* was one of three ships that deposited twelve months' clothing, four months' flour, and eight months' beef and pork for the settlement. On the day following the vessel's arrival, the weekly ration for each convict man was increased to:

- Four pounds of maize
- Three pounds of soujee (Indian semolina)
- Seven pounds of beef, or 4 lbs. of pork
- Three pints of peas
- Half a pound of rice.[31]

Two thirds of these rations were to be issued to each woman and to each child above ten years of age; one half of the man's rations was issued to each child above two and under ten years of age, and one quarter to each child under two. For a long time soldiers, settlers and their families would be under the same laws of rationing.

Governor Phillip was so chuffed by the filling of Sydney's larder that he began remitting sentences. He gave an unconditional pardon to Elizabeth Ruse,[32] the wife of farmer James Ruse. Elizabeth had sailed to New South Wales on the *Lady Juliana* after receiving a seven-year sentence for stealing clothing and a small amount of money.

Phillip's joy turned to chagrin, though. He soon found that not only was there not the amount of salted meat promised on the *Britannia*, but also that the suppliers had sent out cuts that were 'lean, coarse and bony, and worse than [the inspectors] had ever seen issued in his Majesty's service'.[33] The loss was keenly felt, and the convicts and settlers would have to tighten their belts.

MOUNTAINOUS SEAS ROSE up around the *Royal Admiral* as it headed towards southern Africa. At times the prison holds flooded, leaving Mary and others up to their waists in water. The latrine buckets were thrown askew. Despite the efforts of the gunner George Thompson to keep the convicts' quarters clean, fleas, lice, rats and cockroaches often came to visit. And no matter how often the quarters were fumigated and aired, the stench of body odours, human waste and death haunted all those confined there.

Temperatures began to plummet as Captain Bond made brisk time sailing south, and he doled out warm fearnought cloaks, made of thick wool, for all the prisoners.[34] Regardless, the sick bay became more crowded. By 9 August, when the *Royal Admiral* reached the Dutch-controlled territory at the Cape of Good Hope, three convicts and two crewmen had died, but these were low figures for such a voyage at the time. Another convict man died while the ship was in False Bay off Cape Town.

There was a flotilla of Dutch boats in the bay, and Bond acknowledged the Dutch commodore with a nine-gun salute, a compliment that was returned. The captain ensured that there was a ready supply of fresh provisions in an effort to restore the health of all on board: livestock, fresh meat, rice, green vegetables, lemons and coconuts were hauled onto the ship.

Mary stayed put on board as Bond sent the sick to a hospital in Simon's Town where a handful of the convicts tried to make their escape. After her horse theft had landed her in this mess, Mary made sure not to annoy authorities again. She watched on as Bond had two of the recaptured convicts, Owen McCarthy and Robert Blanchflower,[35] flogged for running away from the hospital.

One of the escapees, John Smith, managed to get away, though,[36] and evade capture, but another runaway was found to even the tally.

On 21 August, almost two weeks after the ship had reached the Cape, Mary and the others were amazed to see the runaway convict artist from the *Pitt*, Thomas Watling, being frogmarched on board the *Royal Admiral*. In happier times after he had made his escape, Watling had written to his Aunt Marion to say that he felt the joy of 'the jubilee of creation'; he was 'treading in air', he claimed, with his spirits 'electrified' and his heart beating quicker than ever with 'redoubled fervour and emotion'.[37] Now Watling had his hands and feet manacled, and tears in his eyes. Soon he wrote again to his aunt, adding to the swirl of her emotions back in Dumfries, to say that the Dutch 'mercenaries' had betrayed him in Cape Town, arrested him at his hiding spot and kept him prisoner until the next British convict ship arrived. Watling had a flair for art – and melodrama: 'the nauseous cup was poured out for me, and I was born to drink it to the very dregs', he told his aunt.[38]

For three weeks, Bond remained at the Cape to lift the health of his crew, passengers and human cargo. Many of the convicts were still ailing despite their treatment in hospital, but Bond calculated that the ship now had enough vegetables to reach Sydney. He'd also obtained twenty sheep to help with regular rations of fresh meat. On 30 August 1792, the captain weighed anchor and set off for the final leg of the voyage to the sound of another nine-gun salute from the Dutch.

THE *ROYAL ADMIRAL* MADE record time across the Indian Ocean, powered along by winds known as the Roaring Forties. A week after the ship left the Cape, the convict Sarah Thomas delivered a son named David. Captain Bond baptised the sickly child as his weary mother watched on and wondered listlessly about their fates. Amid the easy spread of disease in her prison hold, Sarah died a week later from dysentery. Her body was sent to the bottom of the ocean as the ship sliced through what would become known as the Great Australian Bight.[39] Another convict woman, Elizabeth Mathews, delivered a stillborn child the next day. The convict women and girls nursed sickly David Thomas, but they despaired a week later as his little body was also wrapped in canvas and dropped over the side.

Watching on with the awful uncertainty of pregnant women in such perilous conditions were Ann Viles,[40] convicted of receiving stolen goods, and Mary Springate, convicted of theft. They hoped that whether they gave birth on land or at sea, their children would be hale and hearty.

On 1 October, with a gale blowing, Mary Haydock and the others saw a sliver of lush green land in the distance – the first land they had seen in a month. The reserves of fresh meat and vegetables had dwindled, and seventy-six people were on the sick list. Bond noted the green outcrop as the south-west cape of Van Diemen's Land, and word of this spread around the ship. The blessed sight of land was accompanied by the screams of Ann Viles as she gave birth to her daughter.[41]

The *Royal Admiral* followed the east coast of New Holland for six days. Then Bond observed a jutting piece of land, twenty kilometres to the west, that Captain Cook had named Cape Solander twenty-two years earlier. Just after dawn on 7 October, Mary watched spellbound as the Union Jack fluttered on the flagstaff of Port Jackson's South Head. Bond sailed through the narrow gap between the Heads.

It was a warm spring day, almost summery, with an easterly wind. At about noon an alcoholic conman, Richard Atkins,[42] who had somehow become a magistrate and registrar of the Vice-Admiralty Court in Sydney, heard the blast of fifteen cannons signalling an approaching vessel.[43] He and many others on shore presumed it was the long overdue slave ship *Kitty*, carrying convicts and 3780 ounces of silver in Spanish dollars to pay many of the colony's creditors.[44] But the *Kitty* was still a month away.

Mary watched with a mixture of excitement and fear as Bond made the most of an easterly wind to navigate the *Royal Admiral* through Port Jackson. As she looked out over the deck at Sydney's harbour, young Tom Reibey was aboard the *Britannia*, anchored in the same waters. His ship was being readied for a private charter voyage to Cape Town, where it would collect 'a freight of cattle'[45] and other goods for the New South Wales Corps, the military force that was starting to flex its muscles and brandish its muskets as the real power in local government.

Bond sailed into Sydney Cove, finally anchoring in ten metres of water in front of the infant settlement that huddled around the water. As Mary glanced excitedly all about her, Bond had the ship washed down thoroughly with vinegar and the prisoners scrubbed clean before preparations began to disembark them. The convict women and girls were told they would be put to work making clothes.

Thompson observed the area closely, writing later that the land of New South Wales, from Botany Bay to Port Jackson, had a level appearance at first sight and could be viewed from the sea at a distance of up to forty kilometres.

> As you come nearer, it appears hilly up the country, and full of trees. The entrance of the harbour is formed by two heads, called the North and South Heads lying nearly in those directions and about three quarters of a mile distant from each other ... The whole abounds with islands, coves, creeks, and harbours, up to Sydney, which is about nine miles from the entrance, and makes the most complete harbour in the universe: there your ships lay within fifty yards of the shore, in five fathom and a half [ten metres], and as smooth as in a fishpond.[46]

The *Royal Admiral* had taken 139 days to reach Sydney from England, clocking the fastest ever time from the Cape of five weeks and three days.[47] Having survived the arduous voyage of twenty thousand kilometres, the convict Samuel Sutherland died the day after the *Royal Admiral* docked, and Bond sent 182 convicts ashore along with Sutherland's body for internment. Mary Springate stayed on board to deliver a daughter, but both died within a few days.

Governor Phillip was planning to return to Britain, sick of the day-to-day struggles he tried to overcome from Sydney while communications with his masters in Britain took months to arrive by ship. He wrote to tell Home Secretary Henry Dundas in London that the *Royal Admiral* had arrived with an alarming number of sick convicts, bringing fever to the young colony that Phillip was trying to protect.

> Of the convicts embarked on board that ship, ten men and two women died on the passage, and four children were born, one of whom died; one male convict escaped at the Cape of Good Hope, and seventy-two men, eleven women,

My Dear aunt   oct 8th 1792 botany bay
We arrived here on the 7th and I hope it will
answer better than we expected for I write this on
Board of ship but it looks a pleasant place—
Enough we shall but have 4 pair of trowser a week to make
and we shall have one pound of rice a week and
th pound of pork besides Greens and other
Velgetoubles the tell me I am for life wich
The Governor told me I was but for 7 years wich
Grives me very much to think of it but I will
Watch every oppertunity to get away in too or 3 years
But I will make my self as happy as I Can In my
Present and unhappy situation I will Give you—
Further satisfaction when I get there and is settled
I am well and hearty as ever I was in my life I
Desire you will answer me by some ship that is
Coming and lett me know how the Children is
and all inquireing friends so I must Conclude
because we are in a hurry to go a shore remember
My Love to my sister and aunt wamsley and
My Cousens so no more at present from
your Dutifull neice Mary Haydock Mr scot
Took 2 Guineas of me and said he would Get me
My Libearty with my sister has been very ungra
To me so I must never see you again

Mary Reibey's letter to her aunt Penelope Hope in Church Street, Blackburn,
written on her arrival at the convict colony in Port Jackson on 8 October 1792.
State Library of NSW FL898510

and five children have been landed sick. I have no doubt but that strict justice has been done them, and hope the sending out [of] convicts and stores by ships employed in the service of the East India Company will answer the end proposed by Government; but, sir, if I was to give an opinion, I think the people have been too much crowded on board this ship.[48]

Little Mary Haydock, though, had survived the passage fighting fit. She might have remained in England had just one family member guaranteed her good behaviour, but she had not been privy to the judge's order. She now thought of her loved ones left behind. Believing the place she looked out upon was Botany Bay and not Sydney Cove, as many convicts did, she composed a fond letter to Aunt Penelope at Church Street, Blackburn, Lancashire. Even at the tender age of fifteen, Mary realised she had made many errors in life, and despite the unkindness of her sister, familial bonds tugged at her heart.

October 8th 1792 bottany bay.

My Dear Aunt,
We arrived here on the 7th and I hope it will answer
better than we expected for I write this on Board of
ship but it looks a pleasant place – Enough we shall have
but 4 pair of trowser to make a week and we shall have
one pound of rice a week and 4 pound of pork besides
Greens and other Vegetables the[y] tell me I am for life
wich The Governor told me I was but for 7 years wich
Grieves me very much to think of it but I will watch
every opportunity to get away in too or 3 year But I will
make my self as happy as I can in my Present and unhappy
situation I will Give you Further satisfaction when I get
there and is settld I am well and hearty as ever I was in
my life I Desire you will answer me by some ship that is
Coming and lett me know how the Children is and all
inquiring friends so I must Conclude because we are in a
hurry to go a shore remember My Love to my sister and

Aunt Wamsley and my Cousens so no more at present,
from your undutiful niece Mary Haydock Mr Scot took
2 Guinnes of me and said he would get me My Libetty
with my sister [he] has been very ungood To me so I must
never see you again —[49]

It seems Mary didn't yet know about full stops, but what she saw
all around the *Royal Admiral* was an exclamation mark underlined
for emphasis. While she yearned for the people and places she
had left behind, she already knew that having escaped the noose
in England she had been given a second chance at life. This vast
waterway was her route to a whole new world of opportunity.

Chapter 5

THE HEALTHY CONVICTS fit for work were rowed upriver to Parramatta, about twenty kilometres from Sydney. Most of the men were to be employed in clearing the land for farming in order to feed the young colony, while the women were to keep huts clean and make clothes. The eighth of October was another hot, sunny and windy spring day,[1] much warmer than the weather Mary was used to. As she travelled slowly down the harbour and into the Parramatta River, she marvelled at the great waterway and the khaki hills, so very different to the Lancashire landscape.

Governor Phillip had ordered that all new prisoners arriving in Port Jackson should be sent to Parramatta immediately 'without permitting them to disembark at Sydney'.[2] Judge Advocate David Collins recalled that until then Sydney was the only place where shipping anchored, and it 'possessed all the evils and allurements of a seaport of some standing'. Phillip wanted the new convicts to be ignorant of those enticements so that they would go to their work camps upriver 'with cheerfulness', glad that their gruelling voyages were over.[3]

During his time in Sydney the governor had hanged nineteen men and one woman for theft, but even the threat of capital punishment couldn't stop pilfering from the limited provisions. Although the storerooms were vigilantly watched while secured with bolts, locks and iron fastenings,[4] they were routinely robbed. Phillip changed tack: he replaced the convict security guards on the stores with a new team, promising them that if they behaved well and protected the supplies, they would eventually be set free. He was confident the plan would work, but for the time being food in New South Wales remained scarce and heavily rationed for soldiers, settlers and convicts alike.

In the year and a half since she'd run away from the boarding school, Mary had found much more adventure than she'd bargained for. But her fascination at her new surroundings was checked by a rising feeling of dread. She could see that men vastly outnumbered women in the new colony – in fact, it was by six to one – and it seemed that women and girls had limited long-term career options apart from convict duties as seamstresses or cooks: they could be sex workers, indentured maids, or wives/mistresses – or a combination of the three.[5] George Bond, an ensign with the New South Wales Corps, recalled that on the arrival of a transport the women and girls were well washed and given a change of clothes.

> The commissioned officers then come on board, and as they stand upon deck, select such females as are most agreeable in their person; who generally, upon such occasions, endeavour to set themselves off to the best advantage. In this state some have been known to live for years, and to have borne children. The non-commissioned officers then are permitted to select for themselves; the privates next, and lastly, those convicts, who, having been in the country a considerable time, and having realized some property, are enabled to procure the governor's permission to take to themselves a female convict. The remainder, who are not thus chosen, are brought on shore, and have small huts assigned them; but, through the want of some regular employment are generally concerned in every artifice and villainy which is committed.[6]

A select committee of the House of Commons later heard that in the distribution of convict women and girls, great abuses prevailed: 'they were indiscriminately given to such of the inhabitants as demanded them, and were in general received rather as prostitutes than as servants; and so far from being induced to reform themselves, the disgraceful manner in which they were disposed of, operated as an encouragement to general depravity of manners ...'[7] Every freeman in New South Wales was entitled to a convict wife, and the talk among the prisoners was that life could be much more bearable for a convict woman if she was chosen by one of them rather than assigned as a maid or seamstress.[8]

As Mary and the others were taken towards Parramatta, the gunner George Thompson recorded detailed observations about the land and water that he and the prisoners were seeing for the first time. He noted that Sydney's harbour and the Parramatta River were teeming with a variety of fish, most of them unknown in England. There were plenty of oysters, cockles and other shellfish, along with snapper, mullet, flathead, salmon and whiting.

Sydney was the site for the first settlement because of the advantage of clean water and the convenience of the harbour, and there were now gardens there sufficient to supply the inhabitants with vegetables. Governor Phillip had a fine two-storey residence with a grand harbour view, and most of the colony's officials lived nearby, all with sufficient convicts to act as servants and to attend the colony's storehouses and fishing boats.[9] About three kilometres away, in what became the suburb of Surry Hills, were fields where convicts baked light-brown bricks and tiles. Buildings constructed of wood were white-walled with pipe clay.

Mary saw all manner of wildlife unknown in England, such as brightly coloured parrots that didn't sing so much as screech. There were mosquitoes everywhere, and she soon learnt that the ubiquitous flies were so aggressive that meat could be full of maggots an hour after the animal was killed.[10]

When Mary arrived in Parramatta, she saw a row of buildings about a kilometre and a half long; this was High Street, the first formed road at the settlement.[11] There was a series of detached houses, each surrounded by enough space that they could be

A view of the Governor's House on Rose Hill in the town of Parramatta by J Heath, engraved in 1798. On the right of the path are stocks used for the confinement and humiliation of prisoners. *State Library of NSW FL8781864*

enlarged when necessary. A large brick hospital was under construction on High Street, as well as a church and storehouse. Mary was surprised by the extent of development in what she'd been told was a harsh prison, and Thomas Watling would soon sketch the scene of budding prosperity. Overlooking it all was the governor's country residence, a large house situated in a sylvan setting upon Rose Hill. The government's cattle grazed at Cumberland Park, and there were forty hectares of grain growing nearby, chiefly a hardy type of maize called 'Indian' or 'flint' corn; there was also some wheat, oats and barley. The crops looked 'remarkably well', promising that at the end of Phillip's reign as governor, the colony would have the most fruitful harvest in its short history.[12]

But the current prosperity of the settlement masked recent calamity. Thompson wrote that food had been so scarce that those now living owed their survival to all those who had died and left them enough provisions.[13]

MARY SOON LEARNT THAT the camp at Toongabbie, a few kilometres from Parramatta, had the greatest number of convict labourers in the colony. They were made to work hard, felling trees, digging up the stumps, rooting up the shrubs and grass, turning up the ground with spades and hoes, and carrying the timber away. Each morning they toiled from five until eleven; they rested during the heat of the day and then worked again until sunset. They were often hungry as they mostly received ill-treatment from the superintendents – men that the observer Thompson called 'a set of merciless wretches'.[14]

At night the prisoners were confined in huts, with as many as eighteen together and with just one woman, who – while fending off their advances – had to cook for all of them and keep the place clean. Bedding was only what the convicts had been permitted to take from the ship, unless they had the means to buy some when they came on shore. Most of the huts had just one small iron pot to cook the pitiful allowance of meat and rice. Many prisoners didn't have a bowl, plate, spoon or knife, their only utensils being what they could carve out of timber.[15] Mary heard that it was not uncommon for seven or eight men to die each day as they were kept in the field when ill, and there were stories of convicts dying at the storehouse door as they waited for their allowance of food. Convict women and girls at Parramatta had a more comfortable life than the men and boys, so long as they didn't misbehave and earn a place working in the fields.

Because of her tender years, Mary was to be protected. Rather than working as a hut keeper, she would be put to work making four pairs of trousers a week for the labourers. She hoped she would soon be assigned elsewhere or find a kindly husband among the free settlers.

MARY HAD ONLY BEEN in New South Wales for two weeks when she and the other prisoners received extra clothing and other necessary articles. She lined up at the government store while a convict with privileges handed every woman and girl a cloth petticoat, one coarse shift (or smock), a pair of shoes, a pair of yarn stockings, a pound of soap, a quarter pound of thread, two ounces of pins, six needles, a thimble, and a pair of scissors. Each man and boy was issued with two tunics made of coarse, light and fragile osnaburg material,[16] which rarely survived more than three weeks of hard work.[17] They were also given two pairs of trousers made from the same material, a pair of yarn stockings, a hat, a pair of shoes, a pound of soap, three needles, a quarter of a pound of thread, and a comb. There were more than a few muttered complaints that the tunics and trousers wouldn't last, but the agent who had bought the fabric for the government had been given limited funds.[18] The men and boys didn't receive scissors because not only were they expensive, but they were also dangerous in the wrong hands – especially if those hands had just held a few strong drinks.

At Sydney and Parramatta, Captain Bond, about to depart for China, opened shops with the help of his agent John Macarthur – who had come over with his family on the Second Fleet. They sold the goods that Bond had carried from England on the *Royal Admiral*. The only significant addition made to the weekly ration of the settlers by the arrival of the *Royal Admiral* was an allowance of six ounces of oil to each person. There had been 9278 gallons of oil derived from animal fats loaded onto that ship and the *Kitty* to be used in lieu of butter, but the bulk of the oil had turned rancid on the voyage, so the colonists mostly burnt it as a substitute for candles.

On 20 October 1792, under Governor Phillip's direction, Judge Advocate David Collins granted Bond the colony's first liquor licence to sell beer and the dark brown porter. Collins would later lament that 'under the cover of this, spirits found their way among the people, and much intoxication was the consequence'.[19] Some of the settlers simply went berserk on 'gibber-juice', and there were all manner of fist fights and incidents of domestic violence.

Several of the settlers, breaking out from the restraint to which they had been subject, conducted themselves with the greatest impropriety. The indulgence, which was intended by the Governor for their benefit, was most shamefully abused and what he suffered them to purchase with a view to their future comfort, was retailed among themselves at a scandalous profit; several of the settlers' houses being at this time literally nothing else but porter-houses, where rioting and drunkenness prevailed as long as the means remained. It was much to be regretted, that these people were so blind to their own advantage; most of them sacrificing to the dissipation of an hour what would have afforded them long comfort and convenience, if reserved for refreshment after the fatigue of the day.[20]

In one of his last messages as governor to the British authorities, Arthur Phillip lamented prophetically that 'The permitting of spirits amongst the civil and military may be necessary, but it will certainly be a great evil.'[21]

Mary quickly discovered that not all the custodians of the law were above reproach. Until his promotion to the Vice-Admiralty Court in Sydney, the thoroughly disreputable Richard Atkins – who was 'addicted to liquor, immorality and insolvency'[22] – had been Phillip's magistrate at Parramatta, while the new man in charge of security at the stores was the reformed Irish pickpocket George Barrington.[23] Gunner Thompson called Barrington 'a very diligent officer', but his past was as shady as a wide verandah: he claimed to have picked the pockets of everyone from his schoolmaster to a Russian count, peers of the British realm and some of 'the brightest luminaries of London'.[24] After his final arrest, Barrington had tried to escape from London's Newgate Prison in his wife's clothes. But in Sydney he had impressed Phillip with his resolve to go straight, and the governor offered him emancipation and twelve hectares to farm.[25]

Good work at Parramatta was rewarded, while punishments could be severe. For a trifling offence, convicts were often placed in the public stocks until they could be properly interrogated. If found guilty, they could immediately be dragged to a cartwheel

Irish pickpocket George Barrington was put in charge of the government stores at Parramatta. *State Library of NSW FL3276571*

and tied to its spokes, and then receive a 'Botany Bay dozen' – twenty-five lashes.[26] A petty crime that might have earned a dozen lashes on the convict transports could earn a few hundred in Parramatta. Crimes tried by a regular court, such as theft, were often punished with a death sentence – or a second transportation to the prison on Norfolk Island, 1400 kilometres away in the Pacific, which some convicts believed was worse than death.

AS MARY WAS SEWING TROUSERS, Tom Reibey was preparing to sail on the *Britannia* for the Cape of Good Hope with William Raven. Raven had accepted a payment of £2000 for the voyage, and Lieutenant-Governor Francis Grose had organised eleven shares of £200 each from investors to purchase £2200 of livestock and merchandise that the officers of the New South Wales Corps planned to sell at a hefty profit. The *Britannia* was well built for carrying livestock, having adequate space between the decks, and tradesmen from the Corps were employed to fit the ship with stalls to safely accommodate the animals. A quantity of hay was put on board to lessen the expense of it at the Cape.[27]

The ship had been caught in a battle between Phillip and Grose, the man who would soon take over the governor's role and who was being influenced by vocal members of the New South Wales Corps. Grose was a malleable commander who bent to the will of strong personalities, such as his friend John Macarthur. The lieutenant-governor was uncertain about making his own decisions, once telling Home Secretary Henry Dundas that 'I cannot but be alarmed at all I purchase, and everything I do, being unaccustomed to business, and fearful of acting so much from my own discretion.'[28]

But Grose was emphatic when he argued with Phillip in this instance. While Phillip was insisting on rations for everyone in the colony, the governor included, Grose believed that the officials and soldiers needed for the safety of the settlements should be above such privations whenever they could easily be avoided. Phillip wanted all supplies for the colony to be provided through the East India Company, which had a royal charter giving it a monopoly on trade east of the Cape; he was wary of what he called 'opening a door to contraband trade'.[29] Grose wrote:

Sir,
The situation of the soldiers under my command, who at
this time have scarcely shoes to their feet, and who have no
other comforts than the reduced and unwholesome rations
served out from the stores, has induced me to assemble
the captains of my corps for the purpose of consulting
what could be done for their relief and accommodation.
Amongst us we have raised a sufficient sum to take up the
Britannia, and as all money matters are already settled with
the master, who is also an owner, I have now to request
you will interest yourself in our favour, that you will, by
representing the necessities of my soldiers, protect this ship

from interruption as much as you can, and that you will
assist us to escape the miseries of that precarious existence
we have hitherto been so constantly exposed to.

> With every respect, &c.,
> FRANS. GROSE,[30]

Phillip suggested Grose was exaggerating the privations of his
men, since Phillip ate the same food as them and had been in
the colony much longer. However, the governor reluctantly
acquiesced, telling Under Secretary Nepean that the voyage
would proceed 'although very much against my inclination'.[31] It
would give Phillip the chance to forward his dispatches to the
British government when the *Britannia* relayed with another vessel
at Cape Town.

Phillip suspected that Grose and the New South Wales Corps
were more interested in profiteering than provisioning, and that
the greed among some members of the Corps could only cause
harm. Grose appointed Macarthur the regimental paymaster,
putting him in charge of investing the officers' money. As Phillip
grew preoccupied with leaving Sydney, Macarthur oversaw the
purchase of all the wine, rum and gin from the American ship
Philadelphia,[32] and 7597 gallons of American spirits from a Rhode
Island ship, the *Hope*.[33] The alcohol added to the crime rates in
Sydney, and Grose's soldiers earned the title of the 'Rum Corps'
as they controlled the liquor trade, selling it at exorbitant prices.

Long before the *Britannia*'s departure, Raven had found Sydney
to be a cesspit of sin. On the night of 10 October 1792, three days
after Mary's arrival in the colony, Raven was sleeping in his hut on
the shore when a burglar broke in at around midnight. The thief,
risking death if caught, tiptoed to Raven's bedside and pocketed a
tin watch and some ornate knee buckles that were used to fasten the
legs of the skipper's breeches. As the thief picked up a jewellery box
containing a more expensive timepiece and some money, Raven
woke in fright. He shouted salty sea curses and leapt at the intruder.
They tussled violently. As Raven clutched at the thief's jacket to
restrain him, he dropped the jewellery box and ran for his very life,

his feet making almost no noise as they slapped against Sydney's dirt streets. Almost instantly he vanished into the blackness of night.[34]

Raven was a mentor to young Tom Reibey. The pair enjoyed something of celebrity status in Sydney, whose inhabitants remained in what they saw as the dark recesses at the end of the world. Ships arriving from England or from any other part of the world not only brought much-needed supplies but also were objects of endless fascination. Their crews were invited into private homes and sought after by public officials for news of what was happening in the rest of the world.[35]

Raven and Reibey had spent the better part of their lives on the sea. Reibey, who also spelt his name 'Raby', was the son of Edward Raby, a ship's officer from Cobham, Kent. Edward was the second officer on the ship *Tannah*, the Bengal Pilot Service schooner for the East India Company, operating out of Calcutta. The pilot service was responsible for guiding ships, particularly East Indiamen, along the Hooghly River between Calcutta and the Bay of Bengal. Edward's base was the Calcutta suburb of Entally, where Tom had spent his formative years. The *Tannah* was captured by the French in 1781[36] off Madras and recommissioned as a ten-gun corvette of the French Navy,[37] and Edward was imprisoned by the French until the Treaty of Versailles in 1783. Tom claimed that at thirteen he'd been shipwrecked and nursed back to health by the locals at Entally.[38]

It had a place in his heart for the rest of his life.

TOM REIBEY AND CAPTAIN RAVEN sailed out of Sydney on the *Britannia* on 24 October 1792 bound for the Cape and the abundance of food it offered. They carried with them Governor Phillip's dispatches for the British government pleading for a year's worth of provisions for the colony.[39]

Three weeks later Captain Bond steered the *Royal Admiral* through Sydney Heads bound for a large cargo of tea in Canton. With John Macarthur's help, Bond had sold £3600 worth of goods in Sydney and Parramatta, and he left behind articles worth £750 for Macarthur to sell on commission.[40] Bond also left behind seven of the *Royal Admiral*'s crew who had decided to take their chances in the new colony; those who stayed in Sydney included George Thompson, Thomas Dargin – who later married Mary Loveridge, one of the convicts who had given birth on the ship – and the brutal Henry Hacking, who hid in the woods until the *Royal Admiral* was out of sight.

In December 1792, Arthur Phillip left Grose in charge of the colony and headed back to England aboard the *Atlantic*, taking with him Bennelong and another Wangal man Yemmerrawanne,[41] who had both volunteered for the voyage to act as diplomats for their people. Watkin Tench wrote of Bennelong's 'bold intrepid countenance, which bespoke defiance and revenge',[42] but the Indigenous man had quickly adapted to the ways of his captors and learnt simple English, telling Phillip and other colonists of Eora customs and language. Tench described Yemmerrawanne as 'a good-tempered lively lad' who had become 'a great favourite' waiting on the table at Government House.[43] Phillip also carried with him at least two skulls of Indigenous people, which Joseph Banks sent on for study to fellow natural scientists: a German, Johann Friedrich Blumenbach[44] – a fellow of the Royal Society who lectured at the University of Göttingen – and a Dutchman, Sebald Justinus Brugmans.[45] Despite claiming that he wanted to protect the Eora, Phillip had little respect for their sacred customs, having his men rob graves in the name of science.

On its way to the Cape, the *Britannia* visited Dusky Sound, New Zealand, in November 1792. Captain Raven left his second mate John Leith and some of his crew there to collect 4500 seal furs and valuable spruce fir timber, which Raven regarded as the best wood possible for shipbuilding. From New Zealand the *Britannia* rounded Cape Horn and proceeded to the Portuguese settlement on the island of Santa Catherina, on the Brazilian coast. Raven and the crew stayed there as welcome guests for eighteen days before sailing across the vast expanse of the Atlantic to the Cape of Good Hope. The Britannia arrived there on 24 March 1793[46] and Raven delivered Phillip's dispatches to Captain Edward Manning aboard the *Pitt*.

Reibey was earning an attractive reputation as a dashing young adventurer, and he was about to see how much profit a trader could make. Following Grose's orders, Reibey oversaw the loading of thirty cows, three mares, twelve goats, and a quantity of flour, sugar, tobacco and spirits, as well as other goods that could be sold for big profits in New South Wales. Despite all the precautions taken with the animals, twenty-nine cows and three goats died as the ship endured rough weather between the Cape and the colony, including an icy gale around Van Diemen's Land.[47] Of course, Grose and the New South Wales Corps were able to sell the surviving goods and livestock at phenomenal mark-ups, when the *Britannia* returned to Sydney in June 1793.

With tensions mounting between Britain and France, Grose decided that the colony's supplies would almost certainly be affected by 'commotions at home'.[48] On 26 August 1793, he again chartered the *Britannia*, this time for a mission to bring back supplies from Calcutta, specifically salted meat – Irish beef or pork. In the event of it not being possible to procure them, the ship was to return loaded with sugar, rice, and the legume dhal.[49] Grose told Lord Cornwallis, Governor-General of India, that he was appealing for provisions because of the uncertainty of British ships coming to New South Wales now there were 'the appearances of war'.[50]

Reibey and Raven set off once more, but in the Straits of Malacca the *Britannia* was intercepted at 8 a.m. on 2 February 1794 by a fleet of fast-moving Malay proa boats loaded with pirates who had murder and looting on their minds.[51] The Malays cornered the *Britannia* and opened fire from heavy cannons mounted on swivels.[52] Some tried to make it onto the decks to use their curved kris daggers in close-quarter battles. For six long hours, Reibey and the others blasted away with cannon fire and muskets, as screams and bloodcurdling threats rang out across the vivid blue sea. Hot lead bullets fizzed past Reibey's head, and the smell of gunpowder filled the air.

The battle raged and raged, until finally, with the *Britannia*'s ammunition almost exhausted, the captain of one of the pirate vessels was killed trying to climb on board the British ship, and Raven managed to get away. He sailed the *Britannia* safely to Batavia, arriving on 11 February. But there was bad news in the Dutch outpost. Raven was warned that French privateers were 'so numerous and strong'[53] that a passage to India wasn't possible without the near certainty that the *Britannia* would become a French possession, just as the *Tannah* had when sailed by Reibey's father a decade earlier. Raven and Reibey addressed the Governor-General and Council of Batavia. After some diplomatic arm wrestling, they obtained permission to load the ship with provisions from the Dutch East India Company's stores, even though it was an opposition business to the British East India Company and what it regarded as a monopoly for the settlement of New South Wales.

On 1 June 1794, the *Britannia* returned to a hero's welcome in Sydney. Not only did Reibey have thrilling, bloodcurdling stories to tell of the gunfight on the high seas, but he and the other men on board the *Britannia* had returned with more than a hundred thousand pounds of beef, eighty-three thousand pounds of pork, sixty-five thousand pounds of sugar, and more than a hundred thousand pounds of rice.[54]

IT BECAME LORE IN HER family that because Mary Haydock was literate, she was assigned to work as a nursemaid for Grose, looking after his infant son Francis Jr.[55] Grose had been granted land known as Grose Farm, on what in later years became the University of Sydney, at the junction of a track that led to Botany Bay and one that led to the farmlands of Parramatta. He was in regular contact with William Raven and Tom Reibey, who at twenty-five was eight years older than Mary.

Reibey saw Sydney, with all the teething problems of its troubled infancy, as a gateway to opportunity for him and the large family he wanted. He was quickly charmed by Mary's good looks and intelligence, and the fact that unlike the many convict women and girls who had known only poverty and degradation, she had been educated and schooled by middle-class standards.[56]

Mary didn't know Tom well, but she could see he was a bold and daring man of adventurous spirit – a man after her own heart. She had managed to dodge the forced marriages that so many convict women and girls had undergone. Now, in this pirate-fighting tamer of the high seas who had a head for figures, Mary had found her man. Tom made up his mind to marry her and settle in the colony, and Grose gave her permission to get married.[57] The name 'Mary Reibey' had a ring to it.

Chapter 6

MARY HAYDOCK BECAME Mary Reibey at just seventeen when she married Tom Reibey in St Philip's Church[1] on 1 September 1794. It was a hot, blustery day,[2] and the couple were preparing to ride the winds of change in the still infant colony. They were making plans to obtain their own farm, raise a family and invest for their future.

St Philip's Church was a T-shaped wattle-and-daub building with a thatched roof and an earthen floor,[3] not far from the harbour. It could hold five hundred people, but as Sydney experienced another spring heatwave the Reibey wedding was a simple affair without any of the pomp that Mary remembered from Aunt Penelope's wedding to Adam Hope in Lancashire.

Mary was a small, petite bride, radiant in a frock of Indian muslin that Tom had secured in one of his cargoes. Her reddish-brown dark curls clustered around her wide, high forehead and her merry, mischievous brown eyes danced with joy under her arched brows.[4] Some of Tom's crewmates from the *Britannia* had warned him that he was 'a quixotic young fool' for marrying a convict, and that he was sacrificing family, career, and a prosperous future.[5]

He thought otherwise.

Tom knew all about Mary's conviction and the shame she had caused her people in Bury and Blackburn, but he also knew that in the two years since the *Royal Admiral* had delivered Mary to her convict superintendents she had proved herself to be strong, loyal, industrious and dependable. The young officer had decided to stake his future and that of his family on those qualities.

As the pungent scent of bush flowers wafted into the church and a flock of magpies serenaded their ceremony, the colony's first chaplain, Richard Johnson, pronounced them man and wife. Outside the church there was the clank of chains as convict road gangs went by.[6]

Tom's shipmates and his mentor William Raven missed the ceremony, having sailed a day earlier[7] on the *Britannia* for the Cape on another transport voyage to bring back horses, cattle and supplies.[8] The official witnesses for the wedding were Sarah Higginson, a thief who had sailed on the *Royal Admiral* with Mary, and another convict friend, William Denman, who had received a fourteen-year sentence for highway robbery. Both were illiterate and signed their names with an 'X'. Tom signed his surname as 'Raby'.[9]

Curious eyes turned towards the young couple as they made their way over the rough road towards a simple honeymoon. Other women convicts watched with envy the consummation of a romance that must have seemed like a fairytale to them,[10] as little Mary had found a good man and a life away from the cruelties endured by most prisoners.

Marriage to a man with prospects was the fastest way for a convict woman to improve her lot in Sydney at the end of the eighteenth century. Thomas Watling complained that young convict women had an unfair advantage over men like him, who were often farmed out to work for despots. If a girl of uncommon spirit should attract the affection of a man in high office in the convict settlement, he wrote, she could become very powerful in Sydney, dressing and living better than ever before.[11]

Construction of St Philip's, the first religious building in Sydney, had been finished in June 1793 under Richard Johnson's direction. He paid for it out of his own pocket, using convict labour. During the week, the church served as a schoolhouse where he and his wife Mary taught as many as two hundred children.

It was compulsory for all convicts to attend church every Sunday because Christianity was seen as crucial to the reformation of their sinful natures. But the reverend was frequently in disputes with Lieutenant-Governor Grose, who saw Johnson as meddling in the personal salvation of the prisoners, and doing harm to discipline and order. Grose falsely accused Johnson of being 'one of the people called Methodists' and branded him 'a very troublesome, discontented character'.[12]

Despite their bitter differences, Grose had assigned Johnson a grant of forty hectares. The lieutenant-governor encouraged as much private farming as possible, in order to reduce the colony's dangerous dependence on imported foods – and his workload in running government operations. Unlike Phillip, who had followed the official policy of only trading with the East India Company, Grose had been encouraging his officers to make fortunes trading with visiting ships from Britain, India, Java and Britain's old enemy, the United States, now that the American republic had been formed and peace had been restored. The Reverend Johnson was given Bidjigal land, and he named his farm Canterbury Vale, after Canterbury in England. Over time it expanded and covered an area that is now part of the suburbs of Canterbury and Ashbury.

Grose increased the weekly ration for soldiers, giving them more food than the convicts and settlers, and he improved their living conditions.[13] He also started doling out land grants of about ten hectares each to serving members of the New South Wales Corps, extending his largesse to bureaucrats, emancipists and free settlers. Military officers received much more land and – contrary to instructions from the Home Office in London – ten convicts provisioned at government expense to work that land.

The big winner of these grants was Grose's friend John Macarthur. The lieutenant-governor had doubled Macarthur's salary as paymaster of the New South Wales Corps. He had also appointed him Inspector of Public Works, which gave Macarthur control of the colony's captive workforce and all its materials and machinery for his own personal use.

Macarthur and his wife had established Elizabeth Farm at Rose Hill, on a forty-hectare grant of land that Elizabeth called 'some of the best ground that has been discovered'.[14] It was near Macarthur's regular job at the barracks, so his daily commute took next to no time. Convict labour helped him become the first man in the colony to clear and cultivate twenty hectares of land, and this earned him another forty-hectare grant. He was on his way to becoming a land baron. At Elizabeth Farm he built 'a very excellent brick building 68 feet in length and 18 feet wide [20 by 5.5 metres], independent of kitchen and servants' apartments'.[15] The house had four large rooms and a big hall, and it was surrounded by a fertile vineyard, fruit trees, and more than a hectare of garden 'abounding in the most excellent vegetables'.[16] Soon Macarthur was writing joyfully that Grose had transformed his life with pay rises and free land.

The changes we have undergone since the departure of Governor Phillip are so great and extraordinary that to recite them all might create some suspicion of their truth. From a state of desponding poverty and threatened famine, that this settlement should be raised to its present aspect in so short a time is scarcely credible. As to myself, I have a farm containing 250 acres, of which upwards of 100 are under cultivation, and the greater part of the remainder is cleared of the timber which grows upon it. My stock consists of a horse, two mares, two cows, 130 goats, and upwards of 100 hogs. Poultry of all kinds I have in the greatest abundance. With the assistance of one man and half-a-dozen greyhounds which I keep, my table is constantly supplied with wild duck and kangaroos; averaging one week with another, these dogs do not kill less than three hundred pounds weight.[17]

Tom Reibey was now a family man with aspirations to mirror Macarthur's success, and he'd applied for a grant of land to farm. Two months after the wedding, on 19 November, Grose awarded

'Tom Raiby' Land Grant 310 in the district of 'Mulgrave Place'.[18] While Tom had made a career on the sea, he now saw the chance to make a life on the land. He and Mary were awarded thirty acres (twelve hectares) in the newly colonised region north of Sydney, alongside a magnificent river that had been named after Charles Jenkinson, First Earl of Liverpool, also known as Lord Hawkesbury.[19]

THE DAY BEFORE MARY'S WEDDING, Grose had told his bosses at the Home Office in London that he had 'caused a very good road to be made from Sydney to the banks of the Hawkesbury'. He said an officer who was 'by no means considered as being particularly active undertook for a trifling wager to walk there from Sydney in nine hours, and with great ease to himself performed a journey in eight hours and two minutes which formerly required an exertion of some days to accomplish.'[20] Back in January 1794, Grose had settled twenty-two farmers beside the Hawkesbury,[21] around what is now known as Pitt Town.[22] Although many of them were reluctant to move there, worried about 'the overflowing of the river', six months later Grose boasted that they were doing well with 'the most luxuriant crops'.[23] The rich silt soil along the banks of the wide, winding river were far more fertile than the stony and sandy patches around Sydney Cove, Botany Bay, and even Parramatta. Grose told the Home Office that while during winter there had been the heaviest rains that the colony had experienced in its six years, fears among the settlers about flooding were unfounded and the Hawkesbury had remained benign.

By the time Mary and Tom were married, there were seventy settlers on the Hawkesbury. All were doing 'exceedingly well', according to Grose, and their wheat promised to be the best yet grown in the colony.[24] Most of the farmers also kept pigs, and they grew wheat, vegetables and maize, making the area the colony's food bowl for many years. In March 1795, the small vessel[25] *Experiment* carted sixty logs of Hawkesbury cedar and some mahogany to India as the area became an important source

The Settlement on Green Hills (Windsor), on the Hawkesbury in 1809, attributed to G.W. Evans. *State Library of NSW FL1151980*

of timber. As a married man, Tom was entitled to another twenty acres (eight hectares), and from his time on the *Britannia* he had the money to hire working men – both convicts and emancipists.

At first most of the European settlers lived in humble two-room cottages. The walls were usually constructed with vertical wooden stakes, or wattles, woven with horizontal twigs and branches, then daubed with clay or mud to form a solid structure. The roofs were thatched and the floors bare earth. Kitchens were mostly skillions, lean-tos attached to the building.

Despite the opening of the road north, most of the transport to the Hawkesbury was still done by a colonial vessel,[26] the *Francis*. The 41-tonne schooner had been partially constructed at the Deptford Dockyard in England, then shipped to New South Wales on the *Pitt* for reassembly as a vessel for exploration. Tom was working on acquiring his own transport vessels.

Mary and Tom had hardly taken up their land grant when Grose resigned as lieutenant-governor, complaining that his health rendered it absolutely necessary that he return to England.[27] He didn't have the experience to become a governor at the time but he didn't leave the colony without talking himself up, submitting a report to the Home Office in London from Augustus Alt,[28] the government surveyor, who with Arthur Phillip had planned the wide streets and huge blocks for the village of Sydney. Under instructions from Grose, Alt had estimated the amount of land cleared since Phillip's departure. 'According to the most accurate observations' Alt wrote, there were 4675 acres and three-quarters of cleared ground in the colony, whereas under Phillip there had been only 1703.[29] Grose had given Alt a hundred of those acres (forty hectares) at what is now Petersham, and Alt took up another 250 between the road to Parramatta and what is now the suburb of Ashfield. Alt Street was named in his honour.

THOMAS WATLING WAS AT FIRST assigned as a servant to the surgeon-general and naturalist John White,[30] who had kept deaths low on the First Fleet and then survived a duel with his assistant William Balmain that left both men only slightly wounded. Watling then worked for David Collins, the judge advocate. Fascinated by his new home, the artist and forger began drawing and painting landscapes, Eora people, and the stunning local fauna and flora. He continued writing his verbose letters to Aunt Marion in Dumfries;[31] he told her that he had seen 'so much wanton cruelty practised on board the English hulks, on poor wretches, without the least colour of justice' and that neither the 'French Bastile [sic], nor Spanish Inquisition' could manifest more horrors. To him, New South Wales was a world upside down.

> Our longest day coincides exactly with your shortest; and vice versa. The climate is an extremely sultry one, especially in summer ... A few European culinary vegetables grow, but never arrive to their pristine maturity, and when re-transplanted dwindle unto nothing. The face of the country is deceitful; having every appearance of fertility; and yet productive of no one article in itself fit for the support of mankind.

Perhaps nothing can surpass the circumambient windings, and romantic banks of a narrow arm of the sea, that leads from this to Parramatta, another settlement about fourteen miles off.

Overhead the most grotesque foliage yields a shade, where cooling zephyrs breathe every perfume. Mangrove avenues, and picturesque rocks, entwined with nondescript flowers.

In the warmer season, the thunder very frequently rolls tremendous, accompanied by a scorching wind, so intolerable as almost to obstruct respiration — whilst the surrounding horizon looks one entire sheet of uninterrupted flame. The air, notwithstanding, is in general dry. Fifteen months have been known to elapse without a single shower.

The vast number of green frogs, reptiles, and large insects, among the grass and on the trees, during the spring, summer, and fall, make an incessant noise and clamour. Birds, flowers, shrubs, and plants; of these, many are tinged with hues that must baffle the happiest efforts of the pencil.[32]

Watling described the huts and canoes of the Eora as 'extremely rude and ill formed', adding: 'but when we consider their non-acquaintance with iron tools, and the hardness of their wood, it is more surprising that they can use it at all'. Sometimes the Eora would sit by Watling as he painted, and he noticed that art was vital to their own culture, observing the way they daubed their faces and bodies with paint, and made markings and carvings on their weapons and tools.[33]

IF SYDNEY AND PARRAMATTA had been a culture shock for Mary after a relatively genteel childhood in northern England, the Hawkesbury was an even more confronting place. Two expeditions had explored the great waterway and its associated river, the Nepean, a year after the First Fleet's arrival, and in 1793 part of the Hawkesbury–Nepean catchment had been named the Grose River and the Grose Valley. Despite Grose's assurances that there was no threat of flooding along the Hawkesbury, Mary and Tom remained concerned every time the skies turned grey.

A year after their wedding there was a spell of heavy rain and tempestuous winds, and the river rose to twenty-five feet (eight metres) above its usual level, submerging the farms of several settlers. The water rose so swiftly that one local settler and many animals were drowned. Despite the uncommonly fertile ground in the area, many farmers offered their land back to the Crown.[34]

Farming far from even the small settlements of Sydney and Parramatta was confronting for Mary and Tom, even though they had already overcome all manner of hurdles in life. The air, the sky and the land were all very foreign. It was hot in December rather than snowing, and kangaroos, goannas and venomous snakes were stark contrasts to the fauna in Britain.

Portrait of Bennelong, the Eora man taken to England.
State Library of NSW FL214557

Colonisation had devastated the lives of the First Peoples and they fought back. Tom had survived a pitched battle with pirates armed with cannons, but the stealth and ferocity of the Indigenous people around the Hawkesbury, the Dharug, struck terror into him and his fellow settlers. The Dharug had repeated skirmishes with the pale strangers who had invaded the land where their people had hunted and fished for thousands of years. The settlers ripped out wild yams on the riverbanks and planted crops, and the Dharug didn't understand why they weren't welcome to partake from the fields of grain where their own food had grown, or why their visits were met with deadly gunfire. Their concept of property was deeply at odds with European ways.[35]

Mr and Mrs Reibey had been on the Hawkesbury for about three months when Bennelong left England aboard HMS *Reliance* after his visit there with Arthur Phillip and Yemmerrawanne. Henry Waterhouse[36] was the skipper. Others heading for Sydney on the ship included the new Governor of New South Wales, John Hunter, who had sailed with the First Fleet; the ship's surgeon, George Bass;[37] and an enterprising midshipman, Matthew Flinders.[38]

Watkin Tench had thought Bennelong would receive celebrity status[39] in Britain, but because England was at war with France again, the novelty of meeting indigenous people from the colonies didn't excite Londoners as much as seeing kangaroos – the animals drew big crowds paying a shilling a ticket at the Lyceum Museum on the Strand. Bennelong and Yemmerrawanne were first billeted in Mayfair, and while it was rumoured that the 'New Holland men' met King George III, this wasn't at an organised royal visit; if it did happen, it was most likely on 24 February 1794, when Bennelong attended the Theatre Royal at Covent Garden during a royal visit there.[40] Two months later, the Wangal men visited the Houses of Parliament, where they met the speaker and future prime minister Henry Addington. They also saw the Tower of London, St Paul's Cathedral, and curiously a display at the Parkinson Museum of artefacts from Cook's voyage to their land.

Bennelong and Yemmerrawanne were dressed in the height of London fashion: coats, silk stockings, blue and buff striped waistcoats, ruffled shirts, and slate-coloured breeches. They were also often sick and morose. They longed for home. 'They seem constantly dejected,' the *London Observer* noted, 'and every effort to make them laugh has been for many months ineffectual.'[41]

After a long illness, on 18 May 1794 Yemmerrawanne had died of a lung ailment aged just nineteen. He was buried in the churchyard of St John's in Eltham, under a modest tombstone that Phillip insisted the Crown provide.[42] Nine months later, on 25 February 1795, Bennelong began his journey home from Chatham on the River Medway in Kent. He arrived back in Sydney that September and was seen by David Collins as an important bridge between the settlers and the colony's First People, but the judge advocate lamented that Bennelong's 'influence over his countrymen' did not extend to the Dharug people of the Hawkesbury,[43] who weren't as friendly to the colonists as those in Sydney.[44]

The Dharug had good reason not to be welcoming. The first settlers along the Hawkesbury were constantly on guard after many of them provoked animosity in the cruellest ways possible. 'Whatever the settlers at the river suffered was entirely brought on them by their own misconduct,' David Collins wrote. 'There was not a doubt but many natives had been wantonly fired upon; and when their children, after the flight of the parents, have fallen into the settlers' hands, they have been detained at their huts, notwithstanding the earnest entreaties of the parents for their return.'[45] Collins blamed much of the trouble on former convicts who 'finding themselves freed from bondage, instantly conceived that they were above all restrictions; and being without any internal regulations'[46] became uncontrollable.

In the month that Mary and Tom were married, a settler on the Hawkesbury and his servant were speared and clubbed in their hut during a raid by the Dharug; both barely survived. After another attack on settlers a few days later, the Europeans formed a posse and killed 'seven or eight of the plunderers' on the spot. Collins heard reports that some of the local farmers had seized a Dharug child and, after tying him hand and foot, dragged him several times through a fire until his back was dreadfully scorched. Then they'd thrown him into the river, where they shot and killed him.[47]

Captain William Paterson[48] cared nought for reconciliation. The Scottish soldier and botanist had succeeded Grose as lieutenant-governor in Sydney while the colony awaited John Hunter. A devotee of Joseph Banks, Paterson had been sending plant specimens to Britain's leading scientist since being stationed in South Africa fifteen years earlier. Paterson had more regard for native plants than Indigenous people.

Six months after Mary and Tom had settled on the Hawkesbury, four hundred Europeans were living there, and their farms extended for fifty kilometres along the riverbank. Paterson complained to his superiors at the Home Office that those settlers had 'for some time past been annoyed by the natives, who have assembled in large parties for the purpose of plundering them of their corn'.[49] He was doing his best to placate his superiors in Britain, who had ordered that colonisation should be carried out as peacefully as possible with regards to the Indigenous inhabitants. The temporary governor said he did not want to destroy any of those Aboriginal people, 'particularly as I have no doubt of their having been cruelly treated by some of the first settlers who went out there'.[50] He made no mention that the First Peoples were starving after their food sources had been taken from them. However, he added that if he hadn't taken drastic measures, the European settlement on 'the banks of so fine a river as the Hawkesbury' would be doomed. According to Paterson, because there weren't enough firearms for the settlers there, several 'accidents [had] happened'.[51] One settler had been speared to death in 1794, and the Europeans had retaliated by killing as many as ten Indigenous people. On 15 June 1795, Paterson told Home Secretary Henry Dundas that within a few weeks, the local Indigenous people had killed five settlers and wounded several.

It therefore became absolutely necessary to take some measures which might secure to the settlers the peaceable possession of their estates, and without which, from the alarm these murders have created, I very much feared they would have abandoned the settlement entirely, and given up the most fertile spot which has yet been discovered in the colony. I therefore sent a detachment of two subalterns and sixty privates of the New South Wales Corps to the river, as well to drive the natives to a distance, as for the protection of the settlers ... I have just received a report from the commanding officer of the detachment informing me that the night after his arrival at the river the party had fired upon and pursued a large body of natives, who had concealed themselves in the neighbouring woods during the day, and at night came to a settler's farm to plunder it; that he supposes seven or eight natives were killed, and that he was taking every measure he thought likely to deter them from appearing there again.[52]

Collins described the battles on the Hawkesbury in far more graphic terms. An 'open war' seemed to have commenced, he wrote. Word was received early in 1795 that two settlers had been killed: a man named Wilson and his labourer William Thorp, a former crewman with Tom Reibey on the *Britannia*. Collins recalled:

The natives appeared in large bodies, men, women, and children, provided with blankets and nets to carry off the corn ... In their attacks they conducted themselves with much art; but where that failed they had recourse to force, and on the least appearance of resistance made use of their spears or clubs. To check at once, if possible, these dangerous depredators, Captain Paterson directed a party of the corps to be sent from Parramatta, with instructions to destroy as many as they could meet with of the wood tribe (Be-dia-gal);[53] and, in the hope of striking terror, to erect gibbets in different places, whereon the bodies of all they might kill were to be hung. It was reported that several of these people were killed in consequence of this order; but none of their bodies being found ... the number could not be ascertained. Some prisoners however were taken, and sent to Sydney; one man, (apparently a cripple,) five women, and some children.[54]

Paterson told Dundas, as diplomatically as he could, that he meant to keep his prisoners until he could make them understand that 'we are readier to be friends than enemies; but that we cannot suffer our people to be inhumanly butchered, and their labour rendered useless by their depredations, with impunity'.[55] Collins recalled that when one of the women prisoners had been shot through the shoulder prior to her capture, the baby at her breast had been wounded. Both of them were carted to a hut near the hospital in Sydney, but the wounded child died. Another woman prisoner gave birth to a son, but he also died. The man said to be 'a cripple' was in fact very active and escaped Paterson's soldiers by swimming across Port Jackson to the north shore.[56]

Soon there was another attack by a Dharug raiding party on the Hawkesbury farm of Cornish-born William Rowe[57] near a place known as Richmond Hill. Rowe had been transported on the First Fleet for burglary and in 1791 at Parramatta had married Mary Ann Hawkins, a convict who had just arrived in Sydney on the Third Fleet after being found guilty of stealing four silver tablespoons. On 15 May 1795, William was granted twelve hectares at Richmond Hill. Eleven days later the Dharug arrived there with spears, and William and the Rowes' 'very fine child'[58] were killed. Mary Ann, who had received several wounds, crawled along the riverbank and concealed herself among some reeds, half immersed in the river. Several hours passed before neighbours found her hiding there. 'This poor creature,' Collins wrote, 'after having seen her husband and her child slaughtered before her eyes, was brought into the hospital at Parramatta, where she recovered, though slowly, of her wounds.'[59] In a cruel postscript, Mary Ann was savagely beaten and strangled to death by burglars at Parramatta eleven years later.[60] Two men were hanged for the crime.

FOR MARY REIBEY, life on the Hawkesbury was as dangerous as life on a convict ship. Tom was frequently away, sailing a sloop between their farm and Sydney as he started a carrying and trading business, and there was little in the way of a neighbourhood watch.

While the Reibeys proved to be among the most industrious couples in the colony, Collins had a low opinion of many of the settlers along the river, saying that some of them simply did not deserve land on a waterway so fertile that it could be termed 'the Nile of New South Wales'.[61] A lot of the Hawkesbury farmers, Collins said, made no preparations for sowing seed, 'consuming their time and substance in drinking and rioting; and trusting to the extreme fertility of the soil, which they declared would produce an ample crop at any time without much labour. So silly and thoughtless were these people.'[62] He claimed that the worst of the Hawkesbury settlers seemed too lazy even to be concerned about protecting their families and crops during the 'open war' with the local Indigenous people, 'seldom or never' showing the smallest disposition to assist each other from the threat of attack.[63] He neglected to mention, though, that some of the settlers might have had good personal relationships with Aboriginal people or might have been working with them, and they may also have felt for their plight.

Crime among the Europeans remained rife in the colony. Public hangings continued in Sydney – mostly for burglary, though in 1795 six men had faced death for the rape of a Dublin-born convict, Mary Hartley, at a farm on the Field of Mars, south of the Hawkesbury near present-day Ermington. The men were found not guilty but retried for assault. Three of the accused were sentenced to five hundred lashes, the other three to three hundred.[64] The case was terrifying to Mary, who was often home alone on the farm with danger all around.

Late in 1795 a convict of African descent, John Caesar – who had come to Sydney with the First Fleet – escaped from custody to become the colony's first bushranger. For weeks, he struck fear into the hearts of free people and convicts alike as 'Black Caesar'. It seemed that every theft committed in New South Wales was ascribed to him and his gang of escapees, who numbered six to eight. On 29 January 1796 the new governor, John Hunter, offered a reward of five gallons of spirits for Caesar's capture; two weeks later, he was shot dead at the village of Liberty Plains, now the suburb of Strathfield.

In January 1796, the Indigenous people of the Hawkesbury had attacked a man who had been allowed to ply a passenger boat between the port of Sydney and the river; he was severely wounded.[65]

David Collins said that two emancipists named Wilson and Knight were living with the Dharug and teaching them that the settlers' single-shot muskets were useless for a minute or so after they were fired because of the slow reloading process. Collins said it 'effectually removed that terror of our firearms with which it had been our constant endeavour to inspire them'.

Because John Hunter felt that many of the settlers on the Hawkesbury were largely 'indolent and improvident even for their own safety and interest',[66] the new governor issued a public order on 22 February 1796: if an alarm was sounded, everyone residing in the different settlements should immediately render to each other assistance, whether or not the alarm was on their own property. Those who didn't help their neighbours would be punished.[67] Hunter also decreed that anyone who wantonly shot and killed Indigenous people would be charged with murder.[68] He didn't officially record that the authorities were willing to turn a blind eye.

Mary was still only eighteen, but she had grown up fast in prison, on the voyage, and now in this strange, beautiful and often brutal land. As she watched the wide expanse of the Hawkesbury flow past her simple cottage, fearing the next heavy fall of rain or the next threat of violence, she also feared for the safety of her unborn child. In February 1796, Mary Reibey would soon be a mother.

Chapter 7

MARY GAVE BIRTH to her first child, Thomas Haydock Reibey,[1] beside the Hawkesbury at 7 a.m. on 6 May 1796. It was six days before her nineteenth birthday. Showing a gift for meticulous record keeping that would be a feature of her adult life, Mary made a note of the details and later wrote them into the flyleaf of a family Bible,[2] one of the few surviving documents she penned. Six weeks later the young family sailed into Sydney for the christening of Thomas Jr in the church where his proud parents had married.[3]

The warfare continued between the settlers and the original inhabitants of the Hawkesbury. In 1796, four more settlers died with jagged spears in them – and their neighbours vowed revenge.

At the same time, John Macarthur was waging war on Governor John Hunter, determined to show the Scottish sea captain that the New South Wales Corps was in charge of the colony. Macarthur had become a very wealthy man. He was building his flock of Spanish merino sheep from a few imported out of the Cape, and he was making vast profits from his monopoly on imported liquor. Grog had become the main currency in New South Wales: with more than half the colony being convicts, Macarthur had a captive market, and many emancipists who were working for settlers accepted rum instead of wages.[4]

On Hunter's arrival at Government House, he had praised the colonists who displayed initiative and industry by raising goats, pigs, sheep and poultry, because they always had food on the table.

He was impressed by his first sight of the locally grown wheat that was 'as beautifully luxuriant' as 'in any part of the world'. The five 'Cape cows' and two bulls that had escaped in the early days of the colony had multiplied into a herd of forty or more near the Nepean, in a lush area Hunter called the 'Cowpastures'. 'Some Settlements which have been lately formd on the Banks of the Hawkesbury River,' he wrote, 'are [also] delightful & promising.'[5]

But the new governor's glowing early reports of Sydney and its surrounding settlements were soon replaced by dimmer assessments. Macarthur was profiting from the colony's addiction to alcohol, and he ensured that much-needed wares were sometimes selling at a thousand per cent mark-up. He and his confederates built huge landholdings by driving the Indigenous inhabitants away and often killing them. Before long, Hunter was describing 'this town of Sydney' as 'a mere sink of every species of infamy'.[6] He wrote to the new home secretary, the Duke of Portland,[7] to complain that the New South Wales Corps was composed of characters considered disgraceful to every other regiment in His Majesty's service.[8] Many of the soldiers and officers, Hunter wrote, were superior in wickedness to the worst of the convicts. '[If] Our stores, provisions, and granaries must be intrusted to the care of those men,' he asked Portland, 'what security can we have in the hands of such people? None ...'[9]

Macarthur and his cohorts had taken control of the courts, as well as the public stores, convict labour and much of the settled land. Hunter knew that his civil administration had to regain control, but Macarthur was always up for a fight – especially when his financial future was at stake. The population of New South Wales when Hunter arrived as governor was 3211: there were 1908 convicts, and the remainder were mostly military and administrative personnel as well as emancipists staying in the colony after their sentences had ended.

Hunter told Portland that 'the debts of the settlers in general are chiefly, altho not wholly, owing to a disposition to indulge in drunkenness', and that Macarthur was the villain fuelling their addiction.[10] It pained Hunter that sometimes the produce of a whole year's labour could be thrown away by working people on booze. The settlers living near the Reibeys were more in debt than those in any other district: 'Their idleness cannot so well be prevented, the distance from hence is so great, and the want of a respectable magistrate to reside upon the spot is very much felt. The ground of their farms is of a superior quality, altho' those which lay low are sometimes inundated.'[11] Thousands of miles from home, Hunter often felt that he was surrounded by enemies.

The new governor wanted the land around Sydney explored as much as possible, because he found it endlessly fascinating. He sent wildlife specimens to Joseph Banks in England, while making sketches of kangaroos and parrots, as well as the platypus, which he called an 'amphibious animal of the mole kind'.[12] Under Hunter's direction George Bass, John Shortland and Matthew Flinders made a series of voyages along the New South Wales coast; Shortland named the Hunter River, north of the Hawkesbury, in the governor's honour.

Bass and Flinders travelled even further. The two young naval officers had grown up near each other in Lincolnshire, and in October 1795 they set off together with Bass's boy servant William Martin, sailing a small boat they called the *Tom Thumb*. They explored Port Jackson, Botany Bay and then the Georges River, and reported favourably to John Hunter that the soil seemed fertile there and that the area was heavily wooded. Two years later Hunter established a community along the Georges River which he named Banks Town in honour of Joseph Banks.[13] In March 1796, Bass, Flinders and Martin sailed the *Tom Thumb II* down the New South Wales coast, investigating what they named Port Hacking and an area they called Tom Thumb's Lagoon but which is now known as Lake Illawarra. Then, in 1797, Bass led a crew of six in an open whaleboat past the area that is now Kiama and its blowhole on their way to what is now called the Mornington Peninsula, not far from present-day Melbourne.

Sydney – and the profits that could be made by exploiting supply and demand in a remote outpost – was enticing more and more traders to its vast harbour, as warehouses and shops began to mushroom around its foreshore. One such trader was Robert Campbell,[14] a Scot who ran the Calcutta-based company Campbell & Clark. In 1796, Campbell sent an Indian ship renamed the *Sydney Cove* to New South Wales, loaded with seven thousand gallons of rum and other goods to be sold at huge profits. The *Sydney Cove* was wrecked off Van Diemen's Land. Three of the crew then survived the fourteen-week overland trek to Sydney. In the process, they discovered large coal deposits south of Botany Bay and explored more of the continent than any Europeans had until that time.

EARLY IN 1798, NOT LONG after she'd helped her son Thomas Jr take his first steps, Mary was pregnant with her second child. She and Tom weren't about to waste time creating their dynasty, and James Haydock Reibey was born at midnight on 2 October 1798. He was baptised six weeks later at St Philip's.[15]

Mary quickly showed that not only was she a hardworking wife and mother, but she was also an astute businesswoman. While misogyny and misery had greeted so many of the early convict women on their arrival in Sydney as degraded sex slaves, some quickly found their lot had improved in the colony. Mary Reibey and other ambitious women saw transportation as a second chance in life; a fresh start in a place where business opportunities seemed boundless with a captive market in a remote corner of the world.

Convict and free women in colonial Sydney had greater legal protection than they would have experienced had they stayed in Britain and many women worked or ran their own businesses, finding employment initially as cooks, seamstresses, and cleaners.

Women remained in short supply in Sydney, and many were able to secure better conditions for themselves than they had before arriving in the colony. The provision to receive government rations, unavailable to even the most desperately poor in Britain, also meant women in the colony did not need a man to avoid starvation.[16]

Single women owned property in colonial New South Wales but according to the common law doctrine of coverture, married women such as Mary were 'one person in law' with their husbands and had no independent legal existence and no economic rights, having ceded them to their husbands upon marriage.[17] Yet this did not apply in the Reibey household as the pair not only were busy raising a family but building their fortune together. Tom's name appeared as the owner on all their possessions including land grants as was the legal custom, but he taught Mary all that he had learned in shipping and trading, and she became his co-worker – his 'first mate' – in everything they did.

Other women were also becoming business leaders in the infant colony. An Irish convict, Jane Maher, who had stolen money from a customer when she was the madam of a Dublin brothel, would soon become one of a handful of licensed bakers in Sydney. She lived with Edward Turley, also an Irish convict, who ran a sly grog shop at the back of her property.

MARY WAS PETITE BUT full of determination. She possessed the temperament and talent required to run both a business and a household under very difficult, rudimentary and sometimes dangerous conditions.[18] She was devoted to her children, remembering how she had been cruelly separated from her own mother – and how her sense of abandonment had contributed to the wild flight of fancy that nearly got her hanged. She did not want them to struggle the way that she had after her grandmother's death.

Not all mothers in New South Wales were as devoted to their offspring. Two months earlier, on 4 August 1798, Priscilla Loveridge – who had given birth to a daughter on the *Royal Admiral* – was 'committed for further exam' on suspicion of murdering her infant son, Thomas Goodman, 'by administering a certain Quantity of Spirituous Liquor'. There was no evidence to incriminate Priscilla, but she was imprisoned for a month for keeping a 'riotous and disorderly house' and concealing suspected wrongdoers in it.[19]

Mary's baby James was just six months old when another devastating flood swamped all the farms along the Hawkesbury.[20] A long dry spell was broken by a heavy downpour that took the settlers by surprise, though some of the Dharug had warned farmers friendly to them of the looming disaster.[21] The river swelled more than fifty feet (sixteen metres) above its banks, and the powerful torrent carried all before it. The government store was washed away, and most of the livestock, pigs and poultry went under. The previous season's harvest was ruined. Many settlers were taken from the ridges of their houses by the few small boats they had among them, just in time to save their lives as the countryside took on the appearance of an ocean. The Reibeys' young Scottish neighbour Andrew Thompson[22] became a local hero for plucking people from roofs as they were about to be submerged. Transported for theft, Thompson had been pardoned and made a constable in the Hawkesbury region.

There were other disasters for Governor Hunter to navigate. His steward, Nathaniel Franklyn, became involved with the criminal element among the free men and women in Sydney and was stealing Hunter's property while the governor was out exploring the countryside. When confronted, Franklyn shot himself in the head.[23]

Before long, Hunter's bosses in London were receiving anonymous letters that claimed the governor was guilty of the very corruption over the liquor trade that he was trying to suppress.[24] He called the attacks on his character the work of a 'dark and infamous assassin; guilty of a diabolical departure from truth' and so wicked he was capable even of 'vilifying the immaculate character of his God'.[25] 'My Lord,' Hunter wrote to Portland, 'by his attack upon my character he shews his cloven foot.'[26]

Despite Hunter's protests, his days at the helm of New South Wales were numbered. Yet he continued to urge Bass and Flinders to chart as much as they could of the colony and the surrounding islands. Bass was convinced that Van Diemen's Land was an island, and in 1798 he and Flinders proved it by circumnavigating modern-day Tasmania in the sloop *Norfolk*. Flinders recommended that the passage between the island and the mainland be called Bass Strait.

The following year, Flinders sailed the *Norfolk* for a thousand kilometres north from Sydney. He was accompanied by an Indigenous man, Bungaree,[27] of the Kuringgai people from the Broken Bay area north of Sydney. Bungaree was a well-known identity in Sydney, moving easily between the Europeans and his own people and he became a mediator with the Aboriginal people of different groups he and Flinders met on their long journey. Flinders explored Moreton Bay, and he rowed ashore at what became known as Woody Point and Coochiemudlo Island. He named one location Red Cliff Point[28] after the colour of its cliffs and named the 'Pumice Stone River', now known as the Pumicestone Passage. He sailed on to Hervey Bay, which Captain Cook had named in 1770, and he proved that the vast expanse of sand that would become known as Fraser Island wasn't connected to the mainland.

Tom Reibey was also making voyages of exploration while carting goods from the Hawkesbury to Sydney and back. As he'd learnt from William Raven, there was good money to be made in transport and trade. Before long Tom was sailing a sloop named the *Raven*, dedicated to his old master.

THE OPEN WARFARE continued between the settlers and the First Peoples on the Hawkesbury, and Hunter tried to show that there was justice for all in the colony, black or white, even though the First Peoples had been treated appallingly. On 14 October 1799, five settlers went on trial in Sydney for killing a pair of Dharug youths known as 'Little Jemmy' and 'Little George'[29] in the small Hawkesbury farming settlement of Argyle Reach. The case was tried before a jury of six comprised of three army officers led by John Macarthur and three naval men including Matthew Flinders and John Shortland.[30]

Dharug people had been hired as trackers for a hunting expedition, for Thomas Hodgkinson and John Winbow, a Second Fleet convict who had survived the horrors of the *Scarborough* and was now living with a Dharug woman, who may or may not have been forced into the arrangement. Certainly it seems the Dharug were not happy with his treatment of her. Not long after the hunting expedition headed towards the Blue Mountains west

An Eora initiation ceremony involved knocking out a front tooth – from David Collins's book on life in New South Wales. *State Library of NSW FL3729339*

of the Hawkesbury, Hodginkson and Winbow were hacked to death. Those responsible included the Dharug warriors known as Major White and Terribandy, who was the father of Winbow's 'wife'.[31] 'Little Jemmy' and 'Little George' came to Argyle Reach, to return Hodgkinson's gun to his wife. They were well known in the village and until then well liked. But now the settlers wanted revenge. Both of the Dharug youngsters had their hands tied behind their backs, and as they struggled desperately against their captors and cried out for mercy, they were slashed with cutlasses. George, who was thought to be about eleven or twelve, suffered huge wounds on his body and hip before he bled to death. Jemmy, who was estimated to be fifteen or sixteen, was shot through the body by a ball from a musket and one side of his head and down his face appeared to have also 'been much cut by a cutlass.'[32] His head was nearly severed from the body. Five local farmers – Edward Powell, Simon Freebody, James Metcalfe, William Timms and William Butler went on trial in Sydney. Lieutenant Thomas Hobby of the New South Wales Corps, the commanding officer on the Hawkesbury, told the court that these killings had taken place at a time when fear gripped homesteads on the river – when there was a belief that at any moment armies of Indigenous warriors would come down from the Blue Mountains to massacre the Hawkesbury farmers.[33] Apart from the deaths of Hodgkinson and Winbow, there had been other recent cases of settlers being killed, though, writing to the Duke of Portland, Hunter assured him that 'much of that hostile disposition which has occasionally appear'd in those people has been but too often provoked by the treatment which many of them have received from the white inhabitants.'[34] The five accused were found guilty of 'wantonly killing two natives'. All the naval men recommended flogging as punishment, but Macarthur and the other officers of the Corps demurred, so the case was referred to London. The five guilty men were freed on bonds and eventually pardoned.[35]

Hunter was livid at the injustice. He told Portland: 'Two native boys have lately been most barbarously murdered by several of the settlers at the Hawkesbury River ... Those men found guilty of murder are now at large and living upon their farms, as much at their ease as ever ...'[36] The governor knew that provoking Indigenous wrath was dangerous, especially at harvest time.

> Fire in the hands of a body of irritated and hostile natives may with little trouble to them ruin our prospects of an abundant harvest, for that is the very season in which they might spread desolation over our cultivated lands, and reduce us to extreme distress; and they are not ignorant of having that power in their hands, for after the destruction of the above two boys they threaten'd to burn our crops as soon as it cou'd be effected ... Their violence against the military proceeded from a soldier having in a most shamefull and wanton manner kill'd a native woman and child.[37]

Tom and Mary knew that living in Sydney would be far safer for their young family, than staying amid the turmoil on the river. Sydney was not proving hospitable for Governor Hunter, though.

His battles with undermining forces in the colony led by John Macarthur worsened. The governor's private secretary and deputy judge advocate Richard Dore[38] proved untrustworthy, then Dore's replacement, Richard Atkins – notorious for not paying his debts – earned Macarthur's wrath as 'a public cheater living in the most boundless dissipation without any visible means of maintaining it than by imposture on unwary strangers'.[39]

Despite Hunter's strident defence of the anonymous claims made against him, Portland ordered his recall.[40] He reluctantly left for England on 28 September 1800, still shaking his head at the machinations of Macarthur and his supporters.

Hunter was replaced by Commander Philip Gidley King,[41] a draper's son who not long after arriving with Arthur Phillip on the First Fleet had been sent to tiny Norfolk Island to establish a settlement. There King had fathered two sons – named Norfolk and Sydney[42] – with his convict mistress Ann Inett, before returning to England to marry his cousin Anna Josepha Coombe.[43] On 15 April 1800, he arrived in Sydney on the slave and convict transport *Speedy*. Before long he was writing home to London about the shocking toll that booze continued to take on the colony. The *Royal Admiral*, which had carried young Mary Reibey to her new home in 1792, had arrived with what King called '8,000 gallons of infamous poison', and the ship *Anne* with even more.[44] In the six months to May 1800, more than thirty-six thousand gallons of alcohol were landed in New South Wales – about seven gallons (32 litres) for every person in the colony.[45]

King found New South Wales a foreboding place, despite its natural beauty. In September 1800, the chaplain and missionary Samuel Marsden[46] and his fellow magistrate, the often sloshed Atkins, sentenced a twenty-year-old Irishman, Paddy Galvin, to three hundred lashes until he gave up information on homemade weapons believed to have been hidden by convicts planning a rebellion. As a fourteen-year-old burglar Galvin had travelled to Sydney with Mary Reibey on the *Royal Admiral*, but their paths had taken very different courses.

Joseph Holt, an Irish rebel who had been exiled to Sydney as a freeman without a conviction, recalled watching the torture of Galvin and other prisoners at Toongabbie as they were whipped with cats o' nine tails. It was the most appalling sight Holt had ever seen.

> The unfortunate man had his arms extended round a tree, his two wrists tied with cords, and his breast pressed closely to the tree, so that flinching from the blow was out of the question, for it was impossible for him to stir ... two men were appointed to flog, namely Richard Rice, a left-handed man, and John Johnson, the hangman from Sydney, who was right-handed. I never saw two threshers in a barn move their flails with more regularity than these two man-killers did, unmoved by pity, and rather enjoying their horrid employment ...[47]

The day was windy and although Holt was watching from a place 'at least fifteen yards to leeward', blood, skin and flesh from the victims flew into his face as the floggers brushed it off their whips. After every fifty lashes a doctor would check the pulse of the bound and bloodied convicts.

When it was Paddy Galvin's turn, his body was quickly reduced to a quivering mess of torn flesh.

> The first hundred were given on his shoulders, and he was cut to the bone between the shoulder blades, which were both bare. The doctor then directed the next hundred to be inflicted further down, which reduced his flesh to such a jelly that the doctor ordered him to have the remaining hundred on the calves of his legs. During the whole time Galvin never even whimpered or flinched ... He was asked 'where the pikes were hid?' Galvin answered that he did not know, and that if he did, he would not tell.[48]

His eyes blazed with defiance as the young Irishman told the floggers: 'You may hang me if you like, but you will have no music out of my mouth to make others dance upon nothing.' Galvin was carted away to the hospital.[49] He eventually recovered from his ordeal and many years later married another former convict, Sarah Wood. Galvin became a farmer[50] on the Cowpastures, the lush grazing area that at the time of his flogging was reserved by the governor exclusively for the colony's cattle herds.

No weapons were found among the Irish prisoners despite the flogging of Galvin and others, but revolution beat strongly among those convicts who were waiting for the chance to burst free. Governor King took office at a time of great turmoil in New South Wales but also at a time when John Hunter's sponsored exploration of the surrounds of New South Wales was going to the next level. In January 1801, in London, Matthew Flinders took command of the ship *Investigator* with a crew of seventy-six, including his younger brother Samuel Flinders as a lieutenant – and his beloved black-and-white cat Trim.[51] He planned to prove that New Holland was an island continent.

AS SETTLERS PAID FOR imports with coins, there developed a troubling shortage of legal tender as goods flooded the colony. This gave rise to the widespread use of promissory notes – IOUs that were often lost, stolen or forged. There was such a wide variety of foreign coins coming from the trading vessels and being exchanged in New South Wales that in November 1800 King tried to ensure honest trade by issuing standard valuations for them. An English guinea would be worth £1 2 shillings of British money circulating in the colony, a Portuguese Johanna £4, and an Indian gold mohur £1 17 shillings. An Indian pagoda was worth 8 shillings, and a rupee 2 shillings sixpence. A Spanish dollar would fetch 5 shillings, and a ducat coin 9 shillings sixpence. King decreed that Dutch guilders were worth 2 shillings; English shillings 1 shilling and eightpence, and one-ounce copper coins, twopence.[52] The Reibeys were willing to trade in any currency.

Mary gave birth to her third son, George,[53] at 1 p.m. on 2 February 1801. In an effort to purchase more goods for sale, she and Tom took out a loan of £160 10 shillings from Robert

Campbell, the Scottish trader. Campbell had taken up land on Sydney's harbour at Dawes Point, and built a private wharf and warehouses there. He established a garden on what had been a burial site for sailors and marines.[54]

Mary and Tom worked hard and invested wisely so their children wouldn't be like so many struggling through the colony's food shortages. Neglected or destitute children, living rough in the streets, were a feature of early New South Wales from the time of the First Fleet's arrival.[55] The Reverend Richard Johnson made plans to start an orphanage at the church where the Reibeys had married, but those plans had been thwarted in 1798 when the wooden building was burnt down by what Hunter believed was 'some wicked and disaffected person or persons' angry at his order that all residents in the colony were to attend Sunday services.[56]

Johnson gained the ear of Governor King, who had previously established an orphanage on Norfolk Island. King saw the situation for homeless children in Sydney, especially girls, as dire, and in 1801 he opened a Female Orphan School on what became known as George Street. At the time, King told the Home Office that the population of New South Wales had grown to about six thousand Europeans, among them 1007 children, with some looking like the most neglected children 'in any part of the world': 'Soon after I arrived here the sight of so many girls between the age of eight and twelve, verging on that brink of ruin and prostitution which several had fallen into, induced me to set about rescuing the elder girls from the snares laid for them, and which the horrible example and treatment of many of their parents hurried them into ...'[57]

Before long, the Female Orphan School housed 103 girls who had been picked up from the streets. King declared that they had been saved from a life of poverty and sin, and that the morals and manners of Sydney would benefit from this.[58] He also saw to it that destitute street boys were apprenticed to Sydney's growing workforce of boatbuilders and carpenters.[59] The governor had no control, though, over John Macarthur and the Rum Corps.

William Paterson had ordered the killing of many Indigenous people – and on 14 September 1801, he felt what it was like to be shot when Macarthur blew away part of his shoulder in a duel.[60] Macarthur was arrested by soldiers loyal to the governor, but while King's order that he be sent to face a court martial in England might have inspired terror in most prisoners, Macarthur saw it as an opportunity to boost business and make strong commercial connections in Britain. He envisioned New South Wales as a prime producer for his homeland, with his wool to be the colony's major export. In the few weeks before he began his voyage – leaving his wife Elizabeth to run their farms for the next four years – Macarthur purchased 1500 more sheep 'besides horses and cattle, with some very extensive farms belonging to individuals'.[61] King warned the British government to beware of this 'rich Botany Bay perturbator' who had a 'diabolical spirit'.[62] He said Macarthur had the eyes of a snake and that, despite earning a captain's salary, he already owned half the colony 'and very soon will get the other half'.[63]

Macarthur certainly knew a good business deal. He had just bought twenty-two hectares at Cockle Bay for a gallon of rum and later gave it the name Pyrmont. He was a far more astute investor than William Balmain, who sold the whole 220-hectare peninsula that now bears his name for just 5 shillings to another Scottish surgeon, John Gilchrist,[64] of Calcutta, who never lived in New South Wales but made a fortune for his heirs when the land was eventually subdivided.

Three months after Macarthur's duel with Paterson, Flinders steered the *Investigator* to the coast of what is now Western Australia.[65] He called the point he saw Cape Leeuwin, meaning 'Lioness', after a Dutch ship that had charted some of the coastline in 1622.

MARY AND TOM'S first daughter, Celia Eliza Reibey,[66] was born at 8 p.m. on 1 February 1802, just 364 days after George had come into the world. By the age of twenty-four, Mary was the mother of four small children, and she and Tom were becoming prominent members of the New South Wales community as landowners and traders. Mary's figure was becoming fuller and though she would always be physically tiny she saw unlimited growth for the family business. Tom had six men working for him on his voyages to the Hawkesbury. He used the Government Wharf, near present-day Customs House, where goods were loaded under the watchful eye of a red-coated sentry. Soon he built a large weatherboard house for his family, overlooking Sydney's harbour at the Rocks, which he could use as a store and trading base. Mary looked after the stores while her husband sailed between Sydney and the Hawkesbury. One of the Reibeys' neighbours was the boatman Billy Blue,[67] a strapping and colourful African-American who served with the British in the War of Independence before being convicted in 1796, at Maidstone, Kent, of stealing raw sugar. He was sentenced to seven years' transportation.

While living at the Rocks he met Elizabeth Williams, a thirty-year-old convict from Hampshire. They were married at the rebuilt St Phillip's and had six children. Blue later became a boatman, ferrying passengers across Sydney Harbour, and he received a land grant of more than thirty hectares at the waterside area named after him, Blues Point.

Three weeks after Celia's birth, John Thistle, the master of Matthew Flinders's *Investigator*, was lost along with midshipman William Taylor and six crew. Their boat capsized at dusk in an area at the south-eastern tip of what is now called the Eyre Peninsula. Flinders named the headland Cape Catastrophe, and the area in which he had anchored, Memory Cove. Sailing east, he named Port Lincoln after his home county, and in his notes he described the Indigenous people as 'Australians',[68] one of the first times the word was used. After charting and naming Kangaroo Island, the Yorke Peninsula and St Vincent Gulf, on 8 April 1802 Flinders encountered the veteran French explorer Nicolas Baudin,[69] who was surveying New Holland for Napoleon Bonaparte, and hoping to find plants and animals that could be brought back to France for cultivation. He and Flinders exchanged notes on their discoveries, and Flinders named the spot Encounter

Matthew Flinders was the first man to circumnavigate the island continent he called 'Australia'. *State Library of NSW FL996590*

Bay before he explored Port Phillip, which Governor King had recently named after himself. Flinders then sailed the *Investigator* on to Sydney, arriving on 9 May 1802.

A month later,[70] Henry Hacking shot dead the Bidjigal warrior Pemulwuy, who had been a constant threat to the Europeans since he'd speared Governor Phillip's gamekeeper back in 1790. For more than a decade, Pemulwuy had mounted a campaign of guerrilla warfare against the Europeans; King had put a bounty on him,[71] dead or alive, claiming he was guilty of two murders.

Like all the early governors, King sent regular shipments to Joseph Banks of the colony's flora and fauna. On a shipment aboard the *Speedy*, the governor included a preserved platypus and, almost as an afterthought, Pemulwuy's severed head preserved in spirits. To King, the great Indigenous warrior was little more than a scientific specimen. The governor told Banks that 'Altho' a terrible pest to the colony', Pemulwuy had been a 'brave and independent character'.[72] Banks kept the head but sent the platypus to his friend and fellow scientist Georges Cuvier at the National Museum of Natural History in Paris, where Napoleon closely examined it, joining discussions about the classification of a mammal previously unknown to Europeans.[73]

Desperate to be reunited with his wife, Flinders and his cat Trim headed to Britain with a crew of ten on a small, dilapidated 29-tonne schooner, HMS *Cumberland*. Flinders was forced to dock at Mauritius[74] for repairs on 17 December 1803 – and was arrested as a spy. He spent seven years as a prisoner there. When Trim vanished, Flinders came to believe that a slave had eaten his cat.

Flinders's long-time colleague George Bass followed Tom Reibey into the maritime trading business. But he set his compass for distant shores rather than the Hawkesbury: on 5 February 1803, he sailed from Sydney for Tahiti on the *Venus*. There were no credible sightings of Bass, his ship or his crew again.

WITH MARY'S CARE in keeping records and accounts, her husband had great success in his trading ventures, land acquisitions, and government connections. She kept her family in England informed of her progress from the time she disembarked in the colony, though her early correspondence back to Lancashire has not survived. On 19 August 1803, Governor King awarded 'Thomas Raby [sic] and his heirs and assigns forever ... 100 acres situate in the district of Mulgrave Place to be called Raby Farm'.[75] The area is now Freemans Reach, and the property became known as Reibeycroft.[76]

King was backing the colony's first weekly newspaper, the *Sydney Gazette and New South Wales Advertiser*, published every Saturday and edited by George Howe,[77] a convicted shoplifter. The paper, produced on a press brought with the First Fleet, was initially printed as a single sheet, folded into four pages of foolscap size. Tom had started advertising his wheat and wood.

CEDAR PLANK.
THOMAS RABY begs leave to acquaint the Public that he
has lately received a large supply of BEAUTIFUL CEDAR

from Hunter's River, which now lies open to Inspection and
SALE, in Boards of all dimensions, adapted to any purpose,
at his House on the Rocks.[78]

The local newspaper had started reporting on the Reibey transport
business as Tom and his men carted wheat from the Hawkesbury
and cedar from the Hunter on his sloops *Raven*,[79] *James*[80] and
Edwin.[81] By now the Reibeys could afford convict servants to help
Mary with the children and to toil as manual labour for Tom.

Andrew Thompson was also bringing down goods on his
boats – wheat, barley and oats – and like the Reibeys was building
a huge portfolio of investments. The Scot had recently built the
first toll bridge in the colony.[82] It crossed South Creek to link
his Hawkesbury home at Green Hills – an area later renamed
Windsor – with the Parramatta Road, removing the need for a
ferry. Thompson was now one of the most prosperous growers of
cereal crops in the colony, and the governor made him the chief
constable on the Hawkesbury. Soon he would boast elegant town
and country houses, several thousand acres of cultivated land, and
three hundred workers year-round on his estates.[83]

With their upwardly mobile trajectory the Reibeys advertised
their house in the Rocks, which they had outgrown, and which
was in an area regarded as being a rough part of the town.

To be Let, or Sold by Private Contract,
A Very CAPITAL and substantial DWELLING HOUSE and
PREMISES, measuring 54 feet front, well weatherboarded,
and shingled; with good Oven, Bake-house, and every
necessary Utensil to carry on the business; containing four
good Rooms and a convenient Loft; a spacious garden
in front, fit for immediate cultivation; the property and in
the present occupation of THOMAS RABY, Of whom
Particulars may be known.
N. B. Any person inclined to purchase will be accommodated
with Six Months Credit for one Half the Purchase money.[84]

As an afterthought, Tom mentioned that the house had lovely harbour views all the way down to South Head.[85] But Sydney real estate could be a hard sell in those days. The little town stank to high heaven with animals being slaughtered in the streets, their blood and entrails left to rot on the ground until the rains came. Sanitation was for a later age, and the unmade roads often became quagmires in the wet. Though vessels with luxury goods from exotic parts of the world were arriving in port with greater frequency, many of Sydney's inhabitants remained in chains – and most of the others looked like they should be. The regular customers of the Rum Corps were permanently drunk. When George Suttor[86] – a market gardener from Chelsea and protégé of Joseph Banks – had arrived at the colony in November 1800 as a free settler in charge of a collection of plants sent to the colony to replace those lost on a supply ship the *Guardian*, the young Englishman was taken aback. 'I was shocked,' he wrote, 'at the state of Sydney, I mean of the people and their hard features – Iron Gangs and low grog shops and generally with the degraded and vice-worn features of my countrymen and countrywomen.'[87]

Still, Sydney had its commercial possibilities. Tom and Mary raised a further credit advance of £150[88] from Robert Campbell by mortgaging three Hawkesbury farms totalling 260 acres (105 hectares) and including the buildings, crops, livestock, and their three boats, along with certain other property and buildings in Sydney.[89] As well as grain and cedar, Tom began carting lime from Botany Bay and Broken Bay,[90] and coal from the Kings Town convict settlement,[91] about a hundred kilometres further up the coast at a place that would be called Newcastle. The Reibey ships would sometimes carry convicts from Sydney to Kings Town[92] – the place where the colony's most dangerous prisoners were sent to work in the coalmines as punishment. A decade after arriving in New South Wales as a frightened young prisoner lucky to be alive, Mary, having served her time, was now making money from organising the transport of convicts.

Chapter 8

BY 1804, MARY REIBEY was a prosperous young mother with four children and plans for more. For many of the convicts, though, New South Wales was no promised land – to them, transportation was akin to a death sentence. Among the Irish, many of whom had been sent to New South Wales for acts of political agitation rather than property crimes, dissent bubbled away violently.

Six years earlier, the Irish had risen up against British rule at Enniscorthy, County Wexford, in what became known as the Battle of Vinegar Hill. Local peasants, armed with wooden clubs and steel-tipped pikes, were easy marks for well-drilled British redcoats with muskets and bayonets. Thirty thousand Irish people lost their lives. Many of the captured rebels were burnt alive,[1] and more than four hundred others were sent to New South Wales. Those who had survived the massacre brooded, promised revenge, and inflamed the minds of other prisoners in the colony. Some of the more vocal Irishmen could sense the fear and vulnerability of their gaolers in this remote place, thousands of kilometres from reinforcements. Proud and determined rebels had overthrown their British masters in North America and formed a new democratic society, so why not in New South Wales?

On 4 March 1804, there were two hundred prisoners in the government farm at Castle Hill, thirty kilometres north-west of Sydney. Just after sunset, a convict hut was set alight as a signal to start a revolution. Philip Cunningham, a stonemason who

The convict uprising at Castle Hill in 1804 was put down brutally. *National Library of Australia nla.obj-135226428*

had been transported for sedition, led the charge with a cry of 'Death or Liberty'. The convicts overpowered the few constables guarding them and fanned out, raiding farmhouses for weapons. Cunningham assured them that the settlements in Sydney and Parramatta would soon fall, and that by the time they reached the Hawkesbury, sixty kilometres north, the escapees would number 1100 men. The plan was to commandeer ships and sail back to Ireland.[2]

The convicts massed together on Constitution Hill, Toongabbie, where there was a panoramic view of approaching trouble, before they moved north towards the Hawkesbury. In Sydney at 11.30 p.m., an alarm was sounded by the firing of cannons and the beating of drums. Governor King declared martial law, and soldiers from the New South Wales Corps – led by a Scottish major, George Johnston,[3] and supported by a posse of armed volunteers – charged out to the fray.

Johnston had fought alongside his father against the Americans at the age of just eleven, and he fought dirty. He chased the convicts to what is now known as Rouse Hill,[4] where he spoke to them under a flag of truce. When the rebel leaders had dropped their guard, Johnston and Trooper Thomas Anlezark[5] ignored the white flag and drew their pistols, dragging Cunningham and another ringleader, William Johnston, away.

During fifteen minutes of shooting from both sides, fifteen rebels were killed; the rest were soon crushed by the soldiers. Cunningham was cut down with a cutlass but survived his wounds long enough to be hanged alongside seven other renegades. Seven more were sentenced to have the skin flayed from their backs by between two hundred and five hundred

Major George Johnston led the military coup against Governor William Bligh. *State Library of NSW FL3273977*

lashes, before they were pressed into a chain gang to work on the Coal River in Newcastle. William Johnston and another ringleader, Samuel Humes, were hanged in chains from gibbets, their rotting bodies dangling for days as a warning to others who might forget their place.[6]

TOM REIBEY HAD SURVIVED his share of close calls with pirates and rough weather while sailing in international waters, and he knew that the seas along the coast of New South Wales held their own terrors. Even so, he and Mary worked their crews and boats hard.

On the morning of Monday, 23 April 1804, their sloop the *James* left Newcastle for Sydney with five crew, bearing a heavy load of cedar and coal. The sloop was already 'very leaky',[7] as Tom put profit above maintenance, and not long out of Newcastle it was assailed by a savage gale and swamped by huge waves. Attempting to preserve the Reibeys' valuable cargo, the crew kept at the pumps relentlessly for thirty-six hours until their arms turned to jelly. On Wednesday morning, both pumps became choked. With the sea running very high and the crew now using buckets to bail out the water, they finally realised the elements had conquered them. On Broken Bay, thirty-five kilometres north of Sydney, they could do nothing but aim the *James* towards a sandy beach. The five drenched seamen leapt off into the safe shallow waters as their sloop was 'dashed to pieces by a tremendous surf'.[8]

The following day, the crew, having walked towards Sydney, were picked up by the ship *Resource* at the North Head and brought into the calmer waters of Sydney's harbour. Tom and Mary promptly sent a party of men to the wreckage in an attempt to save as much of the cargo as possible[9] for a sale in the yard of the Reibeys' home.

The Reibeys were like so many entrepreneurs in New South Wales in the early nineteenth century with businesses that included multiple income streams from shipping, trading, farming and land acquisitions through government grants and the purchase and subdivision of neighbouring properties that were bogged down in debt.

They had the energy of youth and the restless desire to exploit the many opportunities around them in an infant colony that was growing rapidly. While women were still very much in the minority in New South Wales, and King was opening a Female Factory workhouse above the Parramatta Gaol, there were many enterprising free and emancipated women starting their own businesses. The free wives of convicts occupied a unique position in New South Wales as they could own land in their own names, a right typically denied to married women under the common law of coverture. Free women married to convicts were able to become landholders because their husbands were felons and did not have the legal standing against them that free men had. So it was that many women took the chance in business that might have been denied to them in Britain. Ann Mash, for one, took every opportunity the new colony gave her. After she had been abandoned when pregnant by the *Lady Juliana*'s surgeon, Richard Alley, she entered into a relationship with John Irving, a First Fleet convict who was appointed assistant surgeon at Parramatta. Ann was pregnant with their son when Irving died in 1795 and she inherited his property. By 1799 she was living with William Chapman, a plumber, painter and glazier who had been transported for stealing 400 pounds of lead. He had arrived on the *Pitt* in February 1792 and acted in theatre company productions until 1796, when he was appointed a constable. He and Ann opened a bakery, a butchery and a general goods shop in what became lower George Street and from where Ann sold what she advertised as 'excellent and well-constructed mutton pyes.'[10] Sausages could be made to order. Ann also ran one of Sydney's earliest passenger ferry services from the late 1790s.[11]

She was said to have the best boats on the Parramatta River, employing only 'strong and healthy boatmen, who brought good records with them'.[12] She undertook to accompany each boat when there was a valuable cargo on board, and it was a common sight to see her handling one pair of oars while a boatman had the other pair. A stiff breeze was always welcome, as each boat carried masts and a sail. One boat left the hospital wharf in Sydney Cove, next to the King's wharf, every morning, and returned at night from Parramatta. Another boat left Parramatta each morning, and returned at night.

Prices were regulated by Government orders. Each passenger (up or down the river) paid a shilling, children sixpence, though it was said Ann gave many free rides to the poor.[13]

TOM AND MARY HAD BECOME INCREASINGLY FRUSTRATED at not being able to off-load their Rocks home. The area was starting to resemble the old villages of England with narrow laneways, stone houses crowded in together, and grog shops on every corner. For months the Reibeys took out newspaper advertisements and hosted open inspections, talking up the house's aspect, the views, the space, the extensive gardens, the richness of the soil and all the modern fittings, particularly the glazing – something of a rarity in New South Wales at the time. They even promised 'moderate terms of purchase', but still there were no buyers.[14]

The Rocks was an unusual place. From the start of the European settlement, sixteen years earlier, the area had a reputation as a slum frequented by visiting sailors and sex workers. When the well-known Rocks madam Mary Jones passed away at 'a very advanced age', George Howe's *Gazette* reported that the long-time local resident was 'one of the first European Inhabitants of this Colony'.[15] Howe wrote that the funeral was performed the following day, with a 'splendor suited to her avocation during her latest years' and a couple of dozen white-robed working girls leading her procession.[16]

On 1 May 1804, Tom was granted 'Block 70' on the Sydney town plan. This was almost half an acre (two thousand square metres) of waterfront land adjacent to the Government Wharf and Dry Store, and east of the Tank Stream that had been Sydney's first freshwater supply. The land stretched back from the harbour to what is now known as Macquarie Place.[17] The Reibeys were to pay 10 shillings of 'quit rent' or land tax for fourteen years.

That same day, King also granted land to Garnham Blaxcell,[18] who had recently arrived in Sydney as the purser on HMS *Buffalo* and quickly found favour with the governor. He would form a powerful business partnership with John Macarthur.

Another land recipient that day was a former convict from Yorkshire, Simeon Lord.[19] After being transported for seven years for stealing tenpence worth of cloth, he'd turned the sow's ear of his life into many fat silk purses by onselling spirits and merchandise imported by the New South Wales Corps. He owned a large house, a warehouse and other buildings beside the Reibeys' harbour-front block. Neighbouring blocks were owned by other prominent merchants: Thomas Randall, Andrew Thompson, and William Chapman, who lived with Ann Mash and their growing family.[20]

Mary and Tom started work on a large two-storey stone house on their Block 70. The front wall would be fifty feet (sixteen metres) long and twenty feet (six metres) high, allowing for an attic above the dwelling quarters. They had already overseen the construction, behind their new home, of two large buildings that would serve as granaries, offices and housing for workers.[21] All the houses were to be uniform in their front design so that the large row of terrace structures fitted together like a set of building blocks.

Tom called the house 'Entally' after the suburb of Calcutta where he'd spent his formative years. He erected a sign over the front door: 'Entally House – Raby's Warehouse'. The name Entally is derived from the name of the Hintally tree, a palm native to India.[22] Standing in front of Government House, Entally would soon be one of the most conspicuous buildings at the head of Sydney Cove,[23] and finally the Reibeys' new neighbour Simeon Lord auctioned off the Rocks house for them in September 1804,[24] freeing up some capital. Tom advertised for experienced sawyers to keep his lumberyard in constant work.[25] He also bought a couple of 'staunch' greyhounds to take to his depot in

Newcastle; these dogs were 'warranted both to kill and show', not just bringing down their prey but returning it to the master.[26]

ON THE HAWKESBURY WHERE the Reibeys still had their three mortgaged farms, Andrew Thompson was also organising hunts – against the local Indigenous people.

In 1804, Thompson had added to his considerable property along the Hawkesbury when Governor King granted him a 278-acre (110-hectare) parcel of land. Thompson called it Agnes Bank, in memory of his mother.[27] He wasn't about to give it back to the First Peoples or have them threaten his profits from the soil. In April 1805, Thompson led a raid on an Indigenous camp in the foothills of the Blue Mountains, in the vicinity of Shaws Creek.[28] When the settlers came upon what they took to be a weapon-making factory in the bush, thousands of the 'frightfully jagged'[29] spears were destroyed, and at least eight of the Dharug were killed. Aboriginal guides leading the posse of farmers on their killing spree then saved the settlers from marching into an ambush beneath a cliff, where some of the Dharug were preparing to hurl down what the *Sydney Gazette* called 'stupendous rocks' upon their heads.[30]

All the spears and other war implements were burnt, and while the warfare subsided on the Hawkesbury, there was an attack by the First Peoples on a farm on the mountain side of the Nepean the same day. One of the Indigenous men known to the settlers as 'Charley' was shot dead. His companions retreated but the next morning rallied, only to be repulsed again.

A few days later, a party of the New South Wales Corps needing to cross the Nepean availed themselves of an offer from two Dharug men to ferry them over one by one in their canoe. They reported that 'whether from design or accident' the canoe capsized midstream and soldier Robert Rainer drowned.[31]

A few weeks later, John Macarthur returned to Sydney after an absence of almost four years. The enforced time in England had done nothing to curb his belligerence. In London, the case against him for shooting William Paterson had been dropped.

Emboldened in his home country, he charmed his way into the upper echelons of British business, creating demand for his fine merino wool. He gained support from the new colonial secretary, Lord Camden, to occupy ten thousand acres (four thousand hectares) of what they saw as 'unoccupied land' in New South Wales, where Macarthur would produce merino wool for British mills.

Joseph Banks, the unofficial power behind all the governors of New South Wales, had a low opinion of Macarthur – largely because the wounded William Paterson was one of the botanist's most ardent disciples. Banks did all he could to thwart Macarthur's ambitions. But the sheep baron was so confident of his export plans that in London he bought a share of a ship he renamed the *Argo*, attached a large golden fleece figurehead to it and had its master ferry him home to Sydney like a triumphant king.

MARY REIBEY HAD JUST turned twenty-eight when she gave birth to her fifth child, Eliza,[32] on 16 May 1805. Even with convict helpers, Mary was kept extremely busy feeding Eliza and watching her older children run about the water's edge to catch sight of the tall ships and sloops sailing down the harbour, and the Eora canoes coming over from Port Jackson's North Shore. Meanwhile, Tom was always expanding the couple's business interests. Block 70 now not only contained the grand house Entally and outbuildings, but it was also a well-patronised lumberyard, store and boatbuilding facility.

Government House stood behind Entally on a short embankment. There was a small jetty for the governor, with a redcoat pacing to-and-fro beside a sentry box. From the jetty a road led to Government House, and fronting this road stood the Reibeys' two-storey warehouse. Not far from it, the principal officials of the colony had their respective quarters.[33] Tom started advertising for 'a Pair of Sawyers to go as soon as possible to Kings Town, for the purpose of cutting a large quantity of Cedar Plank' and 'a handy Carpenter who understands something of boat-building'.[34]

By mid–1805, the Reibeys had extended their business interests to Bass Strait, where the *Raven* began collecting large supplies of sealskins and oil. Tom was also looking to trade further: all the way to Tahiti and the 'Feejees', the Fijian islands. He had designs on sending his ships all the way to Calcutta and beyond. While Mary ran the day-to-day business from home, raised the children and oversaw the ships plying their trade to the Hawkesbury, Tom formed a seagoing partnership with an ex-convict named Edward Wills.[35] Back in January 1797, a year after Tom and Mary had become parents, Wills and two other desperadoes[36] were arrested for highway robbery in London. They had used arms to rob a man of his watch, a half guinea, a sixpence and 18 halfpence. At their trial in Kingston-on-Thames, Surrey, all three highwaymen were sentenced to death. The sentences were commuted to transportation for life, though one of the gang died before he could leave England with the others on a 'Death Ship', the *Hillsborough*. A convict on board, William Noah, recalled that he and his fellow prisoners were 'ironed two together' and 'ordered below to the Orlop deck, the lowest deck where conditions were grim, because there were no portholes to allow light and fresh air'. On their departure, each man was given a wooden plank two feet wide to sleep on, a blanket, a pillow and a hard brick-like oat biscuit. Many times on the arduous voyage, as convicts died all around him, Noah prayed for his own quick death.[37]

There were six women on board the *Hillsborough*, including Wills's wife Sarah. She was travelling as a free settler with their two-year-old daughter, Sarah Jr, whom the family called Sally.

Skipper James Duncan was paid £18 per convict and £4 10 shillings sixpence extra for every man landed alive. The ship left England with 300 convicts but sailed into Sydney with only 205. Six more died within twenty-four hours of arrival.

Noah wrote that several geographers had claimed New South Wales was an island four thousand miles long, 'but it is not the opinion of the common people, and so obstinate are they of its joining India that several have been lost in trying to find it out'. The most impressive building in Sydney was the governor's neat brick house on a level near the head of the cove, with a large garden and thicket all enclosed with palisades. 'He has a country house at Rose Hill,' Noah wrote. 'The whole town comprises about 1000 to 1400 houses. The hours of the inhabitants being out is till 9, after which you must not pass without the pass-word or you are liable to be put in prison. If you do not attend Divine Service, they warn the Constable, who visits every house, allowing only one to be at home to take care of it and cook. If found idle they send you to prison and you are likely to get 50 lashes.'[38]

Three months after Noah and Wills arrived, the church in which Tom and Mary had married burnt down, but the governor ordered constables to raid the homes of the convicts every Sunday to ensure they attended services in a makeshift church. Defaulters received fifty lashes. 'If found in liquor, 50 lashes,' Noah wrote. 'This you may receive publicly, women as well as men. And if any complaint is made of your being infamous, they shave the women's head and send them up the country ... There is a house done up very neat this year and a billiard room for the gentlemen. I have known liquor to be bought at 2 shillings a gallon and in 2 days fetch 10 shillings a bottle. By this way the money people get so amazingly rich.'[39]

After Governor King gave Wills a conditional pardon on 4 June 1803, he opened a bustling store near Sydney's Hospital Wharf, selling sugar, tea, soap, linen, muslin, gingham, shoes, dungarees, ribbons, nankeen cloth, children's caps and all manner of other merchandise.[40] Old habits were hard to break, though, and not long after his pardon, Wills was ordered to pay £5 for 'incautiously' purchasing seven ounces of stolen silver.[41] At different times, he was a victim of crime. Two men were sentenced to a hundred lashes and three years' hard labour for stealing copper coin from his till in 1804,[42] and the following year a servant woman in Wills's house was gaoled for stealing from his store.[43] He and his wife Sarah set up house opposite the Reibey home across the Tank Stream, in what became George Street, next to the colonial surgeon Thomas Jamison and just down from the Female Orphan School.

Mary's new baby Eliza was only a few weeks old when the *Raven* returned from Bass Strait with a load of sealskins and oil. It also carried a stranded crewman, from the whaler *Ceres*, who had helped a team of eight men club the seals to death on Swan Island.[44] One of the sailors Tom Reibey employed on his skin and oil ventures was an Eora man who lived on the southern side of Botany Bay and was sometimes called the 'Chief of Port Hacking'.[45] He was given the English name William Annan, which was based on the name of a convict transport and whaling ship, the *William and Ann*. The *Sydney Gazette* reported that he offered his services to Tom as 'a Native Volunteer'.[46]

GOVERNOR KING HAD BEEN stunned when the *Argo*, with its golden fleece figurehead and prickly owner, came sailing down Sydney's harbour on 9 June 1805. King was aggrieved that Macarthur had escaped his court martial. Macarthur rubbed salt in the wound by insisting that five thousand acres of the land grant bestowed on him by Lord Camden be taken from the Cowpastures, which had been reserved by the governor for the colony's cattle herds. King refused Macarthur's request, but the Colonial Office in England confirmed his right to the land. He called the property Camden Park, in honour of his benefactor. This fresh victory only spurred Macarthur on to more confrontations. He continued to ride roughshod over King, and the tensions between the governor and the New South Wales Corps bubbled ominously.

In England, the salty sea captain William Bligh was looking for a well-paid government job to take him into retirement, and he appealed to Joseph Banks for help. For a long time Banks had believed King to be too soft in dealing with Macarthur and also with convicts who had been sentenced to death. Banks once told King that while circumstances might make mercy necessary in cases of a wrong verdict, 'mere whimpering soft heartedness never should be heard'.[47] No one could ever say Bligh was too soft.

Regardless of the political manoeuvring going on in London, Tom and Mary were prospering in Sydney. The Reibeys were busy raising their young children while overseeing their new carpenter and sawyers working on their biggest boat yet. Tom advertised for experienced shipwrights to finish the job. At the end of 1805 a bench of magistrates granted the Reibeys a licence to sell wine and spirits,[48] and by February 1806 the hull of a new sixty-tonne vessel was nearly finished. It was being lauded as among the best of its class built in the young colony. The keel measured forty feet (thirteen metres) and the beam sixteen feet (five metres). Soon the partnership of Reibey and Wills was sailing the 130-tonne *Mary and Sally*, named after Mary Reibey and young Sally Wills. The Reibey-Wills partnership reflected the dynamic energy that emancipists were bringing to business in New South Wales in the early part of the nineteenth century. There were 127 registered shipowners in Sydney between 1800 and 1821, and more than a hundred 'were either emancipists, descended from convicts, or otherwise related to convicts.'[49]

The Reibeys were also cashing in on the early stages of industries that would soon be booming export markets. Sealskins, seal oil and timber were prized commodities in Europe. The British transport ship *Lady Barlow*, which had delivered two hundred cattle from Bengal on its first voyage to Sydney in 1804, had recently arrived in England[50] with the first cargo produced entirely by the colonists of New South Wales: 264 tons of elephant-seal oil worth £5280, 13,730 sealskins worth £2746, and 3673 feet of bloodwood timber. But since the East India Company still enforced its trading monopoly in the lands east of the Cape of Good Hope to Cape Horn, the *Lady Barlow* and her cargo were seized by British Customs officers.

In response, Joseph Banks issued a paper titled 'Some Remarks on the Present State of the Colony of Sidney',[51] in which he advocated encouraging an export market from New South Wales. He wrote that 'Sidney' was at first like a newborn infant 'hanging at its Mothers breast', deriving 'its whole nourishment from the Vitals of its Parent', and tolerated by the British only because the American states would no longer take convicts. Now, though, the new colony was like 'a young Lad beginning to attain some learning' and, with the proper care, about to become a 'blessing instead of a burthen to his Family'.[52]

A month later, Banks wrote a 750-word government report encouraging the admission of produce from New South Wales into the United Kingdom.[53] He also recommended that the colony be supplied with its own coinage in order to reduce the corruption caused by a rum-based economy in Macarthur's grip. Banks said New South Wales needed a firm hand so the settlers could stand on their own two feet, and he told the Home Office that Captain Bligh was just the man to sort out troublemakers in the deep south. He advised the British government that King should be recalled. And so the man whose cantankerous personality had sparked the Mutiny on the *Bounty* would soon go head to head with the 'perturbator' Macarthur and his strongarm military supporters. What could possibly go wrong?

THE REIBEY CHILDREN THRILLED to the stories that Tom would tell them about his work: the gun battle with pirates in the Malacca Straits; the exotic destinations of Batavia and Rio and the Cape; the sight of great whales, sharks and schools of dolphins. They were incredulous at his struggles with the wind, rain and high surf on so many of his voyages.

There were spine-tingling adventures close to home too. During the 1806 floods, Tom was out rescuing farmers on the Hawkesbury. At one stage he was in a boat with seven others, hauling people off their roofs or from floodwaters encircling their ground. The Hawkesbury area was largely populated with poor English farmers, and Tom was the only one on the boat who could swim.

In fast-flowing waters littered with dead animals and sharp debris, a man named John Morris was steering the boat when he accidentally drove it across a bough that had fallen into the river. The collision shook everyone on the little vessel and opened a gaping wound in its hull. As water gushed in, panic quickly took hold among the non-swimmers. Tom tried to plug the leak with his handkerchief, in order to give them all time to get on the nearby shore, but the panicking men rushed forward and the boat began to tilt.

All of them called on Tom to save them. Realising that if they seized him in their panic they would all drown, Tom threw himself into the rushing water. He rose under the bow, shook water from his eyes, got a hold of the end of the vessel and began pulling it towards the shore. He towed it within a few yards of shallow water, but the weight of his clothes and the ferocity of the current started dragging him under. He had to let go.

The others continued to scream for help as the boat rocked and rolled and swung around. Tom reached the bank to see all of the men standing in a sinking craft. He told them to hang on. Desperately, he used all the strength he could muster to tear apart a sapling. Wading as far as he could, he pushed it towards his friends. One by one they grabbed the sapling and were hauled to safety. Four times Tom stuck out this tree of life, and four times a man was rescued. A fifth managed to wade across by himself and collapse exhausted on wet but solid ground.

Two others, John Morris and William Green, had waited patiently as their fellows clung to the branch and were hauled to safety. But Morris and Green couldn't bear the exertion any longer. They were still crying out for help as they reached for the end of Tom's sapling, only to be washed away. Even their hats disappeared under the wild water. Green left behind a widow and three infants.[54]

MARY'S SON TOM JR was eleven when she gave birth to her sixth child and third daughter, Jane Penelope Reibey,[55] at 2 p.m. on 14 December 1807. Only four days earlier, Tom had left Mary in the care of Edward and Sarah Wills, then sailed off on another trading venture to Tahiti aboard a new ship he'd bought called the *Mercury*. On 9 December he'd written out his will, giving Mary power of attorney, and his friends Edward Wills and George Howe had acted as witnesses.[56] Mary would be running the business operation in Sydney and the Hawkesbury while he was away, and renting out some of their land to raise money for other property acquisitions and shipping ventures. The couple leased out what Mary called 'two valuable and productive Thirty acre Farms most eligibly and desirably situate on the River Hawkesbury, about half a mile distant from the Green Hills; the whole clear'.[57] Mary and the children spent much of their time on Block 70 awaiting Tom's safe return and more stories of adventure. Meanwhile, a thrilling story was unfolding almost on their very doorstep.

It seemed that trouble travelled alongside Captain Bligh wherever he went. On 28 January 1806, trouble was with him again when he left Portsmouth to begin a seven-month voyage to Sydney. Bligh was skipper of the *Sinclair*[58] with his daughter Mary on board, while her husband, Lieutenant John Putland, was on the ten-gun HMS *Porpoise*, the fleet's escort, under the command of Captain Joseph Short.[59]

Bligh and Short immediately clashed over who was in charge. Short, who had sold up in England for a new life in the frontier colony, was travelling with his wife and six children. He told Bligh that he was in command of the voyage until they reached New South Wales; Bligh thundered that he was the incoming governor and that the role also made him in charge on the water. He called Short 'an evil disposed man', 'wicked and violent' and of 'low character'.[60] Short, said the 52-year-old red-faced Bligh, was a foul-mouthed old seadog.

To show he was the boss, Bligh steered his ship into the lead. Short was insulted to the point of apoplexy. He signalled to Bligh with flags to change course, and the governor ignored him. Short then ordered Putland to fire a cannon blast over Bligh's bow. Reluctantly Putland set one off, making sure he was well wide of the mark as his wife was on the other ship. Bligh ignored that, too. Then he ignored another blast, closer, right across the stern. Short then ordered Putland to put a cannonball through the middle of the ship. Putland explained as politely as he could that he wasn't about to blast his wife and father-in-law out of the ocean because of a clash of egos. Captain Bligh, a man who never forgave an affront,[61] promised revenge on Captain Short.

When the feuding skippers arrived in Sydney in August 1806, Bligh – knowing that Short had sold everything he owned in England to buy farm equipment – refused the man his promised land grant of 240 hectares and instead sent him straight back to London on a leaky ship as a prisoner to face a court martial. Short's wife and one of his children died on the return voyage; her now destitute widower was 'honourably acquitted'.[62]

Bligh began throwing his weight around as the new governor as soon as he arrived, making enemies wherever he went and sowing seeds of discontent among the great wheat and maize fields of the colony. The farmer and merchant John Blaxland[63] complained to the Earl of Liverpool, a future prime minister, that Bligh had no control over his rage – and when that temper was 'unbounded', Bligh 'lost his senses and his speech; his features became distorted; he foamed at the mouth, stamped on the ground and shook his fist … On the recovery of speech, he offered a torrent of abuse in language disgraceful to him as a Governor, an officer, and a man.'[64] Blaxland said Bligh even derived a great and sick pleasure from 'signing a death warrant'.[65]

The governor clashed with the colony's principal surgeon, Irish-born Thomas Jamison,[66] who was defying government regulations by engaging in private trading ventures. Bligh sacked Jamison from the magistracy he held, claiming that he was 'not an upright man, and inimical to government'.[67] In addition, he complained that judge advocate 'Mr [Richard] Atkins has been accustomed to inebriety; he has been the ridicule of the community' and that 'sentences of death have been pronounced in moments of intoxication'.[68]

Bligh took time out from raising hackles to raise his bank balance. As soon as he arrived, he received from the outgoing governor grants of ninety-seven hectares at Camperdown, forty-two hectares near Parramatta, and four hundred hectares near Rouse Hill. He didn't mention them in dispatches home, though regulations required it, nor did he refer to the 320 hectares he gifted to King's wife Anna, before the couple returned to England. Bligh's daughter Mary Putland also received a sizeable land grant, and both she and her father made personal use of government stores and flocks.

Bligh had offended much of Sydney within months of arriving at Government House, but the major conflict he was provoking was with John Macarthur. It seemed the governor had learnt little about diplomacy despite coming off second best from the mutiny on the *Bounty*. Bligh and Macarthur eyed each other like prize-fighters, waiting for the other to make the first mistake. Then Bligh put his foot down hard in an attempt to end Macarthur's monopoly on the importing of rum: Bligh called the richest man in New South Wales an 'arch fiend' who had 'inflamed the minds' of 'wicked monopolising persons'.[69]

The final straw was a breach of the port regulations arising from the escape of a convict on Macarthur's ship *Parramatta*.[70]

Bligh had the ship impounded. Macarthur refused to pay a fine, and on 15 December 1807 – the day after Mary gave birth to Jane – Bligh ordered Macarthur's arrest. But Macarthur played by his own rules, and Bligh claimed that 'the perturbator' proclaimed if anyone tried to take him, 'blood would be spilt'.[71]

Macarthur gathered his troops to fight back against Bligh's censures. He quickly knew he had the support of the senior officers of the New South Wales Corps, including its commander, Major George Johnston, who had brought down the 1804 convict rebellion. Nevertheless, one of the few men who could match Bligh's arrogance was arrested without incident and promptly bailed. Knowing he had nothing to fear, Macarthur wrote a letter highlighting his 'scorn and contempt' for the governor.[72] Bligh had him charged with sedition.

The trial was set down for 25 January 1808. The night before, six of the judges who would be presiding over the case – including the heavy-drinking, debt-ridden judge advocate Atkins – dined with Macarthur, his son and nephew at the new officers' mess. The next day in court, Macarthur protested about Atkins sitting in judgement over him, claiming that the man was actually his sworn enemy and had owed him money for fifteen years.[73] The other six members of the court – all soldiers of the

New South Wales Corps – took Macarthur's side, and the court was dissolved.

Bligh feared that the 'Civil power' was in a 'precarious state'. He accused the six judges of sedition[74] and summoned the Corps commander, Major Johnston, to leave his 'country house ... about four miles from town' at Annandale, which he had named after his birthplace of Annan in Scotland.[75] Johnston sent word back that he was too ill to meet Bligh, having fallen out of his chaise after a good sampling of wine at the officers' mess. Bligh had Macarthur rearrested on the morning of 26 January 1808, but Johnston – apparently recovered from his chaise spill – went to the gaol and released the prisoner on a warrant he signed as 'Lieutenant-Governor', even though he was no such thing.[76]

Macarthur called on Johnston to arrest Bligh and take charge of the colony. On a hot summer's day when contraband rum was flowing freely, Macarthur and Johnston rode about furiously, gathering support for their coup. At 6 p.m., while it was still light, Mary and her children were astounded to see four hundred redcoats formed up under Johnston's command. Their colours were flying, and they stamped their feet to the military band's marching song, 'The British Grenadiers', as they made their way ominously to Government House only a hundred metres up the hill from the Reibey home.[77] Hundreds of spectators followed.

Bligh later claimed that Macarthur's troops broke into all parts of the vice-regal home, even crashing into the ladies' room. There they met armed resistance in the form of Bligh's daughter Mary, who had a temper to match her father's and fought back with a swinging parasol.[78] Her husband John had died of tuberculosis just three weeks earlier, and she was in no mood for an attack on her family.

But Mary was thrust aside. Brandishing their bayoneted muskets, the soldiers marched through the residence, looking for the despot. They later claimed they found Bligh cowering under a bed – something he strenuously denied. Macarthur's friends in the press created the colony's first political cartoon: it depicted the governor being dragged out of his hiding place by the upright heroes of the Rum Corps.

William Bligh and Mary Putland were confined to Government House. To complete what became popularly known as the Rum Rebellion, George Johnston took over as lieutenant-governor, and John Macarthur appointed himself colonial secretary, effectively running the place. Bligh now suspected 'massacre and secret murder'[79] for him and his daughter. The new rulers of New South Wales began burning all records of their rorts and crimes.

Chapter 9

MARY WAS PREPARING her sons to follow their father into a life at sea, and they couldn't help but be inspired by his exploits and the money their parents were making for them all as traders. On 10 July 1808, Tom arrived home on the *Mercury* to meet his new daughter Jane after a hazardous yet fascinating eight-month trading voyage through the South Pacific. Around the fireplace, Mary and the children fought off the winter chills as they listened to Tom's stories of his red-hot adventures.

He had sailed out of Sydney on the *Mercury* four days before Jane's birth in company with the three-masted schooner *King George*, which had been built by James Underwood,[1] a convict turned shipwright who had formed a trading company with Henry Kable,[2] another convict made good. The two ships sailed together for New Zealand's Bay of Islands, where they planned to load extra provisions.

They separated on 3 January 1808, with the *King George* bound for the Feejees. On 24 February, Tom steered the *Mercury* into Tahiti's Matavai Bay. He and the crew spent two months there and on the nearby islands, loading provisions – mostly salted pig carcasses – for sale at a huge profit in Sydney. Tom also delivered to the Tahitian King Pomare II the monarch's gold watch that had been repaired in Sydney.

At Raiatea,[3] the second largest of the Society Islands after Tahiti, the *Mercury* was moored to the very tree that the local chiefs said had been chosen by Captain Cook, thirty-six years earlier, to moor the *Resolution* on his second voyage to the Pacific. A beaming chief named Mahee showed Tom a medallion from King George III; the gilt finish was considerably worn down by time, but it still commanded Tom's attention. Mahee said that his father had received it as a present from Cook. Tom thought it would be a fine souvenir from his voyage, so he drove a hard bargain with the goods he was trading and convinced Mahee to throw the coin into the deal. The reverse side of the medallion featured two ships encircled by the words 'RESOLUTION and ADVENTURE, MDCCLXXII'.[4] The medallion safely in his pocket, Tom oversaw the building of a storehouse to keep goods for the *Mercury*. The storehouse was wooden structure a hundred feet long and fifty wide (thirty-two metres by sixteen), and Mahee organised such a great number of workers that its construction was completed in a day and a half.

On 10 March 1808, Tom wrote in the *Mercury*'s journal that at 2 p.m. he saw the people on the island of Huhaine 'murder a man as a sacrifice, and hang him up in a basket, in a range with four others who had suffered the same fate'.[5] Two days later, Tom saw a canoe take in the murdered bodies at Huhaine, to be conveyed to Raiatea – a distance of forty kilometres – so that they could be buried in the 'grand [marae], or place of worship'. On 14 March, forty or fifty canoes with twenty to thirty men in each arrived from other parts of Huhaine to a bay where the chief hosted a consultation on the subject of war if their vassal islands did not pay a tribute to them in swine.

Tom steered the *Mercury* out of Raiatea. But a few days later, as they neared the Cook Islands, a flotilla of fifty or sixty canoes went out to meet the ship. It was no welcoming party. Each canoe had only one man in it, but each of them was armed with a long spear and several short ones. Beside the fire at Entally, Mary and the children listened intently as Tom told them of this large and 'hostile armada'. These men were ferocious, Tom said, and their aspects 'forbidding'; the Tahitians were big people, but these warriors were even bigger, 'robust, and very muscular'.[6]

About three kilometres from the shore, the canoes came alongside the *Mercury*. Tom and his crew prepared to defend themselves. More and more canoes appeared, but the locals appeared to have no knowledge of firearms. Although Tom and the crew waved their muskets about in a threatening manner and yelled themselves hoarse, the island people weren't alarmed in any way. They made remarks about the size of the *Mercury* and wanted to know whose canoe it was. Then they demanded to take off all the pigs the ship was carrying. Some of the men in the canoes grabbed the *Mercury*'s bowsprit rigging and endeavoured to pull her in towards the shore, while others were trying in vain to undo the bolts from its sides, since iron was precious in the South Pacific and sailors on Cook's voyages had once traded nails for sex with the local women.

To placate these ferocious warriors, Tom offered to buy some of their spears, as these were 'ingeniously carved', but none of the men would part with theirs.[7] Tom told his hushed family that these island men began 'vehemently' to threaten the people on board his ship. Then one of them took a long spear calmly, as though showing its intricate patterns to David Clarke, a crewman. Clarke thought the man was offering it for barter – instead he made a vicious stab at Clarke's belly. Clarke blocked the strike with his right hand, but the spear sliced right through it and cut an inch into his groin. He screamed in pain and fell into the water. Two muskets roared from the ship, and Clarke's assailant was shot dead.

Mary and the children sat wide-eyed as Tom told them that the crew dragged Clarke back on deck, blood gushing from his wound. The gunfire had sparked terror among the local people, who paddled feverishly back to shore where reinforcements waited in case the *Mercury* came any closer.

Tom had no intention of continuing the fight. He told his family that he quickly took leave of 'this little inhospitable island', pointing out that it was 'about 21°38' S. and 158° 20' E. longitude' just in case his sons ever found themselves in that part of the world.[8] It was so beautiful out there, Tom said, and yet it could turn ugly as fast as a cyclone.

The *Mercury* had sailed calmly on to dock at Norfolk Island on 1 June for a five-day stay. There Tom met the crew of an American ship, *Amethyst* – a fortunate meeting, since the skipper was able to supply Tom with additional salt to keep his pork from rotting. The American lamented that he was very short-staffed for the rest of his journey, as many of his crew had jumped ship to live with Polynesian women on some of the islands they'd visited.

Tom brought home a shipload of salted pork to sell at a sizeable profit, and he and Mary put up for sale 'by private contract' their waterfront home. The Reibeys were testing the market with thoughts about leaving the colony for a while to establish a trading base in Calcutta. Mary advertised Entally as 'a capital stone Building, the apartments spacious, with capital cellar, the whole of the workmanship performed in a handsome and truly substantial manner, now nearly finished; together with detached kitchen, store-rooms, and other outbuildings commanding an extensive range by the water-side, next to the Government wharf; the whole occupying a lease, of which 12 years are unexpired being the property of Thomas Reibey of whom further particulars may be known'.[9]

TOM HAD ARRIVED HOME to Sydney while New South Wales was still in the hands of the vindictive military junta led by Macarthur and Johnston. The pair were settling old scores for as long as they could, knowing it wouldn't be long before military officers senior to them arrived and learnt what had happened to His Majesty's colonial representative. Macarthur gaoled magistrates who didn't support his self-appointed role. A rebel court imprisoned William Gore, Bligh's provost-marshal, on trumped-up charges of perjury. Gore was sentenced to seven years' hard labour toiling beside the colony's most dangerous convicts at Coal River in Newcastle. His wife and four children had to beg charity from friends to survive.

A gathering of free settlers protested anonymously to Major Johnston, saying they were alarmed to see 'John McArthur [sic], Esq' as the colonial secretary, and that he had violated the law by assuming this office, violated public faith, and trampled 'on the most sacred and constitutional rights of British subjects'.[10]

> John McArthur does not hold the above-mentioned office by commission from the King; and as the inhabitants of this colony have no confidence in the said John McArthur, we [have] declared our sentiments that John McArthur is the last man we would depute to represent us in any case whatever. We believe John McArthur has been the scourge of this colony by fomenting quarrels between His Majesty's officers, servants, and subjects. His monopoly and extortion have been highly injurious to the inhabitants of every description. We most earnestly pray that the said John McArthur may be removed from the said office of Colonial Secretary, from all other offices, and from all public councils and interference with the government of this colony.[11]

Three weeks after Tom returned from Tahiti, the asthmatic and corpulent[12] Lieutenant-Colonel Joseph Foveaux[13] sailed into Sydney Harbour on 30 July 1808.[14] He was there for a stopover, having agreed to resume his role of lieutenant-governor on Norfolk Island after a period of convalescence in England. Foveaux knew Sydney well; he had first arrived in 1792 and had a farm he called Surry Hills just south of Government House, and for a time he'd been the largest landholder and stock owner in the colony. Foveaux was stunned to find that Governor Bligh had been overthrown and was under house arrest – though he was not surprised as he had been appalled by Bligh's treatment of Captain Short and others.

As the senior military officer in Sydney, Foveaux told Macarthur and Johnston that their services were no longer required: he would assume command until 'His Majesty's pleasure shall be known'.[15] Though Foveaux was no fan of Bligh, Macarthur and Johnston knew that their cards were marked and that London would take a dim view of their actions. When William Paterson, still carrying the scar from Macarthur's bullet, arrived in Sydney in January 1809 to take over from Foveaux as Lieutenant-Governor of New South Wales, Macarthur and Johnston knew it was time to get out of town.

They left Sydney in the *Admiral Gambier*,[16] to explain their actions to the authorities in England. Eventually Johnston would face a court martial. The Reibeys' business partner, Edward Wills, donated £30 towards helping with Macarthur's travel costs – perhaps as an insurance policy in case he ever came to power again. The sheep baron hardly needed the money: he had plans to sell a huge consignment of sandalwood in Rio.

Bligh had spent more than a year under house arrest in Sydney and had refused to go back to Britain, maintaining that he remained the rightful governor. In February 1809, after Paterson's arrival, Bligh finally agreed to go if he was allowed to sail home on his flagship the *Porpoise*. As soon as he was on board he broke his word, claiming that the promise had been made under duress. He and his widowed daughter sailed for Van Diemen's Land in the mistaken belief that they could convince the First Fleet's judge advocate, David Collins – now the lieutenant-governor on the island – to back their cause.

Collins received Bligh graciously and vacated Government House in Hobart Town to make way for the man who said he was still the rightful Governor of New South Wales and Collins's boss. But in the end, Bligh did not stay in Hobart long. He had promised Collins that he wouldn't interfere with his administration – but he did, and he complained to the Secretary of State in London about Collins's low morals: Bligh said that although a married man, Collins walked about Hobart Town with Margaret Eddington, 'his kept woman (a poor, low creature) arm-in-arm'.[17]

Bligh sailed the *Porpoise* into the mouth of the Derwent and made himself lord and master of the waterway, imposing tolls on all incoming ships and ordering his men to fire cannon blasts at any ships that refused to pay.

THE REIBEY CHILDREN were growing into fine, healthy youngsters. They formed an attachment with the sons and daughters of Edward and Sarah Wills, playing together in the yard by the harbour. George and Celia Reibey became especially close with young Tom Wills.[18]

Sydney was only twenty years old but already a goldmine for merchant princes such as their fathers. Tom's old connections with the East India Company and the goods they could supply had helped to establish his place among Sydney's rising class of wealthy traders. As the mercantile power of the Rum Corps waned with Macarthur's absence, the power of adventurous businesspeople such as the Reibey and Wills families, grew even more rapidly. With the exception of Tom, Robert Campbell and a few others, most of the traders were emancipists who had made their own capital by huge profits in business while holding tickets of leave or small government billets. Because of the colony's isolation, the profits on imported goods were so great that fortunes were made in just a few years by merchants willing to risk the high seas for goods in demand. Ambitious speculation in merchandise quickly transferred to wealth in landholdings simply by using heavily mortgaged farms as securities – and having a cash purchaser in the Commissary willing to pay the massive mark-ups for all the grain and salt meat a trader could deliver.

Yet twenty years after the First Fleet's arrival, Sydney still had the appearance of a prison camp and military garrison, with cannons guarding the harbour, and redcoats and chained prisoners all about. Along with Government House, the Reibey home was one of the most impressive in town. Nearby there was now a stone bridge, nine metres long, over the Tank Stream water supply. The road that crossed the bridge was known as Governors Row, but it would soon be called by the obvious name, Bridge Street. The skyline was dominated by the tallest structures in the colony: three windmills essential for the crushing of grain to feed the populace.

With no one able to stump up the cash to buy the Reibey home, it remained one of the busiest markets in Sydney as Tom and Mary continued to sell goods from the East India Company. In one sale in 1809, they offered up 22.5 bags of fine cloth from Kasimbazar in India, silk stockings, hundreds of litres of Madeira wine, chests of Souchong tea from China, muslin and wax candles.[19] Lieutenant-Governor Paterson appointed Tom as a harbour pilot,[20] and he kept selling boats from the front yard. In September 1809 he sold two more sloops, 'with full sets of sails and oars complete, fit for any purpose', as well as a capital chaise carriage, with harness.[21]

Tom and Mary were selling as much stock as they could because Tom had another long voyage planned and wanted the goods off their hands. They advertised in the *Gazette* for 'a Chief Officer and Five Seamen, to engage on a pleasant Voyage to Otaheite, with the advantage of good encouragement and liberal wages'.[22] The crew would be sailing there on the *Mercury* without Tom. Describing himself as a 'Dealer and Chapman' who was 'shortly going on a voyage to the East Indies or China', Tom prepared a revised will and power of attorney given the increase in his family's wealth. Again, he was clear on the one person he wanted to take over the management of all his 'estate, estates, monies, property, interests and advantages'.[23] With 'gratifying consideration', the person he again nominated was his wife Mary, 'his true and lawful Attorney'. In case he 'departed this life while on his said intended voyage', Mary was also to be his sole heir 'knowing and confiding in the natural love and affection which she beareth unto her children and the steadfast assurance he hath that she will always do the best in her power to provide for their future welfare'.[24]

On 10 October 1809, Tom said goodbye to Mary and their six children, and he sailed on the British ship *Lady Barlow*, with his first major stop planned for China. He would be away for about a year. Mary was pregnant with child number seven, but Tom wasn't too sentimental when it came to that sort of thing – business was business. Even with her belly growing by the day, and her pangs of distress about another labour ahead, Mary would have to cope without him. As she always did in his absence, she stepped up in running the family's money-making operations.

Tom's business partner Edward Wills did not go with him. His health was poor, perhaps as a legacy of his hardships on the *Hillsborough*, the convict ship that had killed more than a hundred of his travelling companions. He had to contend with burglars too; in April 1809, one climbed down his chimney to steal goods worth £100. At daybreak a man was seen crossing the rocks to Cockle Bay with two bundles. Eora trackers were called in, and in less than an hour they returned with most of the stolen property, which had been hidden in the rocks.[25]

Mary sought help from the Wills family as the birth of her seventh child neared. By then, Sarah Wills had five as well, of roughly corresponding age.

MARY CONTINUED TO BUILD the family's business empire even though Sydney had been in chaos for the best part of three years: first under the unpredictable hand of Bligh and then during the short, uncertain rule of Foveaux and Paterson.

In the eleven months that Paterson had been running the colony, he'd been plagued by poor health and drunk heavily to cope with the stress of New South Wales slipping into anarchy. He was, in the words of his successor, 'such an easy, good natured, thoughtless man that he ... granted Lands to almost every person who asked them, without regard to their Merits or pretensions'.[26] In less than a year, Paterson granted 67,000 acres (27,114 hectares) of land, more than Governor King had granted in six years. Many of those who received the land had no knowledge of farming, and even fewer had the business drive of Mary and Tom Reibey.

On 29 December 1809, Tom arrived at China's Whampoa Island,[27] now called Pazhou, the chief anchorage for ships participating in Guangzhou's foreign trade. The traders were required to keep their ships at Whampoa while smaller vessels ferried goods to and from the Canton Factories area along the Pearl River. Tom was the sort of man who would have bought all the tea in China if he could, but he was content with bringing home all that he could fit on the 408-tonne *Lady Barlow*.

The Chinese trading city of Whampoa from Dane's Island, drawn by Thomas Allom, engraved by W.A. Le Petit, from *The Chinese Empire Illustrated*, Volume 1. Division 1, London Printing and Publishing Company, 1858.

Mary knew she wouldn't see her husband for a long time. As their seventh child kicked in her belly, keeping her awake at night, another hard-driving man with a burning ambition arrived in Sydney. He was big, brave, charismatic and handsome. And he held the future of Mary Reibey and the rest of the colony in his hands.

TWO DAYS AFTER TOM arrived at the treasure chests that were the Chinese warehouses near Whampoa Island, Mary and the children watched from their front yard as a 48-year-old Scottish lieutenant-colonel, Lachlan Macquarie, commandeered the barge of the storeship *Dromedary*, anchored at Sydney Cove. The vessel had brought Macquarie and his wife from England under escort of the fifty-gun HMS *Hindostan*.

Macquarie was in Sydney to shake the rats from the ranks of the Rum Corps and the Macarthur clique, with the aim of building a new society. Having scraped and scrapped his way out of poverty, Macquarie had an affinity for the poor and downtrodden, especially former convicts such as Mary who were willing to reform, work hard and make the most of whatever opportunities presented themselves. He once described himself as an 'awkward, rusticated Jungle-Wallah'[28] because of all the time he'd spent in the jungles of India when he was an obscure army officer whose career seemed to be fizzling into anonymity.

Macquarie didn't mind the lengthy trip to Sydney: he had spent his whole life waiting for this chance. Until recently he'd regarded himself as an old soldier ready for a military boneyard. He had spent thirty-three years in the British Army, serving in the Americas, the Caribbean, India, Egypt and Ceylon. When told that he would lead a battalion of the 73rd Regiment to New South Wales for the newly appointed governor of the colony, Major-General Miles Nightingall, Macquarie had baulked. He complained to his superiors that he was the oldest lieutenant-colonel in the army and that New South Wales would be too remote to assist any further promotion.

In truth, Macquarie was lucky to still have a job. He had grown up dirt poor on the tiny island of Ulva in Scotland's Inner Hebrides at a time when England had its foot on the throat of its northern neighbour. As a result of the oppression he saw, Macquarie never had qualms about taking money from the English – and he spent as much of it as he could. Senior officers had reprimanded him for corruption during his career, such as investing regimental money for his own pocket and signing up at least two poor Scottish nephews as high-earning reserve officers for the British Army, until both relatives were revealed to be preadolescent schoolboys. By the age of ten, one of his nephews had been receiving an officer's pay for five years and had been promoted to lieutenant, even though no one in command had ever laid eyes on him. In the brutal world of the colonising British Army, the risks Macquarie took to help his struggling relatives make money bolstered his reputation as a romantic with a benevolent streak.

In 1793, while an officer serving in India, Macquarie had married Jane Jarvis, a young woman from a wealthy British family who owned slave plantations in the West Indies. Jane's death three years later plunged Macquarie into an almost suicidal despair; when he recovered, he freed the slaves he had inherited from her and sent them money to start new lives. It took him more than a decade to fall in love again, this time with a much younger distant relative, Elizabeth Campbell, who startled him with her athleticism, grace and beauty. He noted that she was as adept with a long line as any fisherman, and he was inspired to write, 'This girl is quite a heroine! – What a most excellent soldier's wife she would make!'[29] He was so besotted with Elizabeth that when he began to fear rival suitors, he made a mad overland dash from his posting in India across Persia and Russia and finally back to Britain in order to marry her.

When Macquarie was offered a military posting in New South Wales, he and Elizabeth were still grieving the loss of their first child, a daughter Macquarie had named Jane after his first wife. Then he heard that General Nightingall, who had a history of hypochondria,[30] had decided that going to the colony might make him ill. Francis Grose thought he'd have a crack at the job a decade and a half after he'd left Sydney – but that was just wishful thinking, since everyone at Westminster knew that during his stint in New South Wales, Grose had allowed John Macarthur free rein. The Crown was still paying the price.

Macquarie was never backward in coming forward. He wrote to the Secretary of State for the War and the Colonies, Viscount Castlereagh,[31] nominating himself for the position. Candidates were in short supply, and Castlereagh wanted a man of conviction, determination and doggedness. On 24 April 1809 he stopped Macquarie as he was walking at London's Berkeley Square and told him that despite the scandal over his young relatives, he would be the new Governor of New South Wales on £2000 a year.[32] The poor boy made good was being given the opportunity to write his name into the history books.

At 10 a.m. on 19 May 1809, Macquarie and his wife boarded the *Dromedary*. They were accompanied by his staff and more than 350 officers and soldiers of the 1st Battalion of the 73rd

Scottish-born Governor Lachlan Macquarie proved a great
friend to Mary Reibey and other self-made entrepreneurs
from convict backgrounds. Painting attributed to John Opie.
State Library of NSW FL1603135

Regiment, as well as about a hundred women and children. The
2nd Battalion of the 73rd was staying behind to fight Napoleon.

The *Hindostan* carried the remainder of the 1st Battalion – more
than four hundred officers and soldiers – under the command of
a dashing Irishman, Lieutenant-Colonel Maurice O'Connell,[33]
along with at least another hundred women and children.
O'Connell had been appointed Macquarie's lieutenant-governor
after an impressive military career that included battles with the
French in the West Indies. John Pasco[34] was the captain on the
fifty-gun man-o'-war *Hindostan*. Pasco had been Horatio Nelson's
signal officer on board HMS *Victory* at the Battle of Trafalgar
in 1805 – and had advised on the wording of his commander's
famous signal, 'England expects that every man will do his duty.'[35]

On 3 August, the ships met a Portuguese brig sailing from the coast of Guinea to Rio de Janeiro, laden with 436 slave women and girls[36] chained and locked in the dark below deck. The ship was riddled with yellow fever. Elizabeth Macquarie recalled in her journal that to stop the spread of infection, the 'monster'[37] who commanded the ship 'had resorted to a precaution at which humanity shudders, namely, that of throwing the unfortunate slaves overboard as soon as they were taken ill'. Fifty slaves had been drowned in this effort to stop the fever from spreading.[38]

Rough weather plagued the final stages of the voyage. On the morning of 28 December 1809, the two ships entered Sydney Heads but were met with a freak wind from the west and couldn't continue; instead, they anchored at 10 a.m. Half an hour later, the emancipist Isaac Nichols,[39] appointed by Sydney's military rulers to the post of Assistant to the Naval Office, came on board the *Dromedary* to welcome the colony's new master. Nichols, a neighbour of Edward Wills, had arrived in Sydney as a convicted thief; since winning his freedom, he had been building a real estate empire as well as establishing a shipyard and having his own trading vessel constructed, the *Governor Hunter*. He had also become the colony's first postmaster.

At noon, Macquarie was joined on board by the former lieutenant-governor Foveaux and John Mell, Paymaster of the Rum Corps. They were standing in for Lieutenant-Governor Paterson, who had been drunk and sick for months. Foveaux had fresh meat, bread, vegetables and fruit sent out to the ships for dinner, which was more than welcome after so long at sea.

The *Dromedary* anchored in Sydney Cove – close to the Governor's Wharf, and in plain sight of Mary and her children – as Macquarie waited for calm weather to come ashore. On the last morning of 1809, he finally commandeered the ship's barge, and at 10 a.m. he and his entourage were ferried to land, as fifteen cannons on each ship saluted the new governor. The great roar of the cannons echoed around the sparsely inhabited cliffs fringing the majestic harbour, before the soldiers on the ships gave Macquarie three cheers.[40] The battery at Dawes Point answered the salute with more cannon fire, while the ground trembled as though hit by an earthquake.

All of Sydney watched on as the sandy-haired Macquarie, standing more than 180 centimetres tall, 'a clean-shaved, lusty looking man ... and very broad-shouldered',[41] set foot on Australian soil for the first time. He wore the scarlet tunic and white breeches of a British military officer. His skin was tanned by decades of army service outdoors, while his dark, penetrating eyes shone with kindness and strength. He regarded himself as a liberal thinker, but when his brows knitted, he meant business.[42]

On shore, Paterson and Foveaux − along with most of the town's population, from its leading lights to its battlers − saluted their new commander.[43] The New South Wales Corps formed a red-coated line for three hundred metres up the hill, from the Government Landing Stairs to the freshly painted Government House,[44] and there was constant bowing from the onlookers as Macquarie passed. He joined Foveaux on a carriage ride along the tree-lined dirt roads of Sydney. It was still a rustic township huddled around that vast waterway, but Macquarie noted the smattering of grand homes − including the Reibeys' − rising beside the dusty tracks.

The next day, resplendent in scarlet coat and gold braid, and in front of his soldiers on parade at Sydney's military barracks,[45] Macquarie broke open a wax seal and opened the King's Commission. He handed it to the new judge advocate, Ellis Bent,[46] who had sailed with him. Mary Reibey and her children watched on as Bent − a tall, beefy young barrister − unfolded it.[47] The Great Seal of the Territory was displayed. The troops presented arms, and the officers saluted as 'God Save the King' roared out once again from the settlement and assaulted the bushland all around.[48] The soldiers fired three volleys. The summer sunlight glistened on the gold buttons of Macquarie's red coat, and he puffed out his chest. Then, in his rich Scottish burr, he began his address by declaring: 'Fellow citizens, and fellow soldiers!'

Macquarie's commanding presence and booming voice demanded respect. He told his captive audience in a 'short, animated speech', delivered with 'peculiar energy', that following the upheaval of the Rum Rebellion he would exercise his 'authority from the king with strict justice and impartiality', and that he would not tolerate the misbehaviour that had toppled Bligh.[49] He offered an olive branch to the First Peoples: 'I need not, I hope, express my wish that the natives of this country, when they come in the way in a peaceable manner, may not be molested in their persons or property by any one; but that, on the contrary, they may always be treated with kindness and attention, so as to conciliate them as much as possible to our government and manners.' From his troops, he demanded 'a most vigilant discharge of every part of their duty', hoping that their 'strict discipline' would be so exemplary as to 'preclude the painful necessity of resorting to punishment'. He concluded by telling the huge crowd of onlookers that it was 'the earnest wish of our most gracious king, and his ministers, to promote the welfare and prosperity of this rising colony in every way possible'.[50]

Macquarie had plans to transform this colonial outpost into something much grander. It was not only his 'duty', he said, but also his 'chief happiness' to see the colony prosper, and he assured his subjects that 'the honest, sober, and industrious inhabitant, whether free settler or convict, will ever find in me a friend and protector!'[51]

The troops gave the new governor three more cheers, then there was a royal salute of twenty-one guns from Dawes Point and from the two ships. Gunpowder was one of the few commodities not in short supply in Sydney.

Mary Reibey liked the look of Macquarie, and she liked his ideas: he prized industry and effort regardless of someone's background. The cacophony of cannon blasts and cheering to celebrate the new governor was all music to Mary's ears.

Chapter 10

MARY WAS HEAVILY pregnant and caring for six small children in what remained a harsh frontier settlement with poor medical services. Yet somehow she found the energy to oversee every facet of the family business while Tom was in China. One of the first things she did after his departure was to advertise for tenants to take up two of the family's adjoining farms along the Hawkesbury.[1] The properties were known as 'Reibey's Farms', she told readers of the *Gazette*, and they were 'lying and situate between Cobcraft's [sic] and Robert's'.[2] Her advertisement asked prospective lessees to contact her – 'Mrs Reiby' – as for the first time she began to assert herself publicly as a formidable businesswoman, priding herself on the principles of thrift and sobriety.[3] She knew what it was like to have nothing and she counted every penny she and Tom earned.

Tom's long voyage was going to be longer than anyone expected. Unbeknown to Mary, the *Lady Barlow* and a large fleet of homeward-bound East Indiamen were ready to sail from Whampoa early in 1810 but were detained after a Chinese man was found murdered in a local street. The authorities suspected he'd been killed by a visiting sailor, and Tom and hundreds of other foreign crewmen were prevented from leaving for three long months until 1 March, with the crime still unsolved. At least Tom sold a large supply of sandalwood before the *Lady Barlow* set off for Bengal.[4]

Mary had been thrilled by Lachlan Macquarie's appearance in Sydney and the enthusiasm he brought to the future of commerce there. After the governor's arrival speech, his battalion had marched out to stay at Grose Farm, which was then being used as a military camp. Macquarie returned to Government House, where Ellis Bent read out the oaths of allegiance, and where Macquarie issued his first proclamation through the pages of the *Gazette* on New Year's Day.

The proclamation began by declaring that His Majesty felt the 'utmost regret and displeasure on account of the late TUMULTUOUS PROCEEDINGS in this his COLONY, and the MUTINOUS CONDUCT of certain PERSONS therein towards his late representative, WILLIAM BLIGH, Esquire'. Moreover, 'through his gracious anxiety for the welfare and happiness of his loyal subjects of New South Wales, for the complete restoration of quiet and harmony, and to remove every motive for future disturbance', the King was 'graciously pleased' to empower Macquarie as the man to sort it all out. The governor signed the proclamation 'given under my hand, at Government House, Sydney, this First Day of January, 1810.'[5]

After two years of turmoil in the colony, New Year's Day was one of rejoicing in Sydney. That night, celebratory blazes illuminated the settlement, and skyrockets blasted off from the transport ships.[6] Macquarie still had to report back to London, but his bosses were months away by ship; for the time being, his power was absolute for thousands of kilometres in every direction, even out to the islands of the Pacific that the King had included in his jurisdiction.

Macquarie's first census, conducted in the early months of 1810, showed that Sydney had a European population of 6156, Parramatta 1807, the Hawkesbury 2389 and Newcastle just a hundred 'souls'. That made a total of 10,452: 5511 men, 2220 women and 2721 children. In total, there were 1437 prisoners being guarded by 1365 military personnel.[7] The convicts and free settlers of Van Diemen's Land totalled 1321 at the settlements of Port Dalrymple and Hobart Town. Only 177 people lived on Norfolk Island.[8]

They would all have to obey orders. Macquarie did not support what he had once called 'the infernal and destructive principles of democracy' as wielded by the 'savages of France' during their revolution.[9]

A WEEK AFTER MACQUARIE'S arrival, Mary and the children were shaken and shaking during an electrical storm that shocked the colony. Thunder and lightning erupted in the late afternoon. At the office of the *Sydney Gazette*, which was full of metal type, six children ran inside for safety and cowered as lightning repeatedly struck the building. One young man was knocked to the ground by the force of a bolt, which sent a back door flying off its hinges, and reduced the wood and brickwork around it 'to atoms'.[10] The editor, George Howe – who counted the Reibeys among his most valuable advertisers – was reading a page proof of his next edition when he was thrown backwards off his seat by an electric fireball that cannoned into the building, invading every opening with its flaming tongues. Howe rose from the floor to find himself looking like a ghost, enveloped in the dust of lime and mortar from the shattered brickwork.[11]

One week later, the ferocity of the storm was forgotten after a productive meeting between Macquarie and a delegation representing the colonists. The meeting suggested a bright new dawn for the Reibeys and the rest of Sydney's business community. Immediately, there was another grand celebration taking in all of the harbour's waterfront homes. Around Entally that night, illuminated signs went on display. John Macarthur's business partner Garnham Blaxcell, one of the plotters against Bligh, displayed a 'well executed portrait of His Majesty' at his front door.[12] Joseph Underwood[13] – the brother of the boatbuilder James and, like the Reibeys, involved in importing pork from Tahiti, as well as whaling and hunting for sea-lion oil – ignited a huge bonfire in front of his house. He threw open his home for the entertainment of spectators, and 'tables everywhere were covered with refreshments'. A reporter watching the scene remarked that 'youth and beauty joined the lively throng and kept the merry dance alive'. From a corner of Underwood's veranda, a band played 'God Save the King' and 'Rule, Britannia!'.[14]

Despite the euphoria surrounding the promise of Macquarie's regime, the governor knew he had his work cut out for him. He would recall: 'I found the colony barely emerging from infantile imbecility and suffering from various privations and disabilities; the country impenetrable beyond forty miles from Sydney; agriculture in a yet languishing state; commerce in its early dawn; revenue unknown; threatened by famine; distracted by faction; the public buildings in a state of dilapidation and mouldering to decay; the few roads and bridges formerly constructed, rendered almost impassable; the population in general depressed by poverty; no public credit nor private confidence; the morals of the great mass of the population in the lowest state of debasement, and religious worship almost totally neglected.'[15]

Macquarie's immediate job was to make sure his subjects had enough to eat. Regular flooding of the Hawkesbury meant that despite the Reibey ships bringing in their cargos of pork, inhabitants of New South Wales often faced starvation. The governor's first orders were to have three hectares at Castle Hill prepared for planting potatoes and another 150 hectares prepared for sowing wheat.[16] Soon, Macquarie could report that more than eight thousand hectares of New South Wales were under cultivation and almost thirty thousand cleared for pasture, and that between them, the colony's farmers owned 33,818 sheep, 8992 hogs, 6351 cows, 4732 oxen, 1732 goats, 914 horses and 193 bulls.[17] On 15 January, the almost providential arrival of the *Marian* from Bengal – a ship carrying 3500 bags of wheat, 500 bags of rice and 100 bags of sugar[18] – brought what Macquarie called 'a most reasonable relief'.[19] Because of fears that further flooding in the Hawkesbury would destroy crops, he formed a contract in April 1810 with Simeon Lord and his business partner, Francis Williams,[20] to import two hundred tons of Bengal wheat as a safeguard. They charged Macquarie a low price of £16 a ton in return for permission to import twenty thousand gallons of Bengal rum.[21]

Then another storm loomed over Sydney. William Bligh, still prowling the Derwent River in Hobart, heard of Macquarie's arrival from the skipper of a whaling vessel. On 17 January 1810, Bligh and his daughter Mary sailed through the Heads aboard the old and battered *Porpoise*.[22] Macquarie handed back Bligh's sword and flintlock pistols, which the rebels had taken, and returned some of Bligh's papers, although Macarthur and Johnston had kept all the important ones for themselves.[23]

Bligh desired a lot more from Macquarie. He demanded that the new governor treat him regally, and he wanted command of the *Hindostan* and *Dromedary*. While he waited for his demands to be met, he rented a cottage at £10 a month beside the Tank Stream near the Reibey house and had Macquarie assign him a sergeant from the 73rd as his personal bodyguard. Bligh would walk about Sydney with his guard close by, often to the hoots and jeers of the populace. He demanded that anyone who had supported his overthrow be prosecuted and wanted sixteen witnesses to his demise returned to England with him to ensure that Macarthur and Johnston were hanged.[24]

Instead, Macquarie did his best to smooth over the troubles of the past. He removed the bureaucrats appointed in Bligh's absence and restored the men who had held those roles during his reign. He also revoked the land grants, emancipations and pardons awarded by the rebel government. William Gore, the provost-marshal sentenced by the Macarthur regime to seven years on the chain gang, was finally released. Tom Reibey's business partner, Edward Wills, was granted a full pardon.

MARY REIBEY FOUND herself in Macquarie's favour almost from day one of his rule. On 25 January, she wrote to 'the Governor and Commander in Chief etc etc etc', asking for confirmation of the lease on her land underneath Entally.[25] While most women in the colony were relegated to domestic duties, Mary was helping to drive a big business that was really going places. Many of the convict women had been treated as sex slaves in the early days of the colony and there was a lingering stigma around female emancipists such as her which she constantly fought against. Still in her early thirties, she nevertheless had the money and the power to sway government. Although Mary always claimed she never meddled in 'polatics',[26] she was on her way to becoming a skilled lobbyist, trying to influence whoever was in power.

In 'The Memorial of Mary Reibey' addressed to Macquarie, she:

Humbly Sheweth
That Memorialist is the wife of Thomas Reibey, now absent
on voyage to China, and has a family of six children.
That Memorialist and her said Husband have been residents
18 years and upwards in this Territory: and by their joint
industry have become possessed of a valuable stone building
next contiguous to the Government Wharf'.[27]

Mary told Macquarie that the grant had been authorised by Governor King, who had known of her husband's 'universal good character' and the severe losses that Tom had sustained with the sinking of a 'fine sloop and cargo from Hunter's River.'[28] Further losses had been so severe that her husband had needed to journey to China. She asked Macquarie to authorise the lease on the land grant for another twenty-one years because of his 'great goodness and benign consideration to her and her family'. The appeal worked.

Mary also pressed the new government to renew her liquor licence. Sydney was awash with alcohol, and she was not about to miss any of the action. There were only six thousand Europeans in the town but seventy-five licences to run public houses – and though he'd been a heavy drinker as a younger man, Macquarie was calling closing time. Just weeks from giving birth for the seventh time, Mary was informed on 16 February that the governor was slashing the number of persons licensed to sell alcohol in Sydney to just twenty, in an effort to 'arrest the progress of drunkenness'.[29] Macquarie banned what he termed 'the shameful and indecent custom' of working on the Sabbath, and instructed all public houses to shut during divine service. He threatened to take away the liquor licence of any establishment ignoring that edict and to arrest anyone caught working on a Sunday.[30] He ordered that any person retailing or attempting to retail 'Wines or Spirituous Liquors without a License, after the Promulgation of this Order, will be fined in the Sum of Twenty Pounds Sterling, besides forfeiting the whole Stock of Wines or Liquors found in their Possession – Half of which Wines and Liquors to go to the Informer, and the other Half to the Crown'.[31]

Mary breathed a sigh of relief when she saw her name among the chosen twenty, along with those of George Howe and Michael Hayes.[32] She paid £20 for the renewal of the licence and provided the required 'two respectable Inhabitants to go Security' for her good behaviour and the keeping of an orderly house.[33]

Hayes was one of the Irish rebels fortunate not to be hanged after the 1798 Battle of Vinegar Hill. Governor King had given him a conditional pardon, but he'd been convicted of illicit distilling of spirits in his house at Farm Cove and sent to the penal colony at Norfolk Island for three years, where he'd earned a reputation as a ruthless and indefatigable debt collector for merchants.

Macquarie had also been given orders to stop the use of rum as an instrument of barter, but he knew prohibition would be useless. Rum was still vital to the colony as a means of payment, and it would take some time to change that. The governor decided that the best way to regulate the liquor trade was to allow unrestricted importation under a higher duty. From 3 March 1810, he increased the tax on liquor imports from 1 shilling and sixpence to 3 shillings a gallon. He believed this would put an end to any monopoly, to the bartering of spirits for corn, and to the 'very numerous' illegal stills in the colony.

MARY WAS ONLY thirty-two when she gave birth to her seventh child and fourth daughter, Elizabeth Ann 'Betsey' Reibey,[34] at 5.30 p.m. on 8 March 1810. The spirit of optimism that greeted the infant was still blighted by Bligh, who continued to march about town as though looking to make someone walk the plank.

On St Patrick's Day, 17 March, Bligh left town to inspect his farms on the Hawkesbury in Green Hills, the town now called Windsor. Since it was a glorious autumn day, he climbed out of his coach and planted his paunch on a pony for 'twenty miles'. A 'corpulent man and for some time unused to exercise', he became ill with fever and a swollen leg; this made his mood even more prickly than normal and his language even worse, so that he 'overpowered and affrighted every person that might have dealings with him'.[35]

For two years in the colony, Mary Putland had tolerated her father's foul temper and cruel tongue. Now she confronted the old tyrant with a very personal issue. The fiery little 27-year-old widow, who modestly wore trousers under her delicate, almost translucent dresses, had fallen for Macquarie's lieutenant-governor, Maurice O'Connell, who was fifteen years her senior. Bligh gave O'Connell's marriage proposal a 'flat denial', but Mary pressed on. Instead of returning to England with her on the *Hindostan*, Bligh gritted his teeth as he gave her away. His last official act in New South Wales was to attend their wedding at Government House on 8 May.[36] The 'Flogging Parson', Samuel Marsden, performed the ceremony at 10 a.m., and the Macquaries presided with an 'extraordinary degree of pleasure and even exultation'.[37]

Macquarie granted O'Connell 1012 hectares, which he called Riverston Farm, in what is now the suburb of Riverstone. His new wife was granted 427 hectares in what is now the western Sydney suburb of Werrington, adjoining the property Frogmore, which Governor Philip Gidley King had given her. She was a wealthy young bride whose personal fortune included more than 1200 hectares and seven thousand head of sheep and cattle. Broken-hearted and humiliated, Bligh prepared to leave Sydney without the daughter he called 'his inestimable treasure'. Three days after the wedding, he was ferried back out to the *Hindostan*, anchored beside the *Dromedary* and *Porpoise* at the Heads – and ready to set sail at a moment's notice.[38]

On 12 May, Lachlan and Elizabeth Macquarie, along with a large gathering of colonists, took their carriage out to the cliffs overlooking the Heads in order to see the ships sail out into the open sea a little after noon.[39] On board along with Bligh were around half of the Rum Corps and six witnesses for Bligh's prosecution against Macarthur and Johnston,[40] including the colony's principal surgeon Dr Jamison. Also sailing with Bligh was Colonel Paterson, who would die on the voyage, and Judge Advocate Atkins, whom Macquarie wrongly thought unlikely to survive the long journey given his heavy drinking and poor health.[41]

Macquarie stayed there for three hours, watching Bligh disappear over the horizon just to make certain he was gone.

TOM REIBEY, SAILING ON the *Lady Barlow*, arrived in Bengal on 2 April 1810 to load more merchandise at the East India Company's base in Calcutta, his childhood home. Meanwhile, Mary's immediate concern was the health of her new baby and the safe return of the *Mercury*, now under the command of the family's hired skipper, Theodore Walker, and nearing the end of a seven-month voyage through the South Pacific. Mary was having to take on more tasks around the yard, as one of her convict servants Stephen Wycomb had absconded,[42] but she coped as always.

On 3 May, the *Mercury* passed the Heads into Sydney with another large cargo of pork for all those who had hungry mouths and deep pockets. Walker told Mary that they could have brought home even more meat but for the civil wars between King Pomare II and his dissatisfied subjects.[43] The turmoil interfered with their trading deals. While the *Mercury* had been in Matavai Bay, chiefs from neighbouring islands had sent war canoes to help the King 'with every force they could levy', but Walker explained that it was dangerous for any vessel to visit Tahiti, as rebels were determined to capture all boats that came their way. They had a 'great aversion to the English'[44] because of Britain's support for the Polynesian King. Walker told Mary that on the island of Bora

One of the Reibeys' trading customers, 'Pomarre, King of Taheite' 1821, drawn by Samuel Freeman. *State Library of NSW FL8782242*

Bora he'd received a letter from 'Pomare King of Taheite' written in the King's own hand, with a reddish ink, advising Walker to be cautious where he anchored. A pilot boat organised by the King took Walker to a place that was under royal protection.[45]

Once the *Mercury* was safely moored beside the Reibeys' front yard, Mary Reibey and Edward Wills advertised a large quantity of pig flare – the fat from around the loin and kidneys – 'well cured and packed, and in fine condition for keeping'.[46] The sale process was hampered somewhat when four half-hundred weights went missing from Mary's yard; she put up a reward for their return.

Mary was still testing the market with the sale 'by Private Contract' of Entally, 'the new well-built Stone Dwelling House and extensive premises, with suitable out-buildings, the property of Thomas Reibey, situate near the Government Wharf'. 'As a waterside situation,' Mary explained to potential buyers, 'too much cannot possibly be said of the above; and as a further recommendation to a purchaser, terms of accommodation will be attended to or the payment of any sum deficient of the whole purchase money within a reasonable period, on security, being given.[47]

Mary was also getting the most money she could out of the *Mercury*: the schooner was off again on 20 July for a third voyage to Tahiti. To grease the wheels of trade, Mary sent a ceremonial sword as a present to King Pomare.[48] The schooner returned to Sydney laden with meat and vegetables, and it also carried a Tahitian woman named Foo-foo, who became Mary's housekeeper.[49]

MARY'S NEW DAUGHTER Betsey was seven months old when her father saw her for the first time. On 6 October, Tom had arrived home from Calcutta aboard the Reibeys' whaling vessel the *Mary and Sally*.[50] But it was not a happy homecoming. While Mary and the children were ecstatic to see him after such a long time, and there was the prospect of baby number eight, Tom was very different from the man who had sailed away twelve months earlier. He'd been badly sunburnt in India, and this voyage had been especially arduous and left him decidedly unwell.

When the *Mary and Sally* had left Calcutta for home on 10 June, it had shaped a course west of Sumatra in order to avoid the swarm of pirates that still infested the Straits of Malacca.[51] War raged through the East Indies, and the British frigates *Dover* and *Cornwallis* had taken the Dutch settlement on Ambon Island, now part of Indonesia. Tom had once fought a blazing gun battle with pirates, but he no longer had the strength or spirit for a rematch.

Back in New South Wales, he found that another enterprising trader, Alexander Riley,[52] was building a house next to Entally,[53] and that the new governor was planning to build a nation. Macquarie had started a construction spree around Sydney with an ambitious plan to turn the settlement into the jewel of the Crown. The governor had been inspired by a visit to the treasures of the Hermitage in St Petersburg – when he was dashing back to

Wealthy trader Alexander Riley built a house next to the Reibeys' waterfront home, Entally. *State Library of NSW FL3219322.*

Britain overland from India in his race to secure his wife's hand – and he wanted Sydney to be replete with ornate buildings rather than military barracks.

On the day Tom docked in Sydney, he read in the *Gazette* that Macquarie – 'being extremely desirous to do everything in his power' to contribute to the 'ornament and regularity of the town of Sydney, as well as to the convenience, accommodation, and safety of the inhabitants' – had ordered watchhouses to be built for the 'protection of the inhabitants from night robberies'. He was also establishing 'a well-regulated and strict system of police in the town'.

In a first for the colony, Macquarie saw to it that official names would be given to all the streets and ways leading through the town, and that signposts with those names painted on them would be erected in conspicuous places.[54] He decreed that 'the principal Street in the Town, and leading through the middle of it from Dawes's Point to the Place near the Brickfields ... and hitherto known alternately by the Names of High Street, Spring Row, and Serjeant Major's Row, is now named "George Street," in honour of our revered and gracious Sovereign'.[55] Streets were to be fifty feet wide (sixteen metres) and edged by paling fences, while buildings that encroached on the streets would have to be moved back at public expense. Pigs, dogs and goats would have to be fenced in; stray pigs and goats would be sold to benefit the Orphan Fund, and dogs that chased horses would be killed. Men driving cattle through the streets would have to do so on foot but avoid the footpaths under penalty of arrest. Shooting of guns in town, especially on Sundays, was prohibited, as was doing laundry in the Tank Stream or polluting it in other ways.[56]

The home of the former convict Isaac Nichols – 'a most, zealous, active and useful man',[57] and the first to welcome Macquarie to New South Wales – became Sydney's first post office.[58] Soon Nichols created a postmark that read 'Sydney NSW', the precursor of the stamp in Australia.[59]

Macquarie decreed that an area bounded 'by the Spring of Water and Stream on the West' and by the Houses of Simeon Lord, Andrew Thompson, and Tom and Mary Reibey on the north would be an open area named 'Macquarie Place'.[60] The governor was just getting started naming things after himself. He was also setting aside some open ground uphill from Government House for the 'Recreation and Amusement of the Inhabitants of the Town and as a Field of Exercise for the Troops'. The area was known alternately as The Common, Exercising Ground, Cricket Ground, and Race Course; but Macquarie named it Hyde Park, after the area in London he knew well.[61]

On 15 October 1810, during a week of glorious weather, it appeared as though all of the colony's eleven thousand inhabitants had turned out for Sydney's first spring racing carnival at Hyde Park. There had been horseraces in the colony before, but nothing like this event, during which a convict could rub shoulders with a judge, and a thief cheer beside a land baron – in other words, the racetrack was a microcosm of the egalitarian society that Macquarie envisaged for Sydney. While the governor had prohibited the sale of alcohol, as well as 'gaming, drunkenness, swearing, quarrelling, fighting or boxing taking place on or near the race-ground',[62] a good time was to be had by the masses. There was entertainment aplenty between the gallops, with cockfights and several footraces, but none more entertaining than the sight of one Dicky Dowling carrying ninety kilograms on his back for forty-five metres against an unfettered rival who had to run *two* lots of forty-five.[63]

Officers from the 73rd Regiment had put together a program that featured three race days over a five-day festival, held between Monday the fifteenth and Friday the nineteenth of October.[64] Hyde Park's track was one mile and forty yards (1630 metres) in circumference – and, appropriately, the finish line was close to the gallows. Providing the pageantry, colour and thrills were horses owned by prominent citizens Ellis Bent, Maurice O'Connell, Simeon Lord, Captain John Piper[65] and Captain Thomas Cleaveland.[66] Edward Wills staged two balls at his warehouse on George Street, selling tickets at 7 shillings sixpence,[67] and served dinner on his table every day for paying punters.

The race carnival finished with what the *Sydney Gazette* said was 'a universal glow of satisfaction – the celebration of the first liberal amusement instituted in the colony and in the presence of its patron and founder. The ballroom was occupied till about two o'clock when part of the company retired.'[68] The rest partied on until dawn. Macquarie's racing carnival showed a spirit in New South Wales that was missing in Europe; in Sydney, Macquarie wanted the prisoners and the free settlers to know that there was a willingness to forget the wrongs of the past.

MARY REIBEY MIGHT HAVE had enough work on her hands with seven young children and all the business dealings required during Tom's absence, but she still worked overtime during the race carnival to organise the couple's biggest sale yet after her husband's long-awaited return.

Sydney's official market square was being moved to a piece of open ground, part of which had been used by John and Gregory Blaxland as a stockyard next to the town cemetery. Macquarie was building 'Market Wharf' in Cockle Bay for the easy handling of grains and other food from the Hawkesbury. But the sale on the Reibeys' front yard at 'Macquarie Place' and at the Willses' warehouse on George Street, one that had started as soon as Tom came home, was the talk of the town. Mary Reibey and Sarah Wills placed large display ads in the *Gazette* for everything just 'imported per brig *Mary and Sally*'. They included: 'teas of sorts' and pots to boil them in, tortoiseshell combs, metal buttons, sugar and sugar candy, rice and coffee, gilt looking glasses, bait and saltpetre, walking sticks, spices and pepper, beads, bacon, pork and beef, hog's cheeks and lard sausages, curries, long sets of china, calicoes and nankeens, silk handkerchiefs, 'satins of sorts', ready-made shirts, chemises, 'sewing silks of colours', washing 'basons', and chamber vessels.[69] Tom had also brought home a large quantity of spirits from Calcutta, but they went into the government's bonded store for assessment of duty before sale.[70]

Mary had to do most of the selling, as Tom was still recuperating from his sunburn and exhaustion. His skin had become dry, wrinkled and blotched, and his eyes cloudy. Edward Wills was faring poorly too; the hard time he'd had in prison and on the convict hulks, and the even harder time he'd had on the *Hillsborough*, were taking their toll. The thirty-two year old had made out his will, nominating his 'loving wife Sarah Wills' as his executrix and administrix, and leaving everything to her 'in consideration of her constant kindness and affection towards me'. 'It is here my particular request,' he continued, 'that should my daughter Sarah marry contrary to the wish and consent of her Mother Sarah Wills, that the Mother shall cease to give her any further assistance whatever. And I lastly commend my body to the Earth from which it sprang, my spirit to the gracious and most merciful God who gave it hope to die in charity with all men!'[71] Though feeling poorly, Tom and Edward weren't as ill as the Reibeys' neighbour Andrew Thompson.

He had become great friends with Macquarie almost as soon as the governor had arrived. Thompson was made a justice of the peace and magistrate for the Hawkesbury district, the first emancipist to assume that post. Soon the judicial benches were being filled by other men who had once been in irons, while more and more constables knew what it had been like on the other side of the bars. The colony's road system was being put together by James Meehan,[72] a former Irish rebel. Colonists found themselves pleading with former prisoners for land grants.

Macquarie regularly invited Thompson to dinner at Government House, something that offended wealthy free settlers uncomfortable with breaking bread beside a convicted felon no matter how vast his wealth. But all the daring rescues Thompson had made in floodwaters left his immune system exhausted.[73] He died at Green Hills of respiratory failure on 22 October 1810, and Macquarie erected an eloquent and elaborate tombstone over his friend's Hawkesbury grave,[74] lauding the 'generosity of his nature in assisting his fellow creatures'.

In the wider community, there was still a mood of enthusiasm for the future of the colony with Macquarie occupying Government House. He told his bosses in London that he had taken it upon himself 'to adopt a new line of conduct, conceiving that emancipation, when united with rectitude and long-tried good conduct, should lead a man back to that rank in society, which he had forfeited'.[75] Macquarie announced that the Irishman D'Arcy Wentworth[76] – tall, handsome, blue-eyed and charming – would be the colony's principal surgeon until Dr Jamison returned from giving evidence at George Johnston's trial in England. Wentworth had been acquitted of four armed robberies in England, despite having been caught carrying a pistol, black silk mask and wig near the scene of a hold-up in the wilds of London's Hounslow Heath.[77] But Wentworth could wield a scalpel well enough for Macquarie's purposes, regardless of his colourful private life, which included three sons whom he acknowledged and at least seven other children whom he supported.[78]

Wentworth's assistant would be the long-faced William Redfern,[79] a former convict who had been in New South Wales since 1801.[80] Redfern had been transported as a consequence of his part in a mutiny at the Nore, an anchorage in the Thames Estuary; the mutiny had resulted in a death sentence, commuted because of his youth. Foveaux had recommended him to Macquarie 'in the strongest terms, as to his conduct, character and professional abilities'.[81] It was Foveaux who had appointed him the colony's assistant surgeon, and this position was confirmed in 1811 by the Prince Regent, who had taken over the duties of his father George III because of the King's recurring mental illness. Soon Redfern was running Sydney's dilapidated hospital at Dawes Point and building up a profitable private practice, as well as conducting a daily outpatient clinic for men from the convict gangs. Macquarie later pointed out that there were few families in Sydney who hadn't availed themselves of Redfern's considerable skills.

Pursuing this policy of giving convicts a second chance, Macquarie began to commute death sentences for all crimes but murder.[82] He was appalled by the brutal floggings that laid bones bare. There was something almost messianic in his forgiveness of the 'evildoers', with each one's former state 'no longer remembered or allowed to act against him'.[83] Macquarie would later explain that, in his opinion, those most meritorious, most capable and most willing to exert themselves in the public service were former convicts. He extended to them the same considerations and qualifications that they had enjoyed before being transported, and he held out to them the greatest 'incentive to virtue' – freedom and social status.[84] Mary was willing to accept whatever incentives were going.

Macquarie was all for giving ex-convicts a second chance in their new home, provided they were willing to work hard – and Mary Reibey certainly was. Her schooner the *Mercury* was on the way to Tahiti again, and the *Mary and Sally* was heading off on another whaling mission. There were debts to pay, debtors to chase, a mountain of goods to off-load, and properties to lease and maintain.

Mary also had to keep her family looking good.

The Reibeys' trading business allowed her to dress them in the latest fashions as the family's ships, and those of the East India Company, brought home to Sydney the finest linen, muslin, gingham, nankeen cloth, children's caps, dungarees and ribbons.

Embroidered Indian muslin, like that which had gone into Mary's wedding dress, was the height of fashion in Sydney in the early 1800s. The finery illuminated the social life of an early colonial society making the transition from a penal colony to one which provided not only opportunities but luxuries for emancipated convicts and free settlers.[85]

As Mary squeezed a figure that had grown significantly rounder after seven children into elegant muslin and cotton dresses that reached to her ankles, she delighted in the classical women's fashion of the time, a fashion that took its inspiration from the elegance of the draped women depicted in Greek and Roman sculpture.

Lightweight and delicately embroidered cottons in bright colours, usually woven in India, and offset by Kashmir shawls and lace bonnets, were ideal for the climate of New South Wales, in preference to the heavier fabrics favoured in England.

Mary liked to dress her family in the finest clothes in stark contrast to the coarsely woven and ill-fitting slops that most convicts wore, and which she had once donned.

That had been a long time ago when her only job was making trousers for fellow prisoners.

Now, Mary had to organise schooling and private tutors for her children, oversee multiple properties, direct a fleet of ocean-going vessels, run a booming import and export business, and tend to her beloved husband, who remained desperately ill. What other challenges would she have to overcome?

Chapter 11

B Y THE TIME MARY was thirty-three, she had been many extraordinary things: a cross-dresser, horse thief, convict, wife, mother of seven, real estate investor and international shipping boss. On 5 April 1811, she became a widow.

Tom and Mary had been trying to sell Entally for months, and on 2 March, Mary had advertised the property once more, explaining that Tom planned to depart the colony soon.[1] Instead he departed this life, as he and Mary cursed the burning Indian sun. The following day, the *Gazette* reported: 'On Friday evening died, at his house in Macquarie Place, Mr. Thomas Reibey, after a severe indisposition of several months, the origin of which he attributed to a *coup-de-soleil* when in India, from whence he returned to this Colony in October last.'[2] Mary told the *Gazette* editor, George Howe, that Tom, her partner of seventeen years, had been 'an affectionate husband, an indulgent parent', and that he left 'a widow and large family to regret his loss'.[3]

Her heartbreak was colossal. When she married Tom, she was a seventeen-year-old convict servant looking at years of hardship. Back then, she was frightened and largely alone in the world, thousands of miles and vast oceans from her family of origin. Now she had seven children, her own servants and a grand house, and she had inherited a small fortune with the promise of a dynasty to follow her that she and her late husband had created and nurtured together.

Tom was buried in the cemetery next to Sydney's market, where much of his fortune had been made.

Dressed in a long black, high-waisted dress and black bonnet, Mary led her children on the funeral procession through a town, which under Macquarie's guidance was throwing off the shackles of a penal colony to become an important centre of commerce.

Still, as the funeral procession made its way to the burial ground, the different layers of colonial Sydney society reminded her of the convict past she had left behind.

Civil and military officers, soldiers, free settlers, emancipists and chained convicts all co-existed together in what was largely an ordered society.

Government officials marched about in large bicorne hats, trimmed with ribbon rosettes. Most wore three-piece suits of dark cloth comprising tail-coats and waistcoats, buttoned over white linen shirts with pleated fronts.

Trousers were tucked into knee high, tasselled hessian boots.

Free settlers, going about their business on the dusty Sydney streets, typically wore wide-brimmed hats, some made locally of cabbage tree palm, with long, 'duster' coats over waistcoats, and white linen shirts and pointed collars with white moleskin trousers.

Some of the wealthier settlers carried large umbrellas made in India, which Mary sold from her yard.

Emancipists usually wore more basic apparel as they waited to make their fortunes. Men favoured loose-fitting, grey 'slop' suits and low crowned hats and leather shoes; women cotton and muslin dresses with ruffled shoulders.

Soldiers marched about in their red woollen jackets with white trousers and high black 'shako' caps.

Convicts toiled in their brown 'slop' suits and caps, carrying heavy loads under the eyes of the jailers, while repeat offenders wore suits of yellow wool.[4]

Verbose headstones were in fashion at the time, and Mary composed a moving epithet to place over Tom's grave.

Here lie the Perishable Remains of Mr. Thomas Reibey who came into this Colony a Free Mariner and during a residence of twenty years in this Colony always supported a fair and upright character. His conduct as a Husband and a Father needs no better eulogium than his actions have engraven him in the Hearts of His Widow and children who have abundant reason to lament his loss.

He died the 5th day of April 1811 Aged 42 years.

Reader as a Mortal, think of my Mortality.
Survey thy past, and view thy present Life.
Then with thy good, compare thy evil works
And judge if thou canst die.[5]

Life in the colony was too short, too precarious, for any prolonged periods of mourning. It was time to get back to business. With her letters of administration endorsed by Judge Advocate Ellis Bent, Mary got to work. She sorted out debts and creditors in the Civil Court, and started getting her ships underway again.[6]

At a time when independent businesswomen were still a rarity in Sydney, Mary smashed through gender barriers. Not only would she manage the interests and estates that had belonged to Tom, but she would also greatly expand the family empire, becoming adept at handling the voyages of the family's trading vessels, and buying and selling goods from American, Chinese and Indian traders. In Sydney, especially under the new reign of Macquarie, women had more business opportunities than ever, and Ann Mash was another to take advantage of every chance. With her husband William Chapman, Ann, the convict turned ferry operator, also ran the Kings Head Tavern beside the harbour on George Street. It was situated in the old home of Tom Reibey's mentor William Raven.

When Chapman died in 1810, Ann took over the tavern, and Governor Macquarie transferred the wine and spirit licence to her name. Mary instilled in her children early that they could grow wealthy as their young colony prospered.

Five days after his father's death, twelve-year-old James Reibey sailed out of Port Jackson on the whaling ship *Santa Anna*.[7] The ship had been a Spanish Navy vessel transporting a cargo of pitch, tar, and cedar boards to Ecuador when a British privateer had captured her off Mexico in June 1806. Four months later she had arrived in the harbour out the front of the Reibeys' house, carrying a bale of chillies and a bag of limes among other goods.[8] The partnership of Simeon Lord, Henry Kable and James Underwood had bought the *Santa Anna* for use as a whaler travelling between Sydney, New Zealand and Norfolk Island. They'd then sold her to William Dagg, who had been the captain of another whaling vessel, the *Scorpion*.

On 10 April 1811, Mary's ship the *Mary and Sally* and Dagg's *Santa Anna* left Port Jackson in tandem. The men on board the *Mary and Sally* were heading off to wreak havoc on the seals nesting along the shores of the newly charted Macquarie Island, while the *Santa Anna*, with James on board, was heading for the sheltered bays on the coast of New Zealand where sperm whales bred in the winter months and were ripe for the taking.[9] James was a strapping, adventurous twelve-year-old, who though close to his mother, wanted desperately to emulate the heroics and the success of his father, and to learn all he could about sailing. Though still grieving Tom's death, this bold young lad was focused on forging his own path to success. But he knew there would be hurdles in the shipping business. He changed ships in New Zealand, but on the way to England, laden with whale oil, the *Santa Anna* was wrecked in the Straits of Timor. All on board were saved.[10]

Three weeks after Tom's death, Mary let the rest of the colony know that she was forging ahead in business under her own power after settling any debts he had accrued.

NOTICES.

Letters of Administration having been granted to Mrs. Mary Reibey, Wife of the late Mr. Thomas Reibey, deceased, of all his Goods, Chatels and Effects, she requests that all those who have any claims or Demands upon the said Estate, will present the same forthwith for Payment; and all those who are indebted to the said Estate, are requested in like manner to pay their respective Debts within One Month from the date hereof, to avoid legal Proceedings for the recovery of the same.

MARY REIBEY.[11]

Edward Wills had formed a successful business partnership with the Reibeys but his health had been poor for a long time, his breathing shallow and his limbs listless. It was with a forlorn feeling of resignation that he watched Tom's early demise. On 14 May 1811, Edward Wills was only thirty-two when he died in Sydney 'after a painful illness of nearly three months' duration'. In the *Gazette*, George Howe wrote of Wills's 'generosity of his disposition … his integrity was undoubted and he lived universally respected'.[12] Sarah Wills was pregnant at the time and the next year, on what was the first birthday of her son Horatio,[13] she married George Howe. Sarah and Mary then dissolved their business partnership.

Mary's firstborn, Thomas Jr, had just turned fifteen when he planned to join the crew of an American brig for a voyage to his father's old home in Calcutta. Back in July 1809, the *Aurora* had sailed from New York on a trading voyage to Brazil, then on to various islands of the South Pacific. When it reached Sydney it underwent major repairs, financed by Simeon Lord and his business partner Francis Williams,[14] before embarking on a voyage to Macquarie Island for the slaughter of 'an immense number of sea elephants'.[15] Tom Jr planned to join the return voyage from Port Jackson to Calcutta, under the skipper Owen F. Smith, which Lord and Williams were bankrolling. He didn't make it, though – and just as well. The British prevented the brig from returning to Sydney as part of the Royal Navy's blockade on US sea trade, a prelude to the War of 1812. The *Aurora* was forced to sail for Philadelphia, where its cargo was seized as prohibited goods from trade with Britain.[16]

Tom, an ambitious go-getter like his parents and younger brother James, instead boarded the Reibeys' *Mercury* for Tahiti,[17] learning as much as he could about sailing and navigation as he planned to soon skipper his own ships. At the same time, Mary applied to Macquarie to employ a seaman, William Burnett,[18] who had arrived in Sydney on the whaling ship *New Zealander*.[19] She was often advertising for men to join the crews of her whalers for what she called 'pleasant ocean voyages', though the slaughtering work offered few pleasures.[20]

IN FEBRUARY 1811, Macquarie directed that the wealthy merchant and magistrate Alexander Riley[21] take 'every possible pains … to redress the grievance' in the first documented case of an Indigenous person bringing a civil action to a court in New South Wales. The case revolved around a dispute over a sea voyage to Van Diemen's Land. It was dismissed, but the *Gazette* noted that the case showed that Macquarie's government wanted to afford 'every protection and support to the natives'.[22]

Not long after Macquarie had arrived in Sydney, he'd written to Viscount Castlereagh, warning his superior that he was about to 'put the Crown to a very considerable expence in the erection of barracks and other essentially necessary public buildings'.[23] Word had not yet reached Macquarie that Castlereagh had resigned temporarily from his position as Secretary of War and the Colonies after putting a bullet into the thigh of Foreign Minister George Canning in a duel on Putney Heath on 21 September 1809.[24] Macquarie wrote to say that the colony needed new roads and bridges, a new hospital, new granaries, accommodation for a thousand soldiers, and more barracks to deal with the arrival of more convicts. To get all this done, Sydney would also need a new government architect and surveyor-general.[25]

The influx of more workers would create new markets at the Reibey warehouse.

Further afield, Macquarie planned to construct a turnpike road to the Hawkesbury,[26] 32-feet wide with a toll gate at the Parramatta Bridge and one at Rouse Hill.[27] He toured the Hawkesbury and saw the Reibey farms with a party including Simeon Lord and Thomas Moore,[28] a master boatbuilder and devout Anglican who had become one of the colony's biggest

landowners and had a property, Moorebank, on the Georges
River. Moore had been the ship's carpenter sailing on the *Britannia*
with Tom Reibey and William Raven. Macquarie named villages
in the area Windsor, Richmond, Castlereagh, and Pitt-Town. He
then named Wilberforce after 'Wm. Wilberforce Esqr. M.P.', an
anti-slavery campaigner.[29]

While Macquarie had cracked down on the sale of liquor, the
old system of barter continued for some time. Judge Advocate
Ellis Bent bought fifty-seven gallons of brandy for £17 and sold
them for £142 10 shillings. When Macquarie had contracted for a
new bridge over the Tank Stream in September 1811, he paid the
builder with 660 gallons (2500 litres) of spirits.[30] Soon afterwards,
the governor negotiated a much greater liquor deal that he saw as
being vital to the colony's future.

Sydney's hospital was in worse condition than most of the
eighty ailing patients it housed. John Macarthur was still in
England laying low, but his business partner Garnham Blaxcell,
along with Alexander Riley and the surgeon D'Arcy Wentworth,
inexperienced in construction but full of the entrepreneurial spirit
that Macquarie loved, proposed to build a new hospital from stone
and wood that would be 'one of the finest public buildings in any
of His Majesty's colonies'.[31] In return, they would receive twenty
convict labourers, eighty oxen to feed them, twenty draught
bullocks for the hard toil, and – the sweetest part of the deal –
permission to import 45,000 gallons (205,000 litres) of rum from
India and sell it over the three years that the construction would
take.[32] The negotiations for the 'Rum Hospital' deal took several
months. While Macquarie was trying to obliterate liquor as a
currency in New South Wales, he still saw it as a necessary evil.

HARDSHIPS AND HEARTACHE had hardened Mary and
made her a formidable business rival. Twenty years earlier she had
been sentenced to death, but now she welcomed the legal process,
often using it to settle disputes and impose her will.[33]

Just three months after her husband's death, Mary moved
headquarters from Entally to 12 George Street, a public house that

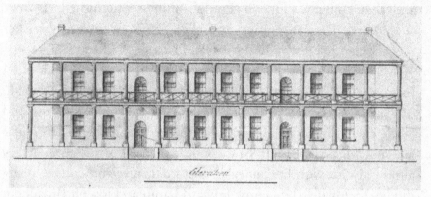

Plan and elevation of the South Wing of Macquarie's Rum Hospital. *State Records NSW. NRS-4335-9-[Plan2342]-[92]*

had been run by Michael Hayes. The Irish rebel and debt collector would soon take up 120 acres (49 hectares) on the Nepean in Airds, a village Macquarie had named after the Scottish family estate of his wife Elizabeth.[34] From there, Hayes frequently wrote to his brother in Ireland to lament the persecution of Roman Catholics in New South Wales; he claimed they were deprived of the right to practise their religion.[35] The rebellion at Castle Hill had made the colony administrators, including Macquarie, nervous of all things Irish, and though Mary and her family regularly attended Anglican services, the Irish would not celebrate mass again publicly in New South Wales until 1820.

Mary rented out Entally and maintained her liquor licence for the Sydney Hotel[36] adjacent to her new home. On 20 July she advertised that from there she would also be selling 'a Variety of Articles recently imported in the *Providence*' – everything from 'Ironmongery in lacquered brass' to 'hammers, drawer handles, hat hooks, slops, blue cloth jackets … and gentlemen's fine black beaver hats'.[37] She told her customers that she was determined to sell all the goods at reasonable prices, as it was 'the best recommendation to public Patronage and Support'.[38]

But Mary could play rough too – very rough. From 1812, New South Wales underwent three years of depression caused by drought and the recall to England of some of the 73rd Regiment and their money. Simeon Lord's business languished, D'Arcy Wentworth was struggling, and even the Reibeys' early backer Robert Campbell was defaulting on loans.

Mary's business suffered along with the rest, and she sent out a threat that 'ALL Persons who stand indebted to Mrs. M. [Reibey], of George-street, Sydney, are requested to come forward and Settle their respective Accounts without delay, to prevent *coercive measures being resorted to*.'[39] In the Court of Civil Jurisdiction, Mary almost always won her appeals – with damages and costs – as she did on 15 April 1812 against Edward Lamb and Joseph Broadbent for the non-payment of goods.[40]

Mary considered herself 'thrifty Correct and Sober'[41] and an astute investor. In return for £12 15 shillings being her 'quit rent' or land tax for nine years, Macquarie granted Mary another forty-five rods of land (1100 square metres) near her home in Macquarie Place on 25 August 1812 – provided she constructed a large building of at least two storeys upon it and kept it for three years.[42] She wrote back to Macquarie, pointing out that she was now a widow with seven young children and that she wished to confirm her long-term lease on a property in George Street, first granted to the surgeon Thomas Jamison and adjacent to the home of Isaac Nichols. 'Your Memorialist,' Mary wrote, 'most humbly prays Your Excellency will be pleased to take into your most Humane Consideration the Advantages that would result to her infant family, thro your Excellencys goodness.'[43] Again, her appeal worked.

Late in 1812, Mary opened another warehouse in George Street,[44] and advertised both passage and freight charges on her vessels.[45] She also made plans to off-load twenty tons of Tahitian salt pork and to trade forty hogsheads and twenty muskets in return 'for a liberal price'.[46] She sold fine wine at 12 shillings a gallon in minimum lots of ten.[47] At age eleven, George Reibey, her third son, started his career on the sea, joining the *Mercury* crew for one voyage along with a Tahitian nicknamed 'Old Raby' and a Hawaiian the Europeans called 'Bobahee'.[48]

MARY FOUND LACHLAN MACQUARIE to be a boon for her businesses, but the Earl of Liverpool was incandescent with rage over the governor's spending. In May 1812 he had written to Macquarie, demanding to know what game he was playing. The earl told the governor that under his watch the burden of New South Wales upon the mother country had so dramatically increased that the Prince Regent wanted 'a more satisfactory explanation' of the 'unusual expenditure' Macquarie had sanctioned.[49] The governor's dramatic building and infrastructure program had racked up bills of £72,600 6 shillings 10¼ pence in 1810, whereas under Governor King's watch, less than £14,000 had been spent in six years. If the expenditure in 1810 wasn't bad enough, Macquarie had asked his superiors to fork out £21,214 11 shillings 8¾ pence from 1 January to 12 March 1811.

Liverpool reminded Macquarie that while he remained in charge of New South Wales he was to undertake no public buildings or works of any description without having the previous sanction of His Majesty's Government for the construction.[50]

'An easterly view of the town of Sydney, the cappital [sic] of New South Wales. Taken from the west side of Benne Long's Point, 1812'. *State Library of NSW* FL1602252

Macquarie's job, Liverpool said, was to relieve Britain of a substantial financial burden in running the colony, not to add to it.[51] Macquarie told Liverpool that New South Wales had undergone a military revolution against Bligh before his arrival, and the colony had been in a state of decay, with convicts barely having enough clothing and food.[52] He explained that he was required to spend big in order to ward off famine while opening up the colony for pasture and cultivation. Knowing it would take months for the British government to learn what he was doing and then months more to complain about it, Macquarie decided to power ahead with his building projects.

Mary subscribed to the public fund that would help to finance Macquarie's new road linking Sydney with Botany Bay.[53] She could certainly spare the money, even though she also had to post a reward of £5 pounds 5 shillings after her Tahitian servant Foo-foo 'unaccountably disappeared' and 'no tidings whatever' had been heard. It was said that the Tahitian woman had become a favourite in the family, especially among the children, whom she attended as nursemaid; and 'when she went out with them for their daily walk to Dawes' Battery or Bennelong's Point, she attracted a great deal of admiration from the men'.[54] Mary was exceedingly fond of her and warned that anyone who should detain her servant 'against her inclination' would be prosecuted 'with the utmost rigor',[55] but it seems her young servant was homesick and gone for good, most likely returning to Tahiti.

A LIFE AT SEA REMAINED a lucrative occupation for savvy merchants, but it was always precarious. While Tom had been able to build boats at Entally, the Reibeys' shipbuilding business had ended. Mary's son George had once sailed on Mary's *Mercury* but there would be no more voyages on that vessel after that ship and Henry Kable's schooner the *Endeavour* were wrecked off the Shoalhaven River two hundred kilometres south of Sydney on 2 March 1813. Both were carrying large cargos of cedar when they were swamped.[56]

The *Endeavour* was wrecked about half an hour before the *Mercury*, which lost its rudder on a sandbank extending across the mouth of the Shoalhaven and became unmanageable in a rough sea.[57] The ship struck a rock, the keel was shattered, and its only boat was lost. The crew floundered amid great waves as they swam to shore. No lives were lost, but it was a close call for many.

When a rescue boat, the *Cumberland*, came down from Sydney, the winds were so damaging that it couldn't moor for some time, but eventually the crew of the *Mercury* and some from the *Endeavour* were hauled on board amid lashing waves. The master of the *Endeavour* and four others, having made it to the safety of land, were unable to make it back to the *Cumberland*. They survived for eleven days on cabbage palm berries, before deciding to walk to Sydney. Without a guide from the local Jerrinja people or even a pocket compass, and without knowledge of the bush they found themselves in, they set off with a couple of muskets and a pistol. Twelve hours into their exhausting journey, some of the Jerrinja helped them by providing fish. Because one of the crewmen couldn't swim – even though he worked on an ocean-going vessel – the Europeans had to construct rafts in order to cross wide rivers. After two days of subsisting on a little fish and grass, they shot and ate a dingo. For five more days they battled through the bush. Some more small fish, this time provided by the Gweagal people, gave them the strength to press on to Botany Bay.[58]

On behalf of his new wife Sarah Wills, George Howe was selling the *Mary and Sally*,[59] Mary having sold her interest in the vessel. It would soon be at Macquarie Island collecting thousands of gallons of oil from elephant seals the crew butchered, and as much fur as they could take from the seals, though the animals' numbers had been almost wiped out in just two and a half years of hunting.[60]

In the same week that five of the survivors of the shipping disaster lumbered home on foot, one of Mary's valuable mares died on the road between Parramatta and Sydney. Several of the poor animal's ribs were found shattered, which was attributed to the 'inhumanity of a driver' who had a few days earlier worked her in a cart.[61]

Mary had lost her prized whaling and sealing ship as well as a horse. In late April, she published a notice in the *Gazette* to inform all of Sydney and surrounds that 'any Part of the Schooner *Mercury*'s Hull or Cargo, which may be brought from Shoal Haven in any Vessel belonging to this Port, will be claimed by the Owner. M. REIBEY'.[62] Mary was in no danger of becoming destitute, though, especially since she had recently been granted a further two hundred acres of farmland at Airds.[63]

IN 1812 THE EARL OF LIVERPOOL, Robert Banks Jenkinson, had become Britain's prime minister after the assassination of the incumbent Spencer Perceval. The heat on Macquarie cooled because Earl Bathurst[64] became the new Secretary of State for War and the Colonies, and he brought a more relaxed attitude to Macquarie's expenses. He still warned the governor about promoting former convicts to the upper echelons of Sydney society, as this would be the 'main point of resistance' among conservative forces in the colony; if Macquarie wanted to bring convicts into the upper ranks, Bathurst advised, he 'should trust to the gradual effect'.[65]

In his younger days in India, Macquarie had been riddled with syphilis requiring copious treatments with mercury. The diseases and the treatment likely contributed to the many miscarriages that his wife Elizabeth suffered. In Sydney, though, Macquarie was working from the ground up as the colony's self-appointed moral guardian. He promised to end, as firmly as possible, the 'scandalous and pernicious custom so generally and shamelessly adopted throughout the territory of persons of different sexes cohabiting and living together unsanctioned by the legal ties of matrimony'.[66] Marriage was the cornerstone for industry and decency, he said, adding that it was also a protection for women, especially when it came to inheriting property after these 'illicit connexions' when a partner died intestate.[67]

Bligh's nemesis George Johnston was back in Sydney after having escaped with his life at his London court martial in June

1811. He'd been found guilty and dismissed from the army with dishonour – but as an old soldier who had provided good service for the marines and the army for many years prior to his run-in with Bligh, he was given his passage back to Sydney, arriving on 30 May 1813. Macquarie greeted him as an old comrade from the American War and gave him six hundred hectares near Lake Illawarra. Only a little earlier, the governor had taken back the eight hundred hectares at Emu Island that Johnston had granted his son George Jr, following Bligh's overthrow. In accordance with Macquarie's edicts on marriage, Johnston finally wed Esther Abrahams.[68] The former convict had already borne him a large family, and he retired to a quiet life. At about the same time, Simeon Lord married the former convict Mary Hyde, the mother of his eight children.

As the governor phased out the use of rum for barter in New South Wales, he began to institute a standard coinage in the colony. A violent hailstorm had hit Sydney in November 1812, heralding the arrival of the leaky[69] HMS *Samarang* from Madras. The vessel brought with it 40,000 Spanish dollars in coins, worth £10,000, which Macquarie used to create the colony's first currency of its own, something he saw as being vital to its development.

Macquarie had a convicted forger, William Henshall, cut the centres out of the coins and counter-stamp them, which made them worthless outside the colony. The central plug, known as a dump, was valued at 15 pence and stamped with a crown on one side and the denomination on the other. Around the hole, the 'holey dollar' received an over-stamp that said 'New South Wales 1813' on one side and 'Five Shillings' on the reverse. The combined value in the colony of the holey dollar and the dump was 6 shillings and threepence, or 25 per cent more than the value of a Spanish dollar, making it unprofitable to export them from the colony.

Converting the forty thousand Spanish coins took more than a year, and only ninety of the coins were wasted during the process. On 1 July 1813, Macquarie issued a proclamation 'that the said Silver Money shall be a legal Tender', and the coins went into circulation in 1814. By then, Macquarie and businesspeople such as Mary could see even greater economic potential for the colony, after the first European crossing of the Blue Mountains promised unprecedented agricultural yields from the fertile plains on the western side.

On 11 May 1813, six days after Elizabeth Macquarie had miscarried yet again, three settlers intent on crossing the mountain barrier – Gregory Blaxland,[70] William Lawson,[71] and William Charles Wentworth,[72] the son of D'Arcy Wentworth and his convict mistress Catherine Crowley – crossed the Nepean onto the fertile Emu Plains.[73] Eight days of climbing and hacking their way through the scrub brought them to a high ridge with a clear view of the settlements below: Seven Hills, Windsor, Mount Banks near modern-day Mount Tomah, and Grose Head near modern-day Yellow Rock. At the Jamison Valley, between modern-day Leura and Katoomba, their progress was halted when they arrived at the edge of an impassable barrier of rock more than 150 metres high, 'which appeared to divide the interior from the coast as with a stone wall, rising perpendicularly out of the side of the mountain'.[74] They gradually worked their way around the great cliffs and passed through what is now Medlow Bath and Blackheath, spellbound by the mists ascending from deep within the valleys.

On the twenty-eighth, they made it to the precipice of Mount York and saw a river below, delighted by the view of what looked like fertile country. The climb down was so steep that their horses stumbled under their loads and the men had to carry the equipment.[75] They found 'two fine streams of water': what would become known as the River Lett and Coxs River. From the summit of a mountain that would be named after himself, Blaxland looked out at the surrounding countryside and thought it would 'support the stock of the colony for the next thirty years'.[76]

VENOMOUS REPTILES WERE hazards that Mary hadn't needed to battle in Lancashire. In March 1814, while her George

Street warehouse was doing a roaring trade, a snake plague in Sydney coincided with the invasion of Russians into France to depose Emperor Napoleon Bonaparte.

In Windsor, a snake bit one of Macquarie's soldiers on the hand. The wounded part was immediately cut open and seared with a hot iron, but the patient underwent several hours of extreme illness and a debilitating stupor; no one was quite sure whether that had been caused by venom from the fangs or the burning flesh. At around the same time, one of the most dangerous species of what locals called 'the viper tribe' bit a farmer on the foot by the Nepean.[77]

A snake was spotted in Mary's warehouse and quickly escaped through a small hole in the floor. Several others were seen in nearby houses by the harbour, causing great alarm. In the property next to Mary's, two snakes were seen in one day but were chased in vain. An old man mixing mortar in the yard felt a sharp pain on his instep, and on looking down saw one of the reptiles between his legs; he severed its head with his spade. He felt no ill effects from the bite and credited his survival to a pair of thick worsted stockings worn loosely about the instep and ankle.[78]

George Howe put the sudden appearance of so many snakes down to the 'very great probability of them being in the hollow parts of trees brought into Sydney as fuel'. He advised *Gazette* readers to examine logs carefully 'when not wholly inconvenient' and to keep them at as great a distance from the more frequented parts of houses as possible.[79]

A week later, on 10 March, another hailstorm assaulted the settlement at Sydney, this time with such force that almost every pane of glass in the town was smashed.[80] Macquarie wrote that Sydney looked like it had been blown apart by an enormous explosion of gunpowder.[81] He could always work an angle for funding, and he warned London that he had two hundred boxes of window glass on order and that there would be other big, unavoidable expenses – he didn't mention all his clandestine building projects.

Despite the wild weather and dangerous wildlife on Sydney's doorstep, Macquarie was succeeding in his efforts to change the face of the colony. His road to Windsor was complete, and while the Sydney–Liverpool turnpike was still unfinished, he had grand plans for a road across the Blue Mountains to the land of milk and honey promised by the vast plains beyond. He estimated that it would take three months to build and require fifty convict labourers; toll roads would help defray some of the costs.[82]

After six miscarriages, Elizabeth Macquarie delivered the couple's second child, Lachlan Jr, two minutes before midnight on 28 March 1814 at Government House in Bridge Street. Dr Redfern helped with the delivery – and with Macquarie's nerves, as he was in a state of panic after all the miscarriages and the death of their first child, Jane. He had high hopes this time. 'A finer child could not be,'[83] he gushed, as his heart soared and tears of pride welled in his 53-year-old eyes at the cries of his firstborn son and heir. The vice-regal birth was the cause for great celebration throughout New South Wales.

The colony was still brimming with optimism, and so was Mary, even though George Lewes, one of her convict servants, had absconded.[84] The economic depression was easing and she was selling mountains of goods from her warehouse, her remaining ships were still carrying all manner of cargo, and she was still maintaining a huge property portfolio, renting out farms and houses throughout the colony.

Then Mary had the idea to visit Lancashire. Two decades after leaving home in disgrace, she planned to return in triumph as a wealthy businesswoman with her daughters. Mary hadn't seen any of her family of origin since she'd sailed out of London in rags and shame, but she had kept them informed of her changing circumstances and the fact that the colony had brought an abundance to her life, even though she had lost her husband and had no plans to replace him.

On Christmas Eve 1814, she advertised to sell 'that valuable House and Premises situated in Macquarie square the Property of Mrs. M. Reibey'. Entally was now being leased by the energetic merchant Robert Jenkins,[85] who had taken over Simeon Lord's job as auctioneer. Mary's 'valuable House Shop and Warehouse, situate 99 George street' was to be let 'for a Term of 3 or 5 years'.[86] She had decided to show all those back home how she had defied her circumstances and triumphed.

Mary began collecting natural curiosities from the colony that she was sure would shock and intrigue her relatives and old friends when she made it home. Among her exhibits was a snake that had been killed in a child's cradle in a house on Pitt Street.[87] Mary wanted to show everyone how she had overcome a deadly situation, too.

Chapter 12

BY OCTOBER 1815, MARY was finalising her preparations for the homecoming to England, but business concerns kept her in Sydney. She moved her family back to Entally House in Macquarie Place that she'd let to Robert Jenkins. With the colony's depression behind it, she was now providing an eager and cashed-up market with all manner of fancy goods from 99 George Street – everything from Chinese silk hats to cut fluted glass butter pots, bed quilts, and souchong teas. She was also offering the potentially volatile mix of Bengal and Jamaica rum, gin, cheroots and gunpowder.[1] After two or three years of depression, it was hard to turn her back on the profits. She had also become something of a favourite of Governor Macquarie, who regularly sought her advice on trade and commerce. She had a great eye for a good horse, as she'd shown as a teenager on the run, and she imported two snow-white Arab stallions for carriage horses for her daily drive round Sydney's Domain park.[2]

All around Mary's home, other fine buildings were seemingly growing out of the sandy soil. East of Macquarie Place, at a spectacular point jutting into Port Jackson, Scottish-born Captain John Piper[3] was planning a mansion on the seventy-seven hectares of waterfront land that Governor Macquarie had granted him. Piper had been one of John Macarthur's seconds in the duel with William Paterson, and he was earning a fortune collecting customs duties, excise on spirits, and harbour dues. He was leaving his stately home, Vaucluse House, for the new home at Point Piper.

Macquarie's expensive development of the town of Sydney – which now had a population of ten thousand – continued, as did his work further afield. The army officer and Hawksbury magistrate William Cox had employed thirty convicts, working in sometimes freezing conditions for the promise of freedom, to complete 101 miles (163 kilometres) of road wide enough for two carriages across the Blue Mountains.[4] The road climbed to almost 1200 metres, and Cox's men constructed a dozen bridges, hewn on the spot from nearby trees. 'The expense of constructing this road,' Macquarie explained to Bathurst, 'would be trifling to

A convict-built road across the Blue Mountains opened up fertile plains to the west. *State Library of NSW FL3200953.*

government', because the cost of labour was only emancipation and rations.[5]

Another of Macquarie's great improvements arrived on his doorstep free of charge. The convict transport *General Hewitt* had reached Sydney on 7 February 1814,[6] carrying seventy soldiers of the 46th Regiment and 266 convict men and boys, including the convicted forger Francis Greenway, a cocky 37-year-old architect from Bristol. Most of the prisoners were in 'a weak and sickly state', and another thirty-four had perished on the voyage,[7] mainly from contagious dysentery.

On 6 April, the same ship sailed for Ceylon bearing Bligh's daughter Mary O'Connell, her husband Maurice and his men of the 73rd Regiment. Even though Maurice O'Connell had always been cordial to the governor, Macquarie was glad to see him leave, believing the officer possessed 'an irritable temper and overbearing disposition'.[8] And there hadn't been much peace with Mary O'Connell bearing a grudge against many people in town over the way she and her father had been attacked.

Macquarie saw much more benefit to Sydney from Greenway, who not long after his arrival was joined in Sydney by his wife Mary and their three children. Greenway had achieved a degree of prominence as an architect but became bankrupt in 1812, and he'd pleaded guilty to forging a financial document. His death sentence was commuted to fourteen years' transportation. The governor noticed Greenway's talent – and temperamental nature – almost immediately. Macquarie granted him such freedom that by the end of his first year in what was supposed to be a hellish prison, Greenway had his own office at 84 George Street, just near the warehouses of Mary Reibey and Sarah Wills. In December 1814, he advertised his services in the *Gazette*, proclaiming he'd practised for many years as an architect 'in some of the most extensive Concerns in England, public, speculative, and private'.[9] His terms were five per cent commission 'on the estimate, for designing the plans, elevations, and sections of the building, from the simple cottage to the most extensive mansion'.[10]

Greenway's first private commission in the colony involved extending the residence of Ultimo House. It was the home of the surgeon Dr John Harris, who had been granted fourteen hectares for helping Governor King stifle the liquor trade of the Rum Corps; Harris had also been on the *General Hewitt*, so he knew Greenway. With Macquarie's guidance, the architect began to transform Sydney's skyline.

PRESSING BUSINESS CONCERNS and constant opportunities for expanding her holdings still kept Mary from travelling to England. She had also started to suffer with asthma and became concerned about how she would fare if she had breathing troubles thousands of miles from home. There were minor matters, too. She issued a public notice against a man named Rainsford who was collecting grain on the Hawkesbury on her account, under the pretext of an authority from her.[11] She also cautioned anyone whose cattle trespassed on her farm 'The Toad Hole, situate in the District of Airds' that the beasts would be impounded.[12]

Her shipping business took up much of her time. Mary had her heart in her mouth every time her sons set sail, but they were headstrong lads determined to be masters of their fate. At just nineteen, Tom Jr had become the master of his mother's new 37-tonne schooner *John Palmer*,[13] ferrying passengers and cargo between Sydney and Port Dalrymple on the Tamar in Van Diemen's Land. His father had seen the commercial potential of trading with the merchants along the Derwent and Tamar, and the fledgling towns growing beside the rivers. The possibilities became increasingly attractive to Mary and Tom Jr.

By April 1816, Macquarie had been governor for longer than any of his predecessors. He was proud of how he was shaping the colony in accordance with his vision for an enlightened, liberal outpost of empire. The year had started in jubilation, with a victory dinner for 120 elegantly attired ladies and gentlemen in one of the new hospital's halls, which were festooned with native flora and exquisitely crafted decorations that spelt out

Surgeon John Harris had a mansion and vast tract of rural land that is now the inner-city suburb of Ultimo. *State Library of NSW FL3267837, FL3322827*

'WATERLOO, WELLINGTON, and VICTORY' as Sydney celebrated the final defeat of Napoleon.[14]

There may have been peace in Europe, but wars with the First Peoples had continued to rage. Soldiers and settlers were still driving Aboriginal people from their land, their food sources had been taken from them, their sacred sites were routinely destroyed, and their women and children molested. In March 1814, Aboriginal warriors had been spearing cattle and raiding farms along the Nepean from Bents Basin to Castlereagh; but settlers and soldiers escalated the violence in a despicable way. Two months later, three European soldiers shot and killed a Gandangara boy who was with a group taking maize from a farm on Mallaty Creek in Appin. One soldier, Isaac Eustace, was speared to death and mutilated.[15] Revenge attacks and atrocities followed: settlers attacked a camp of sleeping Gandangara people, killing and hacking an Aboriginal woman, the wife of the warrior Bitugully. They also killed three children, one of whom was a child of the warrior Yelloming. Macquarie was told that the posse of settlers 'not content at shooting at [the Gandangara people] in the most treacherous manner in the dark, actually cut the woman's arm off and stripped the scalp of her head over her eyes, and on going up to them and finding one of the children only wounded one of the fellows deliberately beat the infant's brains out with the butt of his musket'.[16]

The First Peoples then struck at a hut belonging to Elizabeth Macarthur in Bringelly. A stockkeeper named William Baker and a woman named Mary Sullivan were killed.[17] The settlers used muskets to ward off attacks at William Cox's property in Mulgoa and at the Shancomore estate in Bringelly.[18] Macquarie visited the area as a peacemaker, decided in his own mind that Aboriginal payback justice had been satisfied,[19] and ordered both sides to stop the violence. Understandably, Aboriginal warriors ignored him; they speared to death the men who had killed the Gandangara woman and children. In a public proclamation, Macquarie declared that he 'felt much Regret in having to advert to the unhappy Conflicts which have lately taken place between the Settlers in the remote Districts of Bringelly, Airds, and Appin, and the Natives of the Mountains adjoining those Districts; and He sincerely laments that any Cause should have been given on either Side for the sanguinary and cruel Acts which have been reciprocally perpetrated by each Party.' It was obvious to any unprejudiced man, Macquarie said, 'that the first personal attacks were made on the Part of the Settlers'.[20]

On 2 March 1816, a group of thirty Aboriginal men attacked the servants' quarters at George Palmer's property on the Nepean, near Bringelly. The following day a large group of Indigenous men encircled a small posse chasing them and hailed down 'a shower of spears'.[21] Some of the Indigenous men picked up guns that the settlers had dropped in their escape and used the Europeans' weapons on them. Four settlers 'fell in an instant, either from shot, or by the spear', and an adolescent boy with them received a spear in the back. The next day, sixty Indigenous fighters ransacked and destroyed nearby farm buildings.[22] Soon a great arc around the Cumberland Plain – from Lane Cove on Sydney's north shore to Bringelly in the west and Camden in the south – became a battleground in what the *Gazette* called a coordinated plan of the 'mountain natives' and the 'nearer hordes' to plunder the settlers' maize fields.[23]

At about 5 p.m. on 10 March 1816, at the Hassall family's Macquarie Grove property at Camden, neighbours rode up with a warning that 'the whole body of Gundenoran [Gandangara] natives' intended to attack the Macarthurs' nearby farm to 'plunder and murder all before them'.[24] News spread that three of the Macarthurs' servants at Upper Camden had 'fallen victim to the dreadful atrocities of the savage natives'. On the nearby Razorback Range, 'forty armed [settlers], some with muskets some with pistols some with pitch forks some with pikes and others with nothing', came face to face with their enemy, who had apparently stockpiled spears and lured the Europeans into a trap.[25] Aboriginal warriors were 'posted on a high perpendicular rock'. The settlers fired their muskets, but the Indigenous men – knowing that the guns were good for just one shot – fell down as soon as the weapons were pointed at them, only to 'get up and dance' after the explosion. Spears and stones then rained down on the colonists 'in great abundance'. Realising they had no chance, the farmers ran away as fast as they could.[26]

Three weeks later, the *Gazette* reported: 'At the beginning of the week an attack was made by a body of natives upon the farm of Lewis, at the Nepean, whose wife and man servant they cruelly murdered. The head of the unfortunate woman was sever'd from the body, and the man was dreadfully mangled with a tomahawk. The furious wretches afterwards plundered the house, and wantonly speared a number of pigs ... A number of the natives, supposed 80 or 90 at the least, a few days since made their appearance at Lane Cove, and committed depredations on several farms.'[27] The attacks were becoming more frequent and widespread, and colonists were advised only to travel in numbers.

Macquarie's vision splendid of colonising the country west of the Blue Mountains was being threatened. He had long conceded that most of the attacks by Indigenous people had started when cruelties were heaped upon them by the settlers, but now he would tolerate no excuses for their retaliations. Many settlers had already abandoned their farms.[28] Macquarie wrote to Bathurst to say that he had consistently shown 'much kindness' to the Aboriginal people.[29] In his mind he had been magnanimous in giving them some of their own land back to farm, set up a Native Institution at Parramatta to teach Indigenous children British ways, and always tried to remain on 'friendly terms', overlooking 'many of their occasional acts of violence and atrocity'.[30] After promotions while in Sydney, Macquarie was now a major general in the British Army. He had been a soldier all his life, and this was a war he was determined to win. His plan was to strike the Aboriginal people 'with terror against committing similar acts of violence in future'.[31] He ordered three separate military detachments to march into the 'interior and remote parts of the colony' in order to punish 'the hostile natives'.[32]

So it was that just before dawn on the cold moonlit morning of 17 April 1816, as the waters of the Cataract River rushed through deep canyons near Appin, Aboriginal guides led a party of Macquarie's soldiers, under Captain James Wallis,[33] to an area of dense, dark foliage ending in sheer cliffs sixty metres high above the raging waters. A group of Dharawal people, perhaps fifty or so, were trapped against the cliffs.

The terrified Dharawal people could do nothing as Macquarie's soldiers started shooting. They tried to run for cover as the soldiers cut down some of them with rifle fire. Others fell inadvertently to their deaths or were seen 'rushing in despair over the precipice'.[34] Wallis counted fourteen corpses, but no one could be sure how many men, women and children lay dead in the craggy rocks of the steep cliffs.

Wallis had his men haul up the bodies of Durelle and Cannabayagal. Durelle was said to have been a Dharawal speaker, probably of the Muringong people, and Cannabayagal[35] was a well-known Gandangara warrior and leader from the Burragorang Valley.[36] Wallis said the bodies were taken to a prominent hill on William Broughton's farm, Lachlan Vale. There they were hanged by their necks from tree branches, where they stayed decomposing for days.

William Byrne, a local settler who was a boy of eight at the time, remembered the massacre and its aftermath differently from Wallis. In his old age, Byrne recalled the slaughter, saying, 'The government ... sent up a detachment of soldiers who ran a portion of them into a drive, shot sixteen of them, and hanged three on McGee's Hill.' Byrne said three bodies were strung up and that the soldiers 'cut off the heads and brought them to Sydney, where the government paid 30 shillings and a gallon of rum each for them'.[37]

THE HAWKESBURY AND NEPEAN experienced a great flood at the end of May 1816, wiping out the wheat crops and threatening food shortages. Macquarie turned his attention to this new problem, satisfied that the worst of the fighting was over.

The war wasn't over yet, though. Settlers at the Kurrajong Brush, in the foothills of the Blue Mountains, were attacked with such ferocity and frequency that soon Joseph Hobson was the only one still farming there. On 7 July 1816, he was killed with a spear through the heart.[38] Attacks on William Cox's Mulgoa farm, on the Nepean between Emu Plains and the Cowpastures, resulted in the murder and mutilation of a shepherd, and two hundred 'very fine sheep' were hurled down an 'immense precipice'.[39] At Glenroy on the Coxs River, on the western side of the Blue Mountains, Sergeant Jeremiah Murphy was ordered not to allow Aboriginal people nearer to the settlement than sixty yards and to send any whom he captured – either handcuffed or with their hands tied with rope – to the depot at Springwood and then on to Parramatta.

Macquarie issued another proclamation on 20 July 1816, declaring ten Aboriginal warriors[40] as outlaws and giving anyone – 'whether free men, prisoners of the Crown, or friendly natives' – 'the power to kill and utterly destroy them'.[41] He offered 'a reward of ten pounds sterling' for each of them, dead or alive.[42]

The bounties went unpaid, but the governor announced that several rebel leaders had 'been either killed or taken prisoners', and he called a truce even though Aboriginal people never meekly followed British rule. The ten outlaws would be forgiven if they surrendered, and 'from and after the 8 November 1816, all hostile operations, military or other, against the said native tribes will cease'.[43]

At the annual post-Christmas feast day at the Parramatta marketplace, Macquarie assured the Indigenous people who attended his yearly gatherings and who seemed to co-exist well with the Europeans that meat and drink would be 'plentiful', and that he would personally advise them on the 'plan of life' they might 'be inclined to adopt for their own comfort and happiness'.[44] In his mind he had brought peace to the colony, even if it was with a heavy hand. Before long, he told Bathurst that the Indigenous population of New South Wales was 'living peaceably and quietly in every part of the colony'.[45] The wounds, however, continued to fester and would never heal.

THE DANGERS THAT MARY'S family faced were mostly out on the water. On 19 July 1816, Tom Jr sailed the *John Palmer* into Sydney Harbour after a two-week voyage to Port Dalrymple. He returned with nine children among his passengers to be rejoined with their families. In unpredictable winds he elected to bypass the Heads and go to the calmer seas around Newcastle. The schooner stayed there for five days while tempestuous gales forced the *Lady Nelson* into Port Stevens on its voyage from Newcastle to Sydney.

The *Edwin*, a schooner once owned by the Reibeys, was wrecked just north of there at Cape Hawke, owing to the loss of all her sails. The skipper had been travelling with his wife and their baby, and a crew of two men; he said that after surviving the wreck they had been robbed by the local Indigenous people of all their provisions and clothes, 'leaving them in perfect nudity to make their way through a trackless if not impenetrable scrub, for upwards of 100 miles' on a journey of fifteen days to reach Newcastle.[46]

There would soon be a magnificent lighthouse to guard the Sydney Heads. Macquarie had laid the foundation stone, and the architect Francis Greenway had designed a building sixty-five feet (twenty metres) high with a revolving light and an internal stone staircase.[47] Macquarie, Greenway and others in Macquarie's party drank a toast with cherry brandy to its success.[48] When the stonework for the Macquarie Lighthouse[49] was finally finished,[50] it was the first in Australia.[51] The governor was so pleased with the result that he presented Greenway with conditional emancipation.

The cost of the lighthouse and its revolving lantern was to be paid by a tax on ships entering the harbour – however, as a gift to Sydney, Macquarie declared that local vessels would be exempt.[52] The governor told Bathurst that it was a 'very elegant and strong stone tower' and 'greatly wanted for the use, safety and direction of shipping, trading to and from this port'.[53] Bathurst, becoming increasingly alarmed at Macquarie's expenditure, replied that the governor had been warned about wasting money on a place that was supposed to be a prison.[54]

Macquarie was planning a Greenway-designed obelisk that would mark the distance to other settlements in the colony from a position in front of Mary Reibey's house in Macquarie Place. Just up Bent Street from there was Macquarie's new 'Rum Hospital', the most spectacular building in the colony, with its wide verandahs a nod to his time in India. He regarded it as his sale of the century. He had charged the contractors £9000 in duties on their imported spirits, which eventually amounted to sixty-five thousand gallons (295,000 litres), and provided them with £4200 in convict labour and bullocks. In this way, he'd poured nearly £4800 profit back into the government coffers – and into the bargain he received a series of buildings with an estimated worth of £40,000 that would house a hospital, and eventually the colonial mint and the New South Wales Parliament.[55]

All three contractors complained that Macquarie's masterstroke had sent them to the wall. Mary's neighbour Alexander Riley became a bitter rival of the governor and an ally of Macquarie's enemy Samuel Marsden. D'Arcy Wentworth was flat out paying his son's allowance,[56] and Garnham Blaxcell was only saved from court action because the judge – Jeffery Bent, brother of Ellis – was always at war with Macquarie and had temporarily shut down the court. Blaxcell was broke and unable to pay the government £2385 in import duties. He fled for England, promising to recover money owed to him when he arrived in London. But the man who had once been one of the colony's richest merchants – with a 'fine house' in Sydney, a warehouse in George Street, a windmill at Pyrmont, a farm at Petersham and, at different times, seven trading vessels – drank himself to death in Batavia.[57]

Mary Reibey was of much tougher and more astute stock. She kept putting off her trip to England because the timing with her business still wasn't right. Money was pouring in after the depression, and as an experienced trader she was always searching for a sale. Mary was now a small, plump woman approaching forty and though her sharp eyes would soon need spectacles, she always had a focus on the next big deal. For many years she constantly advertised all her properties and assets, always putting a high price on them, with the belief that in a growing town there would always be someone willing to purchase something at above market value. She was careful with her things, too. When she lost a gold brooch engraved with her initials while touring her properties on the Hawkesbury, she immediately offered a 20 shilling reward through the *Gazette*.[58] She continued to test the market, offering for sale her 'valuable and extensive dwelling house with extensive stores, at the water-side, in George Street, Sydney', and the 'valuable House and Premises in Macquarie Place', twelve farms on the Hawkesbury, eighty hectares at Airds, 'and a House and Premises in Cockle Bay'.[59] The George Street property had a 'large and extensive Shop, and four large Parlours or sitting Rooms on the first Floor, with a commanding Hall'. There were 'five Bedrooms with a comfortable Garret, and Cellaring under the whole of the House'. Mary told prospective buyers that Entally House and its other buildings in Macquarie Place had 'commanding access' to the harbour. The apartments were 'well furnished, with good cellarage, convenient stores and detached kitchen'.[60] It was a grand, genteel home that had the advantage for a trader of being a long-established mercantile house.[61] One of the Hawkesbury properties, Ravil Farm, was 120 acres of 'good land' on the riverbank at Wilberforce, 'out of danger of floods' with about forty hectares cleared. Reibey Farm was twelve hectares with all the land cleared, as was Cross Farm.

Mary was also offering to sell the schooner *John Palmer* for the right price and it had been 'lately refitted, having a new bottom with sheathing, two suit of sails, two anchors and cables'; it had recently arrived from Port Dalrymple with four tonnes of wool and could be made ready for a new owner with a few hours' notice.[62] Terms of the sale were half the purchase price up front and twelve months' credit for the other half on good security.[63] The offers weren't high enough.

The businesswoman also advertised for 'a steady Person who understands the tenanting of Farms and collecting of Rents, and other Debts, who has no Objection to go up the Country'. She was a no-nonsense boss, telling jobseekers that 'None need apply but those who can give satisfactory Proofs of their honesty and integrity.'[64]

Her children were looking to her fortune to help them make a start with homes and careers, but the diminutive Mary demanded obedience as the family matriarch. All three of her sons, the three eldest of her seven children, were headstrong teenagers, like she had once been in Lancashire. James, especially, clashed with his mother.

With considerable experience already gained on the sea, James had set himself up as a merchant in Hobart Town. On 25 March 1816, aged just seventeen and without informing his mother, James married a 21-year-old widow named Rebecca Breedon.[65] Mary was livid when she heard the news, insisting that James was far too young to be wed, even though she had married Tom Reibey at the same age. She wasn't too fussed about Rebecca's family either. Rebecca's mother, Ann Doyle, had been sentenced to death at the Kent Assizes in Maidstone for burglary but instead sailed on the 'floating brothel' *Lady Juliana*. She was sent to Norfolk Island on the *Surprize* and had four children there, most likely all of them with Philip Devine, a First Fleet convict who twice endured floggings – including a whipping of two hundred lashes for selling a shirt.[66] At the age of sixteen, Rebecca had married Joseph Edward Breedon, a lieutenant in the Royal Marines, but he'd died two years later.

After James and Rebecca wed at St David's Church in Hobart Town, the couple sailed for Sydney. There, Rebecca met someone else, who as a girl had been sentenced to death for theft and then after being transported to the colony, had made a new life for herself on foreign shores.[67]

The meeting between Rebecca and her new mother-in-law did not go well, though. Mary was adamant that James's new wife would not get a penny from Mary's hard work. James said that such an arrangement suited him just fine, but he later lamented that he was deeply hurt that for a time his mother 'discarded' him.[68]

Still, he conceded she had her reasons and that they were 'just'. 'I was only Seventeen years of age, and my wife unknown to her,' James later explained to Mary's Lancashire cousin David Hope, who became a Glasgow merchant.[69]

James said the severing of the relationship with his mother for a year or two forced him to stand on his own two feet. Rebecca had a small house left to her by her late husband, 'tho in a very unfurnished state & built of wood'.[70] They managed to get two small rooms habitable and opened a small shop with £40 of stock which James obtained on credit in Sydney. The newlyweds preserved every shilling they earned as though it was a fortune and paid off the debt quickly.

For a time they received no charity from Mary, but on 12 December 1816, James received an early Christmas present of a hundred acres from the government along the Derwent in Hobart Town.[71] Mary joyfully wrote home to her Aunt Penelope Hope to share the good news.[72]

James revealed that when Mary 'found from various reports' that the young couple were settled and responsible, they became 'good friends'.

Despite the happiness that was evident between James and Rebecca, Mary chose not to remarry, most likely to protect her wealth for her children. Under the law of coverture any new husband would have had a claim on her property. Remaining a wealthy, single widow also enabled Mary to make her own business decisions without interference from a spouse.

Married women couldn't sign contracts in their own right, unlike single women,[73] though colonial women had more commercial freedom than their British counterparts, and judges often made decisions based on local circumstances, given the overheated melting pot that mixed aristocratic Englishmen with prisoners who had once been sentenced to death.

MACQUARIE'S BEAUTIFICATION of Sydney included his establishment of the Royal Botanic Gardens,[74] bisected by '3 miles and 377 yards' of Mrs Macquarie's Road. The thoroughfare was designed to transport the vice-regal carriage from Macquarie Place to a chair that convicts had carved into rock, and from which Elizabeth Macquarie could gaze across the harbour. Macquarie envisioned that the garden would grow into a serene setting for the town under the care of his fellow Scot, Charles Frazer[75] of the 46th Regiment, who would soon be known as the colonial botanist.

The beautification of Sydney was also helped by the magnificent facade of Macquarie's Rum Hospital, though there were concerns about shoddy building work caused by the contractors cutting corners. The governor called in Samuel Bradley, the Superintendent of Government Carpenters, and Ambrose Bryan, Foreman of Government Stonemasons, to shore up its structure, along with Francis Greenway to oversee repairs and improve supports.[76]

Greenway also designed a Doric fountain for Macquarie Place,[77] as well as a new courthouse and a new St Matthew's Anglican Church at Windsor. Macquarie then asked his colonial architect to expand the fortifications at Dawes Point with a semicircular battery and a decorative guardhouse that resembled the one on Fort Macquarie, built on the site of Bennelong's hut[78] and incorporating some of the guns from HMS *Supply*.

Greenway designed the Hyde Park Barracks on Macquarie Street to house six hundred convict men in hammocks, and Macquarie would eventually lay the foundation stone on 6 April 1817. There was soon going to be a great influx of convicts, with the end of the Napoleonic Wars creating mass unemployment, and Macquarie wanted to be ready to accommodate them. He granted Greenway a full pardon on the day the barracks were opened.[79]

Across Macquarie Street, Greenway designed the grand St James' Church. For almost half a century it was the tallest building in Sydney, its copper steeple rising to fifty-two metres.[80]

Greenway also designed the courthouse next door, originally intended to be Macquarie's Georgian Public School. The architect's greatest decorative masterpiece, however, was the Government

Stables, a huge project that Macquarie tried to slip in under the nose of the London bean-counters and which Greenway based on Thornbury Castle near his old home in Bristol.[81]

Macquarie had another impressive construction in mind. Ever since his arrival in New South Wales seven years earlier, he'd argued that for the colony to progress it needed its own legal tender and its own bank as a solid foundation for financial success.[82] He wanted all social classes to cooperate with the founding of the bank, especially as some ex-convicts were among the wealthiest people in the colony. He stipulated that all levels of the colonial society should be represented in the bank's direction and management.[83] It would be a bank issuing notes as legal tender and loans for investors. Macquarie called it the Bank of New South Wales – and he wanted Mary Reibey to play a key role in its creation.

Chapter 13

MARY AND OTHER TRADERS regularly made their way to the courts because of disputes over the IOU system of barter still in place despite Macquarie's crackdown on promissory notes. The forgeries and value fluctuations involving the notes had damaged the trade and credit system in New South Wales almost from the founding of the colony. The governor feared that the prevalence of this flawed monetary system would plunge New South Wales into bankruptcy 'unless some remedy [were] speedily applied to this growing evil'.[1] Macquarie had always talked about forming a bank because of the 'infinite frauds, abuses, and litigations' that the promissory notes were causing.[2] He'd seen a colonial trading bank operating in Cape Town, and believed that something similar could create financial independence in his colony and make it less of a burden on the British taxpayer.

Mary was quick to seize on the possibility that the government needed a well-located building – perhaps the one right next to the public park that Macquarie had named in his own honour. She wrote to the governor, offering to sell any of her properties that might be required to house the town's first financial institution. Macquarie's secretary and right-hand man, John Thomas Campbell,[3] a trim, fiery Ulsterman, promptly wrote back on 4 November 1816 to say nice try, but 'His Excellency does not feel it necessary to purchase any Buildings at this time for the use of Government'.[4] Of course, Mary was not one to give up.

Promissory notes such as this one issued by Garnham Blaxcell threatened the economy of the colony. *State Library of NSW FL15878556*

On 20 November 1816, Macquarie held formal talks with Sydney's leading businessmen and bureaucrats about a prospective new bank. He said the bank was 'the only mode of relieving the Colony from the depression, embarrassment, and losses it had sustained by reason of the circulation of a debased colonial currency, or paper money, at an indefinite and fluctuating nominal value.'[5]

Two days later, at the Sydney Courthouse inside the Rum Hospital, Lieutenant-Governor George Molle,[6] from an old Scottish landed family, presided over a meeting of the colony's leading settlers to discuss the bank. The planned board of directors for the Bank of New South Wales was a gentlemen's club. Despite the success of women in business, females still made up less than a quarter of the total adults in the colony, and the vast majority of them were convicts or former convicts with little education or prospects. In this male-dominated society, thirty years after the founding of the colony, women were still seen principally as mothers, wives, mistresses or sex workers. Even though Mary had enjoyed enormous success, since Tom's death, the concept of women investors remained a foreign one to most people in New South Wales. Although Mary wasn't invited to a meeting to form the bank's board, she still wanted a slice of the action.

At the meeting, resolutions were entered into for the purpose of establishing a 'Colonial Subscription Bank', and a list of confirmed subscribers was made, including Molle, Mary's tenant Robert Jenkins, the newly arrived Judge Advocate John Wylde,[7] his father Thomas, D'Arcy Wentworth and Simeon Lord.[8] John Campbell offered his advice on how a Bank of New South Wales could operate; he had spent years employed in various departments of the Bank of Ireland and played a principal role in the establishment of the Cape of Good Hope bank.[9]

Macquarie had grown in confidence when it came to dealing with London. In 1810, he'd vainly sought the permission of the British government to establish a bank; now he relied on his chief tactic for dealing with the bureaucrats. He would start his projects, then seek approval when the government – months away by sea – was alerted and it was too late for them to stop him. Early interest came from investors including Dr Redfern, George Howe, the poet laureate Michael Robinson, and Edward Eagar,[10] a Dublin lawyer who had been sentenced to death but undergone a spectacular conversion to Christianity in the shadow of the noose, then helped to start the first Methodist church in Australia, known as the Wesley Mission.[11]

Not everyone funding the bank shared Macquarie's views on promoting convicts to the upper realms of society. When Dr William Redfern nominated Eagar as a director, four of the other candidates refused to accept office if he was elected. The subscribers accordingly made it a rule of the bank that no person was eligible as a director unless he was 'absolutely and unconditionally free'. Macquarie had to accept this regulation, and shortly afterwards he soothed Eagar's disappointment by granting him an absolute pardon.[12]

On 29 November, a meeting of investors agreed to fix an exchange rate for the local currency of 13 shillings and fourpence to the pound sterling, and Macquarie issued an order that all wages must now be paid in that currency. By early December there were forty-seven subscribers bankrolling this bank.[13] An iron chest was purchased, and banknotes were printed – there were 639 £5 notes, 1794 at £1, 440 at 10 shillings, 1192 at 5 shillings and 809 at 2 shillings 6 pence.[14] Notes for Spanish

Edward Smith Hall became the first cashier at the Bank of New South Wales, which opened inside Mary's home in 1817. *National Library of Australia nla.obj-134350637*

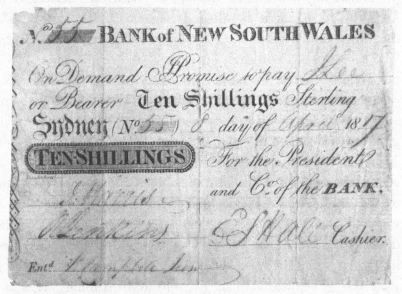

The Bank of New South Wales began issuing its own bank notes, signed by cashier Edward Smith Hall. *Westpac Group Archives*

currency ranging from one to a hundred dollars were also issued but were soon superseded by British money.[15]

Macquarie signed a charter of incorporation[16] and told Earl Bathurst that his idea was for a 'subscription bank with a capital of £20,000, divided into £100 shares', and that 'the bank will be opened for the usual purposes of loan, discount, and deposit' under the management of seven directors,[17] elected on 7 February 1817.[18] They were D'Arcy Wentworth, John Harris, Robert Jenkins, Thomas Wylde, Alexander Riley, William Redfern, and John Campbell, who was unanimously elected the bank's first president. Macquarie assured Bathurst that Campbell was 'likely to uphold the Credit and Respectability of the Establishment by the possession of a character of Strict Integrity, Honour, and Superior talents.'[19] This was despite him having wounded an officer in a duel after the Sydney races in 1811.

Mary kept pressing for the bank to use her real estate assets. At the first meeting of the board on 12 February, the directors empowered President Campbell to 'treat with Mrs Reiby [sic] of Macquarie Place for her House and Premises situated therein for a term not exceeding two years and at a rent not exceeding £150 stg. Per annum.'[20] The decision was pending, though, and the directors advertised in the *Sydney Gazette* for other potential landlords, seeking 'a suitable strong well-built house situate in or near George Street'. The bank was intending to open its doors on 1 March 1817,[21] and Campbell also advertised for 'two persons of respectable Character, who can give good Security for their Fidelity, to fill the Situations of cashier and principal accountant'.[22]

The directors chose thirty-year-old Edward Smith Hall[23] as cashier and bank secretary. Hall had spoken passionately at the public meetings about the value of a Bank of New South Wales. As the son of a London bank manager, he had finance in his blood. He'd arrived in Sydney five years earlier under the patronage of the powerful British politicians William Wilberforce and the future prime minister Robert Peel. Macquarie gave Hall a grant of land, and he became a trader with Simeon Lord and others, with designs on establishing a trading base in New Zealand. In 1813 Hall helped to launch the New South Wales Society for Promoting Christian Knowledge and Benevolence, which later morphed into the Benevolent Society. Mary became a regular donor.[24] Macquarie initially described Hall as 'a Useless and discontented Free Gentleman Settler', claiming that 'without making the least attempt at Industry, [Hall] expressed himself Much disappointed in Not getting his Land cleared and Cultivated for him, and a House built for him at the Expense of Government'.[25] But the governor gradually warmed to Hall's charitable side, and he was appointed to the bank job at a salary of £200 per year. The downside was that he would have to sleep at the bank every night as an extra guard. His quarters at Entally House were so small that he had to leave his wife and children on the farm he'd bought, a few kilometres away in Surry Hills.

While Mary was making great strides in the commercial sphere, having got through an economic downturn and building her trading ventures from the foundation Tom had laid, she was unable to reach the heart of the colony's latest big business venture. Three of the bank directors – Wentworth, Redfern and Jenkins – were delegated to make sure the board was making the right decision in choosing her property. They were sure they had, partly because Jenkins had lived there for some time. On 6 March 1817, they informed the board that Entally House was 'the most suitable' of the candidates as the first home of the Bank of New South Wales; the agreed rent of £150 a year was guaranteed until 1819.[26] The bank, which Macquarie saw as integral to the colony's future, was to be housed in a property owned by a hardworking former convict. This was doubly satisfying to a vice-regal who had always pushed for giving offenders a second chance as the 'friend and protector'[27] of emancipists.

Jenkins was still living in Entally, so on 8 March he announced that he would be vacating the residence and warehouse in a few days,[28] and moving to his own premises on George Street. The opening of the bank was put back to 8 April, and in the interim Mary planned a trip to Port Dalrymple.[29] She had little interest in the lands being opened up for farming west of the Blue Mountains; she was more intrigued by the idea of exploring investment opportunities in Van Diemen's Land, where her two eldest boys, Thomas and James, had found a lucrative base.

Tom Jr had met a striking young woman in Sydney, Richarda Allen,[30] who was looking for some happiness in a new world after so much sadness in the old. Her father Richard Allen had been a doctor in London, and his well-heeled patients had included the Prince of Wales, later King George IV.[31] But when Richard died in 1806, he left a large family behind with little to support them. His widow Mary married Thomas Collicott, who had managed Richard's business dispensing medicines, but in 1813 he was convicted of forgery and transported to New South Wales. Mary Collicott followed him three years later, bringing Richarda and her brothers Richard and George, along with three of Collicott's children from a previous marriage. Mary also brought letters of introduction addressed to Governor Macquarie from influential friends.

The family quickly became active in re-establishing their lives, and they befriended the Reibeys. Richarda opened a 'seminary for young ladies' at her family home at 19 Pitt Street, teaching English, French, geography, writing, accountancy and needlework, subjects that fascinated Mary's daughters. Richarda's stepfather used the building as a retail outlet before he gained a liquor licence and also a land grant of eighty hectares at Lake Illawarra on a property he called 'Campbell Park'. Then Mr and Mrs Collicott were made master and matron of Macquarie's new Female Orphan School in Parramatta. Richarda's brother George became the first solicitor to receive his legal training in the colony, and he went on to found the oldest legal firm in Australia, a business that continues to operate two hundred years later.[32]

ON 25 MARCH THE BANK directors accompanied Mary for an inspection of Entally House and 'the Rooms intended for use of the bank – and to give orders for the necessary preparations'.[33] She pointed out that they were getting a bargain, and not to worry about the damp, because summer would sort that out. On 5 April, three days before the official opening of the bank, Sergeant Jeremiah Murphy of the 46th Regiment – back from a patrol intended to protect the road to Bathurst from people termed 'hostile natives' on the other side of the Blue Mountains – walked into the property with £50 of regimental money in his hand and asked the bank to safeguard it for him. On 7 April, a general meeting of shareholders formally adopted the fifty rules and regulations for the operation of the bank.

At 10 a.m. on 8 April, when the bank was officially opened, Dr John Harris of Ultimo House deposited £138 1 shilling and fourpence. Three days later, the judge Frederick Garling[34] deposited £58, and on 12 April, Dr Redfern banked £51 15 shillings and sevenpence.[35] Their names were entered into a thick ledger bound with kangaroo hide. A week later, the bank wrote out its first mortgage for £25 at ten per cent interest, a favourable rate at the time. It was taken out by a 59-year-old former convict, Owen Connor from Roscommon, who had been aboard the *Marquis Cornwallis* when it brought a shipment of Irish convicts to Sydney in 1796. Connor had become a respectable carpenter at the Rocks.[36] He'd subscribed to Macquarie's fund to build a new courthouse and was farming a 500-acre (200-hectare) land grant from Macquarie near Mary's property in Airds, south-west of Sydney. He used his land as security for the mortgage.[37]

On 27 May, Mary Collits – who had come to Sydney free to join her convict husband, Pierce – applied for a loan of £25 on security of a land grant of seventy acres on the Nepean. The bank only granted the loan 'on said security being joined therein by her husband'.[38] Pierce and Mary eventually built the renowned Collits Inn at the foot of Mount York on the western side of the Blue Mountains.

While Mary was happy to take the bank's money in rent for Entally, she was initially cautious about giving any of it back. It seems she wanted to make sure the Bank of New South Wales was a safe bet before becoming a customer and before long, she had her own passbook[39] for deposits and withdrawals.

Mary and her young children were living in George Street. The military sentries who patrolled her bank building day and night were ordered to prevent any unauthorised persons from entering the premises. To secure the bank, they used the most advanced technology of the time – this involved fastening the building's back door and locking the garden gate.[40] The directors gave instructions that 'the Windows and Doors of the Cellar of the Bank House shall be built up with Stone and Lime – also that the Windows shall be fastened securely – and the Wall covered over'.[41]

Despite the threat of being hanged, thieves in Sydney remained bold, inventive and relentless. One burglar broke into the Kent Street home of William Tarrant, an officer with the 46th Regiment, and made off with four linen shirts, four pairs of white military pantaloons, two pairs of military shoes, a canister of tea, a half-guinea coin, two Spanish dollars, and – the best prize of all – a metre-high kangaroo that was said to have bounded along next to him on a leash.[42]

Macquarie sent the bank directors a letter of encouragement. 'Persevere gentlemen in your exertions to foster this infant establishment,' he wrote, 'and be assured it shall ever have my warmest support and patronage and that the time is not far distant when the bank will on its own merits, obtain the public confidence and gradually flourish to the credit and benefit of the proprietors and to the country at large.'[43] With the promise of the bank boosting trade and the economy even more, Mary again shelved her plans to visit friends and relatives in Lancashire. Always wanting to increase her family's bottom line, she was even selling two live emus from her warehouse in George Street.[44]

Just a few weeks after the official opening of the bank in her old home, Mary paid £750 sterling for the 142-tonne copper-sheathed brig *Governor Macquarie*,[45] moored near another of her properties in Cockle Bay. Known as 'a fast sailing and very complete vessel',[46] it had been making regular trading voyages to Tahiti, bringing home shells, sandalwood and pork. Mastery of the ship made a fine wedding present for Tom Jr, who on 28 May

1817 married Richarda Allen in the new St Philip's Church. Three weeks later, the happy young couple sailed on the *Governor Macquarie*, with Tom Jr at the helm, for their new home in Van Diemen's Land, where he and James had become well-known traders. Soon Tom Jr was sailing the *Governor Macquarie* from Hobart Town to Port Dalrymple with a cargo of Van Diemen's Land convict women for that settlement, before he continued on to Sydney with a load of wheat for his mother to sell.[47]

Owning a ship named in honour of His Excellency didn't hurt Mary's standing with the governor. Macquarie regularly sought her advice 'on the advantages of early colonial manufactures.'[48] Mary became an occasional guest of Macquarie and his wife at Government House – though this didn't save her from being fined £7 for selling spirits after her liquor licence had lapsed.[49] To dine at Macquarie's table was one of the greatest honours in the colony, even though some of the free settlers still turned up their noses at being seated next to emancipists. Elizabeth Macquarie had brought over a Broadwood three-pedal grand piano from England to entertain at her parties and dances, but a critic in Macquarie's own circle had once complained that the Macquaries were 'both Scotch & consequently close fisted', and that they 'kept a shabby table'.[50]

In truth, their dinners involved a variety of fare, even though occasional food shortages sometimes kept the portions small. There was an obligatory curry as a nod to Macquarie's service in India and the presence in his family of George Jarvis, his Indian friend and manservant whom he had rescued from a slave market in Cochin twenty years before. Ellis Bent, Macquarie's first judge advocate, gave a description of one dinner, and the positions of the food on the table, at the Macquarie residence: there was soup 'removed by a very small Boiled Turkey ... There was a piece of Roast Beef. The sides were fricassee, curried Duck, Kidneys & a Tongue, the Corners Vegetables. 2nd Course, at the Top, Stewed Oysters, bottom Wild Ducks, sides & corners tartlets, Jellies & vegetables, in the middle there was an Epergne. – The Table was very large, & one might have danced a Reel between the dishes.'[51]

One man absent from Macquarie's table during his reign was John Macarthur. While in England he had devised ways to improve his profitable Merino wool business in New South Wales. He'd also used his political contacts to lobby Earl Bathurst until he revoked Macquarie's orders to arrest Macarthur on sight for leading the overthrow of Bligh. In September 1817, the sheep baron returned to Sydney.

By the end of the year, after the Bank of New South Wales had been operating for almost nine months, 22-year-old Margaret Campbell became the first woman shareholder. Her husband Robert, ten years older and a wealthy merchant, was the nephew of the trader who had loaned the Reibeys money to help start their business ventures. Robert Jr was employed to oversee the bank's accounts and was prohibited from owning shares while in its employ. When he resigned in 1818 to concentrate on his trading business, Margaret soon transferred her share to him. In 1819, Elizabeth Macquarie, the second female shareholder, acquired three shares for £300, representing almost four per cent of total shareholdings of £7,550,[52] and the board elected to give women shareholders voting rights. The example set by the governor's wife encouraged other women to invest in what was still a male dominated society. Other women – Rachael Moore and Jane Roberts – followed and used their proxy votes to boost the power of Macquarie's secretary John Campbell as the bank's president. Jane Roberts was the first emancipist woman to become a shareholder, buying in to the bank to safeguard her family's future after the death of her husband William Roberts, a former convict who had made a small fortune as one of Macquarie's chief road builders. Rachael Moore was another emancipist and the wife of boatbuilder and magistrate Thomas Moore, who owned the impressive Moorebank estate on the Georges River. Jemima Eagar was the wife of Edward Eagar, the former forger prevented from sitting on the bank's board. He was the largest shareholder in the bank when it was launched, though, and his wife's votes gave him even more power.[53]

By the end of 1821, eleven women owned shares in the bank, although many had bought them to give their husbands greater voting rights by proxy. By 31 October 1823, a third of the shareholdings were held by women. Mary Reibey eventually bought some as well, though she continued trading for some time without a bank account.

MARY CONTINUED WITH the hard sell to off-load as many assets as she could before her departure for England as there was a trade downturn and she thought it the best time to spend a good many months out of the colony. She was sure she could find someone to run her businesses while she was away. Early in 1818 Mary again warned her debtors to pay up with as little delay as possible, to prevent the 'necessity of coercion'.[54] Some men thought they could avoid paying this small and by now bespectacled plump woman who had passed her fortieth birthday – but they did so at their peril. Mary was a tough woman. It was said that when she rather brusquely asked one of her debtors, John Walker of Windsor, to settle his account, he refused and remarked that she was 'no lady'. Mary replied by hitting him over the head with the nearest object, a gentleman's umbrella.[55]

On 19 January 1818, Tom Jr arrived in Hobart Town after a ten-day voyage from Sydney[56] aboard the *Governor Macquarie*. Mary had travelled with him to see the life he and his brothers were making for themselves in Van Diemen's Land. Tom had also ferried a cargo of merchandise to Hobart Town, as well as at least one very unhappy passenger, the bushranger Richard Collyer, who had been sentenced to death in Sydney for murder and was being returned to Hobart Town for execution. Mary knew the terror that the ashen-faced Collyer was feeling; her life had been spared, and she'd never looked back, but the bedraggled bushranger wasn't getting a second chance.

Collyer was a confederate of the notorious bandit Michael Howe, and he endured the penalty originally set out for Mary. After praying fervently and 'exhorting those around him to take warning by his fate, and to avoid the course of life which led to it', he was hanged 'on the rise of the hill at the beginning of the Newtown road' outside Hobart on 26 January 1818.[57] Punishments remained brutal in the colony, despite Macquarie's benevolent attitude to lawbreakers. When two burglars tried to rob Tom Jr's Hobart office in Liverpool Street by taking a shutter from one of the front windows, they each were sentenced to a hundred lashes and to work for two years on a prison chain gang.[58]

On 1 February, Mary and Tom Jr left Hobart Town for Port Dalrymple on the Tamar. But Mary was decidedly unwell, and her son had to turn the *Governor Macquarie* back. Mary elected to travel to Port Dalrymple by carriage before Tom Jr resumed the voyage.[59]

While Mary was in Van Diemen's Land, her sister Betty – who had once been 'very ungood'[60] to her when she was gaoled – sailed back into her life. Mary had long forgiven Betty and was trying to improve her sister's circumstances. Betty and her husband Charles Foster had raised a large family in Lancashire, but life had not been as generous to them as it had to the girl who'd left them in disgrace a quarter of a century earlier. Recently the Fosters had decided to chance their luck on the other side of the world in the hope of following Mary's arc of success. Betty was a skilled milliner with designs on selling hats in Sydney and Hobart Town – if a wild little horse thief could make a fortune in the colonies, why not her? Mary sponsored their relocation, and they arrived in Sydney on 9 February 1818,[61] with their three youngest children, a son and two daughters, after a difficult voyage that left Betty a physical and emotional wreck. Charles had a letter for Macquarie from Henry Goulburn, the Under Secretary of State, which said: 'I am directed by Lord Bathurst to acquaint you that he has given permission to the Bearer, Mr. Charles Foster, to proceed together with his Wife, etc., as a Settler to New South Wales, and I am to desire that you will make to him a Grant of Land in proportion to the means, which he may possess of bringing the same into Cultivation, and extend to him the Indulgences usually granted Settlers of his Class.'[62]

The Fosters had hopes of working the pastures in Van Diemen's Land like Mary's sons were doing in between sea voyages.

Macquarie granted Charles and Betty three hundred acres (120 hectares) near what is now the town of Hadspen, on the South Esk River eight kilometres south-west of Launceston. Charles was assigned two convict workmen and six months' rations along with three cows on credit for eighteen months to be paid for in either money or wheat.[63]

On the same day, Tom Jr was granted three hundred acres nearby under the same deal.[64] At the time he'd been hosting the Arab stallion Young Hector at his Launceston stables. The horse's sire Hector had been owned by the Duke of Wellington and was the most important stallion in the first decade of Australian thoroughbred racing.[65] Tom Jr had ideas to build a large country estate on his land, and the horse's owner, Charles Hook, had shipped Young Hector to Van Diemen's Land for stud duties, offering those services to any suitable thoroughbred mares in the colony for five guineas and a guinea for the groom.[66]

At just twenty, James Reibey was producing thousands of pounds of beef for the government stores in Hobart Town.[67] He and Tom Jr built a major trading concern with large storehouses in Launceston and Port Dalrymple.[68] Soon they would form a partnership as 'General Merchants and Commission Agents' with their business based in Launceston under the name of Thomas Reibey & Company.[69] Despite his youth, James was made a member of the lieutenant-governor's Court of Civil Judicature in Hobart Town.[70]

Their younger brother George, a youth with a literary bent, was working for a private bank and had become heavily involved in the local Bible Society. With his mother's financial backing, he soon became active in the Wesleyan Mission, raising funds to build the first Methodist church in Hobart Town.[71]

Tom and his wife made regular voyages to Sydney where both had extended families. His young family was growing. On 27 March 1818, in Sydney, Richarda Reibey gave birth to Mary Allen Reibey.[72] At the age of forty, Mary was now a grandmother.

Chapter 14

WITH HER OLD HOME now the headquarters for the Bank of New South Wales, Mary was operating out of another building in her extensive collection of properties. The house at 1 George Street was next door to the home of Barron Field,[1] a judge of the Supreme Court.[2] Mary had plenty of space to house her sister's family before they moved to Van Diemen's Land, and the Reibey and Foster cousins attended school together with tutors at private academies. Mary's four pretty daughters – Celia, Eliza, Jane and Betsey – were her four youngest children and were aged from sixteen to nine. They were stylish youngsters, dressed in the fashions of the day, clothing made from expensive fabrics that Mary sold from her home. Now that Aunt Betty the milliner had arrived, their collection of lace bonnets was expected to grow. Mary enjoyed hosting the young Fosters but sister Betty had always been hard work. Still, Mary put on a brave face, treating her with affection and writing about her in glowing terms to Aunt Penelope back home.

Trade in Sydney was dropping off with a glut of imported goods, and Mary was now making detailed plans to visit England during a quiet time for merchants. She wanted to take some of her girls with her, and perhaps her son George, who had Latin training and told her he was interested in some schooling in Britain. Mary had learnt that Aunt Penelope Hope had passed away and left her two houses in the Lancashire town of Salford, and she planned to sort out those details when she arrived in England.

On 12 August 1818, Mary wrote to Penelope's daughter Alice Hope, who had been but a babe when Mary was transported to the penal settlement.

Dear Cousin,
by a Gentleman Who Expects to come to Liverpool and which I believe is a resident thier I avail myself of the opportunity of letting you know that with myself my Family are all well and that of Announcing the safe arrival of my dear sister and Family all well except herself which suffered severely during a passage of Five months and 2 days
   but now thank God she is perfectly Recovered
   and which more added to her dissapointment was when she arrivd I was absent at Vandiemans Land whither I had gone to settle my affairs previous to my Coming home as I had Let my shop and Whare houses as also my Farms
   but her arrival will detain me sometime longer as I do not wish to leave her
   and Mr. Foster Expects to get his Land and Indulgences and proceed with the cultivation of it so that he can either let it or sell it
   I intend bringing my Eldest Daughter Celia and youngest son George and I believe my three little ones ...
   I am present Deveided about my son George.[3]

Mary was considering placing George with a tutor in Manchester known to the Hope family. 'Should we agree and should it lye in your way to mention it to him,' Mary wrote to her cousin, 'I Whould thank you to his Terms so that I may hasten his Comeing home as he is getting so big ... I had him at a Latin School till within this 9 months.'[4]

She told Alice all about James and Tom Jr being married, and Tom Jr and Richarda now being the proud parents of a child named after Mary. James was in Sydney on business, and she had sent George to 'Vandiemans Land as I left him to Collect the Remainder of my Debt and rents'.[5]

when I heard my sister had arrived I was very Impatient …

I went down their [Van Diemen's Land] in a brig of my own commanded by my Son Thomas and brought her up [to Sydney] Loaded with which she is now gone after a cargo of Cedar Wood for Building

Mr Foster is gone in her I expect him in the Course of six or Eight weeks

I have also got a Small Schooner but Trade and Commerce is getting so bad that I cannot sell anything or I should have been Home [Britain] long before now

I have enclosed you a Couple of our *Sydney Gazettes* where you will see an advertisement of mine but their is no person here able to purchase them

so I must give over the Idea of selling and live on my income[6]

Mary revealed that her yearly income was £1000 and that rents on her properties should soon rise to £1800. She had land on the Hawkesbury and at Airds under lease totalling 810 acres (328 hectares), and 2040 more acres (825 hectares) on Van Diemen's Land, as well as houses and stores on George Street, and the bank building in Macquarie Place. Mary told Alice that 'should I Come to England immediately I could have Remitted Home [Britain] seven hundred pounds per Annem after leaving a little for my sons and paying agency – therefore I think it will be as well to leave them as to Sell as to make a sacrifice'.[7]

Penelope's death had deeply saddened Mary and Betty. 'I can assure you my poor sister never mentions your Mother but with Tears and the Deepest Sorrow for her loss,' Mary wrote, 'and altho I had not seen her for 27 years it had a great effect on me for almost the first interchange of words with my sister was to know if my Aunt Hope was alive I do assure you the meeting of her was one of the happiest moments of my life and still more so knowing it was in my power to assist her as I consider her so deserving the protection of me and everybody who knows her.'[8] Betty 'did not meet as good Treatment as might be expected on her passage',

Mary wrote. 'Considering what she paid … had I been at home while the Capt of the ship was here I whould have actioned him but he sailed the day after I came home.' Betty's children Eliza and James were now attending the same school in Sydney as Mary's three youngest girls, who were 'Boarders'. She noted,

> they are fine company for each other. little Eliza is …
> notice by everyone … she is such an agreeable little thing
> … my youngest little girl [Betsey] and her are much alike
> and is remarked almost by everyone …
> my sister begs me to mention a Book Entitle the *History of Wales* that she left with a man Byron's next door to the first House as you turn the Corner
> that is all the description she can give
> she wishes you to get it for her if you Can
> she would do very well here Could she have her own way at her Business and Mr Foster too but no one will do well but is not thrifty Correct and Sober
> this place is not like England
> you are under the Eye of every one and your Character Scrutinized by both Rich and poor although you may have a different Oppinion of it through the Different Characters that Comes here

Mary told Alice that she had nothing but praise for the way the colony was kept 'in regular order by our Good Govenor Lachlan Macquerie' after the disastrous reign of Bligh.[9]

Macquarie had just returned to Sydney from an expedition along the Hunter River near Newcastle, with the surveyor James Meehan and Captain Wallis, the officer who had led the massacre of the Dharawal people on the cliffs above the Cataract River two years earlier. During the recent Hunter River expedition, the vice-regal party had rowed upriver for about fifteen kilometres, passing through several fine long reaches, though the land on both banks for the first ten were either low, swampy or thick brush.

Two days later in Newcastle, the Reverend William Cowper

married ten couples and baptised thirty children in a church that Wallis had built – the first ceremony of the kind ever performed in the town. As part of the celebration, Macquarie directed that all the convicts in Newcastle were to be exempted from work and to receive an extra ration of fresh meat.[10]

At the end of Macquarie's week in Newcastle, he wrote that an Awabakal man known to the Europeans as 'Jack', or 'Burigon, King of the Newcastle Native Tribe', came into town with about forty men, women and children of his people, and at the Government House between '7 & 8, O'Clock at Night … entertained with a Carauberie in high stile [sic] for Half an Hour'.[11] Macquarie said he ordered the Awabakal to be 'Treated with some Grog and an allowance of Maize'.

MARY HAD IMPORTANT business to transact in Lancashire when she finally returned there, and the economic benefits made the visit even more urgent. She told Alice Hope:

> those Houses in Salford which did belong to me & my sister
> and which she has made over her Interest in to your Mother
> I should wish if agreeable to Repurchase on my arrival in
> England
>   the Bill is against me I have Rec'd by the hands of my
> sister which shall be attended too
>   my sister wished me particularly to mention to you how
> my Husband came here
>   he was 2d officer … of the Britannia Whaler which was
> laying in the Harbour when I came here and he prevailed
> on the Captain to let him stay here.
>   I hope dear Cousin altho unknown to you but for
> the sake of your dear Mother you will write by every
> opportunity and by sending your letters to Mrs Smith in
> London where my sister stayd She will be remitted.
>   I have nothing more at present to say except my sons
> and all my children desire their love to you and all your
> brothers

… Jane and Eliza send their love to you
I am Dear Cousin yours affectionately

                                          M. Reibey.

My sister thinks it whould be the best way to pay the
postage to the Lands end of England and they are sure to
come safe.[12]

Mary was clearly set on returning to Lancashire, but she was still busy in Sydney. At the same time she was planning her voyage, she tendered to supply the Sydney government stores with three thousand pounds of fresh meat.

Tom Jr now sailed regularly on the *John Palmer*, ferrying passengers and cargo between Van Diemen's Land and Sydney. In mid-1819, after unsuccessfully trying to sell her ship the *Governor Macquarie* to its namesake,[13] Mary managed to off-load the vessel for a profit. The new owner, Roland Loane[14] – from a family of English landlords living in the south of Ireland – soon refitted the ship for voyages to New Zealand,[15] where missionaries led by Samuel Marsden were bringing teachings of their Christian god.

At least £50 of Mary's profits from the sale of her ship went to bail out her reckless son George. Normally one to hit the books, he'd been fined £100 and threatened with prison if he couldn't pay after assaulting a settler named Henry Brooks. Mary appealed to Macquarie over the case of 'The King v George Reibey', telling him that her son had no savings of his own and that it was clear there had been a degree of provocation in the incident.[16] Macquarie cut the fine in half and had the court refund her £50 on the fine she'd already paid.[17]

Tom Reibey was much less trouble for his mother. While Tom Jr had an office in Liverpool Street, Hobart, he and Rebecca started work on an estate in which they planned to house their extended family on some of the land he had obtained from his uncle Charles Foster's grant at Hadspen. There were only seven hundred people living in and around Launceston at the time. Together with Mary, Tom Jr had 2430 acres of pasture (1000 hectares) and 200 acres (80 hectares) of wheat. They also owned five horses on the island, along with ninety-two head of cattle and six hundred sheep.[18] Tom Jr and James soon began building one of Launceston's first wharves, and their company owned half the land upon which Boag's Brewery now stands.[19]

BY THE END OF 1819, Mary had £1073 10 shillings and 10 pence[20] deposited in the Bank of New South Wales, making her one of the leading customers of the enterprise. Women took to this new way of doing business. More than sixty Sydney women were using the bank by 1819 and as many as nineteen were operating their own businesses, most as shopkeepers, but some as schoolteachers and publicans.[21] Mary was still holding off buying shares though, even though by 1820 eight of the fifty-six shareholders were female.[22] That year, with her business affairs finally in order and her family's future assured, Mary at last booked her passage to visit her old home. The ship she chose to travel on was the American-built *Admiral Cockburn*, which had been captured by the British in 1814 and sold as a war prize.

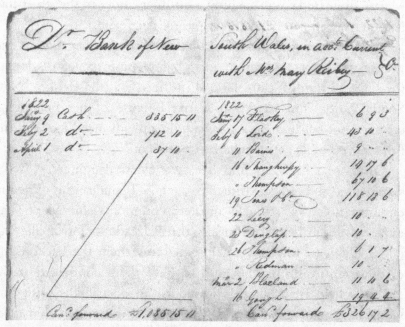

Mary Reibey's original passbook for the Bank of New South Wales.
Westpac Group Archives

Mary would be seeing a very different England to the place she had left behind. Britain had entered a new era. The news was weeks away from reaching Sydney that King George III, the monarch who had overseen the voyages of Cook and the founding of the settlements in New South Wales and Van Diemen's Land, had died on 29 January 1820 after a reign of six decades. His son George IV was the new King after having been Prince Regent for nine years following the first diagnosis of his father's mental illness.

The *Admiral Cockburn* was leaving Sydney with some well-heeled passengers. It also bore a valuable cargo of some of the finest wool produced from among the 120,000 sheep said to be in the colony as a result of John Macarthur driving the industry – wool that would be spun in the mills of Lancashire.

George had ruled himself out of an overseas holiday for now because of the assault charge, and he promised instead to redeem himself by watching over his mother's business interests in Sydney while she was abroad. Her youngest daughters, Jane and Elizabeth (Betsey), would stay with Tom and Richarda in Launceston. Mary's sister Betty was opening a milliner's store in the street that Macquarie had named after Viscount Castlereagh.[23]

Mary was leaving in high spirits, even though her tenants had just rejected her application for a £500 business loan[24] despite the huge amount of cash she had in the safe at the Bank of New South Wales. This rejection wasn't because of her borrowing capacity but because the bank had already advanced loans to the full amount of its entitlement by its charter.[25]

On 1 March, Mary and her two eldest daughters – Celia, seventeen, and Eliza, fifteen – set sail under far different circumstances and much greater comfort than Mary had experienced on her arrival nearly three decades before.[26] She was taking them to England not just to show them the background of their family history but also to have them confirmed at the old church in Blackburn. It would be an open-ended visit that would last many months and Mary hoped the girls would meet as many relatives and see as many sights as possible. If Celia and

Eliza found wealthy suitors while there, that would be a bonus. As Mary sailed down the harbour towards the Heads, she must have been stunned by the way the town had grown from the infant struggles she'd observed when the *Royal Admiral* had reached Port Jackson in 1792.

Convicts from Macquarie's impressive Hyde Park Barracks were busy quarrying stone or cutting timber, and Mary could see that their conditions had improved markedly under the governor's rule. Redcoats marched about, marshalling the captive workforce, and here and there pet kangaroos lolled about eating grass along the streets. At the Rum Hospital, patients rested on the verandahs, hoping the autumn sunshine and sea breezes would bring them back to health.[27] The sails of at least nine windmills made a merry rattling as they danced on the hills, the tallest structures along the Sydney skyline. Here and there congregated small groups of Eora people, still practising their traditional ways in the face of the unrelenting development around them. Fort Macquarie stood guard over Sydney Harbour like an ancient Scottish castle.

Celia and Eliza were dressed in the finery of princesses with long flowing dresses of bright fabric, and Mary took in a view of a town in which she owned a sizeable stake. Due to an influx of convicts and settlers after the end of the Napoleonic wars, Sydney now had a population of just over twelve thousand Europeans,[28] and it boasted 1084 buildings – still mostly single-storey dwellings, though Macquarie's building project had increased the number of more imposing structures. The settlements at Parramatta, Windsor and Liverpool had an additional five thousand settlers each, with one thousand in Newcastle, three hundred in Bathurst, and a hundred or so in the new village of Port Macquarie, named by the settler John Oxley.[29]

Throughout the colony, convicts still outnumbered free settlers. Irish, English and Scottish accents dominated, though there were other accents and languages on the trading vessels in Sydney's harbour. That year alone, twenty more convict transports arrived in Sydney to dump 2574 prisoners: 2278 men and boys, and 296 women and girls. In the public houses, all men were created equal. Most smoked dudeen pipes with short stems; some wore straw hats, others those made of American beaver skin, and still others of untanned kangaroo skin. Drunkenness remained rife.[30]

Inside Government House, just behind the bank building that Mary owned, Governor Macquarie had become a worn-out shell of a man. His battles in Sydney for more than a decade – with enemies such as Samuel Marsden, opposed to his emancipist policies, and with official complaints to London about his lavish spending – had left the governor deflated.

Among the wealthy passengers sailing with Mary and her daughters was Alexander Berry,[31] a former surgeon's mate from Scotland who had become one of Mary's rivals as a leading Sydney merchant, trading in goods from across the South Pacific. Berry had charge of taking Macquarie's letter of resignation back to London.[32]

Mary Reibey, meanwhile, had no intention of retiring from anything. As the *Admiral Cockburn* headed for the open seas on which much of her trading fortune was based, the salt spray assailed her round face and bright, shining eyes. Passing the fruits of her labour, she realised that, with a long journey ahead of her, she had already come very far. She had started with nothing, as a frightened girl in a strange land, and now had a personal fortune of £20,000.[33]

Sydney was much different than it had been in 1792. And so was Mary Reibey, the richest and most powerful woman in the colony.

Chapter 15

BEING A RICH businesswoman was certainly better than being a runaway horse thief. As Mary caught sight of the thin outline that was Britain for the first time in almost thirty years, she counted her many blessings. The *Admiral Cockburn* was a vastly different vessel to the *Royal Admiral*, and its comfortable quarters a stark contrast to the miserable conditions of a convict transport.

Mary and her two daughters sailed into Portsmouth on 20 June 1820, after a voyage of almost four months. They landed at 8 a.m. and took brief refreshments at an inn by the docks, before setting off for London an hour later in a comfortable coach. For the next ten hours, Mary, Celia and Eliza bounced along as the team of horses clip-clopped north-east through Haslemere and Guildford and all the other villages on the way to London's outskirts at Kingston on Thames.

Perched on the leather seats, each next to a window, Celia and Eliza were astonished by the panorama of Britain passing before their eyes – the thatched cottages and haystacks, and a greenness to the grass unlike the sun-bleached fields they knew back home. Even though it was the height of summer, the people looked paler than the populace of Sydney, and the skies were greyer and seemed closer to the earth. The foliage was different to anything the girls had seen before – the ash trees, the birches, the chestnuts and oaks – and they were impressed by the size and grandeur of London. St Paul's Cathedral, the Tower of London and the Palace of Westminster all made their jaws drop.

Mary took in sights and smells from an earlier time, but in the almost thirty years since she had left, changes were all about. The roads were better, wider and firmer than she remembered, and gas lighting was now being used in the bigger towns and cities. Horse-drawn carriages were using tramlines for haulage, and there was talk that soon steam locomotives would be crisscrossing Britain.

Night was falling when the Reibeys reached a historic coaching stopover, the Belle Savage Inn, at Ludgate Hill near the centre of the great city.[1] The Belle Savage had operated since the 1400s, and its guests had included the Native American princess Pocahontas in 1616, and in 1684 the first 'Rhynoceros' ever seen in Britain.

It was the biggest hotel that Mary and the girls had ever seen, four stories high and in the shadow of St Paul's, which only added to the majesty of their lodgings.

Mary wasn't one to sit around. The next morning, following her long, exhausting voyage from Sydney and the taxing ride from the coast, she took a hackney-coach and went to the London office of Bell & Wilkinson, in order to conduct business with the ship owners and merchants.[2]

London was now a city of one and a half million people and a world away from Sydney – geographically and in just about every other sense. It had grown enormously while Mary had been in New South Wales, and was now the largest and wealthiest city in the world, the centre of international finance and trade thanks largely to the East India Company and colonisation. Conditions for the urban poor that would give rise to the tales of Charles Dickens were growing worse, and a new age of technology was ushering in rapid changes to the way of life for millions in Britain. Magnificent buildings reflected the city's economic power.

Amid the marbled walls and leather furnishings of the Bell & Wilkinson office, Mary met her agent and deposited £1000 in Treasury bills with him.[3] She was astounded when the Sydney merchant and sealing magnate Joseph Underwood also arrived in the office. Like Mary, Underwood had made a fortune in New

South Wales and was celebrating with a visit to the country of his birth. He walked back with Mary to the Belle Savage, then took her and her daughters out sightseeing and treated them to ice creams.[4]

Mary was carrying a letter from a master mariner's son, John Atkinson,[5] a friend of her children, to his father. As a boy, Atkinson had sailed with his father to Russia, carrying troops for the fight against Napoleon. He'd arrived in Hobart Town in 1817, and two years later sailed into Sydney, where he had befriended the Reibeys. The old sea captain met Mary in the city. In a journal she kept of her travels, written with little punctuation and much evidence of an abbreviated education, Mary recorded that 'a finer and I think a better man he cannot be ... he was very much affected when he read the letters and I believe it was very favourable to me and daughters as he immediately asked us to his House and have kept our friendship ever since.'[6] Word spread via various ship captains that the wealthy Mrs Reibey was home, and many came to see her and enquire about her using their vessels for her trading ventures. Many friends she had made over the years in Sydney also came to visit her, and she made contact with a family member: she wrote to Aunt Penelope's son, her cousin John Hope in Manchester, and received 'a very kind and affectionate letter' and an invitation to stay at his London home.

There had been theatrical productions in Sydney since before Mary's marriage in 1794, but nothing quite so lavish as the comedy *The Provoked Husband* at the Theatre Royal in Drury Lane, which had entered a new age of audience comfort, being gaslit throughout, and which delighted the Reibeys with the kind of entertainment they had only ever read about. In this euphoric mood Mary went hunting through all the dusty booksellers of London to find tomes for George, having made a list of all those he wanted: David Hume's *History of England*, Dr William Robertson's *History of the Reign of the Emperor Charles V*, Edward Gibbon's *Decline and Fall of the Roman Empire*, Grecian histories, British essay collections, and the narrative poem *Rokeby* by the newly knighted Sir Walter Scott.[7]

Mary and the girls spent twenty-seven days in London, but they all became so ill with respiratory infections after the voyage that they spent most of their last fortnight in the great city bedridden and didn't get to see all the sights. The day before they departed for Lancashire on 17 July, Mary noted that a doctor bled and blistered her, and that Eliza was also very ill. Neither of them could hold their heads up, and Celia was not much better. But they kept moving and arrived in Manchester the next day after travelling a gruelling 186 miles (300 kilometres) 'without stopping except to change horses'.[8]

The ailing trio reached the grand Moseley Arms Inn across from the northern end of Manchester's Piccadilly Gardens, but they felt like they were at death's door. They were not inclined to glance at the Royal Coat of Arms over the hotel's entrance, and they barely had the energy to take in the fast-paced movement going on all around them in Manchester, along the busy roads and the packed canals of the world's first industrial city, a city transformed from a village into an economic giant because of the textile industry. Two of Mary's cousins – John Hope[9] and the surgeon Dr Robert Halstead Hargreaves[10] – were waiting with a hackney-coach. Dr Hargreaves was the son of Mary's aunt the former Jane Haydock, and he had one of four apothecaries operating nearby on Market Street.[11] The cousins ferried their antipodean guests to John's home, 'a very delightful place a little way in the Country' in the sylvan setting of Lancashire. While Manchester choked with factory fumes, the countryside around her cousin's house was a carpet of vivid green everywhere that Mary and the girls looked and the temperature was pleasantly warm. The Hargreaves immediately called for a surgeon friend – Samuel Barton, who lived nearby – to minister to them. Mary wrote:

> He paid all the attention was possible
> [and] we began to recover very fast and Mr Hargreaves
> very often came to take us out a walking. He sent us Jellys
> preserves and fruit and everything he could think of for our

comfort as soon as we could walk about which was about 11 days

we had several invitations the first to Dr Bartons one of the first surgeons in Manchester, Mrs B. a very, Lady-[like], woman and one of the most respectable about that Country, was very glad to see us and treated us very kindly wishing us to renew our visits as often as we could. We took tea with my half cousin Mr Aspinall, dined and tea'd next day with Mr and Mrs Hargreaves they made me promise on my return to Manchester that we should stop at their house. We stayed at Manchester from the 18th of July till the 6th of august being 19 days.[12]

On Saturday, 6 August 1820, with John accompanying them, Mary and the girls bade their hosts goodbye and took the coach for Blackburn – and a reunion she'd been awaiting for more than a quarter of a century. At about three o'clock in the afternoon, the soot-stained outskirts of the town came into view, after Mary and her companions had observed the smoke from the mills some time before.

Blackburn was low and grey and brown, of narrow terrace houses and even narrower cobblestone lanes, but the sun was shining and Mary was instantly transported to a time when she was young, fearless and free.

Mary was physically overwhelmed by the occasion. All about were the small cottages of the town's handloom weavers but as she neared the row of more substantial brick terrace houses on Darwen Street, Mary's steps faltered. Behind her thick round glasses, John observed tears in her eyes.

She jotted down her reaction: 'It is impossible to describe the sensation I felt when coming to the top of Dorwen [Darwen] Street my native home and amongst my Relatives and on entering my once Grandmothers House where I had been brought up, and to find it nearly the same as when I left nearly 29 years ago all the same furniture most of them standing in the same place as when I left but not one person I knew or knew me ...'[13]

Mary's cousin Alice Hope[14] had been in anxious expectation of her return. With a Miss Ward, an old acquaintance of the Haydock and Hope families, Alice met the visitors at the door 'with all the affection and love of a sister'.[15] The house was tiny and dark compared to the mansions in which Mary lived beside Sydney harbour but it had a special place in her heart. Beds were prepared for the guests, and they were made to feel as loved members of the family. Word quickly spread to all the old inhabitants of Blackburn whom Mary had known as a child, and the door to her grandmother's house hardly ever closed with people 'coming either out of Curiosity or Respect'.[16] Among the most welcome visitors was the deaf and mute woman whom Mary had often played with when they were girls; overjoyed to see each other, they embraced as long-lost friends.

On 8 August, Celia and Eliza were confirmed in the church of St John the Evangelist, though only by certificates that John Hope procured because the church was closed for repairs. Over the next few weeks, Mary spent most of her time enjoying an open invitation to bring the girls to all the homes of their relatives, among them her father's brother William Haydock, in his seventy-fourth year, and his son William Jr. There was Uncle Robert Brown and his wife Aunt Hindle, 'a very kind and affectionate' Quaker who told Mary she was seventy-six years old. 'I believe they thought they could not show me enough of attention,' Mary wrote – though they hadn't been so hospitable when she was facing transportation, and the judge had only needed a relative to take her in and guarantee her good behaviour to avoid the heartbreaking voyage to New South Wales. Perhaps no one told Mary about that because she certainly showed her relatives no bitterness.

No place was quite so congenial as Alice's – 'the most affectionate young woman I ever met with,' Mary called her.[17] Family friends put out the welcome mat as well. There was Dr Cork, a Blackburn surgeon, and his wife, and the Reverend William Hope and his wife Sarah, 'a very Genteel woman'. There were the Fletchers and the Littles, the Wrens and the Wraiths.

David Hope, now a lawyer and broker living in a large sandstone house on Brunswick Street in the trading heart of Glasgow, returned to Blackburn for a tearful reunion. On 5 September he went with Mary to St John's, standing in front of the stone that marked its consecration just as they'd done when Mary held his tiny, infant hand thirty-one years before. She and her daughters and some of the Hopes then took a carriage and post-chaise to visit other relatives in Preston, and on 15 September they toured John Horrocks's famous cotton mill.

The heat from the steam engine was too oppressive for Mary. She had to take her leave, becoming ill that night in Blackburn. Her cousins the Browns insisted she stay with their family until she recovered, partly because they wanted to talk to her about everything she had experienced on the far side of the world. Aunt Hindle sat up with Mary until morning, even though she thought the old woman looked like she was about to draw her last breath at any moment. The constant care paid off, and by 24 September Mary was well enough to lead a party of visitors to the palatial Stonyhurst college, a grand school more like an opulent castle with high turrets, twenty kilometres north of Blackburn.[18] 'We was shown through the college and through the Gardens,' she wrote, 'which was very grand.'[19] They all returned via the village of Whalley, inspecting the ruins of the Cistercian abbey there. The Abbey dated from the 1300s and Mary was an eager tourist listening to her companions talk about the murder and intrigues that happened inside those grey crumbling walls. She was now so at home in England's north that it sometimes felt like she had never left.

Next Mary and the girls decided to extend their visit beyond England and they headed for the sights of Scotland aboard the steamboat *Robert Bruce*. It ferried them from Liverpool to Greenock, on the edge of a place Mary called 'Glascow'. Hospitality greeted the Reibeys everywhere, as all their relatives and friends wanted to ask them about the great southern land, the kangaroos, and what convict life had been like.

At the end of October, Mary and Eliza came down with violent colds and were confined to bed for eleven days. They were treated by a Dr King, whose bill of £5 3 shillings and sixpence made Mary feel even worse. She was one of the richest traders in Sydney, but she regarded the Scottish doctor's account as 'a very exorbitant Demand', especially since the treatment had involved being bled by leeches on her temples on 9 November. Her asthma, which had begun to plague her in Sydney, became worse in the cold and damp of Britain.

LACHLAN MACQUARIE was leaving New South Wales after a decade of turning it from a hellish penal colony into an agricultural and trading powerhouse, and a society based on a fair go for any European man − and the occasional woman − willing to work hard, even if they were prisoners of the Crown. While Macquarie waited for his resignation to reach London and for its acceptance to come back, some events in the colony brought him great joy.

On 22 March 1820, at the Greenway-designed St Philip's Church, George Jarvis − the Indian slave whom Macquarie had purchased at Cochin and then treated like a son − married Mary Jelly, a convict chambermaid working at Government House. George accompanied Macquarie on his next grand tour of the colony in October, this time exploring the lush land south of the Cowpastures, and bringing with him wine, biscuits and oranges for their fellow travellers.[20]

Macquarie wanted to gaze upon the great lake that had been seen by Joseph Wild,[21] a former convict burglar employed by the grazier Charles Throsby. On 27 October, Macquarie and his party reached the north shore of the lake, 'most highly gratified and delighted with this noble expanse of water, and the surrounding scenery',[22] though the governor was surprised to learn from Throsby's Indigenous guide, Taree, that it wasn't the source of the 'new river' Murrumbidgee. Joseph Wild sold Macquarie 'four very pretty young emus and a very little rock kangaroo' as well as a young swan, as presents for Macquarie's son Lachlan Jr.[23]

On 28 October, Macquarie sat down to dinner at their bush camp. He and his party drank a bumper toast to the success of the future settlers who would farm around the magnificent sheet of water that he now named 'Lake George', in honour of the King – and perhaps of George Jarvis as well.

JUST FIVE DAYS AFTER Dr King treated Mary in Glasgow, her mood brightened at the many 'Illuminations and Bonfires' erupting around her in the city.

The festivities were taking place across Britain to celebrate the moral victory of Queen Caroline, the estranged wife of the new King, George IV, during a time of great political turmoil.

The King had wanted to divorce Caroline after their only daughter, Princess Charlotte, had died in childbirth, but the vote in Parliament for a bill allowing this had been desperately close. Caroline was widely seen as an oppressed wife at the mercy of a bullying husband, and she had great support among the general public, whose anger towards the King was white-hot. Under immense pressure, the prime minister, the Earl of Liverpool – for so long Macquarie's antagonist – declared that the bill was withdrawn. There were wild public celebrations, and much of the revelry descended into violent riots. In London, the windows of government supporters were smashed, and the offices of newspapers that had supported the King were set ablaze.

But in Glasgow, the celebrations were more festive than furious. Mary wanted to see how the latest fabrics she was selling in Sydney were created, and on 14 November visited a Glasgow factory where a glowing iron ran over stretched muslin cloth but never damaged it. Then she strolled through the Botanic Gardens in Glasgow. Celia and Eliza went to the Trades Hall to hear speeches about a controversial subject that was constantly being debated in Scotland at the time – the education of Roman Catholic children in a Protestant nation.

The next day, Celia sat for a portrait that depicted her as a pretty teenager wearing an expensive evening gown made from royal-blue silk velvet with short, puffed sleeves and a wide, low neckline with fine white lace edging.[24] Mary helped Celia put on her pendant pearl earrings. A corsage of roses in her hair set off Celia's light brown ringlets, and a long fine gold chain was looped loosely several times around her neck. Underneath the vivid blue gown was a sheer white muslin slip which has been carefully arranged in scalloped folds to show off her youthful décolletage.[25] Celia draped a brightly-coloured tartan stole over her shoulder. Mary knew that in Sydney, despite Macquarie's egalitarian views, her convict past prevented her from being among the 'exclusives' in the upper reaches of polite society and that she was always being 'Scrutinized by both Rich and poor'.[26] But no one could deny the status that Mary's wealth brought her and her children. Later in the visit, Eliza had her portrait completed as well; it showed a handsome 15-year-old in the latest fashion, her expensive evening frock a far cry from the garb that 15-year-old Mary Haydock wore at the same age on the *Royal Admiral*. The portraits complete, Mary and her daughters took a walk down the ancient Trongate and Argyle Streets to see the 'splendid illumination' paying tribute to Queen Caroline's victory.

The Reibeys travelled by small two-wheeled Noddy carriages to the homes of many new friends and some old ones. There were parties galore, long games of whist, and dances. The young people enjoyed their Scottish reels late into the night, accompanied by piano and a double flageolet, a wind instrument similar to a recorder.

Newlywed acquaintances invited the Reibeys to dinner in the nearby town of Paisley. After a glass of wine and a little wedding cake, the visitors were taken to see a factory that made fine gauze and then more of the town's manufacturing plants and tourist attractions. Mary was intrigued by Paisley Abbey where in 1316, after a fall from a horse nearby, Marjorie Bruce had delivered a baby who became Robert II, King of Scotland. On the way back to Glasgow they passed Crookston Castle, where Mary, Queen of Scots was said to have wed Lord Darnley under a yew tree.

In Glasgow's recently built St John's Renfield Church, Mary and her daughters listened to fiery sermons by Dr Thomas Chalmers, called 'the greatest Scottish Churchman of the nineteenth century',[27] and his assistant the Reverend Edward Irving. It was stirring stuff as Mary felt nearer to god than ever.

She had always been a churchgoer in Sydney but Chalmers had a zeal that was infectious. A few days later Mary and her girls had breakfast with the pious pair, during which Irving read a chapter from the New Testament and Dr Chalmers offered prayers.

The Reibeys had been in Britain for five months and were still seeing fascinating sights every day. In Garnethill, the Glasgow Society for Promoting Astronomical Knowledge had built Britain's finest observatory after Greenwich. It had a revolving cupola, a sidereal clock used to locate celestial objects, and two Herschelian telescopes, one ten-feet long on the terrace and another fourteen-feet long on the roof. Mary and the girls studied

In Scotland, Mary befriended the fiery preacher Thomas Chalmers.
Free Church College, Edinburgh

the camera obscura and a lens capable of magnifying an image by a multiple of 1400.[28] After that the Reibeys went to see a panorama of the Battle of Waterloo, which had been Napoleon's demise just five years earlier, and the three Australians were spellbound by the depiction of a battle that had changed the world.

The following day, Mary sat for an artist creating her portrait for a watercolour miniature on ivory. He captured the image of a plump, matronly figure with wide brown kindly eyes behind silver spectacles. Her greying hair peeked out from a delicate indoor bonnet made of muslin, fashionable for a woman of her age.

On Monday, 27 November, Mary, Celia and Eliza took a coach ride for about twenty-five kilometres south-east of Glasgow to join a tour of the Duke of Hamilton's magnificent country mansion. Standing before 'a most grand collection of paintings', Mary couldn't help but congratulate herself at the way she had prospered. Among the paintings was *Daniel in the Lion's Den* by the Flemish master Peter Paul Rubens, one of the most striking images Mary had ever seen, and one that depicted someone else who had overcome seemingly insurmountable obstacles. There were also portraits of King George III and Queen Charlotte, and an ornate throne, which Mary and the girls took turns sitting on. They then saw a painting of Bonaparte by Jacques-Louis David; according to the tour guide, it had been done from life recently and was said to be a remarkable likeness.

After touring the grand home for an hour, the Reibeys signed their names in the visitors' book. From that great mansion they went on to visit the medieval Bothwell Castle, taking in a striking view from its position on a high, steep bank above a bend in the River Clyde.

Then, on the morning of 30 November, the Reibeys left Glasgow for a stay in Edinburgh, changing horses after twenty-five kilometres at a village called Cumbernauld. At Grangemouth, a further twenty-five kilometres on, they left their coach for a steamboat ride to the harbour of Newhaven on the Firth of Forth, just five kilometres outside Edinburgh, which was carpeted in snow. They arrived at 7 p.m. on a freezing night to begin the

The only surviving portrait of Mary Reibey, completed when she was in middle age; a watercolour on ivory miniature. *State Library of NSW FL1048687*

Sydney Cove in 1788 when the First Fleet arrived. Mary was eleven years old and living with her grandmother in Blackburn, Lancashire. *State Library of NSW FL1113870*

Justice John Heath, who sentenced Mary to death by hanging in 1791.
Royal Albert Memorial Museum & Art Gallery

Sydney's first Government House stands guard over the harbour at about the time of Mary's arrival as a convict in 1792. Watercolour by John Eyre. *State Library of NSW FL4381727*

Tom Reibey began his shipping ventures taking cargo to Green Hills, now Windsor, on the Hawkesbury River. *State Library of NSW PXD 388 v.3 f.7*

After moving to Sydney, Scottish merchant Robert Campbell helped bankroll Tom and Mary Reibey for their first trading ventures.
State Library of NSW FL3270300

Lieutenant Governor William Paterson (left) ordered the killing of many Indigenous Australians, but found out what it was like to be shot when the pugnacious 'perturbator' John Macarthur (right) blew away part of his shoulder in a duel.
State Library of NSW FL1056085, FL1067725

John Hunter, the second Governor of New South Wales, described early Sydney as 'a mere sink of every species of infamy' and said that many of the soldiers and officers were superior in wickedness to the worst of the convicts. *State Library of NSW FL1051266*

Mary's firstborn, Thomas Reibey Jr, became a prominent merchant in Van Diemen's land and built the Entally Estate outside Launceston.

Ferryman Billy Blue was a neighbour of Mary and Tom Reibey when they lived in the Rocks, then a rough area of Sydney. He is commemorated in the suburb of Blues Point. *State Library of NSW FL3141441*

Simeon Lord, whose grand home and warehouse was next to the Reibeys' Entally House, was another convict merchant who made a fortune in the new colony. *State Library of NSW FL3190314*

Mary's first daughter, Celia. *State Library of NSW FL3201805*

Mary's daughter Jane Penelope Atkinson pictured in 1828. *State Library of NSW FL1059378*

Philip Gidley King, the third Governor of New South Wales. In 1803 he awarded Tom and Mary Reibey 40 hectares on the Hawkesbury to be called 'Raby Farm'. The area is now Freemans Reach and the property became known as Reibeycroft. *State Library of NSW FL1052291*

Captain William Bligh's term as the fourth Governor of New South Wales was aborted in a military coup near Entally House. *State Library of NSW FL3320133*

The arrest of Governor Bligh, Australia's famous first cartoon, or first example of political propaganda. *State Library of NSW FL1021193*

South Head Light House, New S. Wales.

Lachlan Macquarie's lighthouse and Hyde Park Barracks became landmarks in the colony.

State Library of NSW
FL3243483, FL3322832

Mary's long-time family home, Entally House, is the white building on the right, opposite the Macquarie obelisk near Circular Quay. It was the first office of the Bank of New South Wales and then the Royal Admiral Hotel from the 1850s until it was demolished 30 years later. *State Library of NSW FL983404*

The Reibey family's magnificent Entally Estate, built by Thomas Reibey Jr at Hadspen near Launceston, remains a major tourist drawcard. *Creative Commons*

Scottish winter. Then, as snow fell gently all around them, they took another coach to lodgings that the Hopes had arranged. Mary kept detailed notes of all their expenses, and she noted that the trip from Glasgow had cost the family £2 18 shillings and sixpence. Stealing a horse would have been cheaper, but it came with much greater risks.

On 1 December, with David Hope leading the way, the family took a walk around Edinburgh. They observed the castle, gaol, college and several public buildings, though they entered none of them owing to the fatigue they felt after their busy journey. Instead they went to the theatre and saw the tragedy *Douglas* followed by the melodrama *The Vampire*, which had recently premiered on the London stage and begins with a noblewoman asleep in Fingal's Cave on the Scottish Isle of Staffa as spirits try to warn her about Lord Ruthven, an ancient vampire who marries and then drains the blood of young women. It wasn't necessarily the increasingly devout Mary's cup of tea, but she was on holidays and determined to experience as much of Britain as she could.

The following morning the Reibeys climbed the 143 steps to the top of the towering Nelson Monument, high on Calton Hill. It was a steep climb and Mary, no longer the 'lively lass' of her youth, was breathing heavily when she struggled to the top. The tower had been built to commemorate Horatio Nelson's victory over the French and Spanish fleets at the Battle of Trafalgar in 1805, and his death there. The day was cool and frosty, and the visitors carried with them the latest in fast food: basins, like small metal buckets, of hare soup that each cost tenpence. Mary was made giddy by the astonishing view over the harbour of Leith. The next day they watched a display of horsemanship and sat down to enjoy another play, *The Antiquary*, a seventeenth-century farce set in Pisa.

A friend of Reverend Irving gave Mary a letter of introduction to find a good finishing school for Celia and Eliza while they were away from home. They visited Miss Duncan, a boarding-school governess in Edinburgh's Picardy Place, 'a most delightful and airy situation'.[29] Wishing to make her antipodean girls marriageable in the finest circles of society, Mary agreed to one year's tuition only on account of Eliza's respiratory problems that might require a return to the more comfortable surrounds of Sydney. She would gladly pay more for a longer stay if her daughter's 'health proved well'. The fee was £52 10 shillings per annum for board and lodging, while tuition would cost another £24 6 shillings for each young lady.

The business of formal education having been decided, Mary and the girls journeyed to Edinburgh's Palace of Holyroodhouse, taking in the splendour and the majesty. They saw ancient artworks made several hundred years before Christ. They also visited the room where it was said Mary, Queen of Scots had seen her private secretary, David Rizzio, stabbed fifty-seven times by Protestant noblemen on 9 March 1566; stains on the floor were said to be remnants of Rizzio's blood. The girls shuddered at the thought of it.

Mary spent much of 5 December cutting up flannel cloth to prepare school clothes for Celia and Eliza, who were to begin their studies the next day. She could have hired a servant to do it but Mary had been making clothes ever since she had first sown trousers at Parramatta, and it was good to teach her children industry and thrift. Soon she was touring Edinburgh Castle, where she marvelled at the Crown of Scotland 'enclosed by a very superb palasading of iron', along with the sword of state and scabbard, and the mace and sceptre. She also saw the room where King James had been born and the hole through which his mother, Mary, Queen of Scots had conveyed secret letters.[30] 'We then went through the Armoury where there are upwards of a hundred thousand stand of arms beside swords pikes and pistols and other instruments of war,' Mary wrote, 'also the Colours belonging to the different associations and Regiments, a very grand sight.'[31]

It took time for Mary's girls to settle into their new school. On a visit to Miss Duncan's on 7 December, their second day there, Mary found Celia and Eliza taking a drawing class while looking 'rather poorly owing to sleeping in a strange bed and being up sooner than usual'. She gave the girls a day off schoolwork. In the cold and wind, she walked with them around the port of Leith and along its new pier, taking in the full view of the wide harbour as whitecaps whipped along its breadth.

Mary again left her daughters at Miss Duncan's and took a two day coach ride back to William Hope's home in Preston, before heading back to Blackburn. She visited the houses in Salford that her late aunt Penelope had left to family members, including her. Twenty-eight-year-old Thomas Foster,[32] whose mother was Mary's sister Betty, was living in one of them with his pregnant wife Mannie, at 12 Albion Street. Salford was undergoing a population explosion. Just as in Manchester and so many places in Lancashire, factories were replacing cottage industries. The houses bequeathed to Mary were typical of the small, low quality terraces in a city that was becoming grossly overcrowded. The next day, Mary left Blackburn for Manchester, planning to stay a night with her cousin Dr Hargreaves.

She felt eerie on the drive, though. While she had always done her best to placate Betty, meeting Thomas seemed to stir something inside her. She dreamed about all the times Betty had been 'ungood' to her. She dreamed that Betty had died.

In Manchester, Mary saw Shakespeare's *Othello* on stage, along with the century-old comedy *Three Hours After Marriage*. But as captivating as they were, they did not contain the same sort of excitement that Mary felt three days before Christmas when Dr Hargreaves drove her in his gig to Openshaw Fold, about a mile outside Bury. There Mary was reunited with the nurse whom her grandmother had hired to look after her forty years before. The elderly lady was with her husband, and despite their advanced age their eyes shone like beacons for the wayward girl made good. Mary said they were 'both so gratified they hardly knew how to contain themselves with joy'.[33] As tears cascaded down the old woman's lined face, the nurse told Mary she was sure she couldn't have rested in her grave had she not seen her, and that she and her husband were 'in their eightyfirst year of their age', though Mary reckoned they looked as if they would live twenty years longer.

After the emotional reunion, Mary needed a good lie down. It had been an exhausting and tearful day, and the tugging of the heartstrings had left her spent. She stayed the night at Bury's Grey Mare Inn about twenty metres from the house that had been her mother's when her mother was still known as 'Jinny' Law, though all the old homes that Mary recalled from her childhood in Bury had been pulled down to make way for more modern abodes.

Mary had a deep sense of history and wanted to know more about her people – about who they were and where they had come from. She wanted to know more about herself too. Her cousin's wife Elizabeth Hargreaves accompanied Mary to find her birth certificate at the old St Mary's Church in Bury. The church clerk let them look through tattered parchments and the register book, and Mary found the entry in an almost indecipherable scrawl that 'Molly Heydock [sic]' was 'Born in the year of our Lord 1777, May 12th and christened 29th.'[34]

On 23 December, the two ladies went to do their Christmas shopping at the Manchester markets, and they lost each other for some time in the crowd. Christmas was very different away from the summer sun and the blowflies. Mary gave herself a carriage, which she was having built in town for shipment to Sydney.

Three days after Christmas, she took a ride five kilometres west to Salford in order to visit her nephew Thomas Foster and to celebrate the birth of his son Charles Haydock Foster[35] some ten weeks earlier – 'and a very fine Child he was'.[36] Betty was running her millinery on Castlereagh Street in Sydney, but the Fosters still had a property in Van Diemen's Land and Thomas had an idea to move there.

Mary finished the day by visiting a touring exhibition in Manchester of wax figures moulded by a Frenchwoman, Madame Marie Tussaud, who had honed her craft making moulds of executed French royals during the revolution. Madame Tussaud planned to one day open a permanent museum in London.

Chapter 16

THE WINTER SNOW had turned the green hills of Lancashire white, and the frigid Manchester weather hit Mary full blast, as she had become accustomed to the climate of New South Wales. She spent New Year's Day 1821 confined to bed with a bad cold and asthma at the Hargreaves' home outside the city. The doctor and his wife ministered to her and told her that a ship called the *Malabar* had arrived from New South Wales.[1] They would see what news the vessel had brought with it.

Mary was lifted from her sickbed when her old nurse and the woman's husband arrived unannounced, having decided to walk fifteen kilometres from Bury to see her again. Elizabeth Hargreaves gave the elderly couple a bed and 'every Comfort that they required' after so long a walk for two eighty-one year olds. They told Mary they 'hardly knew how to express their joy' at being able to see her once more before they died.[2] Elizabeth packed them some mince pies and a little wine and water, and Mary gave them some money when they set off home the next day, knowing they would never see her again. They all parted with heavy hearts, and Mary continued to send the couple money after she returned to Sydney.[3]

Winter became so dark and gloomy in Manchester that candles had to be lit at midday. Mary was again plagued by bad dreams as she fretted about her family thousands of miles away. In one of her nightmares, Thomas Jr had come to England to tell her that her youngest child, little Betsey, was very ill and subject to fits.[4]

At this time in Sydney, Major Frederick Goulburn[5] – a Waterloo veteran and younger brother of the Undersecretary of State for War and the Colonies – had arrived as the new colonial secretary. He was replacing John Campbell, the president of the bank of New South Wales, who had become the new provost marshal, in charge of the colony's military police. Goulburn brought news that Macquarie's resignation had been accepted.

At the end of January, Mary sold the two small houses in Salford that she'd inherited from Aunt Penelope, receiving £300. She then began preparations to visit London again. At Greenheys in Manchester she stayed with cousin John Hope and his family, and on Sunday, 4 February, she and John went to the All Saints Church on Oxford Road and heard a sermon on the text of Jeremiah 2:13, about a disloyal people who had forsaken their God, something Mary told her girls that they must never do.

The following day, Mary interrupted her packing to buy a hundred pieces of cambric and calico. She politely declined an invitation from the Hargreaves to stay another month or two, but accepted a gift of books for her youngest daughters. Dr Hargreaves gave Mary a book of prayers – Robert Nelson's *Festivals and Fasts* – and a box containing all the potions and medicines that Mary and the girls had taken when they came down with their savage colds. He feared they would need them again.

Mary paid £3 3 shillings for a coach ride to London. Thomas Foster, the Hopes and the Hargreaves were all there to wave goodbye as the coach rattled off at 2 p.m. on a 350-kilometre journey south to the great city. After a day and a half, Mary arrived exhausted at the White Horse Hotel on Fetter Lane in Holborn, close to St Paul's Cathedral, just before 7 p.m. on 7 February.[6]

Captain William Dagg, the whaling ship master from Sydney, happened to be in London. He called around to her hotel to say that he'd seen James and George Reibey in Sydney while she was away, and they were both 'very well'.[7] The news made Mary rest a little easier, though she was missing home. Dagg wasn't to know that Tom Jr's second child, Thomas Reibey III, had died on 7 August 1820 after only two days of life.

After breakfast the next morning, Mary visited her agent's office at 53 Old Broad Street and took a walk through Cheapside and then down Ludgate Hill. As impressive and intoxicating as old London was, it had now been close to a year since she'd set sail from Sydney on this open-ended voyage, and she had a longing to see her other children. The nightmares she suffered about their welfare didn't encourage her to stay in Britain any longer. She inspected the accommodation on a Sydney-bound ship, the *Brixton*, which was lying in the London Dock, but she could get no decisive answer about when it might sail, the broker not being on board.[8] Her cabin would cost 80 guineas, with steerage passengers charged half that. The booking agents wanted £30 to transport her fabulous new carriage, but she thought they were taking a little round woman for a fool and went elsewhere. Thrift was vital for her.[9]

Mary received a letter from her cousin David Hope in Glasgow and replied while taking a break from a shopping expedition. Among the news items from home that she relayed to David, was that the surgeon and settler Charles Throsby – who had recently explored the Illawarra region and revealed grazing land of 'hundreds of Thousands [of] acres without a tree and very rich land' – had discovered another 'very fine track of Land'. It was a pass between the Illawarra and Robertson districts.[10]

As always, Mary's letters were written without punctuation and with phonetic spelling.

'I am afraid you will hardly make this out,' she said by way of apology, 'but I know you will excuse my errors.'

London, feby 14th 1821
From 22 Suffolk street Commercial Road, London
My Dear Cousin,
    You will excuse me not answering your letter of the
2nd feby as I have been so taken up with business, their has
been a ship calld the *Tuscan* arrivd from Sydney lately which
I got letters by from my family and which I had a difficulty
in finding them out as the Come in a private box so that it
took me nearly Three days before I could get them,

however I got very pleasant news they were all very well and happy and has they say they happiness whould be Complete if I near them

I have on this day been on board the *Brixton* laying in the London Docks … the accomadation seems very good … she is expected to sail in a month from this date which you see I Shall not have much time to spare

I wrote my daughters on the 10th so I expect an answer by friday new – they had a wish to stay another three months [in school at Miss Duncan's in Edinburgh] but that they will not be able

but they shall stop their till I go which giving them time to come up to London will be three weeks or a month more as perhaps the ship may not sail by a week so soon as expected[11]

Mary asked her cousin to purchase for her about two hundred yards of the different prized plaids from Kilmarnock, fifty yards of each pattern, as all things Scottish were popular in Sydney because of Macquarie's reign and the growing literary cult around the Scottish poet Robert Burns. Ever the canny businesswoman, Mary asked David to make sure the cloth was good quality but 'as Cheap as you can … and let their be attached to each pattern the Clan they are of, you will know how to send them to me better than I can tell you, direct for me at Mr Jones 53 old broad street, and Draw for the amount on him.'[12]

When Celia and Eliza eventually were 'Comeing of for London', she asked that if David had any business that day in Edinburgh to see them off in the best 'smack' – a traditional fishing boat – and to 'ensdure they were has [sic] comfortable as possible but I should not wish you to go over on purpose.'

She told David she was so busy making purchases in London and that the city was so large that it took her nearly all day to walk from one place to another. She worried that all the stock she was taking home might not sell. 'It is intirely a risk now,' she wrote, 'as their is such an abundance gone out their.'[13] 'I was very proud to hear your account of my daughters being so very well in health I can assure you it added to my recovery, I am extremely obbliged For the attention you have paid to them on every occasion.'[14]

David helped Mary with letters of introduction to trading partners, and she asked if it was possible for him to arrange through friends for a meeting with 'Mr Thomas Brisban [sic]'[15] in London before the Scottish major general sailed off to replace Macquarie as Governor of New South Wales. It wasn't possible, but Mary would see him soon enough.

While Mary mulled over the idea of sailing on the *Brixton*, she toured the ship *Hope*, on 16 February 1821 a couple of days after writing to David. The captain said they would soon be setting sail for the great southern land, but he appeared to be well behind in his refit of the vessel that was moored on the Limehouse Basin in the Thames. One of the *Hope*'s owners was planning to settle in Van Diemen's Land and wanted all the information Mary could give him before she set off for a snack at a pastry shop on the way back to her hotel.

Whatever time Mary had left in London, she planned to see as much of it as she could. The following day, she was touring the Lord Mayor's home, Mansion House, and the Guildhall, the vast, regal building that was the ceremonial and administrative centre of the City of London. She also spent a great deal of time with the Atkinson family over the next few days. Young Miss Charlotte Atkinson accompanied her to a church service, this time at a non-denominational floating chapel called the *Ark* (formerly HMS *Swift*), which was moored on the Thames.[16]

The idea behind the floating chapel was that sailors rarely visited churches on shore, but would feel more comfortable worshipping in a vessel; and these 'floating churches' were soon established in other British ports.

Mary and Charlotte were excited about this new mode of worship as small boats delivered about three hundred sailors to the 'Ark' from ships moored all over the Thames. At 10 a.m. when one of the crewmen on the ark hoisted the 'Blue Peter', a blue flag with a white rectangle in the centre, it was the signal for the church service to begin.[17]

Mary and Charlotte filed into the floating chapel, stunned at the way the ship's hull had been converted into a commodious church, complete with pulpit, galleries and long rows of benches with sailors in suits and ties, holding Bibles, and with reverence on their faces.

Some of the sailors fell to their knees on entering the chapel for a minute or two of silent prayer, perhaps recalling former shipmates and family who did not return from voyages across the deep.

Mary being 'thrifty Correct and Sober'[18] was dead against wasting money. When she received a packet of letters from Betty with the packet attracting double postage after having gone through Manchester, Mary fumed at the 10-shilling expense the postal authorities had imposed.

She moved into new, cheaper lodgings at 9 Postern Row, overlooking the Tower of London, and inspected 'the *Mariner* ship lying in the West India Docks'.[19] Skippers who were planning voyages to New South Wales repeatedly called on Mary to see if they could persuade her to part with her cash and sail with them. She made a second tour of the *Brixton*, which was still waiting to set sail, and checked out the accommodation on another ship, the *Grace*.

But she was more impressed with the *Mariner*, an American vessel launched at Philadelphia twelve years earlier, then seized by the British for illegally trading with France during hostilities. It had been sailing between London and Jamaica but was now making its first voyage to New South Wales, advertised as a 'remarkably fine fast-sailing Ship' with 'elegant and commodious ... Accommodation for Passengers'.[20] Mary met the owner, Mr Evans, in Broad Street; she didn't like the look of him but knew his ship was one of the best available for the voyage.

As Mary waited on news of when the *Mariner* would set sail, Celia and Eliza wrote to her while still in Edinburgh, and she had a visit from Alexander Riley, one of the original directors of the

Bank of New South Wales. Riley had sailed for London at the end of 1817 and was managing his colonial affairs from there with plans to send a large flock of the hardy Saxon Merino sheep to New South Wales.

Mary made plans to visit the widow of Francis Grose to pay her respects to her husband. Grose had married his second wife, Elizabeth, just a month before he died in 1814. His son the Reverend Francis Grose, who had been an infant when his father ran Sydney, had died in 1817. Elizabeth was the widow of Lieutenant-Governor William Paterson, the man wounded by John Macarthur in their duel.

Waiting to set sail was unpleasant. The cold, wet weather played havoc with Mary's lungs, and she again developed a hacking cough. But she was well enough on 9 March to venture out into the drizzle in order to buy a large, heavy edition of *Clarke's Family Bible*, in which she would write out the dates and times of the births of her children. She thought that it would make a wonderful keepsake for them.

On Sunday, 11 March 1821, Mary sat inside the St Mary Magdalen Church across the Thames and listened to 'a very good sermon from the 15th Chapter of St Luke and 3rd verse', which promised that there was more joy in heaven over one sinner 'that repenteth than over Ninety and Nine just persons which need no repentance'. There was something in Mary's own life story that made her think deeply about that lesson.

Mary continued her big shopping sprees, buying all manner of household goods: cutlery, doilies, cloths and mats, stationery, Irish linens, looking glasses, a sofa, a mahogany dresser and a writing case. She also chased after more books and gifts for George, buying him on 14 March a double-barrelled fowling gun and the complete set of *'Incyclopaedia Britanica'*, twenty volumes, which cost her 30 guineas, about six months wages for the averaging labourer.[21] Later she packed away a canteen for him to use on his travels, to go along with all the books she had found for George, forty-five fat volumes of the *British Essayists* and twelve volumes of Edward Gibbon's *The Decline and Fall of the Roman Empire*.

She also collected the frames for the miniatures she'd had painted; hers was gold in an oval shape with a glass front and green velvet backing.

On 16 March 1821, Thomas Thomson[22] – a young Scottish lieutenant of the Royal Marines and a relative of Dr Chalmers – called on Mary, bringing a letter from Celia in Edinburgh. He quickly charmed this little, round business giant from Sydney. Two days later, despite Mary still suffering badly with a heavy cold, Thomson escorted her to the British Museum, which was proudly showcasing its great Egyptian treasures captured from the French after the surrender of Napoleon.

LACHLAN MACQUARIE WAS now sixty years old. On 4 April 1821, while Mary was still in London, he started a farewell tour of his realm with his wife, their six-year-old son and a large entourage aboard the private merchant vessel *Midas*. Their first few days travelling towards Van Diemen's Land 'nearly proved fatal' in heavy winds, after Greenway's lighthouse near South Head had initially been a welcome sight for the skipper, Captain Beveridge.

It took Macquarie's party twenty days to reach Hobart Town, where they were greeted by the glory of Mount Wellington covered in snow. While in Van Diemen's Land, Macquarie received a letter[23] from Henry Goulburn informing him that his fellow Scot, Thomas Brisbane – a graduate of Edinburgh University and almost as well travelled in the military as Macquarie – was on his way to take over as governor. Brisbane, a keen astronomer, had first expressed an interest in Macquarie's job in 1815, keen to chart the stars from the Southern Hemisphere. He'd even built an observatory at his home, Brisbane House in Largs, Ayrshire. Brisbane was close friends with the Duke of Wellington from their days as young subalterns in Ireland.

Macquarie was glad to be going home, but he knew he would miss this great southern land. He would also miss his faithful old carriage horse, Ajax, who impaled himself on the handle of a plough in a Hobart Town street after breaking loose from his

Thomas Brisbane was chosen to succeed fellow Scot Lachlan Macquarie as Governor of New South Wales. *State Library of NSW FL3233443*

stable. 'We have had this useful fine Horse upwards of 11 years in constant use,' Macquarie wrote, 'and therefore I feel it a most severe loss.'[24]

Only a day earlier, after Macquarie had signed their death warrants, ten men had been hanged on a public scaffold at the top of Macquarie Street in a crackdown on bushranging.[25] On 6 May, James Reibey wrote to David Hope in Glasgow to tell him the mass hanging was 'The most awfull Sight that was ever Witnessed on this island.'[26] This affectionate communication reflected the regard James had for his mother and her extended family in Britain as he told David that she had always spoken of the Hope family with great affection and respect; it also provided a glimpse into life in Van Diemen's Land. The letter was written in haste, as James had just made a quick dash overland for 126 miles (210 kilometres) to bring his youngest sisters Jane and Betsey from Port Dalrymple for schooling in Hobart. He was still tired from the trip, and he was sailing at dawn for Sydney. He told David:

I hope we shall not be such strangers as we have been for so many years. The manner in which my Mother always mentioned with you and your Brothers and Sister I was always Lead to Respect you. I sincerely hope this will find you well.[27]

My Brother Thomas to whom I sent your letter promised to write to you. He is the Eldest and Twenty Five old to Day. He is married and one Little Girl as I suppose Mother has informed you of. I have been Married these Five Years but have no Family. My Brother George who was in the Bank [in Van Diemen's Land] has now left it, in Consequence of it nearly failing and they could not keep up such an Establishment. The Cashier had lent all the money out long before my Brother joined but was not found out till lately. He had lent £12,000 to a set of Rascalls who Refused to pay it back to him again knowing He could not make a noise about it, so in fact the Bank had Existed for nearly 3 years Entirely upon the Public Confidence ... You wish to know if there is not something suitable in the way of Produce to send to you. The only Produce New South Wales Exports is Wool which goes to London, about two Ships Cargoes a year

we export very Little Wool from this Island, it being very Coarse, at Present, altho People are now paying more attention to it than they Did. Wheat we export to Sydney about 50 or 60 Thousand Bushells every year with a Large Quantity of Potatoes.

James also told David that Macquarie had been the saviour of morality in Sydney. Hobart had the Reverend Robert Knopwood[28] of the Church of England, but he was 'a very profane man' who had only come out to the colony after running through a fortune in England.[29]

MARY STILL HAD IMPORTANT business to pursue in London before she headed home. She finally organised for Celia and Eliza to leave Miss Duncan's school, and on 7 April visited her contacts at the merchant firm Buckles, Bagster & Buchanan at 33 Mark Lane in London. She was seeking their help in securing a pension for her daughter-in-law Rebecca, whose first husband, a lieutenant in the Royal Marines, had died young. Though Mary was wealthy, she still wanted every penny her family were entitled to from the government.

A few days later, Mary went to Whitehall to fill out the proper forms for securing the pension. Then she dropped into the law offices in Temple Bar to see a friend from Sydney, William Charles Wentworth, who had been in London for the past five years and had hopes of procuring a free constitution for New South Wales as a means of self-government in some form. The man who had crossed the Blue Mountains in 1813 had just published a book almost as long as its title: *A Statistical, Historical, and Political Description of the Colony of New South Wales and Its Dependent Settlements in Van Diemen's Land, With a Particular Enumeration of the Advantages Which These Colonies Offer for Emigration and Their Superiority in Many Respects Over Those Possessed by the United States of America.*

Wentworth had much to share with Mary, including news of his brother John, who had recently died at sea as a petty officer.

Mary told him that she had never meddled in 'polatics',[30] but she was interested in Wentworth's ideas for a representative government; she confessed in her journal that she 'staid' with him 'too long, till twas too late to go'.[31]

While George Reibey was minding Mary's stores in Sydney, he was also keeping an eye on the changing social and political climate. Commissioner John Thomas Bigge had sailed for England after finishing a two-year royal commission in New South Wales into the effectiveness of transportation as a deterrent

William Charles Wentworth had strong views about self-rule in the colony. *State Library of NSW FL3326851*

to felons. Earl Bathurst had given Bigge instructions to ensure that penal transportation should be made 'an object of real terror' without the 'ill-considered compassion for convicts' reflected by Macquarie's humanitarian policies.

Great changes were now expected in the colony, George said. Some in New South Wales saw Bigge as having 'attached himself to a certain Party existing here whose sole object is their own aggrandisement with the depression of those who have once been Prisoners, without any reason to their real Interests of the Colonies'.[32]

In a strike for Wentworth's republican ideas, George wrote his own letter to David Hope to say that 'if an attempt of such a nature should be made it is not impossible that a second

Washington might rise up among us – but by the bye as we are not yet independent perhaps such an expectation may be considered too much of Treason which we read of here is often punished [in Britain] with either an Axe or an Halter and speaking sincerely I should not much relish the performance of such an operation on my own Neck'.[33] He told David that he was writing at the request of his 'very Dear Mother' and 'affectionate Sisters' as a 'tribute of gratitude offered by the loving Son of Her to whom you showed so much kindness and attention'.[34]

Another big news item from Sydney, George told his Scottish relative, was that 'distillation permission' had been granted, which would help end the sly grog trade and the huge mark-ups on imported spirits. Robert Cooper[35] – a convict who came from a family of distillers and hotel keepers in the Stepney area of London – would soon launch 'Cooper's Best Gin' at the colony's first distillery in the 'Black wattle-Swamp' on Parramatta Road.[36]

George was also excited about the prospects of the new colony of 'Port McQuarie', which was 'about two hunds. [miles] to the Northwards of Port Jackson'. He told Mary's cousin that its foundation was for the object of cultivating sugar cane, 'it being much warmer than here … the highest hopes are entertained of its success … if such are realised, very great advantages by its means will accrue to the Country – an important Article for Exportation will be afforded which is much wanted, it will also detain in circulation a great portion of the Colonial Capital which is annually sent out for foreign produce'.[37]

Meanwhile, George kept his brother James informed of the social happenings among their business rivals in Sydney. He wrote of the recent wedding[38] at St Philip's of the 31-year-old French-born merchant Prosper de Mestre[39] to nineteen-year-old Mary Ann Black, daughter of the convict Mary Hyde and stepdaughter of Simeon Lord. Prosper had moved into Macquarie Place, taking up the town home of the late Andrew Thompson. The newlyweds were as small as 'pygmies', George told his brother, but added that de Mestre was 'in my opinion one of the most worthy little fellows in the colony' while young Mary Ann's 'amicable disposition is well known'.[40] The couple went on to have ten children, with their youngest son Etienne[41] developing such an affinity for horses that many years later he trained five winners of a great race called the Melbourne Cup.

George also reported on two marriages at Parramatta. The weddings were European ceremonies between Aboriginal men and two women graduates of Macquarie's Native School.

At the time, George was busy organising his own 'splendid ball' at Mary's home for what the *Gazette* called 'some of the principal officers, merchants, and inhabitants of the town of Sydney'. The ballroom was elegantly decorated, and the band of His Majesty's 48th Regiment attended. 'The utmost hilarity and harmony pervaded the Company,' the *Gazette* reported, 'till the solar beams began to gild the horizon.'[42]

There was some gloom on that horizon, though. George told James that Mary's sister was proving difficult, and he warned Rebecca that Aunt Betty wasn't the friend she pretended to be. Betty was making 'frivolous excuses', he said, for not finishing a set of bonnets she'd promised to send to the Reibeys in Van Diemen's Land. George's advice was not to expect them any time soon.[43]

In April 1821, when Mary and his sisters were still readying themselves for the return voyage, George learnt that his mother would have to find new tenants for Entally in Macquarie Place – the £150 a year in rent would have to come from somewhere other than the Bank of New South Wales. The bank secretary reported to the board that the house was 'damp, in want of repair, and unfit' for their purposes, and asked the president to 'find a more eligible House'.[44]

ON EASTER SUNDAY, 22 April, Mary visited London's Foundling Hospital, which was not so much a hospital as a home for 'deserted young children'. She remarked that it was 'a most gratifying sight to see such a number of little females in such good order and an equal number of boys'; she knew what a horror it was to feel all alone in the world. She joined in the singing of hymns at the building's chapel.

The 27-year-old Lieutenant Thomson was now a frequent visitor to Mary's lodgings, and he and Eliza, just sixteen, were often together. A few days after Easter, Thomson accompanied Mary and the girls as they toured the Naval College at Greenwich, standing awestruck inside the Painted Hall. But Mary was so ill with her persistent cough that not even the strongest brew in the Virginia Coffee House on Threadneedle Street could perk her up. It wasn't until her birthday on 12 May, when she turned forty-four, that the sickness began to lift. The cough came back, though, and there was great stress before she set sail.

Mary sent twenty trunks of luggage onto the *Mariner*, and on 22 May she took a coach to the docks at Gravesend. Thomson had become very attached to Eliza, and he decided that he would sail with the Reibeys. Mary went on board the ship and made a great clearance in the cabin she had taken, shifting many of the trunks down to the hold to give her more room. She saw it as only fair, because the ship's owners were charging her freight while trying to keep the luggage in her quarters. She was not about to waste money.

Mary was anxious to get going, but the ship remained stalled. An advertisement appeared in the *Times* that all passengers should be on board by Sunday, 10 June, but by the twelfth there was still no sign of the ship moving. Mary and Thomson stayed with the Atkinsons while they waited anxiously. One of Mary's fellow passengers told her that the *Mariner* couldn't proceed on its voyage 'for the want of means'. Mary's London agent urged the passengers to seek redress. Thomson and some of the others marched down to the Mansion House and complained in person to the mayor. Mary noted in her diary: 'ever since the 1st of April when [the owner] first ingaged that the ship should sail, I have been living at very heavy expence and in consequence my sickness has increased it and God only knows now when We shall get off, but I will put my trust in Him who alone can judge'.[45]

Ten days later, on 24 June, Mr Evans, the ship's owner, came on board and gave the crew a severe scolding for letting the passengers who stayed on board have provisions. 'A great dispute arose amongst him and the passengers,' Mary wrote, 'and on his leaving he was hissed and hooted not without his deserving it for a more oppressive villain cannot exist.'[46] Finally, on 26 June, Evans found the money to pay the sailors their advance in Spanish dollars so they could get going after such a long delay. The passengers again jeered him as he left the vessel. The skipper, Captain Douglass, weighed anchor and sailed from Gravesend. Mary and the others had travelled only fourteen miles down the Thames when fierce winds forced the crew to drop anchor once more. Most of the ladies, including Mary and her daughters, were sick as the ship rocked and swayed. The next day at 11.30 a.m. the *Mariner* headed for heavy seas. Most of the ladies were violently ill once more.

The rough ride did not bode well for the rest of the journey. On 1 July the *Mariner* anchored at Ryde, a small village on the Isle of Wight. Two days later, Mary finally felt well enough to go ashore with some of the other passengers. She stayed the night in the more comfortable quarters of the Star & Garter Inn at Portsmouth, which did not lurch about like her ship's cabin. The passengers then discovered that Captain Douglass was 'in Difficulties in regard to provisions' and heard that the shifty owner, Mr Evans, was now in gaol. This meant that Mary and all the others would have to buy their own food and drink for the voyage. On Thursday, 5 July 1821, Mary wrote: 'This day the gentlemen went on shore and bought the remainder of the provisions, had to open the Hatch to get at their Dollars to pay for it, sailed from Ryde this evening with a foul wind.'[47]

FOUR MONTHS LATER, the *Hobart Town Gazette and Van Diemen's Land Advertiser* reported that on 8 November 'arrived from England, which she left the 5th of July, the ship *Mariner*, Captain Douglass, with merchandize and passengers; namely, Robert Honner, Esq. and two Misses Honner (his Lady having died on the voyage), ... Lieut. Thompson ... Mrs. Reibey and two Misses Reibey [among others]'.[48]

Mary had brought home half a shipload of goods for sale in New South Wales, and she had also hauled home a new family member. On 20 November, twelve days after the ship's arrival, the Reverend Robert Knopwood presided over the Hobart Town wedding of 'Lieutenant Thomas Thomson, of the Royal Marines, to Eliza, second daughter of the late Mr Thomas Reibey, of Sydney'.[49] Eliza, just sixteen and a half, fell pregnant almost immediately. Her brother George thought that Lieutenant Thomson was 'a very worthy young man'.[50]

The wedding was just one of the many celebrations Mary enjoyed before sailing for Sydney. Mary's first grandchild, Mary Allen Reibey, was now a healthy, bouncing three year old. Following the loss of her infant son, Thomas Reibey III, Richarda gave birth to another son; he was given the name Thomas Haydock Reibey.[51] He'd been born in a cottage on the estate Tom was building at Hadspen, outside Launceston, while Mary and the girls had been sailing home. Little Thomas was now two months old with an extraordinary future before him.

Mary couldn't hide the immense delight she felt for her family when she arrived at Tom Jr and Richarda's country home outside Launceston. Mary was carrying the large family Bible she'd bought in London. On the flyleaf, she wrote, 'Thomas Reibey, a gift from his affectionate mother, M. Reibey, Hobart Town, V.D.L., December 1st 1821.'[52]

On that very day, 1500 kilometres north, the summer sun over Port Jackson turned the most magnificent harbour in the world a golden hue as artillerymen packed black powder and wadding into the nineteen cannons that guarded it. Lachlan Macquarie was about to make his farewell speech to the colony after almost twelve years as the fifth Governor of New South Wales in which a dumping ground for British prisons had become a thriving settlement of second chances – a place where former convicts such as Mary Reibey could become business leaders.

Macquarie wanted to remind every settler, convict and emancipist who would hear his goodbye speech that their land was one of limitless potential and that they had the ability to realise that potential for themselves. The continent was still being referred to as New Holland in official documents, yet Macquarie had been the first to use a different name for it in his government reports. He had included this name in the opening sentence of his farewell to the people and the land he had grown to love.

As his carriage arrived at Hyde Park and a large gathering stood to hear his address, Macquarie alighted and looked around at the community he had helped create. He stepped forward, puffed out his chest, cleared his throat, and in his booming Scottish burr welcomed his people with the greeting: 'Fellow citizens of Australia!'[53] He told his gathered supporters: 'My most fervent prayers will accordingly be offered for the welfare and prosperity of this country, and for the happiness of its inhabitants.'[54]

At her son's property at Hadspen, Mary could hardly be happier. She played with her grandchildren, knowing her life was one of rich blessings. She had no idea of the staggering heartbreaks that were just around the corner.

Chapter 17

BIRTHS, DEATHS AND MARRIAGES – the milestones of the joys, sorrows and struggles of humankind. Like one of her ships on a long voyage, Mary was sailing through placid waters before meeting wild and catastrophic storms in the roaring forties of her life.

Three weeks after Eliza's wedding in Hobart, Captain Douglass brought Mary, her four daughters, her son George, and her new son-in-law Thomas Thomson home aboard the *Mariner*.[1] Despite Mary's wealth, there was still a social stigma in Sydney attached to those with convict origins – especially women, because of the association with sex work. So it was that in the next census and subsequent 'musters', Mary chose to write that she had arrived 'free, on the *Mariner*' rather than as a convict on the *Royal Admiral*.[2]

Tom Jr, James and Eliza were now married, and Mary was working on finding partners for her four other children while getting back into her job as one of the leading merchants in Sydney. Celia, her eldest girl, had always been delicate. Her health had been tested painfully by a cold and wet Scottish winter, but her outlook had brightened in the summer sunshine when she was reunited with the Wills family, the children of her late father's old business partner. The children of both families all had one parent who was a former convict and one who had chosen to come to the colony. When younger, the Reibey children had played with the Wills brood, and Celia had formed a strong attachment to

Tom Wills,[3] who was now twenty-one. He had buried his young stepfather, the newspaper editor George Howe, while Mary and her daughters were in England.[4]

Mary's George Street store was offering the exotic goods that she'd brought back on the *Mariner*: 'ladies and gentlemen's super-fine cloths of colours, of excellent qualities, ladies' fashionable cloaks, white lead [for paint], spirits of turpentine, linseed oil, Hollands' gin, Port and Madeira wine …'[5] The ships *Actaeon* and *Amboyna* had also delivered to Mary's stores a shipment of Indian calico, coir rope, and Isle of France sugar from Mauritius on sale at £45 a ton, though Mary would discount it to £42 a ton for five tons or more.[6]

In Hobart Town, at his store on the Derwent, Tom Jr was selling goods from the *Tiger*, an American ship captured by the British on her first voyage. The vessel had deposited playing cards, silk and cotton handkerchiefs, nankeen pantaloons, and 'very superior negro-head tobacco in 2 oz. figs' as well as 'excellent Irish butter in jars', Cayenne pepper, mustard, birdshot and sago. He insisted everything was on sale 'at very moderate prices'.[7]

Working in the Reibey storehouses was a far safer occupation than working on their farms. Midway through 1822, while the Reibey brothers were all doing good business in Van Diemen's Land, William Evans, a stockkeeper in Tom's employ at Port Dalrymple, went missing while in charge of a flock of sheep. He was found some days later with spears through his body from head to foot.[8]

At Mary's house on George Street, though, there was the prospect of new life. Nineteen-year-old Celia and 22-year-old Tom Wills took out a licence to marry, and they did so four days later before the Reverend Cowper at St Philip's.[9] They made a handsome couple. Celia's brother George later wrote that he and the groom had been the greatest friends from infancy, and that he'd met few people with a character 'more amiable and honourable than his in every respect'; Tom was also handsome and well mannered.[10] Within a few weeks, Celia was pregnant like her sister Eliza.

The flurry of excitement over the wedding, the baby news, Mary's new merchandise and the sale of a shack she had on Cockle Bay kept the Reibeys in a permanent state of celebration – but their giddiness was tempered by the fact that the Bank of New South Wales was moving from the damp house in Macquarie Place to a property on George Street[11] owned by James Chisholm,[12] who had come to Australia as a Scottish soldier with the Rum Corps in 1790. Like Mary, Chisholm had acquired huge landholdings, including a 379-foot (120 metres) frontage along the eastern side of George Street. Chisholm sold his spirits licence to Mary and leased his Crown & Thistle pub building to the Bank of New South Wales; they used it as their headquarters for decades.[13] He became a director of the bank while establishing a country residence on his 23-hectare Newtown Farm, today in the suburb of Redfern.

In 1822, Mary began travelling frequently between New South Wales and Van Diemen's Land with a servant, and sometimes with George, Eliza, Lieutenant Thomson, and some of Betty's children.[14] Early in August, Mary and a servant set sail for Launceston to be with Eliza when she gave birth to Mary's second granddaughter, Mary Helen Thomson.[15] Eliza and her husband had made their home, Rosetta, in the St Leonards area just outside Launceston, not far from her brother James.

The passage of time had allowed Lieutenant Thomson to ease his embarrassment after David Hope had supplied wrong information to the British papers about the wedding in Van Diemen's Land. David had elevated the lieutenant's status by mistakenly informing the press that he was a high-ranking member of Governor Brisbane's staff. Thomson feared his family and friends would think he was a lying braggart. He had a modest salary of not quite £300 a year, but he was thinking of ways to increase it.[16]

GEORGE REIBEY, now twenty-two and rather full of himself, was busy devouring the historical tomes and encyclopedias his mother had brought back from London, among others. He'd also read all the poems and novels of Sir Walter Scott. Despite the widespread lingering animosity towards the French in the wake of decades of conflict, George told David Hope that through books he'd learnt 'that France is a Nation deeply learned and far advanced in literature'.[17]

From Glasgow, David kept him supplied with copies of the highbrow *Edinburgh Review* magazine. Although the magazines were second-hand and well out of date, George didn't mind, since his mother had taught him to 'admire a judicious economy' – though he admitted he wasn't as thrifty as her. In return, George kept his Scottish relatives abreast of the changing social and political climate of his world. He told them about what he saw as the hypocrisy of the colony's foremost religious zealot Samuel Marsden, the 'Flogging Parson' and missionary who had been deeply opposed to Macquarie's policies of promoting convicts and emancipists to important positions.

The 'Flogging Parson' Samuel Marsden was not popular in the Reibey family.
State Library of NSW FL4391686

George was appalled at the attacks being made on Macquarie's reputation through Commissioner Bigge's report into transportation.

Macquarie's lavish use of government money for public works in New South Wales and his support for emancipated convicts in lofty positions had angered many members of the British Government who wanted to keep the distant colony as a harsh penal colony, and a place miscreants would fear.

Bigge's official report, heavily flavoured by condemnation of Macquarie from the likes of Marsden and John Macarthur, was scathing of the former governor's rule as a waste of money and a danger to free settlers.

Macquarie had returned to the grandeur of the mountains, lochs and islands of Scotland, but the stress of trying to clear his name damaged his mood and health.

'McQuarie [sic] as we expected is severely lashed and Marsden much excelled,' George wrote, describing Macquarie as 'our late worthy Governor ... a more strictly upright and Moral Man will never again rule over us, nor one who will show himself more truly alive to the best interests of the colony by his laborious assiduity for its advancement and reformation'. 'I am much astonished,' George wrote, 'to find that the Revd. Mr Marsden has found means to create so general and so strong a feeling in his [own] favour throughout Britain, and at the expence of the worthy Personage abovementioned. We here can best judge which of the two deserves it most.'[18] Macquarie, he said, was a man 'who's most heartfelt pleasure during his arduous administration here was to promote the welfare' of convicts wanting to become productive members of society.[19]

While Marsden had managed to build a good reputation for himself among powerful political allies, George claimed that 'his spiritual Brethren on their arrival here invariably change sentiments towards him'. Marsden, or 'Saint Samuel' as George called him, was 'a portly carcass', round, fat and red-faced. While Marsden had claimed 'mighty things' by taking Christianity to the Maori in New Zealand, George said he'd done nothing for the 'advancement of Religion and civilisation among the Aboriginees [sic]' and, in fact, 'the bad Conduct of the Missionaries' in Australia had caused the First Peoples to be disgusted by the Europeans' religion. 'You will scarcely credit what profligacy that some of these Ministers have attained,' George wrote, 'it is a fact that one of them keeps several of the Native Women under the very eyes of his Wife ... When our native institution was suggested by Govr. Macquarie Mr Marsden could not be prevailed upon to give his assistance or countenance ... it is thought that he was chagrined that any but himself should have been the first promoter of that.'[20]

George told his Scottish relatives that two of the brightest men in New South Wales, Dr Redfern and Edward Eagar, were now in Britain arguing on behalf of all emancipists for political reform. Redfern had made a connection by marriage to the Reibeys, having wed Sally Wills, the sister of Celia's new husband.

George told David about new restrictions on selling grants of land for profit rather than development, though he confessed that his principal business at Port Dalrymple was supposed to involve taking 'possession of Fourteen Hundred Acres of Land', which Governor Brisbane had given him, along with a convict worker for each hundred acres. But George was planning to return to Sydney despite his older brothers imploring him to stay and turn farmer. The business partnership between Tom Jr and James was one of commerce and agriculture, with James overseeing the farms. Under Mary's direction, George said, both 'were too prudent' for any 'wild Speculation', and together they possessed three thousand acres, five hundred head of cattle and two hundred sheep – all without debt. Despite his huge grant of land and the success of his brothers, George wasn't sure if he could 'reconcile myself to such a life' on the land. He was anxious to travel, believing that the world was a book and the person confined to his country of birth had only read a single page.[21]

GRANDCHILDREN BEGAN appearing at regular intervals for Mary, whose eyes shone brightly behind her spectacles at each new descendant of her beloved late husband. She knew that her oldest girl would make a wonderful mother, and on 6 May 1823[22] at Mary's house on George Street, Celia went into labour – but not before she caught 'a violent cold'. Mary's delight at the prospect of another grandchild was checked by her fears for the young mother's fragile health.

Celia delivered a girl that she named after Mary's dear cousin Alice Hope. While Mary fell in love with little Alice, Celia was left deathly ill with exhaustion. 'The cold fastened on the lungs,' Mary explained later, and 'originated a rapid consumption'.[23] Mary ministered to Celia while business continued all around her.

John Atkinson,[24] the young merchant friendly with the Reibey children, had decided to strike out on his own. He told readers of the *Gazette* that he'd now moved into 'Mrs. Reibey's extensive and valuable' property at 9 George Street. He intended very shortly to commence business in the 'several Mercantile Duties of Auctioneer and Commission Agent'.[25] While he had been a partner in the Sydney trading firm MacQueen, Atkinson & Pritchett, he now had designs on becoming Jane Reibey's husband, even though Mary's second youngest child was just fifteen. Jane was tall, clever and 'stout in proportion';[26] her portrait, painted around that time, shows a dark-eyed girl, elegantly dressed, with a mass of dark curls.[27] Atkinson had recently been diagnosed with a liver complaint that his doctor said would prove fatal, but after visiting Eliza and Thomas Thomson in Launceston for a few months, he returned to tell Mary that he was better and that when she would allow it, he wanted to marry Jane.[28]

Mary was in the market for a good man herself. She advertised for a 'steady and sober' one to be the overseer for her business; a man who could write 'a fair hand, and keep Accounts'. 'None need apply,' she declared, 'that cannot give an unexceptionable character.'[29] Mary was the undoubted ruler of her considerable empire, but she had no control over unforeseen circumstance. When the *Mariner* was wrecked on 1 July 1823 off the coast of Chile with the loss of three crew, it was a powerful portent for what was to come on Mary's voyage through life.

On his estate in Hadspen, Tom Jr was enlarging the first simple cottage on the property into a magnificent home called 'Entally House' in honour of his late father. A gang of convicts working on the project beside the South Esk River were housed in an underground cellar at night to prevent them escaping into the bush.[30] On 17 September, James wrote to tell David Hope that the project was costing a whopping £600.

Tom Jr's wife Richarda had just delivered their third child. They named him after James,[31] whose property was about twelve kilometres away.

But Entally wasn't a happy place in September 1823. On doctors' advice over his lung complaints, George had moved back to Van Diemen's Land from Sydney, shelving his dream of travelling to the great sights and museums of Europe. The three Reibey brothers were also lamenting the perilous state of Celia and her fight with consumption; she hadn't been able to suckle her baby, and her health had steadily declined.

Tom Jr and James encouraged George to cut down trees around Entally House for exercise. After a heavy rainstorm he was out in the bush, about a hundred metres from Entally, swinging his axe to work off a hearty lunch, when he decided to climb a tree to gain a better view of the flooded countryside. While astute in many ways, George was no bushman, and the branch he was perched on broke. George fell heavily onto the stump of another tree and was knocked unconscious.[32]

Mary's youngest son lay in the wet grass for more than an hour, nobody having seen him, until at last he recovered enough to crawl back to Entally. Shocked, Tom Jr immediately dispatched a man on horseback to find James at his home in Launceston and to round up medical assistance there. But the South Esk had broken its banks, and the workman could not get across. A canoe that was often used to cross the river had washed away. Conditions were so bad that it took twenty-two hours after George's accident before help was obtained.[33]

The first doctor to treat George took fifty ounces of blood (about 1.4 litres) from him that night. He seemed to recover but then fell desperately ill as a result of the cold, exposure and shock. The massive blood loss didn't help. James and Tom Jr despaired over the slim prospects of their brother, 'Poor George, the Pride and flower of the flock'.[34]

BABY ALICE WAS JUST four months old when her mother Celia died at Mary's George Street house on 28 September 1823, fighting for breath amid her coughing fits. Mary's oldest girl was just twenty. Heartbroken, Mary buried the young mother next to her father Tom, whose coffin had been moved to the new cemetery at Brickfield Hill near Joseph Foveaux's old Surry Hills farm.

Mary made sure that the new editor of the *Gazette*, Tom Wills's brother Horatio, ran a suitable eulogy, asking readers to imagine the 'grief of the astonished widower, and young father'. 'A sweet little girl,' the paper said, '... the deceased is deservedly lamented; the many mental adornments, and attractive virtues, with which she was gifted, will long remain cherished in the bosom of her numerous relatives, and host of surviving friends.'[35]

Mary chose to care for her delicate granddaughter Alice herself. The wounds of Celia's passing were still red raw when news arrived from Launceston that George was now so weak that he couldn't write home. James escorted three more doctors to treat George at Entally, and while their outlook for his recovery was 'unfavourable' they thought the salt air of a voyage to see Mary might help.

George didn't make it. After weeks of suffering, he died on 26 October 1823, aged twenty-two. His sister Eliza was one of the family members with him when he passed. The sight haunted her for years. 'Never, never again may I endure such another trial,' she wrote. 'It was almost too much for my poor heart to see him I loved so tirelessly, laying in an agony of pain, and not a word of Complaint escape his lips.'[36]

The *Gazette* called George a 'truly excellent young Gentleman', with many virtues and 'a mind well stored with intellectual attainments'.[37] 'In our Bible Society, in this Colony, Mr. Reibey occupied for some time the fatiguing duty of Collector, and it is well known that none more amply contributed to these heavenly coffers, by influence and exertion, than the deceased. In Hobart Town he was the first that actively coalesced with the Rev. Mr Horton, Wesleyan Missionary, about two years since, in procuring subscriptions and donations towards the erection of the Wesleyan Chapel in progress in that Colony.'[38]

Within the space of a few weeks, two of Mary's adored children had died. Crestfallen, she moved back to the house in Macquarie Place where she and her husband Tom had raised their children, and which the Bank of New South Wales had vacated. It was there that soon after, baby Alice died at the age of eleven months and five days.[39] Eliza wrote that it seemed the poor baby had 'only been born to be regretted, so perfect a little Angel'.[40]

Mary was shattered, and Tom Jr so badly affected that he took a six-month break from his work in Van Diemen's Land to cope with his depression. Young Jane said the bereavements were enough 'to wring our very souls'.[41]

When news soon arrived in New South Wales of Lachlan Macquarie's death on 1 July 1824,[42] as a broken man weighed down by the attacks on him by government and bureaucracy, a pall was cast over Sydney – especially among the former convicts such as Mary, whose lives and families had flourished under his reign.

As agonising as all those deaths were, and as much as she tried to find solace in prayer and scripture, Mary still had five living children and a growing rollcall of grandchildren who all looked to her as their inspiration. Just as she had always done, Mary Reibey powered ahead.

JOHN ATKINSON WAS persistent in his pursuit of Jane Penelope Reibey, who had now reached the age of sixteen years and nine months. Atkinson had formed a trading partnership, Atkinson & Bingle, and Mary knew that he would keep fighting until he had wed her daughter. On 6 September 1824, Mary made him swear an affidavit that 'John Atkinson maketh oath and sayeth that he is single and unmarried and under no contract or promise of marriage to anyone except Miss Jane Penelope Reibey, daughter of the late Mr Thomas Reibey, to whom this deponent is desirous of being united in Marriage by and with the consent of her mother.'[43] Mary swore out her own affidavit: 'Mr John Atkinson has my Permission to be united in Marriage to my Daughter, Jane Penelope Reibey, Sydney 6th September 1824.'[44]

Five days later, Atkinson married Jane with the Reverend Cowper presiding at St Philip's. Jane told David Hope that she had been 'married rather younger than the generality of my sex but in this Country they marry so much younger than in yours'.[45]

> My dear Friend it [the marriage] was not the whim of a moment but the result of a long meditated and mature deliberation. I made it the subject of Prayer and Meditation by night as well as by day and my Heart told me that I most sincerely loved and that our love was reciprocal. Indeed I think there are not many who considered the marriage state as seriously as I did – I am far from opinion that our Happiest Days are spent in virginity or courtship but on the contrary I think where two Beings are united who have one heart, one mind, one soul the married state is much more lovable.[46]

Mary gave the newlyweds a stunning present to help them begin their lives together. As she neared her fiftieth birthday, she was moving from wealth creation to wealth distribution, and she gifted the newlyweds two hundred acres (eighty hectares) of farmland along the Hawkesbury in Wilberforce,[47] land that included Bushells Lagoon. She had a team of workmen begin construction there of Reibeycroft, a large colonial Georgian farmhouse with a central hall, four rooms downstairs, an attic with two bedrooms and three windows on each side of the house. The men also erected a barn, with huge uprights and crossbeams made from bush timber, as well as a dairy.[48]

Jane had a great desire to visit Britain like her mother and sisters before her, and to experience 'Caledonia's long Famed Lakes & Valleys'.[49] Work at Reibeycroft was taking up all her time, though. The farmhouse had become a glorious place in a peaceful setting, far removed from the wars with the First Peoples, but there was tragedy behind the idyll. The wars were over but only because large numbers of the Dharug had been killed by gunfire or diseases imported by the settlers. The Presbyterian minister and political activist John Dunmore Lang would soon write that 'There is black blood at this moment on the hands of individuals of good repute in the colony of New South Wales of which all the waters of New Holland would be insufficient to wash out the indelible stains.'[50]

Mary often visited the Atkinsons on the Hawkesbury, accompanied by her youngest daughter Betsey and her niece Eliza Foster, who lived with the Reibeys in Sydney whenever her parents were in Van Diemen's Land. Mary always dreaded the scrutiny of Sydney neighbours who looked down on her for her convict past but with her family on the river, she was free. They would while away the afternoons, drifting down the Hawkesbury in a small boat as the sun set over the shining water. Mary would bring bread and butter in the boat, then collect oysters from the rocks and make sandwiches for a cheap family dinner.[51]

It was in this serene setting that Jane's first child, John Reibey Atkinson,[52] was born at Reibeycroft eighteen months after her wedding. In a spirit of benevolence that the family outings fostered, Mary soon became involved in a campaign to establish the Free Grammar School in Sydney, an institution that would eventually become Sydney Grammar.

The idea for the school had been put forward by the thoroughly disreputable sixty-year-old Laurence Halloran, an Irishman who at times pretended to be a priest and had been transported in 1819 for counterfeiting. But Simeon Lord and John Macarthur had befriended the scoundrel, and they regarded him a first-rate schoolteacher. After repeated libel suits and stints in prison brought on by debt, Halloran needed a well-paying job; he advertised in September 1825 for help in establishing a public grammar school under the patronage of the governor. He asked for thirty trustees to subscribe £50.

Halloran was gushing in his praise for his backers, and on his published list of the 'gentlemen' who became trustees was one 'Mrs M Reibey'.[53] The others included Macarthur, Simeon Lord, Gregory Blaxland, William Lawson, and the explorer John Oxley, who had just made his second expedition along a serpentine river that he named after Governor Brisbane.

There were limits to Mary's generosity. She was busy finding tenants for three farms outside Launceston, each of 300 acres (120 hectares) – 'beautiful, fertile spots', she said, with advantages to new emigrants 'too obvious to require any eulogizing'. She warned the public, though, about trespassing on any of the land or other parts of her 2040-acre estate, 'by cattle, carts, or cutting down timber ... as all Persons so offending will be prosecuted with the utmost rigour of the Law'.[54]

THE REIBEY FAMILY, now back at Macquarie place, rallied around young widower Tom Wills, their friend from childhood. Within a few months he had lost his mother, Sarah, wife Celia, only child Alice, best friend George Reibey and stepfather George Howe. There was always work to help him mask the pain. James had formed a partnership with young Wills, and together they had paid £2000 for the East Indiaman trading vessel *John Bull*,[55] which had been built in Calcutta and had carried convicts from Bengal to Port Jackson. In July 1824, the *Sydney Gazette* proclaimed that it was the 'first ship ever belonging, exclusively, to Currency Lads': the first generation of Australians born to settlers, emancipists or convicts.[56]

Before long, Tom Reibey Jr was preparing to follow the example of his father, and undertake a trading voyage to Mauritius and possibly Canton.[57] He wanted to get away from Australia for a while and thought a long sea voyage would help him move past 'the lowness of spirit'[58] caused by the deaths of his brother and sister. He planned to take the *John Bull* on his voyage.

James Reibey, like his mother, played hard in business. In March 1825, Ann Mason – one of his assigned servants in Van Diemen's Land – was charged with neglect of duty, as well as insolence to James's wife Rebecca, herself a convict's daughter; Ann was ordered to be confined on bread and water for a week, then sent to the Female Factory workhouse at George Town.[59] James's mood would grow worse over the next few months.

At the end of April the cutter *Eclipse*, which James also owned with his brother-in-law John Atkinson, sailed from Port Dalrymple for Sydney under his command, and with Rebecca, his sister Eliza, her children, and a load of sealskins and salt. After James disembarked with the passengers, he sent the ship up the coast to take on a load of coal in Newcastle. The *Eclipse* moored in the harbour, and convicts loaded the coal from lighters. But at 9 a.m. on Wednesday, 11 May 1825, a gang of thirteen prisoners – three of them skilled sailors – overpowered the master and crew, smashed the irons from their own legs, and made their escape in brisk winds.[60] The settlement was poorly equipped with vessels. When the sentries realised that the ship was being stolen, every effort was made to send a boat after it at great haste – but all the crews were manned by convicts, and the chase was made in slow motion.[61]

While James waited for news of the pursuit, expecting the *Eclipse* to be overtaken at any time by a government vessel, he and Rebecca stayed with Mary at the house in Macquarie Place. She was glad to have a very big house; she told David Hope on 19 June[62] because she was hosting a large group. Tom Jr, his wife Richarda, their three children and three servants were there after he'd just sailed the *John Bull* back to Sydney with a load of Isle of France sugar and wine from Mauritius.[63] Eliza Thomson and her two children, three-year-old Mary and baby James,[64] along with her servants were also staying with Mary, as well as Mary's youngest daughter Betsey, and Mary's niece Eliza Foster and Mary's three household servants. Any day, John and Jane Atkinson were expected to stop in for a week or two, as well.[65]

Eliza Thomson had brought her daughter Mary Helen to Sydney for an operation after the little girl had badly scalded her hand; the skin had compacted and needed cutting.[66] Her son James was ten months old and 'remarkably stout and healthy', a boy unlike any in the world – at least according to his father Lieutenant Thomson, who was 'not a little proud of him'. Eliza told everyone she was blissfully happy in her marriage to 'a kind and affectionate partner'.[67] She was in for quite a shock.

So too was her brother James. Government officials told him that they suspected the *Eclipse* was headed for Timor, but no sign of it or the thirteen pirates was ever seen again. He and John Atkinson initially claimed a loss of £1000 worth of business when the vessel went missing, but the payout was constantly stalled. After the ship was finally declared gone for good, James and Atkinson had to wait ten years to receive a land grant of 640 acres (255 hectares) as compensation from a negligent government for the lost ship.[68] James considered the amount 'paltry' and the land worth just a fraction of the vessel that had disappeared without trace.[69] He complained that he had made repeated claims to Governor Brisbane but that Brisbane was a 'forgetful man'.[70]

MARY BEGAN TO TAKE a back seat in business, leaving more and more of the trading operations to her sons and sons-in-law. Her 'Astma' attacks were getting worse, and while they were manageable she feared her health was in decline.[71] But Tom Wills was in an even worse state. He had never recovered from the loss of Celia and had started to look so poorly that Mary feared he would soon follow his wife to the burial ground.

Her youngest daughter Betsey, now fifteen, was growing into the spitting image of her late sister. Mary would often take her girls to pray for their dear departed siblings and listen to the fiery sermons of the Presbyterian minister Archibald Macarthur. Mary thought him a good and clever man 'but rather too violent in the pulpit', and feared his powerful oratory would 'Ingure his lungs'.[72]

Mary started 1826 with a huge sale of her merchandise amid rumours that Brisbane's replacement as governor, General Ralph Darling,[73] was willing to pay £5000 for her home in Macquarie Place in order to turn it into a new Customs House.[74] On his way to take charge in Sydney, Darling had arrived at Hobart Town in November 1825 and declared that Van Diemen's Land would now be a separate colony to New South Wales. He reached Sydney on 17 December, two weeks after Brisbane had sailed for Scotland.

The rumour about Darling wanting to buy Mary's house proved hollow, but much of the furniture from the home – a sofa, bedsteads, tables, chairs, elegant window curtains, damask satin sofa and chair covers, an elegant sideboard, a Brussels carpet, and an Indian floor mat – went on the market. So did a set of *Encyclopaedia Britannica*, since George no longer had need of it.[75]

Mary still played the Sydney real estate market when she sensed a good deal. On New Year's Day 1827, she took over a 2700-square metre parcel of land that John Macarthur had along George Street, bounded on one side by 'the stream leading to the Tanks'.[76]

Macarthur's wealth had grown further with the establishment of his Australian Agricultural Company, which had a capital of £1 million. The company would soon open Australia's first railway in Newcastle. Macarthur still frequently clashed with authority, and Governor Darling – a heavy-handed military man who banned theatre and was accused of torturing prisoners – called the sheep baron 'a wayward child' who 'remains at home brooding, but I expect is not altogether idle'.[77]

Mary, however, wasn't bluffed by Macarthur's reputation as a 'perturbator'. For the George Street property she gave him £1000, what she considered a fair price and not a penny more. There were bull sharks in the Parramatta River, and she'd told David Hope there were sharks on land too: that many of the new migrants coming free to New South Wales were worse 'than the most depraved convicts' and went about swindling anyone they could.[78] She would soon find a swindler close to home who would cause her immense grief.

Chapter 18

MARY WAS NOW FIFTY years old, and though much had changed in the thirty-five years since she'd been escorted off the *Royal Admiral*, Sydney remained a harsh and often unforgiving place. Despite Mary's wealth, and her long history in the colony, she was given no openings into the upper reaches of high society, and Governor Darling's social circle was nothing like the egalitarian melting pot that had been Macquarie's table. Mary did not have the speech, or the spelling, or the social background to be invited to the best parties. She didn't mind. James Reibey called Governor Darling 'the most ferocious tyrant that ever governed a Colony',[1] and convicts suffered far more under him than they had under Macquarie or Brisbane – yet crime abounded.

Mary's sister Betty knew that more than most. Australia had not been the promised land for Betty as it had been for her little convict sister. The vagaries of the Australian climate often made farming soul destroying, and Betty and her husband Charles Foster had returned from Van Diemen's Land to try to make a life in New South Wales. Betty's millinery did not fare well – perhaps because of her abrasive personality – and Charles, a worn-out sixty-six year old, found work as a wheelwright along the Nepean.

On the night of 19 August 1827, with a court case approaching in which Charles was to give evidence against cattle thieves, he stumbled out of Delany's public house, near the river at Emu Ford, 'greatly inebriated'.[2] The following day, two men discovered the

James Reibey called Governor Darling (pictured)
'the most ferocious tyrant that ever governed a Colony'.
State Library of NSW FL3239587

body of the old Lancastrian floating in about four feet of water, close to the ferry dock. His corpse was hauled out onto the riverbank, and because of delays in securing a doctor to conduct an examination, it lay there in the open for five days, creating a gut-turning stench.

Finally a doctor examined the body carefully. The face was bruised, and a deep wound 'as if inflicted by some blunt instrument' was obvious on the back of the head, 'wide enough to admit three fingers of a man's hand'.[3] In the doctor's opinion there appeared little doubt that Charles's death had been 'accelerated by violence'. From the appearance of the body, the doctor ruled that Charles had been murdered and thrown into the water. The case remains unsolved.

MANY OF THE LAWS IN Sydney remained just as harsh as they had been in Britain when Mary had gone on trial as James Burrow all those years earlier. On 24 March 1828, William Johnson, a murderer, and George Kilroy and William Smith – highwaymen who were confederates of the Wild Colonial Boy, Jack Donohoe faced the hangman in the parade ground of Sydney Gaol, on the corner of George and Essex streets in the Rocks. Donohoe had been due to join them but had escaped to become the most notorious bandit in the land. Mary read in the *Gazette* that the three ashen-faced prisoners declined the opportunity of addressing 'the multitude assembled for the purpose of witnessing the dreadful spectacle'.[4]

After all three were consoled by religious ministers, they were gathered together on the gallows. At twenty minutes to 10 a.m. the pin that supported the drop was withdrawn, and all three fell. Johnson and Kilroy came to a shuddering halt with snapped necks either side of Smith, but his rope broke halfway along its length. Smith fell senseless against the foot of the gallows with a huge welt across his neck. The other two dangled lifeless above him. Under the sentence of the law, they had to hang for a good half-hour to ensure they were dead.

After a few moments – with the gaolers standing around Smith's crumpled, pathetic, unmoving form, unsure of what to do – the wretched man recovered, shaken but conscious that he had somehow cheated death. Perhaps the padre's prayers for him had worked.[5] The noose was taken off. Breathing a heavy sigh of relief, Smith sat down on one of the three coffins beside the gallows.

Just as Smith was starting to thank his good fortune, the sheriff told him that he'd need to have another dance on the rope. Given the ordeal Smith had just endured, and with the two corpses having gone black in the face as they circled slowly under the creaking beam, the Reverend Cowper – who had married two of Mary's children – rushed over to Government House to seek mercy from Governor Darling. But Darling said he couldn't interfere with the operation of the law.

The bodies of Johnson and Kilroy were lowered from the gallows and placed in coffins, and the drop readjusted. Smith was assisted back up to the platform. A new rope was checked for any damage. A noose was tied, and Smith dropped again. This time, he was dead.[6]

His fate sent a shudder through Sydney, amid calls for executioners to use a better quality of rope.[7] For Mary, the horror story reinforced her appreciation for the good fortune that had landed her in the colonies rather than a shallow grave in Stafford.

The arrival of a new Governor of New South Wales, Major General Richard Bourke,[8] on 3 December 1831, would usher in a more enlightened age for the emancipists and convicts. Bourke would follow Macquarie's example, limiting floggings to fifty lashes and easing the harsh working conditions many convicts had endured under Darling.

AT THE TIME, SYDNEY was going through a real estate boom, and rents were at a premium. While Mary had eased back on her trading activities in imported goods, she always knew the art of a property deal and the right time to cash in. She was now letting out her old home and warehouse in Macquarie Place, the former Bank of New South Wales, to John Macarthur's Australian Agricultural Company[9] on a three-year arrangement, and she'd won public praise for the 'spacious, elegant mansion very recently run up ... adjoining the Custom-house' near the site of the First Fleet's landing place.

The *Gazette* declared that 'between the erection of splendid edifices, and the ramification of children, and grand-children, no respectable Colonist has ever done more than Mrs. REIBEY to "ADVANCE AUSTRALIA"'.[10] The paper declared that 'with a perseverance and spirit of enterprise that truly astonishes us, after having erected many elegant and substantial buildings in Macquarie-place, near the King's Wharf, and in the centre of George-street', Mary had 'now turned her attention towards the improvement of Castlereagh street, where a noble pile of buildings will soon ornament this hitherto neglected part of the capital'.[11] Reibey's Cottages became well known as 'airy and genteel Dwelling-houses'.[12]

There was further public praise from William Charles Wentworth's new newspaper, *The Australian*, for the 'architectural beauty' and 'Ionic elegance' of Mary's 'row of lofty and spacious houses [that] within a very little time' had sprung up in George Street in 1828,[13] on the fifty metres of street frontage land she'd leased from Macarthur and had since taken over. The paper commented that 'the rapidity with which the whole of that fine row of houses in Pitt-street, lately built by Mr. Samuel Terry,[14] as well as those by Mrs Reibey, in George-street, have been let to respectable tenants, and at handsome rents, exhibits proof of astonishing demand for houses, and a spirit for building. Rents in every part of Sydney are now exceedingly high'.[15]

Like Mary, Samuel Terry – known as 'The Botany Bay Rothschild' – was a convict turned wealthy merchant and landowner. While a labourer in Manchester, he'd been convicted of stealing four hundred pairs of stockings and sentenced to transportation for seven years. He had worked under Samuel Marsden's direction in a stonemason gang at Parramatta, cutting rocks for the church, and Terry was both flogged for neglect and rewarded for hard work. By 1828 he was a fabulously wealthy philanthropist with property across the colony, including a bloodstock horse stud in the Illawarra region.

This was where Mary now set her sights, despite the problems she'd had with bushrangers in the area. They had stolen two of her mares from her land at Airds and were using them as packhorses to carry their plunder. In August 1828, bandits robbed one of her servants on the road from Appin to the Illawarra, stealing all his clothes, provisions and money, as well as two mules. 'This reflects disgrace not only on the 13 soldiers stationed at Shoal Haven, but on the imbecile constables of Appin,' opined a reader of a new biweekly Sydney newspaper, *The Monitor*,[16] which Edward Smith Hall was publishing after having left his job – and its long hours – at the Bank of New South Wales.

MARY'S YOUNGEST DAUGHTER Elizabeth – whom the family called Betsey and whom the press called 'an amiable young lady of fortune'[17] – married Irish-born Lieutenant Joseph Long Innes[18] at the elegant Greenway-designed St James' Church on 5 May 1829.[19] Betsey was nineteen and, according to *The Australian*, 'one of the daughters of Mrs. Reibey, who has been not only amongst our oldest, but most valuable Colonists, of which the numerous handsome, edifices about Sydney, and extensive and highly improved farms, in various quarters; up the country, bear ample and honorable testimony'.[20]

Innes, known unkindly by his comrades as 'Pegleg' because he had lost a limb, was the son of a major in the Londonderry Militia and had been raised at a military college in Ireland. Thirteen years older than Betsey, he was the Adjutant of the 39th Dorsetshire Foot Regiment, which had brought convicts to Sydney. As a wedding present, Mary gave the couple the houses she had recently built on George Street as well as a farm; together these provided a guaranteed income of £270 a year before Innes's salary as a soldier, which was about the same.[21] The first of the seven Innes children, Bessey,[22] was born nine months later.

Every large colonial family faced joy and sorrow with the changing seasons. In 1829, Mary's one-year-old grandson George Atkinson died at her George Street home after a 'short and acute illness',[23] aged just sixteen months, leaving the little chap's parents devastated. John Atkinson had never been in the best of health – he had been beset by a liver problem for years – and now his constitution was even worse.

In Launceston, James was given up for dead by three doctors after suffering an inflammation of the bowel; he claimed he only survived by a miracle.[24] He was also plagued by painful, crippling gout,[25] and a 'harassed state of mind'[26] caused by the criminal actions of Eliza's charming husband Lieutenant Thomas Thomson.

James said he'd always been suspicious of the lazy lieutenant. Thomson's income as assistant treasurer[27] in Van Diemen's Land was a little under £300 a year, but he lived as though he was earning three times that.[28] James had spent much of 1829 warning his brother-in-law about his lifestyle, but that had only served to irritate and alienate Thomson. Inevitably the government had begun looking into Thomson's finances, and the axe came down after it was found that he had pilfered thousands of pounds from the treasury.

Thomson was thrown into gaol and told that his theft was a capital crime.[29] Eliza was just about to deliver their fifth child. The government seized much of their property, including everything Mary had given the young family, and sold it – including all the cattle, as well as all the wheat that Mary had planned to sell in Sydney. Even with the sale of the cattle and grain, Thomson was still well short on the money he'd embezzled. Mary came forward to pay off some of the debts to the tune of £2000, only to find that one of Thomson's uncles had also been racking up debts in his name. James and Tom Jr offered to pay off the remaining arrears to keep Thomson out of prison but estimated it would put them £1000 out of pocket.

Thomson and Eliza were still living at *Rosetta*, the home Mary had saved for him, but James said that he had run out of patience with Eliza's husband because he was 'so extravagant and careless' and 'so lazy and useless a being that he cannot turn his hand to anything'.[30] This was in stark contrast to James and especially Tom Jr, who now had possession of twelve thousand acres (4800 hectares).[31] His prized Devon cattle – bred for meat and milk – made up the largest dairy herd in Van Diemen's Land,[32] and he had a reputation as a great philanthropist.[33]

Mary sailed down to help out Thomson, Eliza and their children with living expenses – and kick Thomson in the pants – as often as she could. She complained to her sons, and to cousin David Hope, that the smart young army officer, who had once showed so much promise, remained as 'idle as ever' and that her poor Eliza, saddled with so many youngsters to support, was now 'a young Creature [facing] a miserable prospect' in life.[34] Mary told Thomson to his face that while he was 'kind and affectionate', it took real 'exertions and activity' to support such a large family, and that if he'd had the same work ethic as Eliza 'they might have been amongst the first people in the Colony'. Sadly, Thomson was 'fit for nothing', and his farm was woefully neglected.[35]

Some of the money Mary used to pay off Thomson's debts came from a five-year lease she had recently signed to rent out her Macquarie Place property to the Church of England's School Corporation Trustees. The British government had established a Church and School Corporation in Australia under Archdeacon Thomas Hobbes Scott,[36] and New South Wales had set aside one-seventh of Crown lands to support the clergy and their schools.[37] The rent was £250 a year,[38] but at the end of the term in 1834 Mary threatened legal action, claiming that the Corporation hadn't made the necessary repairs as agreed to in the lease, and that as a result she would have to repair windows, walls and doors to make the property tenantable again.[39]

Mary had initially tried to rent the property to the government again as a new Customs House but had been told by the Collector of Customs that it wasn't close enough to 'the present landing place'.[40] Instead, the Customs House was moved to a building in Argyle Street at the Rocks owned by the solicitor and merchant Frederick Unwin. The collection of customs had been in disarray for some time. Like Mary's son-in-law in Launceston, John Piper – the army officer with the magnificent home on a point of Sydney Harbour – had become mired in debt. He had been forced to resign as chairman of the Bank of New South Wales in 1827 and as the man in charge of customs after an enquiry into his financial affairs. He tried to drown himself off North Head but was rescued and saw out his days on a farm in Bathurst.

Just as Mary had done on the Hawkesbury, she busied herself putting together large farms along the Shoalhaven River, about two hundred kilometres south of Sydney. By 1829 she had a 1600-acre property, Illaroo, on the northern bank of the Shoalhaven, with ten horses, 130 head of cattle, and plenty more to come. Eleven people – four of them convicts – were employed to look after the stock and buildings, which were valued at £350.[41] The property comprised a grant of 1100 acres, along with a further five hundred that Mary had purchased. In the same year she had made moves to buy another 1460 acres at five shillings each. Six years after that, she bought another 640 acres of magnificent coastal country. On the southern bank of the river, she had a further eight hundred acres she called Burrier Farm.

Mary ran a tight ship there as she did on all her properties, demanding hard work from her staff. When one of her overseers on the Shoalhaven, Alexander Mackey, applied for convict labour to be assigned to him to help on what he said was his leased property, Mary objected, telling the colonial secretary that Mackey wasn't leasing Burrier but merely 'superintending' it, and that he didn't have the authority to apply for convict labour. His application was subsequently refused.[42]

Though well past the age of fifty, Mary famously rode on horseback from the village of Bong Bong, near present-day Moss Vale, to inspect her land in Burrier.[43] She eased her way down the mountain spurs in a journey that would make many seasoned riders quake with fear. Mary never forgot how to ride a horse – it's what brought her to Australia in the first place.[44]

MARY'S SISTER BETTY continued to struggle in the years after her husband's murder. Her eldest daughter Jane[45] had married a ship's captain, William Patten, and together they ran a pub in Launceston. But in the words of James Reibey, Patten had turned out to be 'a drunken beast'.[46]

Following the death of her husband, Betty had moved into the Sydney home of her youngest daughter Eliza[47] and wealthy American son-in-law Timothy Pitman,[48] just down George Street from some of Mary's properties there. Pitman was a Bostonian but in Sydney became a naturalised subject of Britain,[49] and he was busy building his own wharf and stores at Darling Harbour.[50] He was 'a most excellent man',[51] according to James, who feared his cousin Eliza would not live long as she was 'in deep consumption'. He was right. On her passing on 26 January 1830, he said that she was 'the only good one of that [Foster] family'.[52]

Betty carried a shipload of bitterness wherever she went. James despaired at the effect she was having on the Reibey family, telling David Hope in Glasgow that his aunt was a 'devil incarnate', and that it was an 'unhappy circumstance for our family' that the Fosters ever came to Australia.[53] Following Eliza Pitman's death, Betty gave Mary a reprieve for a while and moved back to Van Diemen's Land where her eldest son Thomas had arrived with his wife and young family from Salford to work the land.

Mary's son-in-law Tom Wills, still mourning the loss of Celia, left Sydney for a pastoral run, Varroville, in the Minto district south-west of Sydney. For a while, his brother Horatio combined his work on the *Sydney Gazette* and his own newspaper, the *Currency Lad*. But in 1833, Horatio joined his brother at Varroville, believing there was more money in pastoralism than in small-town journalism, even though Sydney now had a population of sixteen thousand.[54]

From 1834, Horatio held a pastoral lease in the Molonglo district, about three hundred kilometres south of Sydney, on an area that became known as Canberra. It was here that his first son was born in 1835. Horatio named the boy Thomas Wentworth Wills,[55] in honour of both his brother and William Charles Wentworth, who shared Horatio's republican ideas of independence from Britain. Soon Horatio began a four-month overland trek to the Grampians region in the Port Phillip District of what is now Victoria, taking with him his wife Elizabeth and their young son Tom, as well as drovers, shepherds and Aboriginal stockmen to tend his five thousand sheep and five hundred cattle. In later years, young Tom Wills would attend Rugby School and Cambridge University in England, become a champion cricketer, and then most famously become a major figure in kicking off a new sport called Australian Rules football, which was perhaps influenced by a game he had played as a child with young Indigenous children.

Jane and John Atkinson and their rapidly expanding family had also uprooted and moved on. They leased out the Reibeycroft farm Mary had given them in Wilberforce and, from 1832, made their new home in Launceston, where John could partner the Reibey brothers in their trading ventures.

AS MARY NEARED HER sixtieth birthday, she continued to speculate in real estate as a way of guaranteeing the financial futures of her children and grandchildren. She still dabbled in business and hoped to open a 'Chymist & Druggist'[56] in Sydney – but her cousin Robert Hargreaves was slow sending out 'a little medicin' from England, and others beat her to the idea.

Mary toured her properties as often as she could. She offered a reward of £20 to capture 'some evil-disposed person or persons unknown' who had torched two stacks of wheat on her Hawkesbury farm near Wilberforce.[57] In December 1835[58] she bought two thirty-acre (12 hectare) land parcels about ten kilometres west of her George Street home, in a country setting on the Lane Cove River; the secluded bush spot was called Hunters Hill. Over time she stretched her landholding there to 110 acres (45 hectares) and made significant improvements.[59] It was a quiet, relaxing place for her and her family to watch the river roll by as convict workmen tended her garden and fruit trees. She named the property Figtree Farm after a Port Jackson fig growing by the river. In 1836 she had two small cottages built to house her convict workers. As she did with most of her properties, she planned to improve them substantially and then sell at a considerable profit.

She found another tenant for Macquarie Place after her unhappy parting with the Church and School Corporation. The New South Wales Treasurer and Auditor General, along with their teams, soon moved into the original Entally.[60] The house would also be used as a temporary office for the Royal Exchange.[61] A house that Mary had built at the rear of the property[62] was taken by the ship's captain John Hardman Lister,[63] whose youngest child was born there.[64]

Mary knew, to the penny, the value of her land. Satisfied with the work at Hunters Hill, she placed the following newspaper advertisement for an auction.

Mrs. Reibey's very pretty Figtree Farm, between Tarban Creek and Lane Cove River,

BY ISAAC SIMMONS & CO., at the Royal Hotel, on WEDNESDAY, the 15th August, 1838, at 12 o'clock precisely, consisting of

All that valuable and exceedingly compact Freehold estate in the County of Cumberland, containing 110 acres, situate in the parish of Hunter's Hill, about two and a half miles distant from Kissing Point Church, the new Lunatic Asylum, and Bedlam Ferry ...

The situation of this Property, and its adaptation for Villas, Orchards, and Market Gardens, exhibits a pre-eminence beyond most others in the neighbourhood, the outlay and improvements thereon have been very considerable and the fertility and produce of the Garden very profitable.

The upper Cottage and Verandah (30 x 24) is built upon a beautiful elevation which overlooks the diversified views and curves of the river; to the north the eye expands over an extensive reach met by romantic bluff Hills, and immediately before the door, on the opposite side of the river, a circular Terrace, called Blackwall, produced by the sinuosities of the Coves; down the river south, you have the same enlivening prospects, with alternate water views of unusual magnificence

Title-Freehold.

TERMS – £200 Cash, and the remainder to lie at interest for any length of time the buyer may propose.[65]

But the auction offers didn't meet Mary's reserve. For the next three years she leased Figtree Farm to the artist Joseph Fowles,[66] newly arrived from England.

At the same time, moves were afoot to erect a circular quay that would stretch across Sydney Cove and cover the Tank Stream that flowed past Mary's home. Some of her Macquarie Place allotment along with the properties of her neighbours – including Simeon Lord and Prosper de Mestre – were to be resumed in order to create roads for the quay, until the

Legislative Council's 'Macquarie Place Property Committee' decided that the land was too expensive. Mary's two houses on the block were valued at £2000 and the land underneath them at £6500; not long after, a reassessment valued the houses and land at £9700.[67]

TOM REIBEY JR WAS ALSO looking for a new home to rent. While Mary was warning Joseph Fowles to treat her property with the utmost care, Tom Jr was in London with Richarda and their two boys: Thomas Reibey III, who was seventeen, and James, fifteen. Tom Jr's daughter Mary Allen Reibey, now twenty, was married to Charles Arthur,[68] the nephew of the former Lieutenant-Governor of Van Diemen's Land.

Tom Jr's boys had been educated at the Longford School, south of Launceston, but he and Richarda were looking to broaden their horizons and give them the best education in the world. Tom Jr could afford to. A few years earlier he'd paid his father-in-law Tom Collicott £250 for the 500-acre farm Bristol Park at Carrick, a few miles from his Entally in Van Diemen's Land.[69] Tom had renamed it Liffey Farm and transferred it to Richarda's sister Jane Kerkham as a gift.

In London, Tom Jr found a cottage at the Canterbury Villas in Edgware Road[70] and made it his family's English base. He visited as many of his Hope relatives as he could.[71] He was unhappy with the schooling his sons initially received in London, as it seemed tailored for much younger boys; he planned to send them instead to the Reverend Barnes in Devonshire, a private teacher highly recommended by his son-in-law and the whole Arthur family. The tuition wasn't cheap at 120 guineas a boy per year, but Barnes treated his students as his family, and there were only six boys in his class, 'all highly respectable'.[72]

While the Reibeys were in England, great changes were again taking place in Australia. At the southern tip of the mainland of New South Wales, along a river called the Yarra, a Van Diemen's Land bounty hunter named John Batman claimed he had swapped forty pairs of blankets, forty-two tomahawks, one hundred and thirty knives, sixty-two pairs of scissors, forty looking glasses, two hundred and fifty handkerchiefs, eighteen shirts, four flannel jackets, four suits of clothes, and one hundred and fifty pounds of flour for 600,000 acres of land belonging to the Kulin people. It was soon a village named after the British Prime Minister, Viscount Melbourne.[73]

While Governor Bourke had championed the rights of convicts and emancipists, he was not so concerned with the welfare of the First Peoples. He declared any land treaties with Indigenous people void and implemented the doctrine of terra nullius by proclaiming that while Indigenous people had lived on the land, it had belonged to no one prior to the British Crown taking possession of it. Indigenous people were not permitted to sell or assign the land, nor could an individual Indigenous person acquire it, other than through distribution by the Crown.[74]

Massacres of the First Peoples still occurred, especially in areas far from authority. In the New England area of New South Wales, about six hundred kilometres north-west of Sydney, a marauding band of a dozen stockmen had been riding about indiscriminately killing as many of the First Peoples as they could in what they saw as retaliation for attacks on settlers and stock. All of the stockmen were convicts or former convicts, except their leader John Henry Fleming,[75] who had grown up not far from the Reibey property in Pitt Town on the Hawkesbury[76] and was now working on a cattle run near Moree.

On 10 June 1838, the band of killers rode into the Myall Creek station, near the present-day town of Inverell. They found a camp of about thirty-five members of the Weraerai group – mostly children and old men and women – who belonged to the Kamilaroi people and who had been living peacefully among the local European settlers for some months. The younger Aboriginal men were away working at another station. Some of the Indigenous people at Myall Creek that day were known by European names. Fleming's raiders didn't care about any of that. Using swords to save on ammunition, they slaughtered twenty-eight of the defenceless Weraerai, beheading most of the children, and forcing their mothers and grandparents to run a gauntlet of self-proclaimed sword-wielding executioners.

While some of the settlers and even some of the Sydney papers applauded the murders, a neighbouring squatter rode for days down to Sydney to report the crime to a new governor, Sir George Gipps,[77] who demanded action. Although five of the killers, including Fleming, managed to avoid punishment, seven of them were hanged together at the Sydney Gaol on 18 December 1838, after the Chief Justice of New South Wales, James Dowling, told the jury that the law made no distinction between the murder of an Indigenous person and the murder of a European person.[78] It wasn't the first time that Europeans were executed for killing Indigenous people,[79] but it was a landmark moment in the New South Wales judicial system.

For Mary Reibey, the brutality of life in New South Wales was a distant memory. For her the colony had always been a place where hard work and a fair share of luck could mend lives and create fortunes. Mary had seen enormous changes in the colony since her arrival, allowing her and her family wonderful opportunities. Now, in Britain, the private tuition for the Reibey boys paid handsome dividends. In 1840, the grandsons of a horse thief were the first Australians to be admitted into Trinity College, Oxford.[80] But they would soon experience great shocks.

Chapter 19

AS MARY APPROACHED her mid-sixties, a retreat to somewhere more bucolic than central Sydney beckoned, along with a welcome rest after a long life of hard work. Her son-in-law Captain Innes was now Sydney's superintendent of police[1] but still able to help her with some of her business interests from his office at the Carters' Barracks prison on Pitt Street in the Brickfields. The prison, comprising several buildings situated near what is now Eddy Avenue, was built to house convict gangs working as carters in the old brick fields and by the 1830s was used for male youth offenders and as a debtors' prison.

For a couple of years, Mary made her home in nearby Elizabeth Street South.[2] But the Sydney traffic was a bit too much for her – what with horses and carriages clip-clopping past her front door at all hours, along with the noise of people rushing to work, and of schoolchildren fighting and skylarking on their morning journey. Mary's asthma was just about killing her, and she was often bedridden, struggling for breath.[3] All around her, it seemed, Sydney had become a miserable place.

For the first time since the early days of settlement, the Australian colonies were facing food shortages and an economic collapse.[4] This upheaval played out against agitation from men such as William Charles Wentworth who were calling for an end to the transportation of convicts. Liberal, humanitarian views were gaining traction, and the British penal code was becoming less harsh. Sending poor, hungry people across the world for stealing a loaf of bread was now seen by Whitehall as manifestly unfair, and transportation was reserved for more serious offences. Consequently, most convicts arriving in Sydney were no longer petty thieves but rather dangerous, hardened criminals whose presence in work parties along the streets beside the harbour threatened the safety of the general population. After protests and agitation from some of Australia's leading citizens opposed to their home remaining a dumping ground for British gaols, an Order in Council was finally signed, in London on 22 May 1840, prohibiting transportation to the east coast of Australia.[5] Convicts continued pouring into Van Diemen's Land for many more years.[6]

Changes to the penal code came at a time when the expansion of the Australian pastoral and whaling industries along with the rapid spread of land settlement had fuelled the establishment of colonial banks and an influx of British investment. But Australia had been producing more wool than it could sell, and a crippling drought in the late 1830s had necessitated wheat imports. Property prices went over the cliff, and insolvencies weakened

Augustus Earle's study of a jail gang in 1830. By the time Earle produced it, most of the prisoners coming to Australia were no longer petty thieves, but dangerous, hardened criminals. *National Library of Australia nla.obj-135316395*

the many new banks: six of them failed.[7] The price of meat fell
to a penny a pound; sheep sold for a shilling a head, cows for
five shillings. Settlers everywhere weren't even attempting to sell
their livestock but instead were killing their animals and boiling
down the carcasses for the fat to export as oil.[8] Cash was king,
and Mary was one of a dwindling number of colonists with plenty
in reserve.

The conditions were ripe for another Reibey real estate coup.
Doctors told Mary that fresh breezes away from the foetid town
air would do her lungs the world of good. She owned large
farms on the Hawkesbury and Shoalhaven Rivers, at Airds, and
on the Liverpool Road towards the Cowpastures,[9] but she had
in mind a country estate much closer to town.

Back in 1840, Sydney's town surveyor, Felton Mathew,[10]
had taken up an appointment as New Zealand's first surveyor
general; he was tasked with mapping out a town named after
George Eden, the Earl of Auckland. Mathew auctioned off his
country home, the Pencilville Estate, situated on the outskirts
of Sydney in Newtown, about six kilometres south-west
from Mary's home in Macquarie Place. The advertisements
for Pencilville described it as 'A desirable Residence comprising
a newly built stone House, with all necessary and convenient
Offices, and about ten acres of land cleared and chiefly under
cultivation; there is an abundant and never-failing supply of
water. The House is fit for the reception of a respectable family,
and immediate possession will be given.'[11] Mathew's 'beautiful
and commodious Villa'[12] and all the land was snapped up for
£3000 by William Montagu Manning,[13] a barrister and real
estate investor who came to own large slices of New South Wales
and went on to be the colony's solicitor general. But Manning's
purchases of 1200 acres (486 hectares) in Mulgoa, another 1000
acres (405 hectares) in the Illawarra, and fifty house allotments
in Kiama left him short of ready funds. In June 1842, he sold
Pencilville to Mary.[14]

It was a lovely property, and everyone said it was the saving
of Mary's health. Before she had lived there very long, her

family rejoiced that she'd become 'well and stout' again.[15] On the ground floor, the home had a dining room, drawing room, sitting room, bedroom, pantry, and store. Upstairs there were three bedrooms. The house also had a detached kitchen and laundry, and servants' rooms, stables, a loft and sheds.[16]

Mary quickly tested the market again with some of her other properties.

TO BE LET OR SOLD

THOSE extensive premises in Macquarie-place, at present occupied by the Royal Exchange Company.

A commodious dwelling house in rear of the above.

An excellent farm at Lane Cove, with a neat cottage and good garden.

A farm on the Liverpool Road, nearly opposite the fifteenth mile-stone.

Terms moderate and liberal. Apply to Mrs. Reibey, Newtown; or to Captain Innes, Carters' Barracks.[17]

Few people had the money to buy such sizeable properties at the time. Of course, following the one remarkably rash decision of her life more than fifty years earlier, Mary had long ago learnt the importance of patience. Looking out across the fields of Newtown with a view stretching past her lush garden and orchard to the ocean, she had every reason to bask in the glow of her business accomplishments.

But while the twilight of her life at Pencilville promised much joy, Mary knew that money could never guarantee happiness.

MARY AND HER ELDEST son Tom Jr were justifiably proud of the young expatriates Thomas and James Reibey when they began their theological studies as part of their arts degrees at Trinity College. Both grandmother and father prayed that the boys would make fine Anglican ministers. Thomas was no scholar, and he was best remembered at Oxford for his rowing and enthusiasm for fox hunts than for academic success.[18] He was busy in other areas too; by October 1842, he was preparing to marry a nineteen-year-old Scottish lass, Kate Kyle,[19] in Plymouth. Her father was the mayor of the East Lothian village of Inveresk.[20] Meanwhile, James was courting Charlotte Bridgett Clack,[21] a reverend's daughter from Devon.

Back at his sprawling Entally estate in Hadspen outside Launceston, Tom Jr told friends that he was over the moon with the calling to God of his sons and that he had never felt better or prouder. Forty-six years had passed since Tom Jr had been born during the wars between the settlers and the First Peoples on the Hawkesbury, and he was now a magistrate and one of the wealthiest farmers in Van Diemen's Land. He was still being lauded for his philanthropy; not only had he made a large donation towards the erection of the new Christ Church in nearby Longford, but in June 1842 he'd forked out the hefty sum of £300 – the equivalent of a very good annual wage – for a peal of bells from England in its new belfry.[22] He was also offering to subsidise a new bridge across the South Esk at Reibey's Ford for the benefit of his local community.[23]

On the morning of 3 October 1842, Tom Jr was at Entally, conversing with a Launceston auctioneer and hotelier named Mainwaring Chitty. He told Chitty that he was never 'in better health'.[24] Almost immediately, Tom Jr collapsed with an apoplectic fit, suffering a brain haemorrhage. Medical assistance was summoned, but Tom Jr remained insensible until 11 a.m., when he died. 'Mr. Reibey was endeared to a large circle of friends, and highly respected by all who knew him,' his local newspaper declared. 'Liberal in his views – affable in his demeanour – and bountiful in his contributions for the promotion of good, there are few whose loss could be more extensively felt or more sincerely deplored.'[25] The news of Tom Jr's passing floored Mary, who was now ensconced in what became known as Reibey's Cottage on her farm in Newtown.

Tom Reibey Jr was buried in the cemetery at the new Longford church that he had helped to finance. His obituary remarked that he was one of the community's 'brightest ornaments, a most liberal and warm hearted leader whose princely fortune was expended with a munificent and unsparing hand for the promotion of public good'.[26] His probate stated that his assets 'did not exceed in value the sum of £12,400', and in his will he left to his wife Richarda an annuity of £300 and to his children – Mary, Thomas and James – his property.[27]

James was the only son Mary had left. At least they were on good terms, after some early estrangement over his marriage to the widow Rebecca. But James had been in poor health for some time, riddled with gout by his early forties and unable to do much work on his huge landholdings. The attacks of gout became more severe and frequent not long after the death of his brother and long-time business partner. Although James bore his 'severe affliction with remarkable fortitude',[28] he became frustrated with the medical advice he was receiving and decided to consult a new team of doctors, hoping they might furnish a solution to the agonising and immobilising pain in his joints.

On the morning of 11 September 1843, two medical men arrived at James's home on William Street, Launceston, to discuss remedies. He asked the doctors what changes he should make to his diet. As his advisers turned away to discuss a meal plan, he dropped dead from a heart attack.[29] He was just forty-five.

The last of Mary's three sons was buried in the afternoon four days later, near his brother George in Launceston's Anglican cemetery, before his mother could even be informed of his passing. His funeral was attended by what the press called 'a large number of the most respectable inhabitants of this town and its vicinity'.[30]

Mary's pain was compounded by the woes of her surviving children and grandchildren. During a break from his studies at Oxford, Thomas Reibey III arrived in Sydney with his new wife Catherine to visit Mary for three weeks, only to be told – as he dropped his luggage, poleaxed – that his father was dead.[31]

Not long after Mary's oldest grandchild stayed with her, she was visited by Eliza Thomson and her large family – including her wayward husband. Eliza was now a worn-out mother of nine, but with Mary's financial aid she and her family had just returned from a voyage to her husband's old home in Scotland so he could see it once more before he died.

Mary was still paying off some of her son-in-law's creditors years after his disgrace had been uncovered. Another of his relatives had placed £1000 in the Bank of Australia on his behalf, but the bank had just failed. There had been hopes that the Thomsons might rent out their Launceston home, Rosetta, but Thomson's daughter Mary Helen complained that no one in that town had a spare farthing during such terrible economic times.[32]

Thomson was a 49-year-old invalid. He had to be carried by two people wherever he went, and he didn't have the energy to lift a spoon to his mouth. His eyesight was gone, and either his long-suffering wife or one of his children would have to read to him.[33] In this sad state, Thomas Thomson died in Launceston on 11 July 1844.

Even after his death, Mary continued to settle his accounts with creditors whom she suspected treated her assets as though they were 'a fountain' of money.[34] 'I am obliged to pay to the last pound to meet them,'[35] she wrote, adding that 'the Bank' was very kind in giving her time to meet the debts that she hoped to clear in two or three years. She was still 'obliged to exercise the greatest prudence and ecconomy still in my old age and [after] so many years of perseverance and industry it is hard to be deprived of the many comforts I have been accustomed too'.[36]

She poured out her heart in a letter to David Hope, telling him that she regarded him more as a brother than a cousin, and that at her age her bereavements had cost her almost all 'enjoyment and social comfort' until she came to reflect that it was 'wicked and sinful to dispair'.[37]

I open my mind to you more than anyone else since the Melancholly death of all my sons – my soninlaw Mr Atkinson is living at Van Deimans Land or he would be of great assistance to me as far as advice etc: he is an excellent man a good husband good Father and the sincere friend and if we may judge by all accounts we hear the character of a honest and just man

he is a Magistrate at Launceston

dont you think that I ought to be proud of all my family turning out so respectable all my sons and soninlaws with the exception of Mr Thomson were Magistrates[38]

By mid-1845, Mary was again having to tolerate the foul temper of her sister. Betty Foster moved into Reibey's Cottage at Newtown, bringing disquiet to the home. With all the tragedies that had befallen Betty, it must have been galling to live in the large country house of the Haydock family's prodigal child.

On 21 June, Mary, now sixty-eight, was awaiting the arrival of Jane Atkinson and six of her children on a visit from Launceston. Jane was thirty-eight and had already borne ten babies; George, named after her brother, had died as an infant, and she had just buried her six-year-old, Celia,[39] named after her dearly departed sister. Several of Jane's other children were in ill health, and Mary hoped the fresh air of the Newtown farm would do them all the world of good.

John Atkinson was planning to visit Sydney in a few months to take his family there, and to accompany Mary on a visit to Launceston so she could put flowers on the graves of her sons and grandchildren. It was a strain for her to leave the comfort of Reibey's Cottage. She had increased the land around it so that she now had twenty-one acres (8.5 hectares) in Newtown, and she was forever working on the 'excellent' garden she had remade.[40]

Mary was determined that Eliza and her large family wouldn't face hardship following Thomas Thomson's death. Most of the children were small, but Eliza's oldest son James[41] was a big help to his mother. He was, Mary said, 'a very good youth and clever', working at the Bank of Australasia in Launceston – despite the scandal surrounding his father – and earning £180 a year.[42] Mary wanted all of them to prosper. She commissioned builders to start work on an impressive double-storey home in the late Colonial Regency design for Eliza and her children on the

Newtown property, near Mary's own dwelling. It would become known as Stanmore House, and it became iconic in the area. She directed the builders to install finely detailed cedar joinery, ornate fireplaces, a geometrical staircase, a fine entrance doorcase with attached columns, and ironwork and plaster ceilings.[43]

David Hope and Mary would send each other newspapers – Mary posting the *Sydney Morning Herald* to her Scottish cousin, and David replying with as many Blackburn journals as he could fit in a parcel because he knew the sheer joy it gave her to read news of her old hometown. She told him that she was completely smitten with the Newtown property; it was the best real estate deal she'd ever made and the reason her health had been so 'renovated'. The land had all been bush when she'd purchased it, with the exception of a small cultivated patch around the house, and she'd had a man erect a paling fence around her yard. 'I am now in the enjoyment of as good health as ever I was, excepting my age and it is to the salubrious air that I account it to,' she told David. 'We have a pleasant view of the Botany Bay Heads and the sea.'[44]

Stanmore House, the home Mary built for her daughters on her country estate at Newtown in Sydney. *Caroline Simpson Library & Research Collection, Sydney Living Museums*

Grandchildren were frequent visitors. At fifteen, Elizabeth Innes's eldest child, Bessey, was two inches taller 'than her mama'. At eleven, Bessey's younger brother George[45] was an outstanding student at William Timothy Cape's school on King Street, Sydney, and was about to enrol at the King's School on George Street, Parramatta. Mary predicted great things for him.

IN 1843 MARY'S eldest grandson, Thomas Reibey III, had taken over his father's Entally estate outside Launceston, and completed Tom Jr's project of building a bridge across the South Esk River; he charged a toll to recover the debt but kept the toll going long after the bridge was paid off.[46] Although he hadn't graduated from Trinity College, he preached in Van Diemen's Land as a layman.

Thomas visited Mary at Newtown in 1845 with his wife Kate and his mother Richarda. Mary had embraced the scriptures more and more as a meeting with her maker loomed, and she was almost overcome with joy when she heard her grandson give a Christian service at her local church, St Peters, on the road to Botany Bay.[47] While Thomas appeared devoted to his rural flock back home, Mary suspected that he would rather live in Sydney than Van Diemen's Land, which was now taking all the convicts coming to the eastern part of Australia. The old lady who had once been a prisoner in chains said the place was 'getting into an awful state'.[48]

After telling Anglican Bishop Francis Nixon[49] that while he did not have a degree in theology he wouldn't require a salary, as his father's properties made him more than enough money, Mary's oldest grandson became the first Van Diemonian to be ordained in the colony.[50] Thomas began his ministry in Carrick and Hadspen, holding services at a blacksmith's shop as there was no local church. He moved his church services to a brick schoolhouse on Reibey land in Carrick, and at his own cost had the building remade as a church.[51] A castellated bell tower was added later, and Thomas ordered a peal of bells from England. Kate supported her husband's ministry by playing the organ during services, with her dog Toby hiding under her skirts.[52]

MARY HAD BECOME FAR more sedate and genteel than she had been as a girl. But turmoil hit her life again with the February 1845 publication of a three-volume illustrated British book: *The history of Margaret Catchpole, a Suffolk girl.*[53] It became an immediate bestseller, and its fame quickly spread to Sydney. The author was a Suffolk clergyman, the Reverend Richard Cobbold, whose parents had once employed a farm worker and skilled horsewoman named Margaret Catchpole.

Margaret had been thirty-five in 1797, when in echoes of Molly Haydock's crime she'd ridden a stolen horse 110 kilometres from Ipswich to London. She was arrested wearing men's clothes while trying to sell the roan gelding to a London horse trader. Her death sentence was commuted to transportation for seven years. While waiting for a ship to the colony, Margaret escaped from London's Newgate Prison and went on the run disguised as a sailor. She was recaptured a few days later, again sentenced to death – and again reprieved, with her sentence this time commuted to transportation for life.

Margaret had arrived in New South Wales on board the convict transport *Nile* in June 1801. She was assigned as a cook for Commissary John Palmer and his wife Susan in Woolloomooloo, and later worked for the Rouse family on the Hawkesbury. By 1808 she was a midwife in Richmond. Five years after Governor Macquarie gave her a pardon in 1814, she died there, unmarried and in virtual anonymity.

A quarter of a century later, the Reverend Cobbold resurrected Margaret. He greatly embellished her story, making her a romantic heroine involved in a steamy love affair with a dashing smuggler. In Cobbold's version of her life, she eventually married a wealthy settler, who died and left her as the mistress of a vast fortune.

The publication had such striking parallels to Mary's own life and chequered past that it rattled her. She was a respected Sydney business leader with important family and social connections in New South Wales and Van Diemen's Land. One grandson was a priest, and another was studying at Oxford to become one. Her daughter-in-law Richarda was from the regal Allen family, her brother George Allen running the biggest legal firm in Sydney. Another son-in-law, Captain Innes, was now the superintendent of police in Sydney. Mary's granddaughter Mary Allen Reibey had married into the family of George Arthur, the former Lieutenant Governor of Van Diemen's Land. Yet despite her constant attempts to hide the true story behind her arrival in Sydney, Mary realised that many of the older colonists knew all about her horse-stealing caper.

Others were concerned about Mary's reputation, too. The Reverend H.D.D. Sparling[54] of Appin, aware of her backstory, concluded – wrongly – that Cobbold had based the story unfairly on a woman who was now a cornerstone of the Anglican community in Australia. Hoping to stop the distribution of the book in the antipodes, he contacted the Bishop of Australia, William Broughton.[55] Without mentioning the name 'Mary Reibey', Broughton wrote that it would be cruel 'to have early offences thus placed permanently on record as a memorial of shame and cause of annoyance to her younger and perfectly innocent connections'.[56] Broughton solicited the support of Bishop Nixon, in Tasmania, who had recently ordained Thomas Reibey III.

Margaret Catchpole depicted stealing a horse in Richard Cobbold's book.
Caroline Simpson Library & Research Collection, Sydney Living Museums

Despite their hopes to thwart publication, the book reached Australia in July 1845, propelled by a massive marketing fanfare. *The Sydney Morning Herald* told its readers that old colonists would have little difficulty deducing the name of the real Margaret Catchpole.[57] There had always been whispers about Mary's previous life as a horse thief – now they were amplified.

Her anxiety heightened further when Cobbold's book was soon dramatised as a play: *Margaret Catchpole, the female horse-stealer.* It was staged in theatres all over London, and on 22 October 1846 it opened at Sydney's 1900-seat Royal Victoria Theatre on Pitt Street. Mary entered 'a painful state of mind'[58] as she feared all of Sydney would not only learn of her convict past but also assume the book's bawdy tale of romance was true. She told Bishop Nixon that she should not be doubly punished for her youthful misdemeanour, and while it was true that she had taken a horse that technically wasn't hers, she explained it away as 'only a childish frolic'.[59] She said it was especially cruel to throw that juvenile misstep back in her face after her more than fifty years of exemplary conduct in the colony, while raising a large and successful family by herself, and, in the words of Bishop Broughton, being 'praiseworthy in a very high degree for exertions in the cause of religion, and of the Church of England'.[60] But the gossip generated publicity for the book, and Mary had to soldier on with her head held high.

MARY'S SECOND GRANDSON James Reibey married Charlotte Clack in Devon. After visiting Mary in Sydney, he returned to Van Diemen's Land with a Bachelor of Arts from Trinity College. He took over from Tom as the priest in Carrick. He and Charlotte were very much in love, and James Clack Reibey[61] was born soon after.

Even as a great-grandmother, Mary remained one of the most influential business identities in Australia. After years of leasing Figtree Farm, she sold it to the French trader Didier Numa Joubert, who had his own storehouse in Macquarie Place. A few years earlier at his office there, Joubert had shown off a daguerreotype camera and the first photograph taken in Australia: an image of Bridge Street taken from the Macquarie Place fountain near Mary's old home.[62] Joubert and his Mauritian wife Louise paid Mary £500 in instalments over four years for her Hunters Hill property, and in 1848 added a two-storey stone wing and paved verandah, making one house out of the two cottages. A tower was added later.

Meanwhile, the Australian Subscription Library rented Mary's original house in Macquarie Place for £300 a year,[63] while a livery stable keeper took the lease on her house behind it.[64] Then a decorator named Andrew Tourang used the rear house for his home and business, with an advertising hoarding out the front. Mary insisted that painting and water for the property were to be supplied at the tenant's expense.[65]

Concerns for her family dominated her thoughts, though. On 11 April 1849, in the 'Family Notices' section of the *Sydney Morning Herald*, Mary placed a small report that pained her enormously despite the clash of personalities that had preceded it.

DIED

At the residence of her sister, Mrs. Reibey, Newtown, on Tuesday, the 10th April, Mrs. Charles Foster, aged 77 years, after a painful and lingering illness.[66]

Fifty-seven years after a frightened convict girl had scrawled on a scrap of paper that her sister had been 'ungood' to her, Mary had comforted, supported and protected Betty in the last years of her life, watching over the sad and bitter old woman until her final breath.

Chapter 20

MARY WAS SEVENTY-FOUR when the biggest upheaval in Australia since the arrival of the First Fleet was sparked in a fast-flowing stream north-west of Bathurst. On 12 February 1851, a burly Englishman named Edward Hargraves and three companions found five specks of gold in the shallow water. When their discovery was made public, rumours of fabulous wealth all around for the taking ignited a stampede across the continent.

In Bathurst, the local newspaper reported that:

The discovery of the fact by Mr. Hargraves that the country from the mountain ranges to an indefinite extent into the interior is one immense gold field, has produced a tremendous excitement ... A complete mental madness appears to have seized almost every member of the community, and as a natural consequence there has been a universal rush to the diggins ... People of all trades, callings and pursuits, were quickly transformed into miners, and many a hand which had been trained to kid gloves, or accustomed to wield nothing heavier than the grey goose-quill became nervous to clutch the pick and crow-bar ... The blacksmiths of the town could not turn off the picks fast enough ... there appears every probability of a complete social revolution in the course of time ...[1]

Gold fever became a pandemic as a rush to Australia began around the world, fuelled by reports of men filling public troughs with champagne, putting gold shoes on their horses and using £10 notes to light their cigars.[2] The latest Governor of New South Wales, Charles Augustus FitzRoy[3] – a former military man wounded at Waterloo – complained that the gold madness had unhinged the minds of all classes in society. Before long – with the discovery of extensive goldfields west of Melbourne in Ballarat and Bendigo – thousands of workmen, in the cities and the bush, were dropping everything and rushing off as 'diggers' in the hope of finding their fortunes.

It has been estimated that within a year of Hargraves's find, more than half a million miners raced to the goldfields of Australia from overseas. Most of them were British, but there were many prospectors from the United States, Germany, Poland, and China. Diggers also arrived in New South Wales and Victoria from all parts of Australia. Wages everywhere doubled, but it was still difficult to find workers as so many had abandoned their jobs to chase their fortune on the goldfields.

Mary was not immune from the 'mental madness' gripping society. In 1852 her granddaughter Celia Innes,[4] now married to a military man named Edward Pym, wrote that people were 'mad about going to the Diggings'.

Sydney I fear for some time will be in a sad state, all the servants and labouring men were leaving and wages enormously high. The [workman] left Grandmama because she would not give him more than a pound a week besides keeping him – rather absurd is it not! … Grandmama often talks of coming to England but I do not think she ever will, indeed at her time of life it would be very foolish to risk such a long voyage. she has a very pretty place a few miles out of town [and] until the last few months has enjoyed excellent health.[5]

But Mary knew her 'excellent health' wouldn't last. She grew very fat in her old age[6] and resembled a cut down version of Queen Victoria. She could not walk far and often had to be carried in a chair by two men.

In Launceston, her ever reliable son-in-law John Atkinson, Esquire, JP, was working for the Tamar Fire Marine Insurance Company.[7] He knew all about marine insurance and the problems involved, his ship *Eclipse* having been lost to convict pirates all those years before. Despite the gloom around his liver complaint as a young man, Atkinson was now prospering and, breathing in the Vandemonian air, in rude health. Atkinson moved his wife Jane Penelope and their children into a Launceston mansion, Bifrons, while renting out the family's hundred spectacular hectares and an impressive farmhouse on Patterson's Plains, five miles from the town.[8] His son John Reibey Atkinson[9] did not enjoy good health, though; the young man had needed to hand in his notice at Launceston's Union Bank because of his coughing fits, and instead he had been helping his cousin James Thomson run Mary's Burrier property on the Shoalhaven.

In her old age Mary would visit them as often as she could, having a skipper sail her from Sydney to the Shoalhaven and her dock at Burrier. One of the grandsons would then drive her to the homestead on a bullock wagon as she reclined on a mattress.[10]

Young John returned to Launceston in 1852 to marry Caroline Anne Wales, the daughter of the police magistrate in Morven.[11] The wedding at St Andrew's Church in Evandale was a family affair, with John's uncle the Reverend Thomas Haydock Reibey performing the ceremony, assisted by his brother, the Reverend James Haydock Reibey.[12] The two pious brothers returned to England soon after.

To Mary's great delight, Thomas received an honorary Master of Arts degree from the Archbishop of Canterbury.[13] James, who wasn't a dedicated letter writer, arrived with his wife Charlotte and their five-year-old son Jimmy for a surprise visit to Charlotte's parents in Devon. '[The young] Mrs. Reibey was much respected by the inhabitants, from whom she has received a hearty welcome,' the local newspaper reported, 'and on this joyful occasion the bells sent forth many a cheerful peal. The band in the town also enlivened the score with many lively airs.'[14]

It was not the same enlivening air for Jane Atkinson in Launceston. Jane was forty-seven, exhausted and in poor health. The death of young John in May 1854[15] was more than she could handle. Jane died in October that year, the fifth of Mary's seven children to pass away before her.

The blow was crippling for Mary. It was tough to bury one child, let alone five, and she had outlived many of her grandchildren as well. Her constitution had been greatly tested through asthma and heartbreak over the years, and it began to fray.

Australia was a very different place to that which Mary had first seen from a convict ship sixty-three years earlier. Then the New South Wales colony was nothing more than a brutal prison camp at the end of the earth; now the Australian colonies were the richest in the British Empire, producing a fortune in wheat,

Mary's final home on Station Street, Newtown. *State Library of NSW FL1656980*

wool, and especially gold. Ornate buildings were constantly being erected around Australia as gold super-charged the treasury coffers. Queen Victoria had recently proclaimed a new colony named after her and was about to sign an order changing the name of Van Diemen's Land to Tasmania. As Mary looked out of Reibey's Cottage at Newtown, across the road a rail line for steam locomotives was being constructed that would soon carry Sydney's first rail passengers to Parramatta under the direction of the recently installed Governor William Denison.[16]

Mary wondered if she would ever see it. She made out her will on 4 March 1855, dividing her property into thirds, one third each for her two surviving daughters, Elizabeth Innes and the widowed Eliza Thomson, and the other third for the children of the recently deceased Jane Atkinson. Mary appointed three executors: John Atkinson; George Miller, from the Savings Bank of Sydney; and the solicitor James Norton, who would have a street through his Leichhardt estate named in his honour. Two domestic servants, Mary Nowlan and Margaret Sullivan, signed the will as witnesses to Mary's final wishes.[17]

In the document, Mary stipulated that money should be set aside for the 'maintenance education and advancement in life' of all of her grandchildren, whether they be boys or girls.[18] She also wanted to ensure her women descendants had every opportunity as the men. With an inkling to what might be happening between Elizabeth and John Innes – their marriage had grown frosty – Mary gave instructions to her executors that the property she was leaving to her daughters belonged only to them, not to their husbands.

Mary had her seventy-eighth birthday on the Pencilville Estate on 12 May 1855. Her body and resistance were breaking down. Her lungs had always been fragile, and her breathing became raspy and difficult. She developed pneumonia and, with it, chest pains, fever and the worst fatigue she'd ever felt. She gasped and fought for every precious breath.

On 30 May in Newtown, she breathed her last. The long ride from Lancashire was over. But what a ride it had been.

MARY LEFT HER CHILDREN well off financially and with a model to follow of being industrious, thrifty and sober. She was buried in the Devonshire Street Cemetery alongside the remains of her long-gone husband Tom, their beautiful young daughter Celia Wills, and Celia's baby Alice.

Mary hadn't been one for sentiment, and her daughters had inherited that quality. Eliza and Elizabeth organised a huge, spectacular sale of items from Mary's home, now registered as being in Station Street, Newtown, and soon to be let on a five-year lease.[19] On Thursday, 16 August at 11 a.m., the auctioneers Rishworth & Co put Mary's personal belongings under the hammer. The train line and stop at Newtown Station was yet to open, but buyers were told that omnibuses ran every half-hour from the corner of King and George streets, and could deliver them to within three minutes' walk of the Reibey premises.

The auction was just like the old days when Mary had used her home to sell all manner of exotic goods from the foreign ships anchored nearby. There were hair-stuffed mahogany sofas with damask covers, Brussels carpets and rugs, bookcases, books, sideboards, lamps, easy chairs, fenders and fireirons, engravings, ornaments, cutlery, plated ware, four-poster beds, mattresses, bedding, towels, kitchen furniture, and cooking utensils of every

By the 1850s Mary's Entally House (far right) had become the Royal Admiral Hotel. *State Library of NSW FL3310895*

description. There was one enclosed carriage, a flash open four-wheeled 'barouche' carriage 'nearly new', saddles and bridles, and harness for gigs, carriages and carts. There was also a dray, a spring cart, a water cart, a roller and three ploughs. Mary's daughters gave potential buyers the hard sell by insisting that one of the ploughs was 'quite new'.[20] There were harrows, spades, and a grindstone, a quantity of building materials including bricks, cut stone, doors, window sashes, a carpenter's bench, water casks, and lumber.[21] There was a cow, 'now in full milk', as well as a dark brown gelding and a bay mare, not dissimilar to the horse Mary had ridden into Stafford in 1791.[22] The two horses were 'used to all kinds of work', Mary's daughters told the auctioneers, and were 'perfectly quiet and in capital condition'. Terms, of course, were strictly cash.[23] It was the kind of sale that would have made Mary proud. For years after her husband's death, she had organised similar bazaars at their home in Macquarie Place.

When Mary passed away, she still owned the Macquarie Place property but she had found another way to profit from Entally House, the home she and Tom had built, and where she had raised her children. Mary had made it a popular hotel. For the sake of her family's reputation, Mary had come to guard the true story of her arrival in Sydney, brushing over her convict past. But her hotel in Macquarie Place reflected a wry sense of humour and a wink to anyone who heard the gossip about her background. Mary had named the pub after the convict transport that had changed the life of a frightened little horse thief from Lancashire and helped make her the richest woman in Australia. She called her pub the *Royal Admiral*.[24]

Epilogue

MONUMENTS AND PLACE names abound honouring Mary Reibey, but none are more prominent than her image, which has adorned the Australian $20 note since 1994 as a tribute to her enterprise, perseverance and philanthropy.

Many of the monuments use the spelling of her name that Mary used when she was first married.

Reiby Place is situated on the site of her old home opposite the Macquarie obelisk in the Sydney CBD; and Reiby Road is a grand street in the Sydney suburb of Hunters Hill, dominated by Figtree House beside the water's edge. There are Reiby Street and Reiby Lane in Newtown, marking the site of Mary's final home at a time when the now bustling inner-city area was a rural estate. Reibeycroft on the Hawkesbury retains its colonial splendour, and properties owned by Mary and her family along the Shoalhaven and in Tasmania – which was known as Van Diemen's Land until a year after Mary's death – regularly fetch multimillion-dollar prices when traded.

The Reiby Youth Justice Centre in Airds, a suburb in south-western Sydney, accommodates up to fifty-five residents under the age of fifteen who are encouraged to change their course in life by following Mary's story of redemption.

There is also the Reibey Institute, a non-profit research centre founded in 2010 to provide information on women in leadership.

A plaque commemorating Mary's life was unveiled on the corner of Argyle and Playfair streets in the Rocks, near her first

The headstone for Mary and her family before it was moved after the closure of Sydney's Devonshire Street Cemetery to make way for Central Station. It has incorrect details about her husband, Tom. *State Library of NSW FL8501885*

weatherboard Sydney home and close to the site of the multiple properties she owned along George Street.

The very first monument to Mary was the gravestone placed over the family plot in the Devonshire Street Cemetery, but the tombstone listed incorrect details of her husband Tom's age and date of death more than four decades earlier. When the Devonshire Street Cemetery was resumed to become Sydney's central train station, the remains of the Reibey family, with their tombstone, were moved to what is now the Pioneer Memorial Park in Botany. Mary is now buried there beside Tom, Celia and granddaughter Alice, and near her old neighbours George Howe and Simeon Lord.

Mary's youngest daughter Elizabeth Innes formally separated from her husband in November 1855, and two months later she advertised for tenants to rent Stanmore House. In later years, that house was occupied by the flour miller and politician James Pemell. The Pencilville Estate was subdivided in 1871, the gardens being replaced by a forest of Victorian terrace houses and shops. Mary's last home, Reiby House facing Station Street, Newtown, was demolished in 1964, but some of Stanmore House remains, having been divided into flats and with shopfronts added facing Enmore Road. The house was classified by the National Trust of Australia (NSW) in 1982, and the Heritage Council of New South Wales placed it under a Permanent Conservation Order in 1989.

In a subsequent edition of the Reverend Cobbold's novel about Margaret Catchpole, published three years after Mary's death, the author regretted the hurt caused to 'Mrs Reibey and her friends and relatives' by the 'misconception of the identity of Margaret Catchpole'.[1]

Mary's grand Entally House in Macquarie Place, the first home of the Bank of New South Wales, became the Sydney Shipping Master's office in the 1870s but was demolished in 1882.[2]

Elizabeth 'Betsey' Innes moved to England soon after separating from her husband, and her children stayed with her at different times at her home in London. In 1870, she died at the Gloucester Gardens in Hyde Park.

Mary always had high hopes for Elizabeth's eldest son George Innes, who had been an outstanding student at the King's School in Parramatta, as well as a champion horseman. A year before Mary's

Since 1994, Mary Reibey's round, kindly face has adorned Australia's $20 bank note. The microprint on the most recent notes, which went into circulation in 2019, include the names of ships she owned: *Edwin*, *Governor Macquarie*, *James*, *John Palmer*, *Mercury* and *Raven*. Reserve Bank of Australia

death, George had become an associate to the New South Wales Chief Justice Alfred Stephen, and in 1856 he entered Lincoln's Inn, London. He was called to the Bar in 1859 and practised law in England before returning to Australia in 1862. He became a Queensland district court judge and Crown prosecutor in New South Wales. He negotiated with the government to buy a George Street property, Chisholm House, which Mary had bequeathed to his mother. It is now the site of the Sydney General Post Office.

In 1872, as the member for Mudgee in the Legislative Assembly, the grandson of a cross-dressing convicted horse thief became solicitor-general of New South Wales. Later he would be the attorney-general and Minister of Justice. In 1875, he became Sir Joseph George Long Innes. His son, Reginald Heath Innes,[3] became chief judge in equity of the New South Wales Supreme Court.

Eight months after the death of Mary's youngest child Elizabeth, Mary's last surviving child Eliza Thomson died in Launceston aged sixty-five. Eliza's oldest son James Thomson, who had worked on Mary's Shoalhaven land for some years, was elected to the New South Wales Legislative Assembly as the local member for the electorate then known as St Vincent.

Like Mary's children, the offspring of her old neighbour Prosper de Mestre prospered in Sydney and also beside the Shoalhaven. De Mestre acquired large landholdings there, and it was from there that the little Frenchman's son Etienne[4] trained the racehorse Archer to win the first Melbourne Cup run in 1861. Etienne's horses would go on to win the Cup five times.

Another of Mary's old neighbours was not so fortunate. Horatio Wills, the son of Mary's friends and business partners Sarah and Edward Wills, and the brother of Celia's husband, became a leading Victorian pastoralist – but in 1861, looking to expand his empire in Central Queensland, he was among a group of nineteen European settlers, ten men, two women, and seven children, killed by the local Indigenous people at Cullin-la-ringo Station north of modern-day Springsure. Cricket star Tom Wills was one of six survivors. It was reported that the attack was revenge for the murder of Gayiri men by Wills' neighbour, Jesse Gregson, who

Three of Mary's prominent grandsons: Sir George Innes (above left), who became the New South Wales solicitor general, attorney general and minister for justice; Thomas Reibey III (above), who was Premier of Tasmania; the Reverend James Haydock Reibey (left) who lived most of his life as a cleric in England. *State Library of NSW FL2215698, State Library of Tasmania SD_ILS:168455, Marg McKeown*

had mistakenly accused them of stealing cattle. Reprisals were swift and merciless. Vigilantes backed by a contingent of the fearsome Queensland Native Police slaughtered as many as 370 members of the Gayiri people.

MARY'S OLDEST GRANDSON, the Reverend Thomas Reibey III, was promoted to archdeacon but resigned after becoming embroiled in a libel case in 1870 after his married goddaughter accused him of trying to seduce her. Despite being represented by the former New South Wales solicitor-general Robert Isaacs, Thomas lost the expensive case that had become a major scandal throughout Australia.

After leaving the church, Thomas devoted himself to politics and horseracing. In 1874 he was elected by a whopping majority to Tasmania's House of Assembly for the seat of Westbury, which he maintained for the next twenty-nine years. For thirteen months he was Premier of Tasmania. His horse Stockwell won the Launceston Cup in 1882, and he once owned Malua, winner of the 1884 Melbourne Cup.

Mary's oldest grandson died in 1912 at Entally, the Reibey family's property in Hadspen. He bequeathed the property to Thomas Reibey Arthur, the son of Mary's first grandchild, Mary Allen Arthur. Entally remains one of Tasmania's oldest and best preserved homesteads, and it's a popular tourist destination. The family Bible Mary bought in England is kept on a writing desk in the Entally library, and the historic home also houses her cutlery, which is in a showcase in the dining room. A suite of furniture from her Sydney home is in the drawing room.

In 1859 Mary's other clerical grandson, the Reverend James Haydock Reibey, was appointed the Vicar of Denbury in Devon.[5] He lived there quietly for the next thirty-eight years. James was sixty-eight when his wife Charlotte died and seventy-three when he married for the second time, exchanging vows on 25 February 1896 at All Saints, Notting Hill, London, with Annie Selina Morris, who was half his age.

When James Reibey died the following year, the *Launceston Examiner* reported that he was 'loved, valued, and esteemed by all who knew him. Not only by the parishioners, but throughout the neighbourhood of Newton Abbot [the] deceased will be long remembered for his genial manner and warm-heartedness. By the villagers he was much beloved for his uniform kindness to them and his care for their welfare, both spiritual and temporal. In Denbury his tall, upright figure will be sadly missed.'[6] James's great-grandson, the gloriously named Vice Admiral Sir Peveril Barton Reiby Wallop William-Powlett, KCB, KCMG, CBE, DSO,[7] joined the Royal Navy as a midshipman in 1914 and served in World War I, then played rugby union for England in 1922 before becoming Captain of the Home Fleet during World War II.

He served as Governor of Southern Rhodesia from 1954 until 1959. Peveril's brother Newton[8] survived the sinking of the destroyer HMS *Tipperary* in the Battle of Jutland during World War I and had command of the Allied ships HMS *Calypso*, *Dauntless* and *Gambia* during World War II.

IN 2016 THE NAME 'MARY REIBEY' was added to the Bradfield Partnership Sydney Honour Roll in the Quadrangle of the University of Sydney. The honour commemorates Sydney's visionaries. Thirty of Mary's descendants travelled from across Australia for the ceremony, and a Bradfield medallion was presented to ninety-year-old Brisbane-based Dr Brian Hirschfield, Mary's great, great, great grandson,[9] one of thousands of Australians who are descendants of the remarkable Mrs Reibey.

Westpac, which grew out of the Bank of New South Wales, also honours the life of Mary Reibey with its museum on George Street, Sydney, and its extensive archives run by Westpac's head of historical services, Kim Eberhard.

Mary Reibey's story is one of the great Australian success stories: the tale of a woman who pushed through gender boundaries to become a business leader as a widow with seven young children at a time when women were at a severe disadvantage against male competitors. She succeeded in the face of incredible odds, powering ahead no matter how difficult her circumstances.

More than two hundred years after Mary Reibey arrived as a convict girl in New South Wales, she created a legacy of strength, resilience and determination for her descendants and for her adopted homeland.

Acknowledgements

THE REMARKABLE Mrs Reibey lived a huge and fascinating life and left behind a legacy of hard work and determination, encouraging all who came after her to rise above the most humbling of circumstances.

My sincere thanks to her relatives Elizabeth Fysh and Eric and Pat Pickering for their work in preserving Mary's story, and for their insights into her astonishing life.

I also owe a great debt of gratitude to Westpac's head of historical services, Kim Eberhard, who oversees the largest privately held archives in the Southern Hemisphere, and who is the custodian of Mary's records from the Bank of NSW.

Thanks also to the staff at the Mitchell Library in Sydney, and the New South Wales State Archives, who safeguard so much of Mary's history.

A special thanks to Dr Meg Foster, Research Fellow of Newnham College at Cambridge University, for her advice on colonial historical accounts. Much of this book is based on the reporting of early British officials and settlers, and Dr Foster provided vital insights into the attitudes that shaped their views in relation to the First Peoples of Australia.

This book would not have been possible without the continued support and encouragement of the marvellous team at HarperCollins: Jude McGee, Brigitta Doyle, Lachlan McLaine, Roberta Ivers, Helen Littleton, Lisa Reidy, Matt Howard, Lara Wallace, Nicolette Houben and my editors Kevin McDonald and Kate Goldsworthy, whose advice and assistance are always invaluable.

Bibliography

BOOKS

Roy Adkins, *Trafalgar: The Biography of a Battle*, Hachette UK, 2011.

Henry Colden Antill, *Early History of New South Wales*, W.A. Gullick, Government Printer, 1914.

Val Attenbrow, *Sydney's Aboriginal Past: Investigating the Archaeological and Historical Records*, University of New South Wales Press, 2010.

Memoirs of George Barrington, M. Smith (ed), 1790.

Henry Grey Bennet, *A Letter to Earl Bathurst, Secretary of State for the Colonial Department*, J. Ridgway, 1820.

Catherine Bishop, *Minding Her Own Business; Colonial Business Women in Sydney*, New South Press, 2015.

F.M. Bladen (ed.), *Historical Records of New South Wales*, Lansdown Slattery, 1978 (f.p. 1892–1901)

Gregory Blaxland, *A Journal of a Tour of Discovery Across the Blue Mountains, New South Wales, in the Year 1813*, B.J. Holdsworth, 1823.

G. Bond, *A Brief Account of the Colony of Port Jackson*, Slatter and Munday, 1806.

J. Brook and J.L. Kohen, *The Parramatta Native Institution and the Black Town: A History*, University of New South Wales Press, 1991.

Richard Broome, *Aboriginal Australians: A history since 1788*, Allen & Unwin, 2010.

Angus Cameron (ed) 'Part One: Capital City Chronologies, A History of Sydney', *The Second Australian Almanac*, Angus & Robertson, 1986.

The Journal and Letters of Lt. Ralph Clark 1787–1792, 3 May 1791, University of Sydney Library, 2003.

Manning Clarke, *A History of Australia*, Melbourne University Press, 1993.

John Cobley, *Sydney Cove 1791–92*, Vol. III, Angus and Robertson, 1965.

T.A. Coghlan, *General Report on the Eleventh Census of New South Wales*, Charles Potter, Government Printer, 1894.

David Collins, *An Account of the English Colony in New South Wales from Its First Settlement, in January 1788, to August 1801*, T. Cadell Jr and W. Davies, 1802.

John Connor, *The Australian Frontier Wars, 1788–1838*, UNSW Press, 2002.

James Cook, *Cook's Voyages Around the World*, Sowler and Russell, 1799.

Adam Courtenay, *Three Sheets to the Wind*, ABC Books, 2022.

T. Crofton Croker, *Memoirs of Joseph Holt: General of the Irish rebels, in 1798*, Vol. 2, Henry Coulburn, 1838.

William Richard Drake, *Heathiana: notes, genealogical and biographical, of the family of Heath*; Baron Heath, 1881.

Cathy Dunn, *Ladies of the Royal Admiral 1792*, Cathy Dunn, 1996.

Tom Dunne, *Rebellions: Memoir, Memory and 1798*, Lilliput Press, 2004.

M.H. Ellis, *Lachlan Macquarie; his life, adventures, and times*, Angus & Robertson, 1952.

Raymond Evans, *A History of Queensland*, Cambridge University Press, 2007.

Herbert Vere Evatt, *Rum Rebellion: A Study of the Overthrow of Governor Bligh by John Macarthur and the New South Wales Corps*, Angus & Robertson, 1965.

Matthew Flinders, *A Voyage to Terra Australis*, Vol. 1, G & W Nicol, 1814.

Antonia Fraser, *Mary, Queen of Scots*, Weidenfeld & Nicolson, 1969.

Mollie Gillen, *The Founders of Australia: A Biographical Dictionary of the First Fleet*, Library of Australian History, 1989.

Alexander Harris, *Settlers and Convicts; or, Recollections of sixteen years' labour in the Australian Backwoods. By an Emigrant Mechanic*, C. Cox, 1847.

Theresa Holtby, *Molly Haydock*, Western Sydney University, 2018.

Clare Hopkins, *Trinity: 450 years of an Oxford College Community*, Oxford University Press, 2005.

Richard Hough, *Captain Bligh and Mr Christian: The Men and the Mutiny*, Hutchinson, 1972.

Nance Irvine (ed), *Dear Cousin: The Reibey Letters*, Hale & Iremonger, 1995.

Nance Irvine, *Mary Reibey – Molly Incognita*, Library of Australian History, 2001.

William James, *The Naval History of Great Britain, Volume 1, 1793–1796* (originally published 1827), Conway Maritime Press, 2002.

Leanne Johns, 'The First Female Shareholders of the Bank of New South Wales: Examination of Shareholdings in Australia's First Bank, 1817–1824', *Accounting, Business & Financial History Vol. 16, No. 2*, Routledge, 2006.

Arthur Wilberforce Jose, Herbert James Carter, *Australian Encyclopedia*, Angus & Robertson, 1926.

Grace Karskens, *People of the River: Lost Worlds of Early Australia*, Allen & Unwin, 2020.

Grace Karskens, *The Colony: A history of early Sydney*, Allen &Unwin, 2009.

Bruce Kercher, *Debt, Seduction and Other Disasters: The Birth of Civil Law in Convict New South Wales*, The Federation Press, 1996.

Carol Liston, *Campbelltown: The Bicentennial History*, Allen & Unwin, 1988.

Frank McCaffrey, *The History of Illawarra and its Pioneers*, J. Sands Limited, 1922.

Sibella Macarthur Onslow (ed.), *Some Early Records of the Macarthurs of Camden*, Angus & Robertson, 1914.

Rob Mundle, *Bligh: Master Mariner*, Hachette Australia, 2010.

John Nicol, *The Life and Adventures of John Nicol, Mariner*, William Blackwood, 1822.

Arthur Phillip, *The Voyage of Governor Phillip to Botany Bay*, John Stockdale, 1789.

J. T. Slugg, *Reminiscences of Manchester Fifty Years Ago*, J. E. Cornish, 1881.

Lyn Stewart, *Blood Revenge: Murder on the Hawkesbury 1799*, Rosenberg Publishing, 2015.

Watkin Tench, *A Complete Account of the Settlement at Port Jackson: In New South Wales*, G Nicol & J. Sewel, 1793.

Watkin Tench, *A Narrative of the Expedition to Botany Bay*, published as *Sydney's First Four Years*, edited by L. F. Fitzhardinge, Library of Australian History, 1979 (f.p. 1789).

George Thompson, *Slavery and Famine, Punishments for Sedition; or An Account of New South Wales, and of the Miserable State of the Convicts*, J. Ridgeway, 1794.

Lynne Vallone, *Becoming Victoria*, Yale University Press, 2001.

Robin Walsh, *In Her Own Words: The Writings of Elizabeth Macquarie*, Exisle, 2011.

Thomas Watling, *Letters From An Exile At Botany Bay, To His Aunt In Dumfries*, Ann Bell, 1794.

Thomas E. Wells, *Michael Howe, The Last and Worst of the Bush-Rangers of Van Diemen's Land*, Andrew Bent, 1818.

John White, *Journal of a Voyage to New South Wales*, J. Debrett, 1790.

INTERNET RESOURCES

adb.anu.edu.au (G.P. Walsh. 'Reibey, Mary (1777–1855)', Australian Dictionary of Biography)

ahsa.asn.au (Arabian Horse Society of Australia)

ancestry.com.au

arc.parracity.nsw.gov.au (City of Parramatta Council Research & Collection Services)

arrow.latrobe.edu.au (La Trobe University Research Online)

australianmerino.net.au

britishnewspaperarchive.co.uk

cambridge.org

capitalpunishmentuk.org ('The execution of children and juveniles') catalogue.nla.gov.au/Record/115107 (Frederick Watson (ed.), *Historical Records of Australia*)

cityartsydney.com.au

cityofsydney.nsw.gov.au

cityofsydney.nsw.gov.au ('History of Macquarie Place Park')

collection.maas.museum (Museum of Applied Arts & Science. Sydney)

dehanz.net.au (*Dictionary of Educational History in Australia and New Zealand*)

dictionaryofsydney.org

historic-uk.com (Charles Duff, 'The History of Hanging')

entallyestate.com.au

experiencesydneyaustralia.com

foundingdocs.gov.au

freesettlerorfelon.com

genuki.org.uk ('St John the Evangelist Church of England, Blackburn')

gutenberg.org

historyandheritage.cityofparramatta.nsw.gov.au

jstor.org

lan-opc.org.uk. ('The Church of St John the Evangelist, Blackburn in the County of Lancashire')

lancastercastle.com ('Executions')

library.sydney.edu.au (University of Sydney Library)

liverpoolmuseums.org.uk. ('Liverpool and the transatlantic slave trade')

nla.gov.au (National Library of Australia)

tww.id.au (R.V. Pockley, 'Ancestor Treasure Hunt: The Edward Wills Family and Descendants in Australia 1797–1976')

nla.gov.au/nla.obj-1126165596 (Royal Admiral Journal, Ships Logs held by the India Office Library [as filmed by the AJCP])

nla.gov.au/nla.obj-228958465 (James Cook, Journal of H.M.S. *Endeavour*, 1768–1771, National Library of Australia)

nla.gov.au/nla.obj-570654388 (Journal of Richard Atkins, National Library of Australia, MS 4039)

records.nsw.gov.au ('Mary Reibey – convict and businesswoman')

simplyaustralia.net (Jim Low, 'Massacre at Shaws Creek')

sl.nsw.gov.au (State Library of New South Wales)

stgite.org.uk (St George-in-the-East Church)

sydneylivingmuseums.com.au

trove.nla.gov.au

visitsydneyaustralia.com.au

warfarehistorynetwork.com

westernsydney.edu.au/femaleorphanschool

Endnotes

Prologue

1   Mary Reibey (nee Haydock) born 12 May 1777, Bury, United Kingdom; died 30 May 1855, Newtown, Sydney.

2   Nance Irvine, *Mary Reibey – Molly Incognita*, Library of Australian History, 2001, p. 7.

3   Theresa Holtby, *Molly Haydock*, Western Sydney University, 2018, p. 200.

4   *Bath Chronicle and Weekly Gazette*, 17 May 1792, p. 2.

Chapter One

1   Her birth name is recorded as Molly Heydock (sic), Bishops Transcripts, Lancashire, England, Church of England Baptisms, Marriages and Burials, 1538-1812, Drm/2/43.

2   'Liverpool and the transatlantic slave trade', liverpoolmuseums.org.uk.

3   Jane Haydock (nee Law) baptised 3 November 1751, Blackburn, St Mary the Virgin, Lancashire, England; buried 27 May 1787, Witton-cum-Twambrooks, Cheshire, England.

4   Charles Duff, 'The History of Hanging', historic-uk.com.org.

5   'Executions', lancastercastle.com.

6   'The execution of children and juveniles', capitalpunishmentuk.

7   James Cook, *Journal of H.M.S. Endeavour*, 1768–1771, National Library of Australia, MS 1, 3 May 1770.

8   He also spelt it 'kanguru', Joseph Banks, *Endeavour Journal*, 25 August 1768–12 July 1771, Series 03:Vol. 2: SAFE/Banks Papers/Series 03.02, *Some Account Of That Part of New Holland Now Called New South Wales*.

9   Later Vice-Admiral William Bligh, born 9 September 1754; died 7 December 1817, London.

10 *Cook's Voyages Around the World*, Sowler and Russell, 1799, p. 358.

11 James Haydock, baptised 10 January 1749, Blackburn, Lancashire; died 28 December 1779, Pleasington, Lancashire.

12 Bishops Transcripts, Lancashire, England, Church of England Baptisms, Marriages and Burials, 1538-1812, Drb/2/7a.

13 On 22 May 1771. Parish register, St Mary the Virgin Blackburn, 1754-1936, p. 92.

14 Elizabeth 'Betty' Haydock, later Foster, born May 1772, Blackburn, Lancashire; died 10 April 1849, Newtown, Sydney, NSW.

15 M. H. Ellis, 'The Lady and the Pony', *The Bulletin*, 12 November 1952, p. 25.

16 Petition for clemency re Mary Haydock, Public Records Office, Kew, ASSI, 2 26 X/L08670.

17 Alice Law (nee Kay), born 1726 Lancashire; buried 7 August 1791, Eccles, Lancashire.

18 Mary Reibey journal, 1820-1821, State Library of NSW, Safe 1/21a, p. 12.

19 Captain Clerke to Secretary Stephens, 8 June 1779, from Historical Records of NSW (*HRNSW*), Vol. 1 Part 1, p. 415.

20 Sir Thomas Charles Bunbury, 6th Baronet (May 1740 – 31 March 1821).

21 Journals of the House of Commons, Vol. 37, 1803, pp. 311.
22 *Ibid.*
23 *Ibid.*
24 Penelope Law, baptised 1 January 1755; died 31 October 1817, Blackburn, Lancashire.
25 Adam Hope, born August 1757, Pendleton, Lancashire; died April 1792, Blackburn, Lancashire.
26 Holtby, *Molly Haydock*, p. 203.
27 Arthur Phillip, *The Voyage of Governor Phillip to Botany Bay*, John Stockdale, 1789, p. 80.
28 Thomas Townshend, 1st Viscount Sydney (24 February 1733 – 30 June 1800).
29 'Governor Phillip's First Commission,' 12 October 1786, *HRNSW*, Vol. 1 Part 2, p. 24.
30 'The Act of Parliament Establishing the Colony,' from *HRNSW*, Vol. 1 Part 2, p. 67.
31 State Library of NSW, ML 124.
32 Records were inexact. 'First Fleet Convicts,' State Library of NSW, guides.sl.nsw.gov.au
33 David Collins, *An Account of the English Colony in New South Wales*, T. Cadell Jun. and W. Davies, 1804, p. iii.
34 The receipt dated 28 May 1787 is at the State Library of NSW, MLDOC 972.
35 Phillip to Sydney, 15 May 1788, *HRA*, Series I, Volume I: 1788–1796, p. 18.
36 *Ibid.*
37 Arthur Phillip, *The Voyage of Governor Phillip to Botany Bay*, John Stockdale, 1789, p. 58.
38 Riaz Hassan, 'Whores, damned whores and female convicts: Why our history does early Australian colonial women a grave injustice', theconversation.com, 11 January 2012.
39 Letter from a Female Convict, Port Jackson, 14 November 1788, *HRNSW*, Vol. 2, pp. 746-7.
40 Watkin Tench, born c. 1758, Chester, England; died 7 May 1833, Devonport, Devon, England.
41 Watkin Tench, *A Narrative of the Expedition to Botany Bay*, J. Debrett, 1789.
42 David Collins, born 3 March 1756 London; died 24 March, 1810, Hobart.
43 David Collins, *An Account of the English Colony in New South Wales*, p. 597.
44 *Ibid.*
45 'St John the Evangelist Church of England, Blackburn', genuki.org.uk.
46 'The Church of St John the Evangelist, Blackburn in the County of Lancashire', lan-opc.org.uk.
47 Mary Reibey journal, 1820-1821, State Library of NSW, Safe 1/21a.
48 David Hope, born 9 September 1786, Blackburn, Lancashire; died 6 September 1857, Glasgow, Scotland.
49 Later Vice Admiral John Hunter (born 29 August 1737, Leith, Scotland; died 13 March 1821, Hackney, London).
50 Phillip to Banks, 16 November 1788, State Library of NSW, SAFE/Banks Papers/Series 37.08.
51 'Mary Haydock', *Evening News* (Sydney), 30 October 1897, p. 3.
52 Holtby, *Molly Haydock*, p. 133.

Chapter Two

1 'Mary Haydock', *Evening News* (Sydney), 30 October 1897, p. 3.
2 James Borrow, born 11 April 1777 Lancashire, Blackburn. Parish Register, St Mary the Virgin, Blackburn, PR 3073/1/8.
3 The Petition of Friends to King Geo. III., 5 November 1791, National Archives, Kew, HO 47/13/140.
4 *Chester Chronicle*, 12 September 1791, p. 3.

5   Evidence of Robert Silvester, Report from Mr Justice Heath to Lord Grenville, Secretary of State for Foreign Affairs, 18 November 1791, from Irvine, Mary Reibey – *Molly Incognita*, p 135.

6   *Ibid.*

7   *Ibid.*

8   Evidence of Francis Emborton, *Ibid.*

9   *Ibid.*

10 Evidence of John Commander, taken on oath before John Wright, Mayor, Stafford, 18 August 1791, PRO ASSI 5 III, Part 1 X/L08687.

11 Evidence of William Moore, Report from Mr Justice Heath, from Irvine, *Mary Reibey – Molly Incognita*, p 135.

12 Stafford Historic Charter Assessment, Staffordshire County Council, August 2011, p. 55.

13 'Miss Muff's Molly House in Whitechapel', eastendwomensmuseum.org.

14 Evidence of John Hughes, PRO ASSI 5 III, Part 1 X/L08687.

15 'Phillip's Instructions,' 25 April 1787, from *HRNSW*, Vol. 1 Part 2, p. 84.

16 *Ibid.*

17 Raymond Evans, *A History of Queensland*, Cambridge University Press, 2007, p. 11.

18 'Phillip's Instructions,' 25 April 1787, from *HRNSW*, Vol. 1 Part 2, p. 89.

19 'Governor Phillip's Instructions 25 April 1787 (UK),' foundingdocs.gov.au, quotingmanuscript dated 20 April 1787 from Public Record Office in London (CO 201/1ff 29–45v).

20 Henry Hacking, born c. 1750; died 21 July 1831, Hobart, Tasmania. He gave his name to Port Hacking, south of Sydney.

21 John Connor, *The Australian Frontier Wars*, 1788–1838, UNSW Press, 2002, p. 26.

22 Mary Wade, born 17 December 1775, Westminster, London; died 17 December 1859, Fairy Meadow, NSW. Her descendants include former Australian Prime Minister Kevin Rudd.

23 John Nicol, born 1755, Currie, Scotland; died 1825, Scotland.

24 John Nicol, *The Life and Adventures of John Nicol*, Mariner, William Blackwood, 1822, p. 119.

25 Ann Mash, aka Ann Marsh, born 1767, Buckland Brewer, Devon; died 7 March 1823, Parramatta.

26 'Voyage of the Lady Juliana', Extract from a letter by one of the female convicts transported', 24 July 1790, *HRNSW* Vol 2, p. 767. Reprinted from the *Morning Chronicle* (Dublin), 4 August, 1791.

27 *The Journal and Letters of Lt. Ralph Clark 1787–1792*, 3 May 1791, University of Sydney Library, 2003, setis.library.usyd.edu.au/ozlit/pdf/clajour.pdf.

28 Camden, Calvert and King, which traded in London from 1760 to 1824, shipping slaves and later convicts.

29 Captain Hill to Wathen, 26 July 1790, *HRNSW*, Vol. I Part 2, p. 367.

30 John Macarthur, born 1767 near Plymouth, England; died 11 April 1834, Camden, NSW.

31 Elizabeth Macarthur (nee Veale), born 14 August 1766, Bridgerule, Devon, England; died 9 February 1850, Clovelly, NSW.

32 Lieutenant-General Sir Edward Macarthur, born 16 March 1789, Bath, Somerset; died 4 January 1872, London.

33 'Old Sydney', *Truth* (Brisbane), 13 June 1909, p. 11.

34 Mrs Macarthur's Journal, 23 November 1789, from Sibella Macarthur Onslow, *Some Early Records of the Macarthurs of Camden*, Angus & Robertson, 1914.

35 Captain Hill to Wathen, 26 July 1790, *HRNSW*, Vol. I Part 2, p. 367.

36 R. Johnson to Mr Thornton, July 1790: *Ibid*, Vol. I Part 2, pp. 387–9.

37 *Ibid.*

38 *Ibid.*
39 Phillip to Banks, 17 November 1791, State Library of NSW, SAFE/Banks Papers/Series 37.18.
40 Woollarawarre Bennelong, born about 1764; died 3 January 1813, Kissing Point, Sydney.
41 Willemering, born c. 1755; died c. 1800.
42 William Balmain, born 2 February, 1762 Rhynd, Scotland; died 17 November, 1803, London.
43 Bennelong Point became the site of the Sydney Opera House.
44 Watkin Tench, *A Complete Account of the Settlement at Port Jackson: In New South Wales,* G Nicol & J. Sewel, 1793, p. 90.
45 PRO ASSI 5 III, Part 1 X/L08687.
46 Sir James Eyre, born 1734; died 1 July 1799.
47 John Heath, born 1736 Exeter, Devon; died 16 January 1816, Hayes, Middlesex.
48 William Richard Drake, *Heathiana: notes, genealogical and biographical, of the family of Heath;* Baron Heath, 1881, p. 6.
49 *Ibid.*, p. 7.
50 'London, Monday, May 14', *Bath Chronicle and Weekly Gazette,* 17 May 1792, p. 2.
51 PRO ASSI 5/ III, 4181.
52 *Ibid.*

Chapter Three
1   *Chester Chronicle,* 2 September 1791, p. 3.
2   Walter Lane hanged 3 September 1791, capitalpunishmentuk.org.
3   Jane North's Reprieve, from Irvine, *Mary Reibey – Molly Incognita,* p. 18.
4   Report from Mr Justice Heath, PRO ASSI 2 26 X/L08670, *Ibid.*, p. 135.
5   'Certificate/memorial of James Eyre and John Heath on prisoners attainted on the last Oxford Circuit, reprieved on 'favourable circumstances' and recommended for mercy on the conditions set against their names: Public Records Office, Kew, HO 47/13/69
6   *Chester Chronicle,* 2 September 1791, p. 3.
7   Governor Phillip to Under Secretary Nepean, 18 March 1787, *HRNSW,*Vol. 1 Part 2 (1783-1792), p. 59.
8   British Newspaper Archive.
9   *Aris's Birmingham Gazette,* 5 September 1791, p. 3.
10 State Archives & Records New South Wales, NRS 1155 (2/8276, p134). From the Musters and papers per the Royal Admiral which arrived in Sydney on 7 October 1792.
11 Lancashire, England, Church of England Marriages and Banns, 1754-1936, Bishop's Transcripts, Prestwich, 1790-1799.
12 Charles Foster, born July 1761, Bolton, Lancashire; died August 1827 Castlereagh, NSW.
13 PRO ASSI 2 26 X/L08670
14 Archibald Menzies, born 15 March 1754, Perthshire, Scotland; died 15 February 1842, London
15 Menzies to Banks, 26 September 1792, State Library of NSW, SAFE/Banks Papers/ Series 61/Item 14.
16 James Ruse, born 9 August 1759, Lawhitton, England; died 5 September 1837, Campbelltown, NSW.
17 Governor Phillip to Lord Grenville, 5 November 1791, *HRNSW,*Vol. 1 Part 2 (1783-1792), p. 540.
18 Governor Phillip to Secretary Stephens, 16 November 1791, *Ibid.*,Vol. 1 Part 2 (1783-1792), p. 553.
19 Later Lieutenant-General Francis Grose, born 1758, Greenford, Middlesex, England; died 8 May 1814, Croydon, Surrey, England.

20 Captain Manning to Alderman Macaulay, 24 October 1791, *HRNSW*,Vol. 1 Part 2 (1783-1792), p. 528.

21 Thomas Watling, *Letters From An Exile At Botany Bay, To His Aunt In Dumfries*, Ann Bell, 1794.

22 *Ibid*.

23 The petition was signed by Adam Hope, Woollen Draper, John Parker, John Fisher, Surgeon, David Gardiner, Tea Dealer, John Thomson, Cotton Manufacturer, Donald M. Lean, Cotton Manufacturer, Peter Wylie, Linen Draper, Christian Irving, Linen Draper, Hugh Jamieson, Cotton Manufacturer, two Messers Smalley, Merchants, Geo. & Thos. Walmsley, 'Attornies at Law', S. McQuhae, Dissenting Minister, Revd. Samuel Dean, Headmaster of the Free Grammar Schl., Charles Waugh, Woollen & Linen Draper, James Tiplady, Tallow Chandler and Soap Boiler, Robert Smalley, Gentleman and the Revd. Richard Smalley.

24 Petition of friends to the King, 5 November 1791, from Irvine, *Mary Reibey – Molly Incognita*, p. 134.

25 *Ibid*.

26 *Ibid*.

27 *Ibid*.

28 Report from Mr Justice Heath to Lord Grenville, Secretary of State for Foreign Affairs, 18 November 1791, from Irvine, *Mary Reibey – Molly Incognita*, p 135.

29 *Ibid*.

30 Report from Mr Justice Heath to Lord Grenville, Secretary of State for Foreign Affairs, 18 November 1791, from Irvine, *Mary Reibey – Molly Incognita*, p. 135.

31 Governor Phillip to Lord Grenville, 22 November 1791, *HRNSW*,Vol. 1 Part 2 (1783-1792), p. 559.

32 *Ibid*, 24 November 1791, *Ibid*, p. 564.

33 *Ibid*, 21 November 1791, *Ibid*, p. 559.

34 Phillip to Nepean, 2 September 1797, *HRNSW*,Vol. 1 Part 2, p. 111.

35 *The Times* (London), 28 May 1792.

36 'London, Monday, May 14', *Bath Chronicle and Weekly Gazette*, 17 May 1792, p. 2.

37 David Collins, *An Account of the English Colony in New South Wales*, p. 182

38 Mary Loveridge, born 17 November 1776 in Hampshire, England; married Thomas Dargin, 17 Nov 1795 in St Phillip's Church of England, Sydney; died 30 April 1854 at age 77 Windsor, NSW.

39 *Oxford Journal*, 7 January 1792.

40 *Reading Mercury*, 12 March 1792.

41 John Jamieson, born 1765 Scotland; died 7 October 1850, Parramatta, NSW.

42 Royal Admiral: Journal, Captain Essex H. Bond, Ships Logs held by the India Office Library (as filmed by the AJCP) [microform] : [M1620-M1627] 1759-1827./Series IOR/L/MAR/B/File 338F/, 14 May 1792.

43 'Navy Office Accounts', 13 June 1794, *HRNSW*,Vol. 2 (1793-1795), p. 220.

44 'Stores and Provisions', *Ibid*, p. 467.

45 Essex Henry Bond, born 1762; died 19 July 1819, Ditchteys, Essex, England.

46 Royal Admiral Journal, 16 May 1792.

47 *Ibid.*, 1 June 1792.

Chapter Four

1 James Lacey (aka James Smith), 'A Convict's Letter', 19 August 1792, *HRNSW* Vol. 2 (1793-1795), p. 479.

2 'Essex Henry Bond', Bond Family Members in the East India Company, blogs.ucl.ac.uk

3 Royal Admiral Journal, Ships Logs held by the India Office Library (as filmed by the AJCP) [microform] : [M1620–M1627] 1759–1827./Series IOR/L/MAR/B/File 338F/, 2 June 1792.

4 *Ibid*, 3 June 1792.

5 David Collins, *An Account of the English Colony in New South Wales*, 1798.

6 Commissioners of the Navy to Phillip, 17 May 1792, *HRNSW*, Vol. 2, p. 470.

7 *The Waaksamheyd*: translation 'Vigilance'

8 Australia, Births and Baptisms, 1792–1981, Salt Lake City, Utah: FamilySearch, 2013.

9 John Cobley, *Sydney Cove 1791–92, Vol III*, Angus and Robertson, 1965, p. 93.

10 Royal Admiral Journal, 3 June 1792.

11 James Lacey (aka James Smith), 'A Convict's Letter', 19 August 1792, *HRNSW* Vol. 2 (1793–1795), p. 479.

12 Royal Admiral Journal, 7, 14 June.

13 George Thompson, *Slavery and Famine, Punishments for Sedition; or An Account of New South Wales, and of the Miserable State of the Convicts*; J. Ridgeway, 1794, p. 23.

14 James Lacey (aka James Smith), 'A Convict's Letter', 19 August 1792, *HRNSW* Vol. 2 (1793–1795), p. 479.

15 *Ibid*.

16 *Ibid.*, p. 480.

17 Royal Admiral Journal, 30 July.

18 James Lacey (aka James Smith), 'A Convict's Letter', 19 August 1792, *HRNSW* Vol. 2 (1793–1795), p. 480.

19 Royal Admiral Journal, 17 June 1792.

20 James Lacey (aka James Smith), 'A Convict's Letter', 19 August 1792, *HRNSW* Vol. 2 (1793–1795), p. 480.

21 Royal Admiral Journal, 19 June 1792.

22 *Ibid.*, 26 June 1792.

23 *Ibid.*, 17 June 1792.

24 *Ibid.*, 3 September 1792.

25 *Ibid.*, 27 June 1792.

26 *Ibid.*, 1, 2, 3 July 1792.

27 *Ibid.*, 19 July 1792.

28 William Raven, born October 1756; died 14 August 1814.

29 Thomas Reibey, born 1869; died 5 May 1811, Macquarie Place, Sydney.

30 David Collins, *An Account of the English Colony*, p. 174.

31 *Ibid.*, p. 175.

32 Elizabeth Ruse (nee Perry). Also known as Elizabeth Parry, born 1768 England; died 27 May, 1836, Campbelltown, NSW.

33 David Collins, *An Account of the English Colony* p. 177.

34 Royal Admiral Journal, 2 August 1792.

35 *Ibid.*, 23 August 1792.

36 *Ibid.*, 25 August 1792.

37 Thomas Watling, *Letters From An Exile At Botany Bay, To His Aunt In Dumfries*, Ann Bell, 1794.

38 *Ibid*.

39 Royal Admiral Journal, 18 September 1792.

40 Ann Viles, born c. 1768, Bristol, England; died 1839, NSW.

41 Royal Admiral Journal, 1 October 1792.

42 Richard Atkins, born 22 March 1745, England; died 21 November, 1820, London.

43 Journal of Richard Atkins, National Library of Australia, MS 4039, 7 October 1792.

44 David Collins, *An Account of the English Colony*, p. 188.

45 *Ibid.*, p. 181.

46 George Thompson, *Slavery and Famine*, p. 1.
47 David Collins, *An Account of the English Colony*, p. 182.
48 Governor Phillip to The Right Hon. Henry Dundas, 11 October 1792, *HRNSW*, Vol. 1, Part 2, p. 665.
49 Mary Reibey (Molly Haydock), Letter to her aunt Penelope Hope 1792, MLMSS 5934 (Safe 1/155), State Library of NSW.

Chapter Five
1 Journal of Richard Atkins, National Library of Australia, MS 4039, 8 October 1792.
2 David Collins, *An Account of the English Colony in New South Wales*, p. 183.
3 *Ibid.*
4 *Ibid.*
5 Riaz Hassan, 'Whores, damned whores and female convicts: Why our history does early Australian colonial women a grave injustice', theconversation.com, 11 January 2012.
6 G. Bond, *A Brief Account of the Colony of Port Jackson*, Slatter and Munday, 1806, pp. 9-10.
7 'Report from the Select Committee on Transportation', House of Commons, 1812, FRM F543, National Library of Australia, p. 14.
8 Thompson, *Slavery and Famine*, p. 4.
9 *Ibid*, p. 8.
10 *Ibid.*, p. 16
11 It was approximately between today's Marsden and O'Connell Streets, set back from the original track, which later became the formed street (from historyandheritage. cityofparramatta.nsw.gov.au)..
12 Thompson, *Slavery and Famine*, p. 7.
13 *Ibid.*
14 *Ibid*, p. 6.
15 Thompson, *Slavery and Famine*, p. 6.
16 Osnaburg originated in the German city of Osnabrück
17 Collins, *An Account of the English Colony*, p. 185.
18 *Ibid.*
19 *Ibid.*, p. 184
20 *Ibid.*
21 Governor Phillip to Henry Dundas, 11 October, 1792, *HRNSW*, Vol. 1 Part 2, p. 665.
22 J. M. Bennett, 'Atkins, Richard (1745–1820)', Australian Dictionary of Biography, Australian National University, 1966.
23 George Barrington, born 14 May 1755, Maynooth, County Kildare, Ireland; died 27 December 1804, Parramatta, NSW.
24 *Memoirs of George Barrington*, M. Smith, 1790, p. 74.
25 Collins, *An Account of the English Colony*, p. 187.
26 Thompson, *Slavery and Famine*, p. 9
27 David Collins, *An Account of the English Colony in New South Wales*, T. Cadell, 1798, p. 236.
28 Lieutenant-Governor Grose to Henry Dundas, 3 September 1793, *HRNSW*, Vol. 2, p. 62.
29 Governor Phillip to Henry Dundas, 4 October, 1792, *HRNSW*, Vol. 1 Part 2, p. 651
30 Major Grose to Governor Phillip, 4 October 1792, *Ibid.*, p. 652.
31 Governor Phillip to Henry Dundas, 16 October 1792, *Ibid.*, p. 669.
32 Collins, *An Account of the English Colony*, p. 243.
33 *Ibid*, p. 254.
34 *Ibid*, p. 201.
35 *Ibid.*, p. 377.
36 On 24 January 1781.
37 It sank in 1782.

38   'The House', entallyestate.com.au.

39   Collins, *An Account of the English Colony*, p. 240

40   *Ibid.*, p. 205.

41   Yemmerrawanne, born c. 1775; died 18 May 1794, Eltham, England.

42   Watkin Tench, *A Complete Account of the Settlement at Port Jackson, in New South Wales, Including an Accurate Description of the Colony; of the Natives; and of Its Natural Productions*, G Nicol and J Sewell, 1793, p. 34.

43   *Ibid.*, p. 86

44   Johann Friedrich Blumenbach FRS, born 11 May 1752, Saxe-Gotha-Altenburg; died 22 January, Gottingen, Lower Saxony.

45   Brugmans to Banks, 22 September 1793, British Library, Add. MS. 8098, 259–60.

46   Collins, *An Account of the English Colony*, p. 293.

47   *Ibid.*

48   *Ibid*, p. 307.

49   *Ibid.*

50   Lieutenant-Governor Grose to Lord Cornwallis, 28 August 1793, *HRNSW*, Vol. 2, p. 60.

51   Captain Raven to the Commissioners of the Navy, 16 February 1794, *Ibid*, p. 120.

52   *Ibid.*, 25 March 1794, *Ibid.*, p. 193.

53   Captain Raven to the Secretaries of the Treasury, 23 March 1794, *Ibid.*, p. 192.

54   Collins, *An Account of the English Colony*, p. 205.

55   Later the Reverend Francis Davis Grose, born 1789; died 16 December 1817.

56   'The True Story of Margaret Catchpole,' *Windsor and Richmond Gazette* (NSW), 20 November 1897, p. 9.

57   *Ibid.*

Chapter Six

1   The original church was on a site that is now the corner of Hunter and Bligh Streets.

2   Journal of Richard Atkins, National Library of Australia, MS 4039, 5 September 1794.

3   'Church Hill', visitsydneyaustralia.

4   'Women Whose Names Will Live', *The Australian Women's Weekly*, 29 January 1938, p. 3.

5   *Ibid.*

6   *Ibid.*

7   Journal of Richard Atkins, National Library of Australia, MS 4039, 31 August 1794,

8   Lieutenant-Governor Paterson to Henry Dundas, 21 March, 1795, *HRNSW*, Vol. 2, p. 286.

9   Registers of St. Philip's Church of England, Sydney, NSW, 1787-1937, Bib 6022845.

10   'Women Whose Names Will Live', *The Australian Women's Weekly*, 29 January 1938, p. 3.

11   Thomas Watling, *Letters From An Exile*.

12   Lieutenant-Governor Grose to Henry Dundas, 4 September 1793, *HRNSW*, Vol. 2, p. 64.

13   Collins, *An Account of the English Colony in New South Wales*, pp. 254, 265.

14   Elizabeth Macarthur to Relatives and Friends in England, 21 December 1793, *HRNSW*, Vol. 2, p. 508.

15   'The Macarthur Papers', 22 August 1794, *HRNSW*, Vol. 2, p. 508.

16   *Ibid*, p. 509.

17   *Ibid.*

18   Land Grants and Leases, Colonial Secretary's Office, 1788-1809, p. 38

19   Charles Jenkinson, 1st Earl of Liverpool, born 26 April 1727, Winchester, England; died 17 December 1808, London.

20   Lieutenant-Governor Grose to Henry Dundas,, 31 August 1794, *HRNSW*, Vol. 2, p. 254.

21   *Ibid.*, 29 April 1794, *HRNSW*, Vol. 2, p. 210.

22   discoverthehawkesbury.com.au

23   Lieutenant-Governor Grose to Henry Dundas, 5 July 1794, *HRNSW*, Vol. 2, p. 238.

24   *Ibid.*
25   Lieutenant-Governor Paterson to Henry Dundas, 21 March 1795, *HRNSW*,Vol. 2, p. 286.
26   Lieutenant-Governor Paterson to Henry Dundas, 21 March, 1795, *HRNSW*,Vol. 2, p. 286.
27   Lieutenant-Governor Grose to Governor Hunter, 8 December 1794, *HRNSW*,Vol. 2, p. 274.
28   Augustus Theodore Henry Alt, born 1731, England; died 9 January 1815, Parramatta, NSW.
29   Surveyor Alt to Lieutenant-Governor Grose, 26 April, 1794, *HRNSW*,Vol. 2, p. 210.
30   John White, born 1756; died 20 February1832, Worthing, Sussex.
31   Thomas Watling, *Letters From An Exile*, 1794.
32   *Ibid.*
33   *Ibid.*
34   Captain Paterson to Henry Dundas, 16 September 1795, *HRNSW*,Vol. 2, p. 320.
35   *The Sydney Gazette and New South Wales Advertiser*, 14 May 1814, p. 2.
36   Henry Waterhouse, born 13 December 1770, London; died 27 July 1812, London.
37   George Bass, 30 January 1771, Aswarby, Lincolnshire, England; died 1803, at sea.
38   Captain Matthew Flinders, born 16 March 1774, Donington, Lincolnshire, England; died 19 July 1814, London.
39   Watkin Tench, *A Complete Account*, p. 87.
40   Keith Vincent Smith, 'Woollarawarre Bennelong', 2013, dictionaryofsydney.org
41   *London Observer*, 29 September 1793.
42   Kate Fullagar, 'Bennelong in Britain', *Aboriginal History*,Vol. 33 ANU Press, 2009, p. 40.
43   Collins, *An Account of the English Colony in New South Wales*, p. 453.
44   *Ibid*, p. 390.
45   *Ibid.*
46   *Ibid*, p. 394.
47   *Ibid.*
48   William Paterson, born 1755, Montrose, Scotland; died 21 June 1810, at sea aboard HMS Dromedary off Cape Horn.
49   Lieut.-Governor Paterson to Henry Dundas, 15 June, 1795, *HRNSW*,Vol. 2, p. 307.
50   *Ibid*, p. 308.
51   *Ibid*, p. 307.
52   *Ibid.*
53   Better known as Bidjigal.
54   Collins, *An Account of the English Colony in New South Wales*, p. 416.
55   Lieut.-Governor Paterson to Henry Dundas, 15 June, 1795, *HRNSW*,Vol. 2, p. 308.
56   Collins, *An Account of the English Colony in New South Wales*, p. 416.
57   William Rowe, Born Lanivet, Cornwall, England 1755; died May 1795, Richmond Hill.
58   Collins, *An Account of the English Colony in New South Wales*, p. 416.
59   *Ibid.*
60   'Court Of Criminal Jurisdiction', *The Sydney Gazette and New South Wales Advertiser*, 12 October 1811, p. 2.
61   Collins, *An Account of the English Colony in New South Wales*, p. 413.
62   *Ibid.*
63   *Ibid.*, p. 458.
64   R. v. Marshall [1795] NSWKR 1; [1795] NSWSupC 1, Court of Criminal Jurisdiction, Collins J.A., 15 April 1795.
65   Collins, *An Account of the English Colony in New South Wales*, p. 453.
66   *Ibid.*, p. 458.
67   'Government and General Order', 22 February 1796, *HRNSW*,Vol. 2, pp. 25-6.
68   *Ibid.*

Chapter Seven

1   Thomas Haydock Reibey, born Hawkesbury district, 6 May 1796; died 3 October 1842, Hadspen, Tasmania.
2   'Family History In A Bible', *The Australian Woman's Mirror*, 24 May 1950, pp. 7, 36.
3   T. D. Mutch papers, 1907-1957, State Library of NSW, MLMSS 426.
4   Waterhouse to Phillip, 24 October 1795, State Library of NSW, SAFE/Banks Papers/Series 37.28.
5   John Hunter to Joseph Banks, 12 October 1795, *Ibid.*
6   Hunter to The Duke of Portland, 12 November, 1796, *Historical Records of Australia (HRA)*, Series 1, Vol. 1, p. 676.
7   William Cavendish-Bentinck, 3rd Duke of Portland, (14 April 1738 – 30 October 1809).
8   Hunter to Portland, 10 August 1796, *HRA*, Series 1, Vol. 1, p. 574.
9   *Ibid.*
10 'Condition of the Settlements,' *HRNSW*, 20 August 1796, p. 81.
11 *Ibid.*
12 David Collins, *An Account of the English Colony in New South Wales*, 1802 edition.
13 Matthew Flinders, *A Voyage to Terra Australis*, Vol. 1, G & W Nicol, 1814, p. xcvii. It is now the Sydney suburb of Bankstown. Flinders wrote it as 'Bank's Town'.
14 Robert Campbell, born 28 April 1769, Greenock, Scotland; died 15 April 1846, Duntroon, NSW.
15 T. D. Mutch papers, 1907-1957, State Library of NSW, MLMSS 426.
16 Grace Karskens, *The Colony: A history of early Sydney*, Allen and Unwin, 2009, p. 329, Kindle Edition.
17 Jenny Hocking and Laura Donati, 'Obscured but not Obscure: How History Ignored the Remarkable Story of Sarah Will Yorkshire Howe', The Journal of the European Association for Studies of Australia, Vol. 7, No. 2, 2016.
18 'The True Story of Margaret Catchpole,' *Windsor and Richmond Gazette* (NSW), 20 November 1897, p. 9.
19 'Suspicion of murdering infant son', R9: Judge Advocates Office, William Balmain Esq, State Records of NSW, COD 76 (1798), p.35
20 Hunter to Portland, 1 May 1799, *HRA*, Series 1, Vol. 2, p. 354.
21 *Ibid.*
22 Andrew Thompson, baptised 7 February 1773, Town Yetholm, Scotland; died 22 October 1810, Green Hills Windsor, NSW.
23 Hunter to Portland, 1 May 1799, *HRA*, Series 1, Vol. 2, p. 356.
24 Hunter to Portland, 15 November 1799, *Ibid.*, p. 395.
25 *Ibid.*, p. 394.
26 *Ibid.*
27 Bungaree, born c. 1775; died 24 November 1830, Garden Island NSW.
28 That place is now known as Clontarf Point, while the suburb Redcliffe is now to the north.
29 Governor Hunter to The Duke of Portland, 2 January 1800, *HRA*, Series 1, Vol. 2, pp. 416, 420.
30 King v. Powell, Freebody, Metcalf, Timms and Butler for wantonly *killing* two native men of this territory, R. v. Powell [1799] NSWKR 7; [1799] NSWSupC 7
31 Hunter to Portland, 20 April 1800, *HRA*, Series 1, Vol. 2, p. 412.
32 *Ibid.*, p. 404.
33 *Ibid.*, p. 408.
34 *Ibid.*, pp. 401-2.
35 Lyn Stewart, *Blood Revenge: Murder on the Hawkesbury 1799*, Rosenberg Publishing, 2015.
36 Hunter to Portland, 20 April 1800, *HRA*, Series 1, Vol. 2, pp. 401-2.
37 *Ibid.*, p. 403.

38   Richard Dore, born 21 March 1749, Essex, England; died 13 December 1800, NSW.
39   Captain Macarthur to Governor Hunter, 25 July 1796, *HRA*, Series 1, Vol. 2, p. 103.
40   *Ibid.*, p. 487.
41   Philip Gidley King, born 23 April 1758, Launceston, Cornwall, England; died 3 September 1808, London.
42   They both became Naval officers.
43   Anna Josepha King, née Coombe, born 11 March 1791, Hatherleigh, Devon, England; died 26 July 1844, Parramatta, NSW.
44   Acting-Governor King to Under Secretary John King, 29 November 1800, *HRA*, Series 1, Vol. 2, p. 695.
45   Adam Courtenay, *Three Sheets to the Wind*, ABC Books, 2022, p. 251.
46   Samuel Marsden, born 24 June 1765 at Farsley, Yorkshire, England; died 12 May, 1838, Windsor, NSW.
47   T. Crofton Croker, *Memoirs of Joseph Holt: General of the Irish rebels*, in 1798, Vol. 2, Henry Coulburn, 1838, pp. 120-122.
48   *Ibid.*
49   *Ibid.*
50   Adrian Nesbitt, 'A renovation with conviction', *The Sydney Morning Herald*, 14 January 2010, smh.com.au
51   Trim was black with white paws, white chin, and a white star on chest.
52   Government and General Order, 18 November 1800, *HRNSW*, Vol. 4, p. 256
53   George Haydock Reibey, born 2 February 1801; died 26 Oct 1823, Hadspen, Tasmania.
54   visitsydneyaustralia.com.au
55   John Ramsland, 'Children's institutions in nineteenth-century Sydney', dictionaryofsydney.org
56   Hunter to Portland, 1 November 1798, *HRA*, Series 1, Vol. 2, p. 236.
57   *HRNSW*, Vol. 4, p. 658.
58   *Ibid.*, Vol 5, p 115.
59   *Ibid.*
60   State Records of NSW, Reel 6037; SZ988 pp.68, 70-2.
61   Acting-Governor King to Under Secretary John King, 14 November 1801, *HRA*, Series 1, Vol. 2, p. 347.
62   *Ibid.*, 8 November 1801, *Ibid*, p. 322.
63   *Ibid.*, 14 November 1801, *Ibid*, p. 347.
64   John Borthwick Gilchrist, born as John Hay Gilchrist, 19 June 1759, Edinburgh, Scotland; died 8 January 1841, Paris, France.
65   On 6 December 1801.
66   Celia Eliza Reibey, born 1 February 1802 Sydney; died 28 September 1823, Sydney.
67   William Blue, born c. 1767, Jamaica, New York; died 7 May 1834, Sydney.
68   Matthew Flinders, *A Voyage to Terra Australis*, Vol. 1, G & W Nicol, 1814, p. 146.
69   Nicolas Thomas Baudin, born 19 February 1754, St-Pierre-de-Ré, France; died 16 September 1803, Mauritius.
70   On 2 June 1802.
71   On 22 November 1801,
72   King to Banks, 5 June 1802, *HRNSW*, Vol. 4, p. 784.
73   'Napoleon and the Platypus,' ngv.vic.gov.au, 2 September 2012.
74   Then called Isle de France.
75   Register of Land Grants, 1803, Colonial Secretary's Papers, State Archives and Records NSW, NRS 13836 [7/445], Register 1, Page 147; Reel 2560.
76   Now located at 141 Blacktown Road, Freemans Reach.

77   George Howe, born 1769, Saint Christopher Island (now known as Saint Kitts); died
      11 May 1821, Sydney.
78   'Classified Advertising', *The Sydney Gazette and New South Wales Advertiser*, 17 July 1803, p. 1.
79   *The Sydney Gazette and New South Wales Advertiser*, 26 March 1803, p. 4.
80   *Ibid.*, 2 April 1803, p. 4.
81   *Ibid*, 10 April 1803, p. 4.
82   In May 1802.
83   Joseph Arnold to his brother, 25 February 1810, A1849 vol. 2, State Library of New
      South Wales.
84   *The Sydney Gazette and New South Wales Advertiser*, 23 October 1803, p. 4.
85   *Ibid.*, 4 March 1804, p. 4.
86   George Suttor, born 11 June 1774 at Chelsea, London.
87   Memoirs of George Suttor, F.L.S., 1774-1859, State Library of NSW, A 3072.
88   In October 1803.
89   G. P. Walsh, 'Reibey, Mary (1777–1855)', *Australian Dictionary of Biography*, Australian
      National University, 1967.
90   'Remainder of Port News', *The Sydney Gazette and New South Wales Advertiser*, 4 December
      1803, p. 4.
91   'Ship News', *Ibid.*, 8 May 1803, p. 4.
92   *Ibid.*, 13 May 1804, p. 1.

Chapter Eight
1   Tom Dunne, *Rebellions: Memoir, Memory and 1798*, Lilliput Press, 2004.
2   'Insurrection', Sydney Gazette and New South Wales Advertiser, 11 March 1804, p. 2.
3   Later Lieutenant-Colonel George Johnston, born 19 March 1764 Annan, Dumfriesshire,
      Scotland; died 5 January 1823, Sydney.
4   The site is commemorated at Castlebrook Memorial Park, Rouse Hill.
5   Thomas Anlezark, born c. 1765, England; died 3 April 1834, Liverpool NSW.
6   'Insurrection', Sydney Gazette and New South Wales Advertiser, 11 March 1804, p. 2.
7   'Ship News', *Ibid.*, 29 April 1804, p. 4.
8   *Ibid.*
9   'Sydney', *Ibid.*, 6 May 1804, p. 2.
10   'Classified Advertising', *The Sydney Gazette and New South Wales Advertiser*, 25 November
      1804, p. 4.
11   *Ibid.*, 17 July 1803, p. 4.
12   Mary Salmon, 'First Sydney Ferry Woman', *The Gosford Times and Wyong District Advocate*,
      5 March 1925, p. 16.
13   *Ibid.*
14   *The Sydney Gazette and New South Wales Advertiser*, 1 April 1804, p. 3.
15   *Ibid.*, 3 June 1804, p. 2.
16   *Ibid.*
17   State Records NSW, Index to the Colonial Secretary's Papers, 1788-1825, Citation:
      [9/2731], p.204, 1 May 1804.
18   Garnham Blaxcell, baptized 27 May 1778, Suffolk, England; died 3 October 1817, Batavia.
19   Simeon Lord, born 1771, Yorkshire, England; died 29 January, 1840, Botany, Sydney.
20   'History of Macquarie Place Park', cityofsydney.nsw.gov.au.
21   *The Sydney Gazette and New South Wales Advertiser*, 23 October 1803, p. 2.
22   'The House', entallyestate.com.au.
23   'The True Story of Margaret Catchpole,' *Windsor and Richmond Gazette* (NSW),
      20 November 1897, p. 9.
24   *Ibid.*, 16 September 1804, p. 4.

25 *Ibid.*, 24 March 1805, p. 4.

26 *Ibid.*, 27 May 1804, p. 4.

27 *Ibid.*

28 Jim Low, 'Massacre at Shaws Creek', simplyaustralia.net, 27 July 2019.

29 *The Sydney Gazette and New South Wales Advertiser*, 12 May 1805, p. 2.

30 *Ibid.*

31 *Ibid.*

32 Eliza Reibey, born 16 May 1805, Sydney, died 25 December 1870, Launceston, Tasmania.

33 'The True Story of Margaret Catchpole,' *Windsor and Richmond Gazette* (NSW), 20 November 1897, p. 9.

34 'Classified Advertising', *The Sydney Gazette and New South Wales Advertiser*, 10 November 1805, p. 1.

35 Edward Spencer Wills, born 13 Aug 1778, Finsbury, London; died 14 May 1811, Sydney.

36 James Dashper and William Woodham.

37 William Noah, 'A Voyage to Sydney in New South Wales in 1798 & 1799' and 'A Few Remarks of the County of Cumberland in New South Wales, 1798-1799, State Library of NSW, SAFE/DLMS 32.

38 *Ibid.*

39 *Ibid.*

40 *The Sydney Gazette and New South Wales Advertiser*, 28 April 1805, p. 4.

41 'Examinations Before The Lieutenant-Governor', *Ibid*, 2 October 1803, p. 2.

42 'Examinations ', *Ibid*, 7 October 1804, p. 2.

43 'Examinations Before the Magistrates', *Ibid.*, 20 January 1805, p. 4

44 'Ship News', *Ibid.*, 21 July 1805, p. 2.

45 'Annan, William', dictionaryofsydney.org

46 'Sydney', *The Sydney Gazette and New South Wales Advertiser*, 3 November 1805, p. 2. His name was often recorded as 'Wilhamanan'.

47 Banks to King, 29 August 1804, State Library of NSW, Banks Papers, Series 39.090.

48 'Sydney', *The Sydney Gazette and New South Wales Advertiser*, 15 September 1805, p. 2.

49 Grace Karskens, *The Colony: A history of early Sydney*, Allen and Unwin, 2009, p. 173, Kindle Edition.

50 On 19 June 1805.

51 Joseph Banks, 'Some Remarks on the Present State of the Colony of Sidney [sic] in New South Wales & on the Means Most Likely to Render It a Productive instead of an Expensive Settlement', 4 June 1806, State Library of NSW, Banks Papers, Series 35.35.

52 *Ibid.*

53 Joseph Banks, 'Some Observations on a Bill Admitting the Produce of New South Wales to Country at the Customs Houses of the United Kingdom', 7 July 1806, State Library of NSW, Banks Papers, Series 35.38.

54 'Sydney', *The Sydney Gazette and New South Wales Advertiser*, 6 April 1806, p. 2.

55 Jane Penelope Reibey, born 14 December 1807, Sydney; died 9 October 1854, Launceston, Tasmania.

56 Thomas Reibey, Power of Attorney, State Library of NSW, ML A 5327.

57 'Classified Advertising', *The Sydney Gazette and New South Wales Advertiser*, 8 Mar 1807, p. 2.

58 Also known as Lady Madeline Sinclair.

59 Joseph Short, born c. 1760 in Portsmouth, Hampshire, England; died c. 1830.

60 William Bligh to Sir Joseph Banks, 1 April 1806, State Library of New South Wales, Banks Papers, Series 40.013.

61 *HRNSW*, Vol. VI, p. xlvi.

62 *Ibid.*

63 John Blaxland, born 4 January, Fordwich, Kent, England; died 5 August, Newington, NSW.

64   Blaxland to Earl of Liverpool, 27 November 1809, *HRNSW*,Vol.VII, p. 237.

65   *Ibid.*

66   Thomas Jamison, born c. 1753; died 25 January 1811.

67   William Bligh to William Windham, 31 October 1807, *HRA*, Series I,Volume VI, p. 150.

68   *Ibid.*

69   Bligh to Viscount Castlereagh, 30 April 1808, *HRNSW*,Vol.VI, p.608.

70   *Ibid*, p. 609.

71   *Ibid*, p. 610.

72   'The Trial of John Macarthur', from Colonial Secretary's Papers, 2 February 1808, *HRNSW*,Vol.VI, p. 475.

73   Bligh to Viscount Castlereagh, 30 April 1808, *HRNSW*,Vol.VI, p. 611.

74   *Ibid*, p. 613.

75   *Ibid*, p. 615.

76   *Ibid*, p. 617.

77   *Ibid.*

78   'Arrest of Governor Bligh', *Clarence and Richmond Examiner and New England Advertiser* (Grafton, NSW), 24 January 1888, p. 3.

79   Bligh to Viscount Castlereagh, 30 April 1808, *HRNSW*,Vol.VI., p. 617.

Chapter Nine

1   James Underwood, born 4 September 1771, Bermondsey, London; died 19 February, 1844 Brixton, Surrey, England.

2   Henry Kable, born 1763, Laxfield, Suffolk, England; died 16 March 1846, Pitt Town, NSW.

3   Referred to as 'Ulitea' in the 19th century.

4   'Ship News', *The Sydney Gazette and New South Wales Advertiser*, 17 July 1808, p. 2.

5   *Ibid.*

6   *Ibid.*

7   *Ibid.*

8   *Ibid.*

9   'Classified Advertising', *Ibid.*

10   Settlers to Major Johnston, *HRNSW*,Vol.VI, p. 597.

11   *Ibid.*

12   Ellis Bent to his mother, 4 March 1810, MS 195/3, National Library of Australia, p. 74.

13   Joseph Foveaux, baptized 6 April 1767, Ampthill, Bedfordshire, England; died 20 March, 1846, London.

14   *HRNSW*,Vol.VI, p. 698.

15   Proclamation by Joseph Foveaux, *The Sydney Gazette and New South Wales Advertiser*, 31 July 1808, p. 1.

16   On 29 March 1809.

17   William Bligh to Viscount Castlereagh, 10 June 1809, *HRA*, Series I,Vol.VII, p. 128.

18   Thomas Spencer Wills, born 5 August 1800, Sydney; died 29 July 1872, 'Willsmere', Kew, Victoria

19   'Classified Advertising', *The Sydney Gazette and New South Wales Advertiser*, 16 April 1809, p. 1.

20   'Government and General Order', *HRNSW*,Vol.VII, p. 86.

21   'Classified Advertising', *The Sydney Gazette and New South Wales Advertiser*, 24 September 1809, p. 1.

22   *Ibid*, 10 September p. 2.

23   Thomas Reibey will, State Library of NSW, ML A 5327-3, No. 108.

24   *Ibid.*

25   'Sydney', *The Sydney Gazette and New South Wales Advertiser*, 30 April 1809, p. 2.

26 Governor Macquarie to Earl of Liverpool, 13 November 1812, *HRA*, Series 1, Vol. VII, p. 548.

27 'Ship News', *The Sydney Gazette and New South Wales Advertiser*, 6 October 1810, p. 3.

28 Lachlan Macquarie to Dorothea Morley, 'Letterbook 22 November 1802 to 14 February 1804', 5 May 1803, Vol. Z A792, Lachlan Macquarie and Macquarie Family Papers, State Library of New South Wales, pp. 31–33.

29 Macquarie, Journals, 20 August 1804, Vol. Z A770, Item 2, State Library of New South Wales.

30 Michael Glover, 'The Nightingall Letters', Journal of the Society for Army Historical Research, Vol. 51, No. 207 (Autumn 1973), p. 129.

31 Robert Stewart, Viscount Castlereagh, Marquess of Londonderry, born 18 June 1769, Dublin, Ireland; died 12 August 1822, Kent, England.

32 Macquarie to Viscount Castlereagh, Letterbooks, 1 May 1809, Vol. Z A796, State Library of New South Wales; p. 3.

33 Sir Maurice Charles O'Connell, born 1768, County Kerry, Ireland; died 25 May 1848, Sydney.

34 Later Rear-Admiral John Pasco, born 20 December 1774; died 16 November 1853 East Stonehouse, England.

35 Roy Adkins, *Trafalgar: The Biography of a Battle*, Hachette UK, 2011.

36 Henry Antill, 3 August 1809, from Henry Colden Antill, *Early History of New South Wales*, W.A. Gullick, Government Printer, 1914.

37 Elizabeth Macquarie, Journal, 5 July 1809, Vol. Z C126, State Library of New South Wales.

38 *Ibid.*

39 Isaac Nichols, born 29 July 1770, Calne, Wiltshire, England; died 8 November 1819, Sydney.

40 Macquarie, Memoranda, 31 December 1809, Vol. Z A772, State Library of New South Wales.

41 Sydney Gazette and New South Wales Advertiser, 7 January 1810, pp. 2–3.

42 *Ibid.*

43 *Ibid.*, 7 January 1810, pp. 2–3.

44 *Ibid.*

45 Now Wynyard Park.

46 Ellis Bent, born 1783 Surrey, England; died 10 November 1815 Sydney.

47 Though officially 'Deputy Judge Advocate', Bent was usually called 'Judge Advocate'.

48 Sydney Gazette and New South Wales Advertiser, 7 January 1810, pp. 2–3.

49 *Ibid.*

50 *Ibid.*

51 *Ibid.*

Chapter Ten

1 *The Sydney Gazette and New South Wales Advertiser*, 31 December 1809, p. 1.

2 *Ibid.*

3 Letter from Mary Reibey to her cousin Alice Hope, 12 August 1818, State Library of New South Wales, Safe/MLMSS 4534 (Safe 1/210).

4 *Ibid*, 6 October 1810, p. 3.

5 'Proclamation', *The Sydney Gazette and New South Wales Advertiser*, 7 January 1810, p. 1.

6 Macquarie, Memoranda, 1 January 1810, Vol. Z A772, State Library of New South Wales.

7 Macquarie to Viscount Castlereagh, 30 April 1810, *HRA*, Series I, Vol. VII, pp. 280–281.

8 *Ibid*, p. 285.

9 Macquarie to Christopher Lundin, Letterbooks, 20 March 1795, Vol. Z A788, State Library of New South Wales.

10   *The Sydney Gazette and New South Wales Advertiser*, 7 January 1810, p. 3.

11   *Ibid.*

12   'Address to His Excellency', *The Sydney Gazette and New South Wales Advertiser*, 21 January 1810, p. 1.

13   Joseph Underwood, born 12 July, 1779, London, England; died 30 August 1833, Ashfield, Sydney.

14   'Address to His Excellency', *The Sydney Gazette and New South Wales Advertiser*, 21 January 1810, p. 1.

15   Macquarie to Earl Bathurst, 27 July 1822, *HRA*, Series I, Vol. X, pp. 671–672.

16   Macquarie, Memoranda, 10 January 1810, Vol. Z A772, State Library of New South Wales.

17   *Ibid.*, 30 April 1810, Vol. Z A772, State Library of New South Wales.

18   Macquarie to Viscount Castlereagh, 30 April 1810, *HRA*, Series I, Vol. VII, p. 321.

19   Macquarie, Memoranda, 15 January 1810, Vol. Z A772, State Library of New South Wales.

20   Francis Williams, born 1780; died 6 October 1831, near Newcastle. Williams had married Lord's adopted daughter.

21   Macquarie to Viscount Castlereagh, 30 April 1810, *HRA*, Series I, Vol. VII, p. 275.

22   *Ibid.*, 8 March 1810, *Ibid.*, p. 218.

23   Macquarie, Memoranda, 26 January 1810, Vol. Z A772, State Library of New South Wales.

24   Macquarie to Viscount Castlereagh, 8 March 1810, *HRA*, Series I, Vol. VII, p. 219.

25   State Records and Archives of NSW, NRS 897 [4/1822, no. 276].

26   Mary Reibey to David Hope, 5 August 1825, State Library of NSW, Safe/MLMSS 5512/1 (Safe 1/261), MLMSS 5512/2.

27   *Ibid.*

28   *Ibid.*

29   Macquarie to Viscount Castlereagh,, 30 April 1810, *HRA*, Series I, Vol. VII, p. 250.

30   'Government and General Order', 27 January 1810, *Ibid*, p. 281.

31   *Ibid.*

32   Michael Hayes, born 1767 Wexford, Ireland; died 7 September, 1825, Sydney.

33   *Ibid.*

34   Elizabeth Anne Reibey, born 8 March 1810, Sydney, died 19 April 1870, Kensington, London.

35   Joseph Arnold, 'Letters, 18 March to 10 May 1810', A1849 vol. 2, Joseph Arnold Papers 1808–1817, State Library of New South Wales.

36   Macquarie, Memoranda, 8 May 1810, Vol. Z A772, State Library of New South Wales.

37   William Bligh to Elizabeth Bligh, 11 August 1810, Safe 1/45, State Library of New South Wales, pp. 279–286.

38   Macquarie, Memoranda, 11 May 1810, Vol. Z A772, State Library of New South Wales.

39   *Ibid*, 12 May 1810, *Ibid.*

40   William Bligh to Sir Joseph Banks, 11 August 1810, *HRA*, Series 1, Vol. VII, p. 404.

41   Macquarie to Viscount Castlereagh, 8 March 1810, *Ibid*, p. 219.

42   *The Sydney Gazette and New South Wales Advertiser*, 19 May 1810, p. 1

43   *Ibid*, 5 May 1810, p. 1.

44   *Ibid.*

45   *Ibid.*

46   *Ibid.*, 9 June 1810, p. 2.

47   *Ibid.*, 14 July 1810, p. 4.

48   *Ibid.*, 21 July 1810, p. 2.

49   *Ibid.*, 4 December 1813, p. 2.

50   *Ibid.*, 6 October 1810, p. 3.

51   *Ibid.*

52 Alexander Riley, born 1778, London, died 1833, London.
53 Colonial Secretary to Alexander Riley, 23 May 1810, Index to the Colonial Secretary's Papers, 1788-1825, [4/3490C], pp.50, 76-7 | Reel No: 6002.
54 'Government and General Orders', *The Sydney Gazette and New South Wales Advertiser*, 6 October 1810, p. 1
55 *Ibid.*
56 *Ibid.*
57 Macquarie to Viscount Castlereagh, 30 April 1810, *HRA*, Series I, Vol. VII, p. 272.
58 'Government and General Order', 23 June 1810, *HRNSW*, Vol. VII, p. 389.
59 'First Post Office', Defining Moments in Australian History, National Museum of Australia, nma.gov.au/defining-moments.
60 'Government and General Orders', *The Sydney Gazette and New South Wales Advertiser*, 6 October 1810, p. 1.
61 *Ibid.*
62 *Ibid.*
63 *Ibid*, 20 October 1810, p. 3.
64 'Sporting Intelligence', *Ibid*, 20 October 1810, p. 2.
65 John Piper, born 8 August 1774, Maybole, Ayrshire, Scotland; died 8 June 1851, Macquarie River district, NSW.
66 Thomas Sadlier Cleaveland, born 1785; died 1812.
67 *The Sydney Gazette and New South Wales Advertiser*, 13 October 1810, p. 2.
68 'The Subscribers' Ball', *Sydney Gazette and New South Wales Advertiser*, 20 October 1810, p. 2.
69 *The Sydney Gazette and New South Wales Advertiser*, 20 October 1810, p. 4.
70 Colonial Secretary's Papers, 1788-1825, | Citation: [4/3490D], p.26, Reel No: 6002, State Records of NSW.
71 R.V. Pockley, *Ancestor Treasure Hunt: The Edward Wills Family And Descendants in Australia 1797–1976*, pp. 11-12.
72 James Meehan, born 1774, Ireland; died 21 April 1826, Macquarie Field, NSW.
73 'Died', *The Sydney Gazette and New South Wales Advertiser*, 27 October 1810, p. 3.
74 At St Matthew's Anglican Church, Windsor.
75 Macquarie to Viscount Castlereagh, 30 April 1810, *HRA*, Series I, Vol. VII, p. 276.
76 D'Arcy Wentworth, born 1762, Portadown, Armagh, Ireland; died 7 July 1827, Homebush, Sydney.
77 Old Bailey Session Papers, 1787 to 1788, pp. 15-20, cited in Kathleen Mary Dermody, 'D'Arcy Wentworth 1762–1827: A Second Chance', Australian National University PhD thesis, April 1990, pp. 23–24, openresearch-repository.anu.edu.au/handle/1885/114504.
78 J.J. Auchmuty, 'Wentworth, D'Arcy (1762–1827)', Australian Dictionary of Biography, MUP, 1967.
79 William Redfern, born 1774; died 17 July 1833.
80 'Government and General Order', 20 February 1810, *HRNSW*, Vol. VII, p. 291.
81 Macquarie, A Letter to the Right Honourable Viscount Sidmouth in Refutation of Statements Made by the Hon. Henry Grey Bennet, M.P. in a Pamphlet 'On the Transportation Laws, the State of the Hulks, and of the Colonies in New South Wales', Richard Rees, 1921, NK4111, Rex Nan Kivell Collection, National Library of Australia, p. 38.
82 Macquarie, memo, 6 January 1821, *HRA*, Series IV: Legal Papers, Section A; Vol. 1, p. 879.
83 Lachlan Macquarie, A Letter to the Right Honourable Viscount Sidmouth, p. 79.
84 Macquarie to John Thomas Bigge, 6 November 1819, *HRA*, Series I, Volume X, p. 222.
85 Laura Jocic, *Anna King's dress: trade and society in early colonial Sydney*, emajartjournal.files. wordpress.com

Chapter Eleven

1   *The Sydney Gazette and New South Wales Advertiser*, 2 March 1811, p. 2.
2   *Ibid.*, 6 April 1811, p. 4.
3   *Ibid.*
4   Edward Charles Close, 'The Costume of the Australasians', watercolour 1817, State Library of NSW, SAFE/PXA 1187.
5   Original tombstone for Thomas Reibey, Series 02: Glass negatives of headstones in Devonshire Street Cemetery, Sydney, and other cemeteries, ca. 1900-1914 / Mrs. Arthur George Foster, No. 439, State Library of NSW, FL8501903. Following Mary's death four decades later a new tombstone was erected, giving an incorrect age and date of death for Tom.
6   Reibey, Mary, administratrix of Thomas Reibey - Shannon, Elizabeth, Court of Civil Jurisdiction index 1799-1814, NSW State Archives, Series: NRS 2659 | Item No: 5/1106, 8 July 1811
7   *The Sydney Gazette and New South Wales Advertiser*, 23 March 1811, p. 1.
8   *Ibid.*, 30 November 1806, p. 1.
9   *Ibid.*, 13 April 1811, p. 2.
10 *Ibid.*, 12 December 1812, p. 2.
11 *Ibid.*, 27 April 1811, p. 1.
12 *Ibid.*, 18 May 1811, p. 2.
13 Horatio Spencer Howe Wills, born 5 October 1811, Sydney; died 17 October 1861, Cullin-la-ringo, Queensland.
14 Francis Williams, born c. 1780; died 6 October 1831, Newcastle district.
15 *The Sydney Gazette and New South Wales Advertiser*, 5 January 1811, p. 1.
16 *Cargo of the Brig Aurora v. United States*, 11 U.S 7 (Cranch), 382 (1813), Justia, Library of Congress.
17 *The Sydney Gazette and New South Wales Advertiser*, 31 August 1811, p. 2.
18 Also known as Bennett.
19 Colonial Secretary's Papers, 1788-1825, Citation: [4/1726], p.252 | Reel No: 6043, State Records NSW.
20 *The Sydney Gazette and New South Wales Advertiser*, 19 June 1813, p. 4.
21 Alexander Riley, born 1778, London; died 17 November 1833, London.
22 *The Sydney Gazette and New South Wales Advertiser*, 23 February 1811, p. 1.
23 Macquarie to Viscount Castlereagh, 8 March 1810, *HRA*, Series I, Vol 7, p. 223.
24 'Pistolling Privy-Counsellors', Cobbett's Weekly Political Register (London), 7 October 1809, p.481.
25 Macquarie to Viscount Castlereagh, 8 March 1810, *HRA*, Series I, Vol. VII, p. 224.
26 *Ibid*, 30 April 1810, *Ibid*, p. 275.
27 Old Windsor Road now follows the approximate route.
28 Thomas Moore, born 1762, England; died 24 December 1840, NSW. He gave his name to Moore Theological College, Sydney.
29 Macquarie, Memoranda, 6 December 1810, Vol. ZA772, State Library of New South Wales.
30 'Contract for Rebuilding Bridge Facing Sydney Cove', 24 September 1811, *HRNSW*, Vol. 7, p. 591.
31 'Hospital Contract', 6 November 1810, *HRNSW*, Vol. VII, pp. 449–453.
32 *Ibid.*
33 'Mary Reibey - convict and businesswoman', records.nsw.gov.au.
34 Macquarie to Earl of Liverpool, 18 October 1811, *HRA*, Series 1, Vol. VII, p. 400.
35 Vivienne Parsons, 'Hayes, Michael (1767–1825)', Australian Dictionary of Biography, MUP, 1966.
36 *The Sydney Gazette and New South Wales Advertiser*, 12 December 1811, p. 2.

37 *Ibid*, 20 July 1811, p. 2.
38 *Ibid*.
39 *Ibid*, 8 February 1812, p. 1.
40 Minutes of Proceedings, Court of Civil Jurisdiction 1812, Cases 138 and 139, NRS 2659 [5/1107], State Records of NSW.
41 Letter from Mary Reibey to her cousin Alice Hope, 12 August 1818, State Library of New South Wales, Safe/MLMSS 4534 (Safe 1/210).
42 State Library NSW, A 5327.
43 *Ibid*, ML MSS, 1757/ Item 2.
44 *The Sydney Gazette and New South Wales Advertiser*, 12 December 1812, p. 2.
45 *Ibid*., 4 July 1812, p. 1.
46 *Ibid*., 6 June 1812, p. 4.
47 *Ibid*., 26 September 1812, p. 2.
48 *Ibid*., 27 June 1812, p. 2.
49 Earl of Liverpool to Macquarie, 4 May 1812, *HRA*, Series I, Vol. VII, p. 477.
50 *Ibid*.
51 Earl of Liverpool to Macquarie, 4 May 1812, *HRA*, Series I, Vol. VII, p. 481
52 Macquarie to Earl of Liverpool, 9 November 1812, *Ibid*., pp. 597–598.
53 *The Sydney Gazette and New South Wales Advertiser*, 27 March 1813, p. 1.
54 *Evening News* (Sydney), 27 November 1897, p. 2.
55 *The Sydney Gazette and New South Wales Advertiser*, 27 November 1813, p. 2.
56 *Ibid*., 13 March 1813, p. 2.
57 *Ibid*, 20 March 1813, p. 2.
58 *Ibid*.
59 *Ibid*, 5 June 1813, p. 1.
60 W. L. Crowther, *Voyage of the 'Mary And Sally' to Macquarie Island for the purpose of obtaining Sea Elephant Oil and seal skins (November 16, 1813-March 13, 1814)*, Royal Society of Tasmania, 1933.
61 *Ibid*.
62 *Ibid*, 24 April 1813, p. 1.
63 Macquarie to Liverpool, 17 November 1812, *HRA*, Series 1, Vol. VII, p. 652.
64 Henry Bathurst, 3rd Earl Bathurst, born 22 May 1762; died 27 July 1834.
65 Earl Bathurst to Macquarie, 3 February 1814, *HRA*, Series I, Vol. VIII, p. 135.
66 'Proclamation', 24 February 1810, *HRNSW*, Vol. 7, p. 292.
67 *Ibid*, p. 293.
68 Esther Johnston née Abrahams, born 1767, England; died 26 August 1846, Sydney.
69 Macquarie to John Wilson Croker, 3 August 1813, *Ibid*., p. 32.
70 Gregory Blaxland, born 17 June 1778, Fordwich, Kent, England; died 1 January 1853, NSW.
71 William Lawson, born 2 June 1774, Finchley, Middlesex, England; died 16 June 1850, Prospect NSW.
72 William Charles Wentworth, born 1790, England; died 20 March, 1872, Wimborne, Dorset, England.
73 They called it Emu Island, because early explorers thought the land was totally cut off by water. It actually occupies a semi-circular bend of the river.
74 Gregory Blaxland, *A Journal of a Tour of Discovery Across the Blue Mountains*, New South Wales, in the Year 1813, Australian Historical Society, 1900, pp. 24–25.
75 *Ibid*, p. 32.
76 *Ibid*, p. 36
77 *The Sydney Gazette and New South Wales Advertiser*, 4 March 1814, p. 2.
78 *Ibid*.
79 *Ibid*.

80 Macquarie to Earl Bathurst, 24 May 1814, *HRA*, Series I, Vol. VIII, p. 261.
81 *Ibid.*
82 *Ibid*, 28 April 1814, *Ibid*, p. 150.
83 Macquarie, Memoranda, 28 March 1814, Vol. Z A772, State Library of New South Wales.
84 *The Sydney Gazette and New South Wales Advertiser*, 24 December 1814, p. 1.
85 Robert Jenkins, born 1777, Arlingham, Gloucestershire, England; died 4 May 1822, Sydney.
86 *The Sydney Gazette and New South Wales Advertiser*, 24 December 1814, p. 1.
87 *Ibid*, 5 August 1815, p. 2.

Chapter Twelve
1   *The Sydney Gazette and New South Wales Advertiser*, 15 April 1815, p. 2.
2   'The Convict Girl', *Brisbane Telegraph*, 20 November 1954, p. 14.
3   John Piper, born 20 April 1773 at Maybole, Ayrshire, Scotland; died at his property Westbourne, near Bathurst, NSW.
4   The road was finished in January 1815.
5   Macquarie to Earl Bathurst, 7 October 1814, *HRA*, Series I, Vol. VIII, p. 315.
6   Francis Greenway, born 20 November 1777, Mangotsfield, near Bristol, England; died September 1837 near Newcastle, New South Wales.
7   Macquarie to Earl Bathurst, 14 April 1814, *HRA*, Series I, Vol. VIII, p. 140.
8   *Ibid.*, 22 March 1815, *Ibid.*, p. 461.
9   *The Sydney Gazette and New South Wales Advertiser*, 17 December 1814, p. 1.
10 *Ibid.*
11 *Ibid*, 14 January 1815, p. 2.
12 *Ibid*, 3 Jun 1815, p. 1.
13 *Ibid*, 20 July 1816, p. 2.
14 *The Sydney Gazette and New South Wales Advertiser*, 20 January 1816, p. 2.
15 *Ibid.*, 14 May 1814, p. 2.
16 Charles Throsby to Wentworth, 5 April 1816, Wentworth Papers, A752/CY699 Mitchell Library, pp. 183-6.
17 *The Sydney Gazette and New South Wales Advertiser*, 14 May 1814.
18 *Ibid.*, 7 May 1814.
19 Grace Karskens, 'Appin massacre', dictionaryofsydney.org.
20 Government and General Orders, Sydney Gazette, 18 June 1814.
21 *Sydney Gazette and New South Wales Advertiser*, 9 March 1816, p. 2.
22 *Ibid.*
23 *Ibid.*
24 Samuel to Thomas Hassall, 16 March 1816, Hassall Family Correspondence, ML A1677/3, 619–22, 627–30, State Library of New South Wales.
25 *Ibid.*
26 *Ibid.*
27 *The Sydney Gazette and New South Wales Advertiser*, 30 March 1816, p. 2.
28 Macquarie to Earl Bathurst, 18 March 1816, *HRA*, Series I, Vol. VIII, pp. 53–54.
29 *Ibid.*
30 *Ibid.*
31 *Ibid*, p. 54.
32 Macquarie Diary, 10 April 1816.
33 James Wallis, born c. 1785, Cork, Ireland; died 12 July, 1858, Prestbury, Gloucestershire, England.
34 James Wallis diary, Colonial Secretary's Papers, 4/1735, pp. 55-57.
35 Also written as 'Kinnahygal'.
36 Carol Liston, *Campbelltown: The Bicentennial History, Allen & Unwin*, 1988, p. 23.

37   William Byrne, 'Old Memories: General Reminiscences of Early Colonists – II', *Old Times*, May 1903, p. 105.

38   *Ibid.*, 13 July 1816, p. 2.

39   *Ibid.*, 31 August 1816.

40   Their names were Murrah, Bunduck, Kongate, Wootan, Rachel, Yelloming, Myles, Wallah alias Warren, Carbone Jack, alias Kurringy, and Narrang Jack.

41   'Proclamation', *The Sydney Gazette and New South Wales Advertiser*, 3 August 1816, p. 1.

42   *Ibid.*

43   *Ibid.*

44   *Ibid.*, 9 November 1816, p. 1.

45   Macquarie to Earl Bathurst, 4 April 1817, *HRA*, Series I, Vol. IX, p. 342.

46   *The Sydney Gazette and New South Wales Advertiser*, 20 July 1816, p. 2.

47   *Ibid.*

48   Lachlan Macquarie Diary, 10 April 1816 – 1 July 1818, Original held in the Mitchell Library, Sydney. ML Ref: A773. [Microfilm Reel CY301, 11 July 1816.

49   Also known as South Head Upper Light.

50   The stonework was completed in December 1817 and the lighthouse began operating in November 1818. It was later pulled down and a stronger near-replica built in 1880.

51   Macquarie Diary, 11 July 1816.

52   *The Sydney Gazette and New South Wales Advertiser*, 12 December 1818, p. 1.

53   Macquarie to Earl Bathurst, 12 December 1817, *HRA*, Series I, Vol. IX, p. 719.

54   Earl Bathurst to Macquarie, 24 August 1818, *Ibid.*, p. 833.

55   The central building was for hospital wards (demolished in 1879), a northern wing (now Parliament House) was for the Principal Surgeon D'Arcy Wentworth, a rare visitor, and a southern wing (now The Mint) housed William Redfern, the assistant surgeon who ran the hospital.

56   Wentworth Papers A 752, p. 188, State Library of NSW.

57   On 3 October 1817. From E.W. Dunlop, 'Blaxcell, Garnham (1778–1817)', Australian Dictionary of Biography, Australian National University, 1966.

58   *The Sydney Gazette and New South Wales Advertiser*, 3 February 1816, p. 1.

59   *Ibid*, 25 May 1816, p. 1.

60   *Ibid*, 29 July 1815, p. 2.

61   *Ibid.*

62   *Ibid*, 21 December 1816, p. 2.

63   *Ibid.*

64   *Ibid*, 9 November 1816, p. 2.

65   Rebecca Breedon, nee Doyle, born May 16 1794, Norfolk island; died 3 July 1854, Launceston, Tasmania.

66   Mollie Gillen, *The Founders of Australia: A Biographical Dictionary of the First Fleet*, Library of Australian History, 1989, p. 352.

67   *The Sydney Gazette and New South Wales Advertiser*, 1 June 1816, p. 2.

68   James Reibey to David Hope, 17 September 1823, State Library of NSW, Safe/MLMSS 5512/1 (Safe 1/261), MLMSS 5512/2.

69   *Ibid.*

70   *Ibid.*

71   James Haydock Reibey, Colonial Secretary's Papers, 1788-1825, State Records of NSW, Citation: [4/3495], p. 363, Reel No: 6005, 12/12/1816.

72   Letter from Mary Reibey to her cousin Alice Hope, 12 August 1818, State Library of New South Wales, SAFE/MLMSS 4534 (Safe 1/210).

73   Bruce Kercher, *Debt, Seduction and Other Disasters: The Birth of Civil Law in Convict New South Wales*, The Federation Press, 1996.

74 Macquarie Diary, 13 June 1816. The seat is still known as Mrs Macquarie's Chair.
75 Charles Frazer, born c. 1788 Blair-Atholl, Perthshire, Scotland; died 22 December 1831, Parramatta, NSW, also reported as Fraser and Frazier.
76 Colonial Secretary Letters Sent, SRNSW 4/3494, reel 6004, pp. 412-413.
77 It was built in 1819 by stonemason, Edward Cureton and demolished about 1883 to make way for a statue of Thomas Sutcliffe Mort.
78 Now the site of the Sydney Opera House.
79 On 20 May 1819.
80 The church was completed in 1824 and finally superseded in height by the Sydney Town Hall clock tower completed in 1873.
81 The building is now The Sydney Conservatorium of Music.
82 Macquarie to Castlereagh, 12 March 1810, *HRA*, Series 1, Vol. VII, p. 242.
83 *HRA*, Series 1, Vol. IX, p. xii.

Chapter Thirteen
1 Macquarie to Castlereagh, 12 March 1810, *HRA*, Series I, Vol. VII, p. 242.
2 *Ibid.*
3 John Thomas Campbell, born Newry, County Armagh, Ireland, 1770; died Sydney 7 January 1830.
4 J.T. Campbell, Secretary, to Mrs Reibey, 4 November 1816, New South Wales Archives, Colonial Secretary's Letter Book 1816–1817, 4\3495.
5 *The Sydney Gazette and New South Wales Advertiser*, 30 November 1816, p. 2.
6 George James Molle, born 6 March 1773, Chirnside, Berwickshire, Scotland; died 9 September, 1823, Belgaum, India,
7 Sir John Wylde, born 11 May 1781 at Warwick Square, London; died Cape Town, 13 December 1859.
8 *The Sydney Gazette and New South Wales Advertiser*, 30 November 1816, p. 2.
9 Macquarie to Earl Bathurst, 29 March 1817, *HRA*, Series I, Vol. IX, p. 220
10 Edward Eagar, born 1787 near Killarney, Ireland; died 2 November, 1866 London.
11 The Wesley Edward Eagar Centre in Surry Hills was named in his honour.
12 *HRA*, Series 1, Vol. IX, p. xii.
13 *The Sydney Gazette and New South Wales Advertiser*, 14 December 1816, p. 1.
14 Macquarie to Earl Bathurst, 29 March 1817, *HRA*, Series I, Vol. IX, p. 231.
15 'First Australian Bank', *The Argus* (Melbourne), 11 April 1908, p. 7.
16 'Bank of New South Wales', *The Sydney Gazette and New South Wales Advertiser*, 22 March, 1817, p. 2. The charter was later rendered invalid. Bathurst told Macquarie he had no power to grant a charter, and was to inform the shareholders that they operated on the principles of an unlimited liability partnership.
17 Macquarie to Earl Bathurst, 29 March 1817, *HRA*, Series I, Vol. IX, p. 219.
18 Westpac Banking Corporation, Bank of NSW Board Minute Book, No. 1.
19 Macquarie to Earl Bathurst, 29 March 1817, *HRA*, Series I, Vol. IX, p. 220.
20 Westpac Banking Corporation, Bank of NSW Board Minute Book, No. 1.
21 *The Sydney Gazette and New South Wales Advertiser*, 15 February 1817, p. 1.
22 *Ibid.*
23 Edward Smith Hall, born London 28 March 1786; died 18 September 1860, Sydney.
24 *The Sydney Gazette and New South Wales Advertiser*, 4 September 1819, p. 1.
25 Macquarie to Earl Bathurst, 7 October 1814, *HRA*, Series I, Vol. VIII, pp. 302-303.
26 Bank of NSW Board Minutes, 6 March 1817.
27 Sydney Gazette and New South Wales Advertiser, 7 January 1810, pp. 2–3.
28 'Bank of New South Wales', *The Sydney Gazette and New South Wales Advertiser*, 8 March 1817, p. 2.

29   *The Sydney Gazette and New South Wales Advertiser*, 22 February 1817.

30   Richarda Allen, born 2 September 1798; died 18 May 1888, Entally House, Hadspen, Tasmania.

31   'Founding the firm', allens.com.au

32   Allens was founded on 22 July 1822, the day after 21-year-old George Allen was admitted as an attorney and solicitor of the Supreme Court of New South Wales.

33   Bank of NSW Board Minutes, 25 March 1817.

34   Frederick Garling, born 1775; died 2 May, 1848, Sydney.

35   First Bank of NSW Ledger, Westpac Archives.

36   *The Sydney Gazette and New South Wales Advertiser*, 25 November 1804, p. 1

37   First Bank of NSW Ledger, Westpac Archives.

38   Russell Craig and Leanne Johns, 'Female customers of the Bank of New South Wales, 1817-1820,' *Journal of the Royal Australian Historical Society* (Vol. 88, Issue 2), December 2002.

39   She began using it on 5 August 1819.

40   *Ibid.*, 24 March 1818.

41   Bank of NSW Board Minutes, 8 April 1817.

42   *The Sydney Gazette and New South Wales Advertiser*, 25 January 1817, p. 2.

43   *Ibid.*, 26 April 1817, p. 2.

44   *Ibid.*, 13 December 1817, p. 2.

45   *Ibid.*, 17 May 1817, p. 1.

46   *Ibid.*, 25 January 1817, p. 1.

47   *The Hobart Town Gazette and Southern Reporter*, 6 September 1817, p. 2.

48   Arthur Jose, 'Mary Reibey: Australia's First Business Woman', *The Brisbane Courier*, 26 August 1933, p. 18.

49   *The Sydney Gazette and New South Wales Advertiser*, 15 August 1818, p. 2.

50   Joseph Arnold to his brother, 25 February 1810, A1849 vol. 2, State Library of New South Wales, p. 3.

51   Ellis Bent to his mother, 27 March 1810, MS 195/3, National Library of Australia.

52   Leanne Johns, 'The First Female Shareholders of the Bank of New South Wales: Examination of Shareholdings in Australia's First Bank, 1817–1824', Accounting, Business & Financial History Vol. 16, No. 2, Routledge, 2006, pp. 293–314.

53   *Ibid.*

54   *The Sydney Gazette and New South Wales Advertiser*, 3 January 1818, p. 4.

55   'Mary Haydock Reibey 1777 – 1855', entallyestate.com.au/its-people

56   *The Sydney Gazette and New South Wales Advertiser*, 24 January 1818, p. 2.

57   *Hobart Town Gazette and Southern Reporter*, 31 January 1818, p. 2.

58   *Ibid.*, 29 August 1818, p. 2.

59   *Ibid.*, 7 February 1818, p. 1.

60   Mary Reibey, Letter to her aunt Penelope Hope 1792, MLMSS 5934 (Safe 1/155), State Library of NSW.

61   Macquarie to Earl Bathurst, 3 March 1818, *HRA*, Series I, Vol. IX, pp. 749.

62   Under Secretary Goulburn to Governor Macquarie, 13 June 1817, *HRA*, Series I, Vol. IX, p. 438.

63   Lieut.-Governor Sorrell to Major Cimitiere, *HRA*, Series 3, Vol. II, 24 October 1818, p. 492.

64   *Ibid.*, p. 491.

65   'A Brief History of the Arabian Horse in Australia', Arabian Horse Society of Australia, ahsa.asn.au.

66   *Hobart Town Gazette and Southern Reporter*,, 31 October 1818, p. 2.

67   *Ibid.*, 7 February 1818, p. 2.

68   Port Regulations, 3 April 1819, *HRA*, Series 3, Vol. II, pp. 507, 703.

69   *Hobart Town Gazette and Van Diemen's Land Advertiser*, 2 November 1822, p. 2.

70   *Hobart Town Gazette and Southern Reporter*, 20 March 1819, p. 1.

71   *The Sydney Gazette and New South Wales Advertiser*, 27 November 1823, p. 3.

72   Mary Allen Reibey, born 27 March 1818; married Charles Arthur 28 June 1836, Longford, Tasmania; died 4 July 1895 Longford, Tasmania.

Chapter Fourteen

1   Barron Field (23 October 1786 – 11 April 1846)

2   *The Sydney Gazette and New South Wales Advertiser*, 18 September 1819, p. 2.

3   Letter from Mary Reibey to her cousin Alice Hope, 12 August 1818, State Library of New South Wales, Safe/MLMSS 4534 (Safe 1/210).

4   *Ibid.*

5   *Ibid.*

6   *Ibid.*

7   *Ibid.*

8   *Ibid.*

9   *Ibid.*

10   *Ibid*, 3 August 1818.

11   *Ibid*, 6 August 1818.

12   Letter from Mary Reibey to her cousin Alice Hope, 12 August 1818, State Library of New South Wales, Safe/MLMSS 4534 (Safe 1/210).

13   Reibey Mary, Index to the Colonial Secretary's Papers, 1788-1825, Ship: Per "Royal Admiral" | Citation: [4/3499], p.81 | Reel No: 6006 | Start Date: 24/09/1818.

14   Roland Walpole Loane, born about 1778; died 8 October 1844, Hobart.

15   *The Sydney Gazette and New South Wales Advertiser*, 31 July 1819, p. 2.

16   Reibey Mary, Index to the Colonial Secretary's Papers, 1788-1825, Ship: Per 'Royal Admiral' | Citation: [2/8130], pp.197-201 | Reel No: 6020 | Start Date: 29/06/1819.

17   Reibey George, Index to the Colonial Secretary's Papers, 1788-1825, Citation: [4/1758], pp.66a, 67a | Reel No: 6054 | Start Date: 01/06/1819.

18   The Cornwall Landholders Muster, State Archives of NSW, NRS-1271, Population musters, Dependent settlements, 01-01-1811 to 31-12-1821.

19   'The House', entallyestate.com.au.

20   'Personal accounts and balances held by BNSW as of 31 December 1819', Westpac Archives.

21   Russell Craig and Leanne Johns, 'Female customers of the Bank of New South Wales, 1817-1820,' *Journal of the Royal Australian Historical Society* (Vol. 88, Issue 2), December 2002.

22   *Ibid.*

23   *The Sydney Gazette and New South Wales Advertiser*, 21 August 1823, p. 2.

24   On 16 February 1820.

25   Westpac Banking Corporation, Bank of NSW Directors' Minute Book 2, 16 February 1820.

26   *The Sydney Gazette and New South Wales Advertiser*, 4 March 1820, p. 2.

27   Panorama du Port Jackson et de la ville de Sidney, National Library of Australia, Rex Nan Kivell Collection, NK651.

28   Angus Cameron (ed) 'Part One: Capital City Chronologies, A History of Sydney'. *The Second Australian Almanac*, Angus & Robertson, 1986, p. 4.

29   T.A. Coghlan, *General Report on the Eleventh Census of New South Wales*, Charles Potter, Government Printer, 1894, p. 66.

30   Alexander Harris, *Settlers and Convicts; or, Recollections of sixteen years' labour in the Australian Backwoods. By an Emigrant Mechanic*, C. Cox, 1847, pp. 12-13.

31   Alexander Berry, born 30 November, 1781 Fife, Scotland; died 17 September, 1873, Crows Nest, Sydney, NSW.

32 Lachlan Macquarie Diary, 1 March 1820, Mitchell Library, Sydney, ML Ref: A774 pp.174-194; [Microfilm Reel:CY301 Frames #580-602].

33 'Old Sydney – Mrs. Mary Reibey at Reibey Cottage', *Truth* (Brisbane), 5 December 1909, p. 11.

Chapter Fifteen

1 Mary Reibey journal, 1820-1821, 20 June 1820, State Library of New South Wales, Safe 1/21a, p. 11.

2 The English Reports:Vice-Chancellors' courts (1815-1865),Vol. LVII,William Green & Sons, 1905, p. 280.

3 Mary Reibey journal, 1820-1821, 22 June 1820 State Library of New South Wales, Safe 1/21a, p. 5

4 *Ibid*, 20 June 1820, *Ibid.*, p. 11.

5 John Atkinson, born 26 October 1795, Kings Lynn, Norfolk; died 20 December 1893, Launceston, Tasmania.

6 Mary Reibey journal, 1820-1821, State Library of New South Wales, Safe 1/21a, p. 12.

7 *Ibid.*, p. 10.

8 *Ibid.*, p. 13.

9 John Hope, 9 September 1789, Blackburn; died January 1871, Chorlton, Lancashire.

10 Dr Robert Halstead Hargreaves, born November 1774, Blackburn, Lancashire; died 17 May 1847, Manchester.

11 J.T. Slugg, *Reminiscences of Manchester Fifty Years Ago*, J. E. Cornish, 1881, p. 64.

12 Mary Reibey journal, 1820-1821, State Library of New South Wales, Safe 1/21a, p. 14.

13 *Ibid*.

14 Alice Hope, born 1792 Blackburn; died October 1853, Liverpool, England.

15 Mary Reibey journal, 1820-1821, State Library of New South Wales, Safe 1/21a, p. 14.

16 *Ibid.*, p. 15.

17 *Ibid.*, p. 16.

18 *Ibid.*, p. 18.

19 *Ibid*.

20 Macquarie Diary, 26 October 1820.

21 Joseph Wild, sentenced on 21 August 1793 in Chester for burglary, together with his brother, George; died 1847.

22 Macquarie Diary, 27 October 1820.

23 *Ibid*.

24 '1821 – Mrs Celia Wills', portraitdetective.com.au.

25 *Ibid*.

26 Letter from Mary Reibey to her cousin Alice Hope, 12 August 1818, State Library of New South Wales, Safe/MLMSS 4534 (Safe 1/210).

27 LynneVallone, *Becoming Victoria*,Yale University Press, 2001, p. 126.

28 Mary Reibey journal, 1820-1821, State Library of New South Wales, Safe 1/21a, p. 33.

29 Mary Reibey journal, 1820-1821, State Library of New South Wales, Safe 1/21a, 4 December 1820, p. 36.

30 *Ibid.*, 6 December, p. 40.

31 *Ibid*.

32 Thomas Haydock Foster, born 26 August 1792, died 1832,Van Diemen's Land.

33 Mary Reibey journal, 1820-1821, 22 December 1820, State Library of New South Wales, Safe 1/21a, p. 44.

34 Mary Reibey journal, 1820-1821, 22 December 1820, State Library of New South Wales, Safe 1/21a, p. 46.

35 Charles Haydock Foster, born September 1820, Manchester; died 21 March 1879, Casterton, Victoria.
36 Mary Reibey journal, 1820-1821, 28 December 1820, State Library of New South Wales, Safe 1/21a, p. 47.

Chapter Sixteen
1 Mary Reibey journal, 1820-1821, 31 December 1820, State Library of New South Wales, Safe 1/21a, p. 48.
2 *Ibid.*, 1 January 1821.
3 Mary Reibey to David Hope, 5 August 1825, State Library of NSW, Safe/MLMSS 5512/1 (Safe 1/261), MLMSS 5512/2.
4 Mary Reibey journal, 1820-1821, 28 January, State Library of New South Wales, Safe 1/21a, p. 50.
5 Frederick Goulburn, born 1788, London; died 10 February, 1837, London.
6 Mary Reibey journal, 7 February, p. 52.
7 *Ibid.*, 8 February, p. 52.
8 *Ibid.*, 14 February, p. 53.
9 Mary Reibey to David Hope, 14 February 1821, State Library of NSW, Safe/MLMSS 5512/1 (Safe 1/261), MLMSS 5512/2
10 *Ibid.*
11 *Ibid.*
12 *Ibid.*
13 *Ibid.*
14 *Ibid.*
15 Major General Sir Thomas Makdougall Brisbane, born 23 July 1773, Largs, Ayrshire, Scotland; died 27 January 1860, Largs.
16 Episcopal Floating Church, St George-in-the-East Church, stgite.org.uk
17 *The Christian Herald and Seaman's Magazine,* Vol. 8, For the Years 1821-22, p. 377-9.
18 Letter from Mary Reibey to her cousin Alice Hope, 12 August 1818, State Library of New South Wales, Safe/MLMSS 4534 (Safe 1/210).
19 Mary Reibey journal, 1820-1821, 19 February 1821, State Library of New South Wales, Safe 1/21a, p. 55.
20 *Hobart Town Gazette and Van Diemen's Land Advertiser,* 10 November 1821, p. 2.
21 Mary Reibey journal, 1820-1821, 14 March 1821, State Library of New South Wales, Safe 1/21a, p. 59.
22 Thomas Thomson, born 14 August 1794, Dysart, Fife, Scotland; died 11 July 1844, Launceston, Tasmania.
23 Macquarie diary, 11 June 1821.
24 *Ibid.*, 29 April 1821.
25 *Ibid.*, 28 April 1821.
26 James Haydock Reibey to David Hope, 6 May 1821, State Library of NSW, Safe/ MLMSS 5512/1 (Safe 1/261), MLMSS 5512/2.
27 *Ibid.*
28 Robert Knopwood, 2 June 1763, Threxton, Norfolk, England; died 18 September 1838, Tasmania.
29 *Ibid.*
30 Mary Reibey to David Hope, 5 August 1825, State Library of NSW, Safe/MLMSS 5512/1 (Safe 1/261), MLMSS 5512/2.
31 Mary Reibey journal, 1820-1821, 14 April 1821, State Library of New South Wales, Safe 1/21a, p. 62.

32   George Reibey to David Hope, 29 May 1821, State Library of NSW, Safe/MLMSS 5512/1 (Safe 1/261), MLMSS 5512/2.

33   *Ibid.*

34   *Ibid.*

35   Robert Cooper, born 15 May 1777, London; died 25 May 1857 at his home 'Juniper Hall', Paddington, Sydney.

36   *The Sydney Gazette and New South Wales Advertiser*, 22 May 1823, p. 2.

37   George Reibey to David Hope, 29 May 1821, State Library of NSW, Safe/MLMSS 5512/1 (Safe 1/261), MLMSS 5512/2.

38   On 1 March 1821.

39   Jean Charles Prosper de Mestre, born 15 August 1789, Lorient, Brittany, France; died 14 September 1844 at his property Terara, at Greenwell Point, Shoalhaven, NSW.

40   Letter from George to James included, in the correspondence of James Reibey to David Hope, 6 May 1821, State Library of NSW, Safe/MLMSS 5512/1 (Safe 1/261), MLMSS 5512/2.

41   Etienne Livingston de Mestre, Born 9 April 1832, George Street, Sydney, died 22 October 1916, 'Mount Valdemar', Moss Vale, NSW.

42   *The Sydney Gazette and New South Wales Advertiser*, 14 July 1821, p. 2.

43   Letter from George to James included, in the correspondence of James Reibey to David Hope, 6 May 1821, State Library of NSW, Safe/MLMSS 5512/1 (Safe 1/261), MLMSS 5512/2.

44   Bank of NSW Board Minutes, 17 April 1821.

45   Mary Reibey journal, 1820-1821, 14 June 1821, State Library of New South Wales, Safe 1/21a, p. 22.

46   *Ibid.*, 24 June 1821, p. 76.

47   *Ibid.*, 5 July 1821, p. 79.

48   *Hobart Town Gazette and Van Diemen's Land Advertiser*, 10 November 1821, p. 2.

49   *Ibid.*, 24 November 1821, p. 2.

50   George Reibey to David Hope, 14 February 1823, State Library of NSW, Safe/MLMSS 5512/1 (Safe 1/261), MLMSS 5512/2.

51   Thomas Haydock Reibey, born 24 September 1821 at Entally House, Hadspen, Van Diemen's Land; died at Entally House 10 February, 1912.

52   'Family History in a Bible', *The Australian Woman's Mirror*, 24 May 1950, p. 7.

53   'His Excellency's Address', *Sydney Gazette and New South Wales Advertiser*, 1 December 1821, p. 2.

54   *Ibid.*

Chapter Seventeen

1   *The Sydney Gazette and New South Wales Advertiser*, 15 December 1821, p. 3.

2   District Constables Notebooks, Sydney and Parramatta, 1822-4, NSW State Archives and Records, NRS-1263, Reel 1254, Image 8.

3   Thomas Spencer Wills, born 5 August 1800, Sydney; died 29 July 1872, Melbourne.

4   Howe died on 11 May 1821.

5   *The Sydney Gazette and New South Wales Advertiser*, 4 January 1822, p. 2.

6   *Ibid.*, 11 January 1822, p. 4.

7   *Hobart Town Gazette and Van Diemen's Land Advertiser*, 2 February 1822, p. 1.

8   *Ibid.*, 13 July 1822, p. 2.

9   *The Sydney Gazette and New South Wales Advertiser*, 21 June 1822, p. 2.

10   George Reibey to David Hope, 14 February 1823, State Library of NSW, Safe/MLMSS 5512/1 (Safe 1/261), MLMSS 5512/2.

11   *The Sydney Gazette and New South Wales Advertiser*, 21 June 1822, p. 1.

12 James Chisholm, born 23 January, 1772, Mid-Calder, West Lothian, Scotland; died 31 March 1837, Newtown, Sydney.
13 Until 1853.
14 *The Sydney Gazette and New South Wales Advertiser*, 9 August 1822, p. 2.
15 Mary Helen Thomson, born 24 August 1822, Launceston; died 11 November 1866, Launceston.
16 Janes Reibey to David Hope, 17 September 1823, State Library of NSW, Safe/MLMSS 5512/1 (Safe 1/261), MLMSS 5512/2.
17 George Reibey to David Hope, 14 February 1823, State Library of NSW, Safe/MLMSS 5512/1 (Safe 1/261), MLMSS 5512/2.
18 *Ibid.*
19 *Ibid.*
20 *Ibid.*
21 *Ibid.*
22 *The Sydney Gazette and New South Wales Advertiser*, 8 May 1823, p. 3.
23 *Ibid.*, 2 October 1823, p. 3.
24 John Atkinson, born 26 October 1795, Kings Lynn, Norfolk, England; died 20 December 1893, Launceston.
25 *The Sydney Gazette and New South Wales Advertiser*, 10 July 1823, p. 4.
26 James Reibey to David Hope, 17 September 1823, State Library of NSW, Safe/MLMSS 5512/1 (Safe 1/261), MLMSS 5512/2.
27 Mrs Jane Penelope Atkinson, daughter of Mrs Mary Reibey, ca. 1828 – watercolour on ivory miniature, State Library of NSW, MIN 54.
28 'The Late Mr John Atkinson', *Launceston Examiner*, 21 December 1893, p. 5.
29 *The Sydney Gazette and New South Wales Advertiser*, 24 July 1823, p. 1.
30 'The House', entallyestate.com.au.
31 James Haydock Reibey, born 22 August 1823, Launceston; died 10 July 1897, Devonshire, England.
32 'Family Notices', *The Sydney Gazette and New South Wales Advertiser*, 27 November 1823, p. 3.
33 Janes Reibey to David Hope, 17 September 1823, State Library of NSW, Safe/MLMSS 5512/1 (Safe 1/261), MLMSS 5512/2.
34 *Ibid.*
35 *The Sydney Gazette and New South Wales Advertiser*, 2 October 1823, p. 3.
36 Eliza Thomson to David Hope, 6 July 1825, State Library of NSW, Safe/MLMSS 5512/1 (Safe 1/261), MLMSS 5512/2.
37 'Family Notices', *The Sydney Gazette and New South Wales Advertiser*, 27 November 1823, p. 3.
38 *Ibid.*
39 *Ibid*, 15 April 1824, p. 2.
40 Eliza Thomson to David Hope, 6 July 1825, State Library of NSW, Safe/MLMSS 5512/1 (Safe 1/261), MLMSS 5512/2.
41 Jane Penelope Atkinson to David Hope, 7 February 1823, State Library of NSW, SAFE/MLMSS 7790 (Safe 1/274).
42 On 1 July 1824, at St. James's, London.
43 REIBEY Mary, Index to the Colonial Secretary's Papers, 1788-1825, Citation: [2/8305], pp.77-80 | Reel No: 6028 | Start Date: 06/09/1824.
44 *Ibid.*
45 *Ibid.*
46 *Ibid.*
47 The address is now 141 Blacktown Rd, Freemans Reach.
48 'Reibeycroft', hawkesbury.org.

49   Jane Penelope Atkinson to David Hope, 7 February 1823, State Library of NSW, SAFE/ MLMSS 7790 (Safe 1/274).

50   John Dunmore Lang, *An Historical and Statistical Account of New South Wales*,Vol. I, CocHRAn and McCrone, 1837, p. 37.

51   *Ibid.*

52   John Reibey Atkinson, born 28 March 1826,Wilberforce, NSW; 7 May 1854, Launceston,Tasmania.

53   *The Australian* (Sydney), 20 October 1825, p. 1.

54   *Hobart Town Gazette and Van Diemen's Land Advertiser*, 30 July 1824, p. 4.

55   *The Sydney Gazette and New South Wales Advertiser*, 15 July 1824, p. 2.

56   *Ibid.*

57   *Hobart Town Gazette and Van Diemen's Land Advertiser*, 17 December 1824, p. 2.

58   Mary Reibey to David Hope, 19 June 1825, State Library of NSW, Safe/MLMSS 5512/1 (Safe 1/261) , MLMSS 5512/2.

59   *Tasmanian and Port Dalrymple Advertiser* (Launceston), 30 March 1825, p. 3.

60   'The Eclipse', *The Australian* (Sydney), 26 May 1825, p. 2.

61   *Ibid.*

62   Mary Reibey to David Hope, 19 June 1825, State Library of NSW, Safe/MLMSS 5512/1 (Safe 1/261) , MLMSS 5512/2.

63   'Shipping Intelligence', *The Sydney Gazette and New South Wales Advertiser*, 19 May 1825, p. 2.

64   James Thomson, born 26 August 1824; died 7 June 1899, Burrier, NSW.

65   Mary Reibey to David Hope, 19 June 1825, State Library of NSW, Safe/MLMSS 5512/1 (Safe 1/261) , MLMSS 5512/2.

66   Eliza Thomson to David Hope, 6 July 1825, State Library of NSW, Safe/MLMSS 5512/1 (Safe 1/261) , MLMSS 5512/2.

67   *Ibid.*

68   Lord Glenelg, Secretary of State for War and the Colonies, to Governor Sir Richard Bourke, *HRA*, Series 1,Vol. XVIII, pp.68.

69   James Reibey to David Hope, 18 April 1832, State Library of NSW, MLMSS 4200.

70   *Ibid.*

71   Mary Reibey to David Hope, 5 August 1825, State Library of NSW, Safe/MLMSS 5512/1 (SAFE 1/261), MLMSS 5512/2.

72   *Ibid.*

73   General Sir Ralph Darling, born 1772, died 2 April, 1858, Brighton, Sussex, England.

74   *The Australian* (Sydney), 6 June 1827, p. 2.

75   *Ibid.*, p. 4.

76   Mary Reibey papers, State Library of NSW, A-5327, 3045.

77   Governor Darling to Under Secretary of the Colonial Office Robert Hay, 2 September 1826, *HRA*, Series 1,Vol. 12, p. 522.

78   Mary Reibey to David Hope, 5 August 1825, State Library of NSW, Safe/MLMSS 5512/1 (Safe 1/261), MLMSS 5512/2.

Chapter Eighteen

1   James Reibey to David Hope, 18 April 1832, State Library of NSW, MLMSS 4200.

2   'Suspected Murder', *The Australian* (Sydney), 31 August 1827, p. 3.

3   *Ibid.*

4   'Execution', *The Sydney Gazette and New South Wales Advertiser*, 26 March 1828, p. 2.

5   *Ibid.*

6   *Ibid.*

7   *Ibid.*

8   Sir Richard Bourke, born 4 May, 1777, Dublin, Ireland; died 12 August 1855 County Limerick, Ireland.

9   *Ibid.*, 15 August 1828, p. 3.

10 *Ibid.*, 19 December 1827, p. 2.

11 *Ibid.*, 2 June 1828, p. 2.

12 *Ibid.*, 12 April 1831, p. 4.

13 'Civic Improvements', *The Australian* (Sydney) 23 July 1828, p. 3.

14 Samuel Terry, born c. 1776, England; died 22 February 1838, Sydney.

15 *The Australian* (Sydney), 6 August 1828, p. 2.

16 *The Monitor* (Sydney), 9 August 1828, p. 2.

17 *The Australian* (Sydney), 8 May 1829, p. 3.

18 Joseph Long Innes, born 19 November 1806, Leitrim, Ireland; died 29 May 1885, Sydney.

19 *The Australian* (Sydney), 8 May 1829, p. 3.

20 *Ibid.*

21 James Reibey to David Hope, 10 August 1829, State Library of NSW, MLMSS 4200.

22 Elizabeth Jane Long Innes born 1830, Sydney; died January 1893, Kensington, London.

23 'Family Notices', *The Sydney Gazette and New South Wales Advertiser*, 27 January 1829, p. 3.

24 James Reibey to David Hope, 10 August 1829, State Library of NSW, MLMSS 4200.

25 Mary Helen Thomson to David Hope, 11 January 1843, State Library of NSW, Safe/ MLMSS 5512/1 (Safe 1/261) , MLMSS 5512/2.

26 James Reibey to David Hope, 10 August 1829, State Library of NSW, MLMSS 4200.

27 'Government Order, No. 11', *The Hobart Town Gazette*, 8 March 1828, p. 1.

28 James Reibey to David Hope, 10 August 1829, State Library of NSW, MLMSS 4200.

29 *Ibid.*

30 *Ibid.*

31 *Ibid.*

32 entallyestate.com.au

33 *The Cornwall Chronicle* (Launceston), 16 July 1842, p. 2.

34 Mary Reibey to David Hope, 20 October 1829, State Library of NSW, MLMSS 4200.

35 *Ibid.*

36 Thomas Hobbes Scott, born 17 April 1783 at Kelmscott, Oxford, England; died 1 January Durham England.

37 Craig Campbell, 'Church and Schools Corporation New South Wales, 1820-1835', *the Dictionary of Educational History in Australia and New Zealand*, dehanz.net.au.

38 *The Australian* (Sydney), 12 May 1829, p. 3.

39 NSW State Archives, NRS 905 [4/2221.2 letter 34/4682].

40 M Reibey to Colonial Secretary 4 March 1829, State Archives NSW, In Letters No. 1697.

41 NSW State Archives, NRS 907 [2/7956].

42 In 1839. *Ibid.*, From NRS 905 [4/2457.5 letter 39/10030].

43 Frank McCaffrey, *The History of Illawarra and its Pioneers*, J. Sands Limited, 1922, p. 151.

44 'The Name of Mary Reibey', *The Shoalhaven Telegraph*, 21 June 1933, p. 3.

45 Jane Foster, born November 1796, Blackburn, Lancashire; died 12 December 1853, Launceston, Tasmania.

46 James Reibey to David Hope, 10 August 1829, State Library of NSW, MLMSS 4200.

47 Eliza Foster, born 29 Aug 1808, Blackburn, Lancashire; died 26 January, 1830, George Street, Sydney.

48 Timothy Goodwin Pitman, born 1794, Boston, Massachusetts, USA; died 29 March 1832, Oahu, Sandwich Islands (Hawaii).

49 An Act to Naturalize Timothy Goodwin Pitman [5th July, 1825.], legislation.nsw.gov.au

50 'Mr. Pitman's New Wharf', *The Sydney Gazette and New South Wales Advertiser*, 19 Dec 1829, p. 3.

51   James Reibey to David Hope, 10 August 1829, State Library of NSW, MLMSS 4200.

52   *Ibid.*, 18 April 1832, *Ibid.*

53   *Ibid*, 10 August 1829, *Ibid.*

54   'Late Colonial Sydney: 1822-1838', visitsydneyaustralia.com.

55   Thomas Wentworth Wills (19 August 1835 – 2 May 1880).

56   Mary Reibey to David Hope, 20 October 1829, State Library of NSW, MLMSS 4200.

57   *The Sydney Gazette and New South Wales Advertiser,* 12 April 1832, p. 2.

58   'Sale Of Land', *New South Wales Government Gazette* (Sydney), 22 June 1836 [Issue No.227], p 463.

59   huntershilltrust.org

60   'Appointments and Employment', *Ibid.,* (Sydney), 4 January 1837 [Issue No.256], p. 1.

61   'Sydney News', *Colonial Times* (Hobart), 19 November 1839, p. 5.

62   *The Sydney Herald,* 14 February 1840, p. 1.

63   John Hardman Lister, born Scarborough, Yorkshire, 21 August 1803; died in a road accident in the vicinity of Bathurst, NSW, 12 July 1850.

64   famtrees.info/captainlisterframe.htm

65   *The Sydney Herald,* 8 August 1838, p. 3.

66   Joseph Fowles, born 24 Dec 1809, Stroud, Gloucestershire, England; died Sydney, 25 June 1878.

67   Patricia Mary Quinn, 'Bank of NSW – First Premises', State Library of New South Wales, ML MSS 1757, p. 13.

68   Charles Arthur, born 5 February 1808, Plymouth, Devon, England; died 29 July 1884, Longford, Tasmania.

69   On 10 November 1832.

70   Thomas Reibey to David Hope, 8 September 1838, State Library of NSW, Safe/MLMSS 5512/1 (Safe 1/261), MLMSS 5512/2.

71   *Ibid.*

72   *Ibid.*

73   William Lamb, 2nd Viscount Melbourne (15 March 1779 – 24 November 1848).

74   *Proclamation of Governor Bourke,* 10 October 1835, National Archives of the United Kingdom, Kew, England, foundingdocs.gov.au.

75   John Henry Fleming, born 27 March 1816, Pitt Town, NSW; died 20 August, 1894, Wilberforce, NSW.

76   'Mr. J. H. Fleming', *Windsor and Richmond Gazette* (NSW), 25 August 1894, p. 6.

77   Sir George Gipps, born 23 December 1790, Kent, England; died 28 February 1847, Canterbury, England.

78   *The Sydney Gazette and New South Wales Advertiser,* 20 November 1838, p. 2.

79   John Kirby was hanged on 18 December 1820 for the murder of Burragong, also called Jack, an Indigenous tracker, in the Newcastle district.

80   Clare Hopkins, *Trinity: 450 years of an Oxford College Community,* Oxford University Press, 2005. p. 306.

Chapter Nineteen

1   'Journal and Proceedings', *Royal Australian Historical Society,* Volumes 9-10, 1924, p. 293.

2   *The Sydney Herald,* 14 February 1840, p. 1.

3   Mary Helen Thomson to David Hope, 11 January 1843 (4), State Library of NSW, Safe/MLMSS 5512/1 (Safe 1/261) , MLMSS 5512/2.

4   *Ibid.*

5   'Order-in-Council ending transportation to New South Wales, 22 May 1840', State Records New South Wales, SRNSW: 4/1310.

6   The last convict ship arrived in Hobart in May 1853.

7   Bryan Fitz-Gibbon and Marianne Gizycki, 'The 1840s Depression', Reserve Bank of Australia, rba.gov.au
8   Mary Helen Thomson to David Hope, 11 January 1843 (4), State Library of NSW, Safe/MLMSS 5512/1 (Safe 1/261) , MLMSS 5512/2.
9   *The Australian* (Sydney), 2 January 1843, p. 1.
10 Felton Mathew, born 1801, London; died 26 November 1847, Lima, Peru.
11 *The Sydney Herald*, 15 January 1840, p. 4.
12 *The Sydney Monitor and Commercial Advertiser*, 17 January 1840, p. 2.
13 Later Sir William Montagu Manning, born 20 June 1811 at Alphington, Devon, England; died 27 February, 1895, Sydney
14 'Stanmore House', Heritage NSW, S90/05914 & HC 32397.
15 Mary Helen Thomson to David Hope, 11 January 1843 (4), State Library of NSW, Safe/MLMSS 5512/1 (Safe 1/261) , MLMSS 5512/2.
16 *The Sydney Morning Herald*, 18 August 1855, p. 1.
17 *Ibid*, 27 December 1842, p. 1.
18 Peter Bolger, 'Reibey, Thomas (1821–1912)', *Australian Dictionary of Biography*, Australian National University, 1976.
19 Catherine Macdonald Kyle, born 1823; died 1896.
20 entallyestate.com.au
21 Charlotte Bridgett Clack, born 1826; died 1891.
22 *The Cornwall Chronicle* (Launceston), 11 June 1842, p. 3.
23 'Legislative Council', *Launceston Examiner*, 1 October 1842, p. 7.
24 *Launceston Examiner*, 8 October 1842, p. 3.
25 *Ibid*.
26 'Thomas Haydock Reibey II', entallyestate.com
27 *Ibid*.
28 *The Teetotal Advocate* (Launceston), 18 September 1843, p. 3.
29 Mary Helen Thomson to David Hope, 11 January 1843 (4), State Library of NSW, Safe/MLMSS 5512/1 (Safe 1/261) , MLMSS 5512/2.
30 *The Teetotal Advocate* (Launceston), 18 September 1843, p. 3.
31 Mary Helen Thomson to David Hope, 11 January 1843 (4), State Library of NSW, Safe/MLMSS 5512/1 (Safe 1/261) , MLMSS 5512/2.
32 *Ibid*.
33 *Ibid*.
34 Mary Reibey to David Hope, 21 June 1845, State Library of NSW, Safe/MLMSS 5512/1 (Safe 1/261) , MLMSS 5512/2.
35 *Ibid*.
36 *Ibid*.
37 *Ibid*.
38 *Ibid*.
39 Celia Alice Atkinson, born 3 April 1839, Launceston; died 17 April 1845, Launceston.
40 Mary Reibey to David Hope, 21 June 1845, State Library of NSW, Safe/MLMSS 5512/1 (Safe 1/261) , MLMSS 5512/2.
41 James Thomson, born 26 August 1824, Launceston, Tasmania; died 7 June 1899, Burrier, NSW.
42 Mary Reibey to David Hope, 21 June 1845, State Library of NSW, Safe/MLMSS 5512/1 (Safe 1/261) , MLMSS 5512/2.
43 'Stanmore House', New South Wales State Heritage Register. Office of Environment & Heritage. H00662.
44 Mary Reibey to David Hope, 21 June 1845, State Library of NSW, Safe/MLMSS 5512/1 (Safe 1/261) , MLMSS 5512/2.

45 Sir Joseph George Long Innes, born 16 October, 1834, Sydney, died 28 October, 1896, London.

46 Entallyestate.com.au

47 Mary Reibey to David Hope, 21 June 1845, State Library of NSW, Safe/MLMSS 5512/1 (Safe 1/261) , MLMSS 5512/2.

48 *Ibid*.

49 Francis Russell Nixon, born 1 August 1803, North Cray, Kent, England; died 7 April 1879, Italy.

50 On 28 October 1845, from 'Ordination', *Launceston Examiner*, 29 October 1845, p. 4.

51 *The Courier* (Hobart), 22 March 1845, p. 2.

52 Entallyestate.com.au

53 Richard Cobbold, *The history of Margaret Catchpole, a Suffolk girl*, Henry Colburn, London, 1845.

54 Hart Davis Draper Sparling, born c. 1812 in Essex, England; died 20 February 1884 Auckland, New Zealand.

55 William Grant Broughton, born 22 May 1788, London; died 20 February 1853 London.

56 Richard Cobbold, *The history of Margaret Catchpole, a Suffolk girl*, Simpkin, Marshall and Co, London, 1858, pp. 369–78.

57 *The Sydney Morning Herald*, 10 July 1845, p. 3.

58 'The True Story of Margaret Catchpole', *Windsor and Richmond Gazette*, 13 November 1897, p. 9.

59 *Ibid*.

60 *Ibid*.

61 James Clack Reibey, born 13 December 1848, Westbury, Tasmania; died 25 August 1870, Denbury Rectory, Devon, England.

62 The photo was taken on 13 May 1841, by Auguste Lucas, a visiting French sea captain. It disappeared soon after.

63 *Sydney Morning Herald*, 22 October 1845, p. 3.

64 Lease, 29 November 1848, Norton Smith Papers, State Library of NSW, A 5327, No. 62.

65 Lease, 2 September 1850, *Ibid*, No. 63

66 *Sydney Morning Herald*, 11 April 1849, p. 4.

Chapter Twenty

1 'The Gold Fever', Bathurst Free Press, 17 May 1851, p. 4.

2 Manning Clarke, *A History of Australia*, Melbourne University Press, 1993, p. 234.

3 Lieutenant Colonel Sir Charles Augustus FitzRoy, born 10 June 1796, Derbyshire, England; died 16 February 1858, London.

4 Celia Long Innes, born 16 September 1831, Sydney; died 22 February 1920 Reading, Berkshire, England.

5 Celia Pym to David Hope, 14 March 1852, State Library of NSW, MLMSS 5512/1, Filed at Safe 1/261.

6 'Women's Column,' *The Sydney Morning Herald*, 17 November 1923, p. 14.

7 *Launceston Examiner*, 27 September 1853, p. 2.

8 *Ibid*.

9 John Reibey Atkinson, born 28 March 1826, Wilberforce, NSW; died 7 May 1854, Launceston.

10 'Women's Column,' *The Sydney Morning Herald*, 17 November 1923, p. 14.

11 *Launceston Examiner*, 31 July 1852, p. 3.

12 *Ibid*.

13 On 22 October 1853.

14 *Exeter Flying Post*, 30 June 1853, p.5.

15 *The Cornwall Chronicle* (Launceston), 10 May 1854, p. 4.

16 William Denison (3 May 1804 – 19 January 1871).

17 State Archives NSW, NRS 13660 [Series 1, #3279]

18 *Ibid.*

19 *The Sydney Morning Herald*, 18 August 1855, p. 1.

20 *Ibid.*, 11 August 1855, p. 7.

21 *Ibid.*

22 *Ibid.*

23 *Ibid.*

24 Lease of the Royal Admiral, 13 October 1853, Norton Smith Papers, State Library of NSW, A 5327, No. 64.

Epilogue

1 Richard Cobbold, *The history of Margaret Catchpole, a Suffolk girl*, Simpkin, Marshall and Co, 1858, pp. 369–78.

2 Patricia Quinn, 'Bank of New South Wales: First premises – Mrs Reibey's House', 1967, State Library of NSW, ML MSS 1757/ Item 1.

3 Reginald Heath Innes, born 17 November 1869, Sydney; died 26 May 1947, Meadlow Bath, NSW.

4 Etienne Livingston de Mestre, born 9 April 1832, Sydney; died 22 October 1916 22 October 1916, Moss Vale, NSW.

5 *Exeter and Plymouth Gazette*, 2 April 1859, p. 5.

6 *Launceston Examiner*, 26 August 1897, p. 5.

7 Vice Admiral Sir Peveril William-Powlett, born 5 March 1898 Abergavenny, Monmouthshire, Wales; died 10 November 1985, Honiton, Devon, England.

8 Captain Newton James Wallop William-Powlett, born 26 June 1896, Bournemouth, Hampshire, England; died 10 November 1963; Cadhay, Devon, England.

9 'The Sydney entrepreneur behind the famous face', sydney.edu.au, 29 November 2016.

Also by Grantlee Kieza

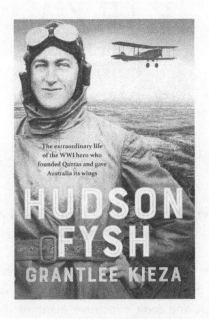

**The extraordinary life of the Gallipoli veteran and WWI
Flying Corp gunner who founded Qantas and gave
Australia its wings.**

This is a fascinating, lively and thoroughly researched portrait of a
modest, resolute family man with a steady hand during turbulence,
a man who guided Australia's national airline from its humble
beginnings through the dark days of the Great Depression, the
perilous years of World War II, when the airline flew dangerous
missions for the Allies, and into the great boom in international
tourism that followed with the jet age.

Hudson Fysh was a decorated World War I hero who not only
founded Australia's national airline, Qantas, but steered it for almost
half a century from its humble beginnings with two rickety biplanes
to the age of the jumbo jets. More than anyone, Fysh shaped the way
that Australians saw the world.

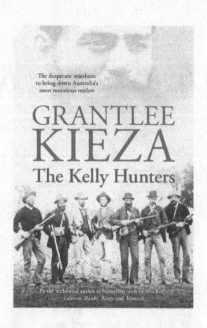

**The desperate manhunt to bring down Australia's
most notorious outlaw.**

When Ned Kelly and his band of young tearaways ambushed and
killed three brave policemen in a remote mountain camp in 1878, they
sparked the biggest and most expensive manhunt Australia had seen.
The desperate search would end when Kelly and his gang, wearing suits
of armour, tried to derail a train before waging their final bloody gun
battle with police in the small Victorian town of Glenrowan.

In the 20 months between those shootouts and aided by a network
of informers, hundreds of lawmen, soldiers, undercover agents and a
team of Aboriginal trackers combed rugged mountains in freezing
conditions in search of the outlaws. The police officers were brave,
poorly paid and often ailing, some nearing retirement and others
young with small children, but they risked death and illness in the
hope of finding the men who had killed their comrades.

The hunt for the Kelly gang became a fierce battle of egos between
senior police as they prepared for the final shootout with Australia's
most infamous bushrangers, a gun battle that etched Ned Kelly's
physical toughness and defiance of authority into Australian folklore.

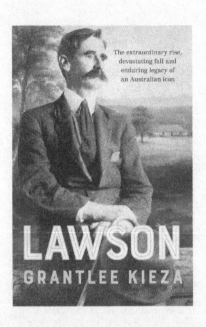

The extraordinary rise,
devastating fall and
enduring legacy of
an Australian icon

LAWSON
GRANTLEE KIEZA

**The extraordinary rise, devastating fall and enduring
legacy of an Australian icon**

Henry Lawson captured the heart and soul of Australia and its people
with greater clarity and truth than any writer before him. Born on
the goldfields in 1867, he became the voice of ordinary Australians,
recording the hopes, dreams and struggles of bush battlers and slum
dwellers, of fierce independent women, foreign fathers and larrikin
mates.

Lawson wrote from the heart, documenting what he saw from his
earliest days as a poor, lonely, handicapped boy with warring parents on
a worthless farm, to his years as a literary lion, then as a hopeless addict
cadging for drinks on the streets, and eventually as a prison inmate,
locked up in a tiny cell beside murderers. His heroic figures such as
The Drover's Wife and the fearless unionists striking out for a better
deal helped define Australia's character, and while still a young man, his
storytelling drew comparisons on the world stage with Tolstoy, Gorky
and Kipling.

But Henry Lawson's own life may have been the most compelling
saga of all, a heart-breaking tale of brilliance, lost love, self-destruction
and madness.

**Lust, science, adventure – Joseph Banks and his voyages
of discovery**

Sir Joseph Banks was a man of passion whose influence spanned the
globe. A fearless adventurer, his fascination with beautiful women was
only trumped by his obsession with the natural world and his lust for
scientific knowledge.

Fabulously wealthy, Banks was the driving force behind
monumental voyages and scientific discoveries in Australia, New
Zealand, the South Pacific, Europe, North America, South America,
Asia, Africa and the Arctic. In 1768, as a galivanting young playboy,
he joined Captain James Cook's *Endeavour* expedition to the South
Pacific. Financing his own team of scientists and artists, Banks battled
high seas, hailstorms, treacherous coral reefs and hostile locals to
expand the world's knowledge of life on distant shores. He returned
with thousands of specimens of plants and animals, generating
enormous interest in Europe, while the racy accounts of his amorous
adventures in Tahiti made him one of the most famous and notorious
men in England.

The remarkable life of Australia's greatest storyteller
'A detailed and sympathetic account … fascinating'
– *The Australian*

A.B. 'Banjo' Paterson is rightly recognised as Australia's greatest storyteller and most celebrated poet, the boy from the bush who became the voice of a generation. He gave the nation its unofficial national anthem 'Waltzing Matilda' and treasured ballads such as 'The Man from Snowy River' and 'Clancy of the Overflow', vivid creations that helped to define Australia's national identity.

But there is more, much more to Banjo's story, and in this landmark biography, Grantlee Kieza chronicles a rich and varied life, one that straddled two centuries and saw Australia transform from a far-flung colony to a fully fledged nation.

Born in the bush, as a boy Banjo rode his pony to a one-room school. As a young man he covered the second Boer War as a reporter. He fudged his age to enlist during World War I, ultimately driving an ambulance before commanding a horse training unit during that conflict. Newspaper editor, columnist, foreign correspondent and ABC broadcaster, he knew countless luminaries of his time, including Rudyard Kipling, Winston Churchill, Field Marshal Haig and Henry Lawson. The tennis ace, notorious ladies' man, brilliant jockey and celebrated polo player was an eye-witness to countless key moments in Australian history.

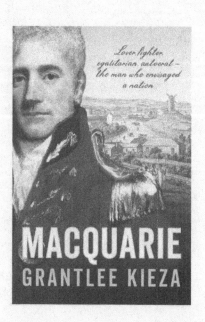

A lively and engaging portrait of a towering and complex figure of Australian colonial history.

Lachlan Macquarie is credited with shaping Australia's destiny, transforming the harsh, foreboding penal colony of New Holland into an agricultural powerhouse and ultimately a prosperous society.

He also helped shape Australia's national character. An egalitarian at heart, Macquarie saw boundless potential in Britain's refuse, and under his rule many former convicts went on to become successful administrators, land owners and business people.

In this, the most comprehensive biography yet of this fascinating colonial governor, acclaimed biographer Grantlee Kieza draws on Macquarie's rich and detailed journals. He chronicles the life and times of a poor Scottish farm boy who joined the British army to make his fortune, saw wars on five continents and clawed his way to the top. Ultimately, Macquarie laid the foundations for a new nation, but, in the process, he played a part in the dispossession of the continent's original people.

Lover, fighter, egalitarian, autocrat – Lachlan Macquarie is a complex and engaging character who first envisaged the nation we call Australia.